Personal Headset Radios • Personal Radios • Personal Minidisc Players • Boom Boxes • Clock Radios

CAMERAS 157

35mm Manual-Focus SLR Cameras • 35mm Autofocus SLR Cameras • 35mm Autofocus Cameras • 35mm Compact Cameras • 24mm Advanced Photo System (APS) Cameras • Instant-Print Cameras • Digital-Still Cameras

TELEPHONES AND ANSWERING MACHINES 182

Feature Telephones • Cordless Phones • Cellular Phones • Answering Machines

COMPUTERS 194

Home & Small Office Computers • Business/Hi-Powered Computers • Portable Computer • Data Storage Devices • Monitors • Modems • Printers

HOME OFFICE PRODUCTS 221

Desktop Copiers • Scanners • Desktop Fax Machines • Handheld Personal Computers (HPCs) • Electronic Organizers

HOME FITNESS 234

Exercise Cycles • Rowing Machines • Treadmills • Home Gyms • Stair Climbers • Ski Machines • Total Body Machines • Elliptical Machines

HOME IMPROVEMENT 251

Safety Equipment • Garage Door Openers • Power Hand Tools

SNOW REMOVAL 271

LAWN CARE 276

Lawn Mowers • Lawn Tractors • String Trimmers • Blower/Vacs

FOOD PREPARATION 291

Food Processors • Electric Mixers • Blenders • Toasters and Toaster Ovens • Juicers/Juice Extractors • Steamers • Ice-Cream Makers • Bread Makers • Coffee Makers and Tea Makers

MICROWAVE OVENS 329

Full-Size Microwave Ovens • Family-Size Microwave Ovens • Medium-Size Microwave Ovens • Compact Microwave Ovens • Microwave/Convection Ovens • Over-the-Range Microwave Ovens • Over-the-Range Microwave/Convection Ovens

RANGES 343

Gas Ranges • Electric Ranges

REFRIGERATORS AND FREEZERS 360

Refrigerators • Freezers

DISHWASHERS 377

Built-In Dishwashers • Portable Dishwashers

ConsumerGuide™

CONSUMER BUYING GUIDE

1999 EDITION

Cover photos: W.B. Donner/Yard Machines; Graco; Krups; Nokia; The Rowland Company/Canon; Samsung; Sharp; Sparks.

PUBLICATIONS INTERNATIONAL, LTD.

CONTENTS

INTRODUCTION 6

TELEVISIONS AND TV/VCR COMBINATIONS 8

35- to 41-Inch TV Sets • 32-Inch TV Sets • 27-Inch TV Sets • 20-Inch TV Sets • Front-Projection TVs • Rear-Projection TVs • TV/VCR Combinations • Digital Satellite Systems (DSS) • Universal Remote Controls

VCRS, DVD, AND LASER DISC PLAYERS 45

VCRs • Digital Video Disc (DVD) Players • Laser Disc Players

CAMCORDERS 63

8mm Camcorders • Full-Size VHS Camcorders • Compact VHS (VHS-C) Camcorders • Digital Video (DV) Camcorders

STEREO COMPONENTS 78

Speakers • Subwoofers • Headphones • Stereo Receivers • Compact Disc Players • Cassette Decks • Minidisc Decks

STEREO SYSTEMS 124

Home Theater Systems • Mini-/Midi-Systems

PERSONAL STEREOS 135

Portable CD Players • Personal Radio-Cassette Players • Personal Radio-Cassette Player/Recorders • Personal Cassette Players •

FLOOR CARE 385

Upright Vacuum Cleaners • Powerhead Canister Vacuums • Compact Canister Vacuums • Mini Vacuum Cleaners and Brooms • All-Purpose Cleaning Machines

LAUNDRY CARE 399

Washers • Dryers • Compact Washer • Combination Washer/Dryer

SEWING MACHINES 412

Computerized Machines • Noncomputerized Machines

ENVIRONMENTAL APPLIANCES 417

Ceiling Fans • Air Conditioners • Air Care Appliances • Portable Heaters

BABY EQUIPMENT 430

Portable Cribs and Play Yards • Swings • Nursery Monitors • Car Seats • Strollers • High Chairs

INTRODUCTION

Are you finally ready to buy that full-size stereo system with a CD player? Do you know what the difference is between a carousel and magazine disc changer? Looking to replace your aging television set with a new one? Are you sure you know what "cable ready" means?

In short, do you know how to determine what features you'll want in a product? Then, do you know how to get the most features for your money?

It takes experience and expert knowledge to spend your hard-earned dollars wisely in every facet of today's marketplace. Intelligent choices become more difficult when you consider rapid advances in technology and shifts in the world's economy. These factors can quickly change price, availability, and long-term usefulness, making your buying decisions very confusing.

That's where we at CONSUMER GUIDE™ can help. We recognize the challenge in picking a Best Buy, a product that meets your high standards of quality, performance, and value. Our experts in the major product fields have taken the guesswork and confusion out of making major purchases. CONSUMER GUIDE™ has no affiliation with any manufacturers or retailers, we accept no advertising, and we are not interested in selling products. Our sole purpose is to provide you—the consumer—with the information needed to make informed, intelligent decisions.

In this publication, we have tried to review a wide variety of products to address diverse consumer needs. The products reviewed range from small personal items, such as clock radios, cellular telephones, and automatic-drip coffee makers, to major purchases, such as televisions, refrigerators, computers, and home theater systems. We have not limited the choices to low-end products or top-of-the-line merchandise. We know that a product is only a Best Buy if it meets your needs and budget. Keeping this in mind, we have selected products in a variety of sizes and prices to match the requirements of different shoppers. In fact, this year we have attempted to meet the needs of more consumers than ever. Our Budget Buys, for instance, are affordable products that may not have all the bells and whistles of the top-of-the-line models but are still well constructed and perform well.

Many consumers will find they benefit from exercising patience. When a new product first hits the market, it generally commands a premium price. However, if you wait, instead of rushing right out to make the purchase, you will probably observe that not only does the price come down but changes and improvements will have been incorporated into the product. Prime examples include products such as CD players, personal cassette players, computers, and food processors. These items are much less expensive today than when they first came on the market, and the progression of refinements has been steady.

To make the best use of this book, first review the introductory material at the beginning of each chapter. These introductions contain important information about the product categories, describe product features, and explain the terminology you need to know when you shop. Determine what features will be most useful to you and those using the item. Once you are acquainted with the criteria we use to select products, go on to our product reviews. Items rated Best Buys were chosen for their usefulness, high quality, and overall value. A Best Buy isn't necessarily the least expensive model; it's the highest quality product available at a reasonable price. Recommended selections are also good products, but for one reason or another, they do not measure up to our Best Buy standards.

When you shop, compare prices and models. We provide an Approximate Low Price to serve as your price guide. If a dealer quotes a price close to the Approximate Low Price in this publication, then you know that you are getting first-rate value for your money. **All the prices listed are accurate at the time of printing, but are subject to manufacturer's changes.** In some rare cases, the products are so new that prices were not yet available. All products were checked to make sure that they would be available to consumers in 1999, but product manufacture and distribution is beyond our control.

For additional information and product reviews, visit our web site at www.consumerguide.com.

TELEVISIONS AND TV/VCR COMBINATIONS

It seems that the American public has a voracious appetite for color televisions. There is also a love affair with bigger and bigger screens above 27 inches. Large-screen and projection TV sales continue to grow, as consumers buy the biggest set that they can (or cannot) afford in pursuit of the best picture quality available.

EVALUATING TVs

How does one evaluate a TV? The obvious criteria are picture quality, brightness, contrast, detail, and lack of signal or video noise. Then combine good sound, a user-friendly remote, and connection options appropriate to your level of use. The colors should be pure and natural. Whenever possible, try to look at programs that offer images you are familiar with for comparison. Try to look at black-and-white images, since these will reveal the quality of the contrast and brightness of the set's picture. DVDs (and laser discs and prerecorded VHS tapes) that display the THX logo have been mastered and duplicated to the highest standards and will provide you with an excellent vehicle to evaluate picture quality. You can even do this at your local dealer because they normally have DVD players hooked up to various TVs. Although many major motion pictures already display their THX logo, more and more discs are receiving the THX logo of quality control. Ask your dealer to play one of these discs so you can evaluate the set you are thinking about buying. VHS tapes displaying the THX logo also offer pristine images. Consider checking out images from either DSS or EchoStar, for they can also display superior picture quality.

Screen size is a matter of personal preference and budget. Ideally, you should view a TV image from a distance roughly twice as far from the screen as the screen is high. You should also consider TVs with front A/V jacks, which allow easy hook-up to video games and camcorders. Sets 27 inches and above are now the primary set in most homes. The majority of sets sold are monitor/receiver or tabletop models. These TVs offer the greatest versatility. Models up to 40 inches can be placed into designer cabinets, which are now offered by major furniture companies and specialty manufactuers. Big floor-standing consoles are quickly diminishing, but upright consoles now represent most of this market. Upright consoles take up about the same floor space as a tabletop model, but offer built-in storage for a VCR and videotapes. While 27-inch TVs are popular for the living room/family room, direct-view sets with screen sizes from 30 to 36 inches are selling in record numbers.

Since differences in brand-name televisions are slight, manufacturers have added all sorts of special features to their sets in an attempt to differentiate them. Deciding which television to buy is a matter of matching a set's features with your needs. Except for small LCD mini-TVs and a few portables, virtually all sets include a 181-channel tuner (either quartz or frequency synthesized). Many TVs also offer a feature called either Parental Block or Channel Block. This feature allows parents to program the set so their younger children cannot tune in to certain channels, such as cable channels that offer adult programming.

TVs are becoming more automated. Many sets now offer auto programming, in which you indicate whether your set is attached to either an antenna or a cable system. At the flick of a button, it will automatically tune in all viewable channels. Most sets also include a sleep-timer function, which lets you nod off to late-night television. The set will automatically shut itself off at a preselected interval: 15, 30, 60, 90, or 120 minutes. Other sets can be programmed to turn themselves on at preselected times, either to wake you up or to be sure that you don't miss your favorite show. Many sets now include on-screen help, which includes definitions of features plus explanations on how to accomplish different functions.

SIZE AND QUALITY

Dark-tint picture tubes now dominate virtually all sets 13 inches and above. Dark-tint screens offer higher contrast and brighter colors, which is what most people desire in their TV sets. Clearly, other features are desirable, but brightness and contrast rank on top.

When TVs were a novelty, a diagonal measurement was introduced as the standard designation of screen size. This was done to make round picture tubes seem larger, even though a fair amount of round tubes were masked and didn't provide a useful picture. Flat, square TV screens have made the diagonal measurement more honest. Flatter tubes also reduce glare and provide less distortion at the corners of the set.

In the last few years, we have seen wide-screen TVs appear on the market utilizing a 16:9 aspect ratio instead of the standard 4:3 aspect ratio of a normally square TV. A 16:9 aspect ratio offers a somewhat rectangular screen, mimicking the shape of your local cinema.

HOME THEATER

"Home Theater" is no longer a buzzword. It is becoming a way of life for many people. As more people cocoon and spend time with family and friends at home, everyone gravitates toward the television to watch the latest movie or video. Home theater can be as simple or as complex as you want it to be, as long as you are marrying your television to better audio.

Many people begin their home theater by purchasing a large-screen TV (either direct-view or projection). To get the fullest benefit from home theater, however, you will need various other components, including a hi-fi VCR and a Dolby Pro Logic or Dolby Digital receiver. (For more information on audio equipment, see the chapter on Stereo Components.)

If you want the best possible picture quality, a laser disc or DVD player may also be in your future. These are the basic building blocks of home theater. The beauty of home theater is that you can buy each component separately or in multiples to enhance your listening and viewing experience. In some cases, a good home theater system can look and sound better than your local cinema.

STEREO SOUND

Stereo sound is a significant feature in TVs today. There are many sets that offer digital sound processing (DSP), Dolby surround decoding, or other sound enhancement options. SRS, for example, is a psycho-acoustic effect that makes the sound emanate from different parts of the room, providing more spacious sound. Spatializer sound offers a similar effect. More than one-third of all TVs sold are now stereo models, and all sets 27 inches and above include stereo as a standard feature.

REMOTE CONTROLS

Most sets include either a basic, standard, universal, or learning remote. A basic remote controls functions such as volume or channel up/down and power on/off. A standard remote is an enhanced basic model with a keypad for direct access that allows you to use on-screen menus and displays. Universal remotes are becoming the most common remote included with televisions. They come with preprogrammed codes for both VCRs and cable boxes. Some brands offer models that are ergonomically designed with keys of different shapes, colors, and sizes. On top of that, a handful of brands include devices with illuminated keys. Learning remotes can be programmed to operate other types of components, such as an A/V receiver or surround processor. If you are trying to tie all your components together, a learning remote might be the best option. However, at best, they can only learn primary functions of each component. Normally, you cannot get into menus from other products to adjust surround settings, for example. A learning remote from an A/V receiver or an aftermarket universal/learning unit provides versatility and access to many functions.

TV/VCR COMBOS

A relatively recent category is the TV/VCR combo, which combines a television set with a VCR. Initially conceived of as a business product, it has found its niche in the home with sales topping two million units annually. While offered in a variety of screen sizes, 13- and 20-inch sets are the most popular. The sets are equipped with either a two-head or four-head VCR and are great for the bedroom or den. Newer models include a stereo TV and hi-fi VCR. While you may not save any money by purchasing a combo, you save in convenience by not having to deal with cables and wires. It is the fastest growing TV/video category.

PROJECTION TVs

There are two basic types of projection televisions: front and rear. Although the perfection of these televisions was slow in the beginning, picture quality today verges on exceptional for both types. Projection TVs have become mainstream products, selling approximately one million units annually. Wide-screen has found a home with projection television.

Front-projection TVs need to be viewed in a dark room, lending itself to what some people feel is a true home-theater experience. Units can be either ceiling-mounted or floor-standing. Besides the purchase of the TV itself, a screen is required that will add another $1,200 to $5,000 to the set's purchase price. Front projectors range in screen size from 20 to 300 inches, offering various aspect ratios. To improve picture quality even more, line doublers and line quadruplers are available from the major front-projector manufacturers. These can also add another $10,000 to $20,000 to the package. Front projectors need a dedicated media room just for themselves.

Front LCD projectors are also available, which utilize an LCD wafer and a powerful projector bulb to project an image onto an external surface. The higher the pixel (picture element) count, the better an LCD image will appear on the screen. Remember, though, you need a completely darkened room to enjoy the LCD image. LCD projectors are currently available from only a handful of manufacturers.

Rear-projection models are bigger and brighter than they have ever been, sporting sizes up to 80 inches, up to 1,000 lines of resolution, and brightness topping 500 footlamberts. Rear-projection TVs use CRTs, mirrors, and complex lens systems to project an image onto a translucent screen for viewing. The sets are so bright that they can be viewed in normal room light without appreciable loss of picture quality. Many models include tinted transparent plastic screens that offer contrast as well as protection for their lenticular lens. Rear-projection sets are not the behemoths that they were in the past; their depth, in some cases, has been reduced to approximately 20 inches. Thanks to casters, these sets are easy to move around the room. While wood-tone cabinetry is still found on many models, black cabinets have become the norm.

Projection TVs provide more flexibility in dealing with the considerable variety of aspect ratios since there is no absolute standard for wide-screen image sizes. While tube-projection TVs (both front and rear) use three built-in CRTs (for red, green, and blue), LCD sets have now become somewhat more sophisticated. LCD sets rival their tube counterparts in quality and high resolution, but they need to be viewed in a darkened room. You will also need an LCD set with a high pixel count to offer a seamless picture.

SATELLITE TELEVISION

Satellite broadcasting, which fell out of vogue several years ago because of large dishes (up to ten feet wide) and descrambling by HBO and the other pay services, has made a strong comeback in recent years. This has happened because many people are dissatisfied with their local cable service. While larger dishes have hung on over the years, it has been the introduction of direct-to-home (DTH) satellite broadcasting that is revolutionizing the satellite industry.

Digital Satellite Systems (DSS) and EchoStar (DishTV) are characterized by a small 18-inch (in circumference) dish, superior picture quality, and CD-like sound. While initially marketed to rural areas and smaller cities, it is now becoming popular in many suburban communities. Previously, these communities had banned large dishes from backyards and subsequently added zoning laws. Now, however, the small dish may be unobtrusively attached anywhere on a dwelling. It only requires a southern exposure free of tall trees to receive signals directly from the satellite. DSS can currently receive up to 200 channels (from three satellites) from two programming providers: DirecTV and USSB. EchoStar receives about 150 channels with similar programming. DSS equipment can be purchased from several manufacturers. The differences among manufacturers come down to on-screen graphics, remotes, and accessories. Picture quality from all brands is virtually identical, so shop for price and features.

Other DTH services are being offered by Primestar, which will rent their equipment to you. Unlike DSS, Primestar provides you with a three-foot dish. There is, however, a $200 installation fee, plus you pay for programming each month. Primestar also offers about 160 channels. The major selling point for this option is that you do not have to buy the hardware. This is all expected to change, as Primestar will start selling its equipment just like its competitors.

In any event, we can look to satellite television to stake its claim in the marketplace. Currently, there are more than eight million subscribers to satellite systems. Telephone and cable companies are in the process of outfitting their entire systems with fiber-optic cable in hopes of providing the best possible interactive TV or telecommunications signals. Satellite television has the potential to deliver the best quality signals and sounds—including wide-screen and HDTV. Movies in different aspect ratios are beamed by satellite as well. Some cable channels are expected to be added as well as pay-per-view channels.

In the coming years, we can expect to see increased digital transmissions and signal processing. Digital signals are already being broadcast via direct-to-home (DTH) satellite in the form of DSS (Digital Satellite System) and EchoStar. Telephone and cable companies are in the process of outfitting their entire systems with fiber-optic cable in hopes of providing the best possible interactive TV or telecommunications signals.

HDTV

The first true consumer HDTV sets will appear in short supply within the next two years. These sets will obviously offer wide-screen aspect ratios. We should note that the broadcasters will not rush to convert to HDTV, as it will cost them millions of dollars to upgrade to new equipment. There will be a limited number of programming hours in the fall of 1998. There is still a question or two on the signal's delivery. DirecTV, an 18-inch satellite delivery system, will offer HD programming limited to two pay-per-view (PPV) movie channels and we can expect to see HBO in HD. By early 1999, we will probably see some set-top converter boxes that will cost approximately $1,500. True HDTV sets, however, will cost between $7,000 and $10,000.

CABLE TERMINOLOGY

A major cause of confusion for shoppers is the term "cable ready." Many people incorrectly believe that a cable-ready set will allow them to receive pay services, such as HBO, free of charge. A cable-ready set only eliminates the need for a converter box to receive basic cable programming. Except for sets 13 inches and smaller, every TV sold today is cable ready. To receive premium channels, which are scrambled, you will probably need the converter box. To this end, many high-end sets offer dual antenna inputs. Through the use of a signal splitter (available from your cable company or Radio Shack), you split the signal before it goes into the cable box. One signal goes directly to your TV and the other to your cable box (in). Then the second signal goes out from your cable box (out) and into the second antenna input of your TV. In this way, all unscrambled programming is available on antenna A, and scrambled/premium services are available on antenna B. As long as your TV has a universal remote, it will control your cable box. Therefore, you do not need your cable company's remote (which is usually supplied at an additional cost).

FEATURES AND TERMINOLOGY

The following are some of the terms you should familiarize yourself with before you shop for a television.

Audio and Video (Inputs/Outputs): Normally there are more audio outputs than video outputs. More audio and video outputs are desirable as they allow you more versatility in signal switching of multiple VCRs, laser disc players, and other components. Depending on how you decide to hook up your A/V system, either the TV or your A/V receiver can be used for video switching. Audio and video input jacks are more desirable for hooking up a VCR than putting the signal through your RF antenna connector as they will provide you with better audio and video quality.

Comb Filter: This feature improves resolution and picture quality, and reduces objectionable color patterns. Low-end to midline sets utilize a glass comb filter. High-end sets utilize a CCD or digital comb filter, which greatly enhances resolution.

Component Video (Inputs/Outputs): Also called Color Difference or ColorStream, this is the latest (and superior) input/output to date. While similar to RGB (red/green/blue) connections, it provides superior images of 500 lines of resolution or better. Most DVD players now include component video outputs, which will also be included on most HDTV set-top boxes. Many TV manufacturers are now including these inputs on their mid- to upper-line TVs.

Dual-Antenna Inputs: By having dual inputs, it allows you to switch easily between antenna sources as opposed to using switching devices. This means that your set can accommodate two antenna sources, such as master antenna and cable box or master antenna/cable box and DSS decoder.

External Speaker Jacks: These allow you to attach separate speakers directly to a TV for improved sound quality, or to attach rear speakers that allow you to experience surround sound. The downside to this equation is based on the wattage of your internal television amplifier.

Front A/V Jacks: This jack pack found on the front of a TV (usually hidden under a panel) is a handy feature, especially for hooking up a camcorder or a video game.

Horizontal Resolution: This is the number of horizontal lines that can be displayed on the television. Theoretically, the more lines that can be displayed, the better the picture. Broadcast television has 330 lines, VHS tapes have about 240 lines, S-VHS tapes about 400 lines from a prerecorded video (330 from broadcast), and laser discs about 425 lines. On the other hand, when broadcast, satellite, DSS, or video sources become available with greater resolution, your set will be able to receive an enhanced signal.

Invar: The invar shadow mask gives the picture more brightness and punch. Invar is considered to be a premium feature. When sets are very bright, a side effect called "blooming" occurs. To counteract this bleeding of colors, some manufacturers include the invar shadow mask.

Notch Filter: This filter helps remove a small part of the signal that contains excess color information. By doing so, it helps eliminate some objectionable color effects from less-than-desirable signals. However, by utilizing the circuit, there is a slight loss in resolution of picture.

Parental Lock-Out or Channel Block: By punching in a special code (that the parent creates), you can lock out your children or anyone from specific channels on the television, or disable it from being used for a specified time of day or period of hours. It is designed to help parents manage their children's viewing time.

Picture-in-Picture (PIP): Picture-in-picture allows you to view two sources simultaneously. You have the primary picture displayed on the screen. The second is normally a smaller box located in one corner of the screen. To utilize PIP, you need a second video source, such as a VCR. There are both basic and advanced PIP. Advanced PIP allows you to display multiple channels on the screen at the same time (all are frozen except the channel that it is presently scrolling through), change the size or location of the smaller box, or swap back and forth between main and PIP. A handful of high-end models include a second tuner for PIP, thereby eliminating the need to utilize the VCR tuner as the second video source.

Premium Sound Systems: Manufacturers are looking for ways to come up with better sound enhancement systems. RCA and Sony, for example, include SRS (Sound Retrieval System) developed by Hughes in their high-end sets. SRS adds depth and more realistic sound without adding additional speakers. Similar systems have been developed by Toshiba, such as their Cyclone Sub-Bass System with four-channel DSP, and Zenith with SEQ. Recently, some manufacturers are adding Spatializer sound to enhance their audio.

Scan Velocity Modulation: Scan velocity modulation adjusts the rate of horizontal movement of the beam as it "draws" the scan lines, which gives black-and-white picture transitions more punch. This results in a sharper picture.

16:9 Aspect Ratio TV: These sets are designed to provide widescreen pictures without the letterbox effect (black bars found on the top and bottom of the screen) or greatly reducing it. Sets are available in 28W(ide), 30W, 34W, 55W, 56W, and 57W screen sizes. That's great for letterboxed movies, but for conventional pictures you will either end up with a cropped picture on the top or bottom, black bars on both sides of the picture, or picture-outside-picture on one side. Some projection sets will stretch a standard 4:3 picture to fit the screen, in which case there could be some distortion.

Special Picture Tubes: A recent innovation that has taken the industry by storm is the inclusion of either dark-tint or dark-glass picture tubes. By darkening the face plate, the tube provides greater contrast between black and white. The brands that include darkened picture tubes have had to increase brightness levels so that the picture does not appear too dark. Brightness more than color accuracy is preferred by most consumers. Other advancements include flat screens (or flattened picture tubes; or FST for flat, square tube), sometimes called "SuperFlat" or "FSTPerfect," which offers less distortion on the outer edges of the picture. Some manufacturers use special coatings such as RCA/ProScan and Mitsubishi to help cut down on glare and dust buildup, giving the appearance of a richer picture. Some manufacturers use a combination of techniques to tweak out the highest performance from their picture tubes, for example Panasonic's SuperFlat System, Mitsubishi's Diamond-Vision, Toshiba's FSTPerfect, and Sony's XBR2 Super Trinitron tube. These sets, while costly, offer the viewer a picture with the highest resolution and provide the most lifelike appearance.

Stereo (Watts-Per-Channel): Some manufacturers' literature is a bit deceptive if it indicates that the TV has a 20-watt internal stereo amplifier. This normally means that the set can produce 10 watts of stereo per left and per right channels. All sets included in this category include an MTS decoder, which receives and decodes all stereo signals broadcast by the networks or cable channels.

Surround: Many manufacturers include matrix surround sound or other psycho-acoustic effects to enhance the audio. It may also be called ambiance or extended stereo effects. More sets are now including Dolby Pro Logic as a means to enhance the audio quality; you must add rear speakers, however, to obtain the desired effect. A major drawback with these sets is their underpowered amps. Even with five or ten watts-per-channel, it just does not achieve the desired effect. Virtually all sets in this category, however, include variable audio outputs for connection to an A/V receiver. And, we might add, a few sets offer ample wattage. Some sets also include a center-channel input, which allows you to use the TV's internal speakers for the center channel.

S-Video (Inputs/Outputs): Many components besides S-VHS VCRs now include S-video jacks. S-video separates the luminance (Y) and chrominance (C) signals, offering better picture quality than standard video inputs. While increasing resolution, it helps color reproduction and helps reduce jitter during scene transitions. On some televisions, you will find as many S-jacks as you have video inputs. Clearly, to get the most out of your video source, you must use an S-video jack for the highest resolution (if it has one).

BEST BUYS '99

Our Best Buy, Recommended, and Budget Buy TV sets and TV/VCR combinations follow. Products within each category are listed according to quality. The unit we consider the best of the Best Buys is listed first, followed by our second choice, and so on. A Best Buy, Recommended, or Budget Buy designation only applies to the model listed—it does not necessarily apply to other models from the same manufacturer or to an entire product line.

35- TO 41-INCH TV SETS

Toshiba CN-36H97

✓BEST BUY

The Toshiba CN-36H97 is one of the best examples of 36-inch screen size technology. The set includes the FST Perfect picture tube that is the flattest and blackest of any 36-inch on the market today. Clearly the flagship of Toshiba's line, this set claims 800 lines of resolution of sparkling color, thanks to its digital comb filter and dynamic quadruple focus. The colors are vibrant and natural, with sharpness, brightness, and clarity not found elsewhere. Depending on your color preference, the H97 includes adjustable color temperature: cool, medium, and warm. Audio boasts 20 watts of stereo power. Sound is further enhanced by its use of front surround and sub-bass system, which provides more of a bass presence. The H97 features dual antenna RF inputs, three A/V inputs with one front and one rear S-video input, and one A/V output. Added to this year's model is a component video input to further improve picture quality. The front jacks allow for the effortless hook-up of a camcorder or videogame. The H97 also features a dual-tuner picture-in-picture. Audio output is fixed or variable for the attachment to an A/V receiver. Besides the rear speaker jacks, external speaker jacks are also included for the attachment of more speakers. The set features a sleekly designed 37-key universal illuminated remote that will control a VCR, cable-box, DVD player, and an audio component. On-screen menus are easy to use and read.

Specifications: height, $30\frac{3}{4}$"; width, $36\frac{5}{8}$"; depth, $25\frac{5}{8}$"; weight, 172 lbs.
Warranty: 90 days, labor; 1 year, parts
Manufacturer's Suggested Retail Price: $2,100
Approximate Low Price: not available

Sony KV-35XBR88

✓BEST BUY

The KV-35XBR88 is part of Sony's new 35-inch color TV line. The set is housed in a sleek and stylish grey cabinet with side-firing speakers. Utilizing a Deep Black Trinitron picture tube with a vertically flat screen, the set produces clear, clean, and bright images free of background video noise. This is one of the flattest tubes available. Reduced-curvature screens help reduce in-room glare and minimize picture distortion. The set includes a digital comb filter, along with scan velocity modulation that sharpens definition detail with reduced dot crawl. Other video enhancements include dynamic focus (accurate focusing from corner-to-corner), dynamic picture (accurate light-to-dark values), and a wideband video amplifier (minimizes noise and distortion). Convenience features include advanced dual-tuner picture-in-picture, bilingual (English and Spanish) on-screen displays and menus, and XDS (extended data service) reception. XDS provides information services (if broadcast) that display time, station call letters, and program information. The KV-35XBR88 has parental control that will block out all preset channels. The set further includes five presets (standard, movie, sports, news, and game), which change brightness, tone, and picture settings, depending on the type of program you are watching. Audio is piped through four side-mounted dynamic acoustic chamber (DAC) speakers that are each rated at 15 watts per channel. Audio enhancements include simulated surround and SRS, which help provide realistic surround sound without the addition of extra speakers. To round out the package, Sony includes a universal remote that will control a VCR or laser disc player and a cable or DSS box. You should be aware, however, that the remote only controls Sony DSS. The KV-35XBR88 features dual antenna inputs, two A/V inputs (one S-video), front A/V jacks (found behind a drop-down door), and three audio (fixed/variable) and two video (including monitor) outputs. This set also includes Sony's new S-Link circuitry, which allows other Sony equipment (with S-Link outputs) to be attached together. S-Link provides one-button access. The KV-35XBR88 is an upright console cabinet, which includes component storage beneath the set.

Specifications: height, 47⅜"; width, 36⅞"; depth, 26⅞"; weight, 199 lbs.

Warranty: 1 year, parts and labor
Manufacturer's Suggested Retail Price: $2,799
Approximate Low Price: not available

RCA F36695BC

Recommended

The RCA F36695BC provides excellent picture quality for an excellent price. Outfitted with RCA's new 36-inch OCS (Optimum Contrast Screen) tube with several step-up picture enhancement features, the set will display up to 770 lines of horizontal resolution, thanks in part to its three-line digital comb filter. The OCS tube displays a clean picture free of video noise and artifacts. Housed in a stylish black cabinet, the F36695BC includes front-firing speakers situated below the screen. Audio performance is rated at five watts per channel, utilizing SRS (sound retrieval system) to increase the spatial presence of sound. A nine-jack panel on the back of the set provides two A/V inputs with one S-video input and one A/V output (both fixed and variable). The set also sports several convenience features including a "sound logic" audio leveler (which lowers volume level on commercials), commercial skip to picture-in-picture (which allows you to channel surf as your program stays), and dual-tuner picture-in-picture that allows you to watch two programs without having to hook up a VCR for the second signal source. The set receives up to 181 channels and includes a Guide+ Gold on-screen program guide, which allows you to see multiday program listings. It also allows you one-button record as long as you have a VCR attached. The F36695BC includes an illuminated, ergonomically designed 46-button universal remote with color-coded keys for DSS, VCR, and cable-box control. Rounding out the system is a complete parental control system, which allows parents to "lock out" specific channels or "lock out" the front panel controls of the set so that it can't be turned on. An optional stand is available for VCR/component storage.

Specifications: height, 30⅛"; width, 33⅝"; depth, 24⅜"; weight, 177 lbs.
Warranty: 90 days, labor; 1 year, parts

Manufacturer's Suggested Retail Price: $1,699
Approximate Low Price: $1,450

Sony KP-41T65

Budget Buy

The Sony KP-41T65 is Sony's third generation tabletop rear-projection TV. The 41-inch screen boasts 790 lines of resolution with 720 footlamberts of brightness and a wide viewing angle of 130 degrees horizontal and 55 degrees vertical. Using Sony's advanced Pro-optic system coupled with a microfocus CRT and a bipolar video processor, images are vibrant and rich. Colors are natural and offer a nice balance of hues, thanks to additional video circuitry that includes a three-line digital comb filter, scan velocity modulation, dual color filter system, dynamic picture and focus, wideband signal processor, adjustable color temperature with an NTSC setting, and video noise reduction. The fact that Sony uses seven-inch instead of five-inch CRTs also helps improve image quality on a set this size. The KP-41T65 includes the DAC speaker system with two front-firing speakers rated at ten watts per channel along with matrix surround sound. There are three A/V inputs and one S-video input combined with one video (fixed and variable) and two audio outputs. The set also features A/V jacks. It receives 181 channels from its tuner, and comes with a stand-up universal remote that controls both the VCR and cable box. Included as well are easy-to-use trilingual menus, icon displays, and a channel-block feature that "locks out" two preset channels. Convenience features include dual-tuner picture-in-picture. Also included with this year's model is a built-in protective screen, which gives the set a direct-view appearance. Overall, this set offers exceptional value.

Specifications: height, 40¼"; width, 37½"; depth, 23¾"; weight, 122 lbs.
Warranty: 1 year, parts and labor
Manufacturer's Suggested Retail Price: $1,800
Approximate Low Price: $1,700

JVC AV-36980

Budget Buy

The JVC AV-36980 is a fully loaded 36-inch stereo TV that includes *TV Guide+* as a standard feature. Picture quality is excellent on this model, producing 750 lines of resolution from its comb filter. Colors are exceptionally natural. You can change its settings via the Video Choice menu, which features three different settings: standard (factory presets), theater (NTSC standard), and choice (your preference settings). The AV-36980 offers three watts per channel of stereo power from two side-firing speakers. For added ambiance, the set includes matrix surround. A switch shuts off its internal speakers so that the variable audio output jack can be utilized or external speakers can be attached. The set includes two A/V inputs. The fixed/variable audio output is switchable via the remote as well. Equipped with a 181-channel tuner, this model features one RF input and dual-tuner picture-in-picture. Its trilingual (English, Spanish, and French) on-screen menus and displays are easy to use. The set also features auto clock set, which means that it always displays the correct time. Linking you to the television is a 45-button illuminated universal remote, which controls your VCR and cable box. The remote is well laid out with the color-coded *TV Guide+* keys situated at the bottom. *TV Guide+* is a free on-screen programming service. It will display all-channel programming for up to 48 hours. A description of that channel's programming is displayed in the upper right-hand side of the screen. On the upper left-hand corner of the screen, the actual channel is displayed. All in all, the set is a solid performer.

Specifications: height, 30⅛"; width, 33⅞"; depth, 23¾"; weight, 153 lbs.
Warranty: 1 year, parts and labor; 2 years, picture tube
Manufacturer's Suggested Retail Price: $1,399
Approximate Low Price: $1,299

32-INCH TV SETS

Sony KV-32XBR48

✓BEST BUY

The Sony KV-32XBR48 is a 32-inch TV that is part of a new breed of television that offers component video inputs for improved signal reception. Some of the new DVD players now offer component video outputs, allowing you to view a full 500 lines of horizontal resolution upon playback of a DVD. The set comes in a black cabinet with top-mounted control buttons for easy access to the set's function buttons. Utilizing a Trinitron picture tube with a deep black screen, this set produces clean and bright images free of background video noise. It includes a 3D digital comb filter with vertical aperture compensation along with scan velocity modulation that sharpens definition. The set also features a dual-tuner picture-in-picture for added convenience. Audio is piped though two side-mounted dynamic acoustic chamber speakers that are rated at 15 watts per channel. Audio is enhanced via Auto SRS, which adds greater realism to many scenes along with more depth of the sound. The set also includes a trackball universal remote, which is capable of controlling four video products including DSS. The set also features five A/V inputs (five S-video), front A/V jacks, and three audio (fixed/variable) and two video outputs.

Specifications: height, 25¾"; width, 33"; depth, 23¾"; weight, 158 lbs. 12 oz.
Warranty: 1 year, parts and labor; 2 years, picture tube
Manufacturer's Suggested Retail Price: $1,799
Approximate Low Price: $1,699

Hitachi UltraVision 32UX58B

Recommended

A black cabinet houses Hitachi's UltraVision 32UX58B. The 32-inch set features Hitachi's UltraBlack dynamic focus picture tube, which has a dark tint (almost black). Because of the dark tint, contrast and brightness levels are greatly increased, consequently producing an exceptional picture that displays up to

750 lines of resolution; video noise reduction, a digital three-line comb filter, and advanced scan modulation circuitry built-in also enhance picture clarity. The set includes three home theater modes for movies, sports, and TV, and is capable of receiving 181 channels. Convenience features include dual-tuner picture-in-picture with a quick-freeze capability. This stereo set includes two speakers located in the front of the screen that provide ten watts per channel. External speaker jacks are provided for the attachment of additional speakers. Enhancing the audio package, SRS (sound retrieval system) system offers increased aural presence. The set also features three sets A/V jacks (one front and two rear), including one S-video rear jack. There is one variable audio output jack for hookup to an external audio source. Included with the 32UX58B is a 35-key, illuminated universal remote that controls both VCR and cable box. The trilingual on-screen guide is one of the easiest to use. A child lock option is available to monitor your child's TV viewing. A new feature added this year is volume correction circuitry, which will automatically lower the volume of especially loud TV stations or channels.

Specifications: height, $26\frac{7}{16}$"; width, $30\frac{5}{16}$"; depth, $23\frac{3}{8}$"; weight, 118 lbs.
Warranty: 1 year, parts and labor; 2 years, picture tube
Manufacturer's Suggested Retail Price: $899
Approximate Low Price: $860

RCA F32690BC

Budget Buy

The RCA F32690BC provides decent picture quality at an excellent price. Outfitted with RCA's optimum contrast screen (OCS) tube, this set includes several video features including a digital comb filter, a wideband video amplifier, video noise reduction, and scan velocity modulation. With these video features combined, the set has the capability to display up to 765 lines of horizontal resolution. It receives 181 channels with advanced auto programming. The OCS tube displays a crisp, clean picture free of video noise and artifacts. The set is housed in a stylish black cabinet with front-firing speakers. Audio performance is rated at five watts per channel, for superb sound. A nine-jack panel on the set provides two A/V inputs with (including one S-video) and one audio output (both fixed and variable). Convenience features include picture-in-picture, 30-second commercial skip (that allows you to surf for 30 seconds and then returns you to your channel), trilingual displays, and parental control. The F32690BC includes an ergonomically designed illuminated 46-button universal remote with color-coded keys for DSS (or cable box), VCR, VCR/LD, and audio (RCA only) components. New this year is the Guide Plus+ Gold on-screen program guide, which provides multiday program listings along with descriptions and on/off timers. Included with Guide Plus+ is "one-button record," which is a handy way to tape programs. A matching optional stand (VS64932) is available for VCR/component storage.

Specifications: height, 29"; width, 30⅛"; depth, 22½"; weight, 120 lbs.
Warranty: 90 days parts; 1 year, labor
Manufacturer's Suggested Retail Price: $899
Approximate Low Price: $750

27-INCH TV SETS

Sony KV-27V45

✓BEST BUY

This full-featured Sony 27-inch television produces sharp and clean images with little video noise, thanks in part to its Trinitron Picture Tube. It also includes a digital comb filter, capable of producing 700 lines of horizontal resolution. Colors are natural. Scan velocity modulation, wideband video amplifier, dynamic picture, and CRT amplifier are also used to improve overall picture quality. This midline set includes many desirable features including picture-in-picture and steady sound (that keeps commercials at their proper sound levels). Its 181-channel tuner features auto programming. Sony also provides this set with an exceptional bilingual on-screen display and menu that is easy to use. The KV-27V45 uses a DAC (Dynamic Acoustic Chamber) speaker system (five watts per channel) combined with a built-in SRS (Sound Retrieval System) circuitry for enhanced sound. The set features two A/V inputs (including one S-video input) and a variable audio output. The easy-to-use illuminated universal remote will also control a VCR, a cable box, DSS, and DVD. A matching optional base (SU-27A3) is available for VCR and component storage.

Specifications: height, 22¾"; width, 27¼"; depth, 19⅞"; weight, 93 lbs. 8 oz.
Warranty: 90 days, labor; 1 year, parts; 2 years, picture tube
Manufacturer's Suggested Retail Price: $949
Approximate Low Price: $799

JVC AV-27980

Recommended

Plenty of features are included on this 27-inch set from JVC that will make television viewing an experience. Picture quality is superior, displaying 600 lines of resolution. Colors are natural and have ample brightness levels. You can adjust brightness and clarity via the Video Choice menu, which features three settings: standard (factory presets), theater (NTSC standard), and choice (your preference settings). Audio is rated at three watts per channel from two front-firing speakers. For added ambiance, the set includes hyper surround. A switch shuts off its internal speakers so that the variable audio output jack can be utilized or external speakers can be attached. The set comes with two A/V inputs including a front jack pack and an S-video input. Linking you to the television is a 51-button universal remote that will also control your VCR and cable box. The fixed/variable audio output is switchable via the remote as well. The AV-27980 includes *TV Guide+* and a 181-channel tuner; it also features dual antenna inputs and dual-tuner picture-in-picture. The means that the set is able to display two different programs simultaneously. Its trilingual on-screen menus and displays are easy to use, and it includes handy on-screen help. All in all, this set is a solid performer.

Specifications: height, 23⅜"; width, 25¾"; depth, 20½"; weight, 72 lbs.
Warranty: 1 year, parts and labor; 2 years, picture tube
Manufacturer's Suggested Retail Price: $580
Approximate Low Price: $499

Philips/Magnavox MX2791B

Recommended

The MX2791B is part of Philips' new upscale MX line. And it makes sense, because this top-of-the-line 27-inch set is a versatile performer. It features a dark glass flat square picture tube, a dynamic comb filter, and video noise reduction circuitry, which enable it to display up to 800 lines of resolution (using S-video). Picture quality is above average. Philips uses its MagnaVue Plus video circuitry to improve contrast, making whites appear whiter and blues look bluer. You also have the option to turn it off if you are not satisfied with the image. The somewhat average audio is powered by two five-inch oval side-mounted front-firing speakers, which frame the set, rated at five watts per channel each. To improve sound, however, the MX2791B uses "Incredible Stereo," which is spatial surround sound circuitry that gives the sound more ambiance. Also included are external speaker jacks for the attachment of outboard speakers. The TV has one A/V input with S-video capability. The 42-button illuminated universal remote will also control a VCR and cable box. The MX2791B is equipped with several helpful features including remote locator (by hitting the power button on the TV, the remote will beep until found), smart sound (which lowers the sound level of commercials), smart picture (which has four settings for optimum video settings), and advanced dual-tuner picture-in-picture. It also includes a 181-channel tuner. The trilingual on-screen menus and displays have a 3-D appearance. They are clean and concise. The menus also include an on-screen help feature that explains operation functions.

Specifications: height, 22¾"; width, 30"; depth, 19⅞"; weight, 78 lbs.

Warranty: 90 days, labor; 1 year, parts; 2 years, picture tube
Manufacturer's Suggested Retail Price: $550
Approximate Low Price: $511

Toshiba CF-27H50

Budget Buy

The Toshiba CF-27H50 is an excellent example of an upscale 27-inch color TV that offers superb picture quality at an economical price. Using their BlackStripe II picture tube, a digital comb filter, and a black level expander, the set has the capability of displaying 560 lines of horizontal resolution. Images are sharp and crisp. Flesh tones are natural looking. The tuner has the capability of receiving up to 181 channels. Audio is average at five watts per channel from bottom-mounted front-firing speaks. It is enhanced, however, by front surround, which adds some ambiance to the sound. Inputs include one RF (antenna), one audio and video (along with one S-video), and one variable audio output. The 32-button universal remote is nicely laid out and easy to use. Although the CF-27H50 includes picture-in-picture (PIP), you will have to attach it to your VCR so that you can view a second image. Convenience features include a parental lock that will "lock out" up to four channels. Rounding out this set are easy-to-use trilingual on-screen graphics and menus.

Specifications: height, 24"; width, 26"; depth, 22⅜"; weight, 73 lbs.
Warranty: 90 days, labor; 1 year, parts
Manufacturer's Suggested Retail Price: $500
Approximate Low Price: $399

20-INCH TV SETS

Panasonic CT-20G32

✓BEST BUY

The Panasonic CT-20G32 is a solid performer that offers the features and performance found on more expensive models. It includes a PanaBlack picture tube that provides excellent contrast. The set also features a notch filter and SAW (surface acoustic wave) filter that improves picture quality, displaying up to 500 lines of resolution. Equipped with a 181-channel tuner, the set will perform auto programming of its channels and provide channel captions for up to 30 channels. It comes in a modern graphite gray cabinet. As with many 20-inch sets, the CT-20G32 stereo speakers are front-firing and located on the sides of the screen. Stereo is decoded via its MTS decoder and sent to its internal amplifier that provides 1.5 watts per channel. For audio enhancement, the CT-20G32 includes a Dome speaker system, which improves the spaciousness of the sound. One pair of audio/video inputs are included. Other features include a trilingual on-screen icon menu system, on-screen clock, sleep/on/off timers, and game guard (which protects the set from keeping games displayed on the screen too long). Lastly, the set features an easy-to-use 34-button universal remote that also controls both VCR and cable box.

Specifications: height, 18"; width, $21\frac{2}{3}$"; depth, $18\frac{11}{16}$"; weight, 49 lbs.
Warranty: 90 days, labor; 1 year, picture tube
Manufacturer's Suggested Retail Price: $400
Approximate Low Price: $350

Toshiba CF-19H32

Budget Buy

This stellar performer offers top-notch picture performance, thanks to Toshiba's BlackStripe II picture tube with black level expander that boosts contrast. In terms of performance and features, this 19-inch should be a Best Buy. Featuring a 181-channel tuner with auto programming, this set can receive both broadcast and cable stations either with or without a cable box. The set sports one set of rear A/V inputs for the attachment of a VCR. It is equipped with a well-designed 32-button universal remote with blue color-coded keys that will control both VCR and cable box. The on-screen menus and displays are clearly written and easy to use. The CF-19H32 features two front-firing speakers with audio rated at two watts per channel. That's better than the many of 19- or 20-inch sets currently available. To increase aural presence, the set includes front surround for added ambiance. Convenience features include a 180-minute sleep timer and parental channel lock that will "lock-out" four channels. Housed in a black cabinet, it takes up little space on your shelf.

Specifications: height, 16⅜"; width, 19$\frac{5}{16}$"; depth, 16$\frac{9}{16}$"; weight, 40 lbs.
Warranty: 90 days, labor; 1 year, parts
Manufacturer's Suggested Retail Price: $269
Approximate Low Price: $249

RCA ColorTrak F20640BC

Budget Buy

The RCA ColorTrak F20640BC is a 20-inch television that is housed in an attractive black cabinet with top-rounded edges. The set features a dark glass optimum contrast picture tube and includes a 181-channel tuner. Its trilingual (English, French and Spanish) on-screen menus and displays are clear and easy to use. The F20640BC also features an on-screen clock and sleep and alarm timer. Picture quality is good for a set in this size. Audio is piped through two front-firing speakers. Stereo sound quality is also satisfactory, enhanced by its proprietary stereo circuitry, which makes the sound imaging appear larger than it is. There is a three-jack audio/video monitor panel that allows direct audio and video connections for a VCR or any stereo video source. New this year is a 36-button unified remote that will also control RCA VCRs. This set is a perfect for the bedroom.

Specifications: height, 19⅛"; width, 20¼"; depth, 18⅞"; weight, 54 lbs.
Warranty: 90 days parts; 1 year, labor
Manufacturer's Suggested Retail Price: $299
Approximate Low Price: not available

FRONT-PROJECTION TVs

Runco DTV-852

✓BEST BUY

The Runco DTV-852 is one of the finest examples of the next generation of front-projection televisions, displaying images from 60 to 240 inches (measured diagonally). Housed in a black cabinet that can be either floor- or ceiling-mounted (ceiling mount kit included), it holds three seven-inch tubes—one for red, one for green, and one for blue. A screen (not included) is also needed to complete this package. The DTV-852 features three lens assemblies with high-definition, color-corrected multilayer coatings and hybrid lenses that produce strikingly clear images. Depending on the video source, this unit will display 900 lines of resolution from a TV signal, 800 lines from a video source using an S-video jack, or 1,080 lines using the RGB/component input (HDTV), thanks in part to its digital comb filter. Brightness is rated at 850 footlamberts, making this unit among the brightest front-projection models available. The DTV-852 will properly display wide-aspect ratio movies correctly in either 4:3 images or 16:9 images. Images that are more severely letterboxed at 2.35:1 will show smaller black bars at the top and bottom of the screen. The unit includes one composite video input, one S-video (separate Y/C) input, and one RGB/component video input. It comes with a 12-function remote control for accessing key controls. Front-projection sets are designed to watch movies, videos, or sporting events in a darkened room. This set is clearly designed for anyone wanting a true home theater experience.

Specifications: height, 12½″; width, 25¼″; depth, 33″; weight, 102 lbs.

Warranty: 1 year, parts and labor

Manufacturer's Suggested Retail Price: $15,000

Approximate Low Price: $15,000

Zenith PRO900X

Recommended

The PRO900X has the ability to display HDTV's 1,920×1,080 lines resolution with brightness levels reaching a spectacular 800 footlamberts. It can display projected images from 60 to 240 inches. (Normal resolution is 800 lines of horizontal resolution.) The PRO900X features three seven-inch High Performance Liquid Cooled Data Grade Tubes, which include a high-resolution color-corrected multilayered coating hybrid lens system. The set utilizes a comb filter with a 2D picture sharpness circuitry, and several other video features and video noise-reduction circuitry. This set also includes several types of video connectors, such as RGB inputs, component video, and S-video. There are VGA and SVGA inputs, plus an RS232 serial port. The PRO900X may be front-, rear-, floor-, or ceiling-mounted. Unlike other projectors, which you have to converge the RGB manually, the PRO900X features digitally-controlled convergence. To complete the package, Zenith includes their Z-Trak trackball remote, which can also double as a wireless mouse.

Specifications: height, $12\frac{9}{10}$"; width, $25\frac{3}{4}$"; depth, $33\frac{7}{25}$"; weight, 95 lbs.
Warranty: 1 year, parts and labor; 2 years, picture tube
Manufacturer's Suggested Retail Price: $12,600
Approximate Low Price: $10,500

REAR-PROJECTION TVs

Sony KP-53XBR200

Recommended

The Sony KP-53XBR200 is a spectacular 53-inch rear-projection TV. It is an excellent value for the money considering the performance it delivers. Utilizing a Microfocus CRT, the lens system produces a superior image from all viewing angles and in all types of light. What separates this set from other comparable sets is its center-to-corner brightness. While claiming a lower brightness level than other projection TVs, the set provides excellent contrast and good detail. Included with the KP-53XBR200 is a plastic screen that offers protection, increases contrast, and even cuts down on reflection. Also included in the video package is a thee-line digital comb filter, which can display up to 1,080 lines of resolution. Two new video features have been added to this year's model: Digital Reality Creation (DRC) and Multi Image Driver (MID). DRC acts almost like a line doubler, greatly improving resolution, and MID gives you the ability to display multi-images from different sources simultaneously. Included is a 90-watt stereo package that features a Dolby Pro Logic decoder offering 20 watts across the front (left, center, and right) and 15 watts to the rear. Left- and right-hand speakers are side-firing with the remaining speakers housed in the base. There is also a center-channel input that enables you to transform the internal speakers to one center channel if you are using external speakers in a home theater setup. Convenience features include dual-tuner picture-in-picture, an intuitive on-screen menu system that uses icons, dual antenna inputs, front A/V input, four A/V inputs (all with S-video), and three A/V outputs. The set also includes a component video input so that you can attach a DVD player (with component video outputs). The set includes a 39-button universal remote that will control four video components including DSS. The remote also includes an eight-position trackball/joystick (with a built-in enter key) that controls all on-screen functions. Like other Sony components, the set includes S-Link, which allows for complete control of all Sony equipment from one remote. The KP-53XBR200 is attractively housed in a two-piece cabinet.

Specifications: height, 52"; width, 55½"; depth, 24½"; weight, 264 lbs.
Warranty: 1 year
Manufacturer's Suggested Retail Price: $4,499
Approximate Low Price: not available

Philips/Magnavox MX5472C

Budget Buy

The 54-inch Magnavox MX5472C is the company's top-of-the-line rear-projection TV. The set displays 800 lines of resolution via a digital comb filter, a brightness level of 550 foot-lamberts, and a viewing angle of 160 degrees. The set also comes with a tinted protective screen for increased contrast, and it features three seven-inch CRTs attached to its Delta 77/78 lenses with curved face plates. Besides having easy-to-use on-screen menus and graphics, the set projects better-than-average images thanks to its three-line digital comb filter. An innovative feature found on this set is *TV Guide+*, which is a free on-screen program guide service. For easy recording of your favorite shows, simply scroll to a particular program in the guide and press the record button. (Make sure that you have configured the system to your local cable system and attach the included signal blaster to your VCR.) *TV Guide+* is activated via your remotes. The tuner receives 181 channels. Audio is rated at 25 watts per channel via four internal speakers. The set includes center-channel input jacks so that you can use the four internal speakers as "one" center-channel speaker in a Dolby Pro Logic set-up. The MX5472C features an illuminated universal remote that will control VCRs and cable boxes. The set also includes features such as Smart Sound (for toning down loud commercials); four preset settings (sports, movies, weak signal, and video games); and Smart Surf, which remembers your favorite channels. It also includes parental control, which can lock out channels and times. Inputs include two audio and two video. Outputs include one video and two audio, including variable audio-out. Two S-video input jacks are also provided for the attachment of either an S-VHS VCR, DSS, Internet TV box, laser disc player, or a DVD player. And in case you are unable to find the remote, simply touch the "power" button on the TV and activate the remote locator, which will "beep" until you find it. The MX5472C is housed in a black Euro-design cabinet in which the screen appears to sit on a pedestal.

Specifications: height, 59 31/50"; width, 49 3/5"; depth, 24 9/10"; weight, 240 lbs.
Warranty: 90 days, labor; 1 year, parts; 2 years, picture tube
Manufacturer's Suggested Retail Price: $2,499
Approximate Low Price: $2,400

TV/VCR COMBINATIONS

Toshiba CV32G68

BEST BUY

The Toshiba CV32G68 is the company's largest TV/VCR combo with a 32-inch screen. It offers an exceptional picture derived from Toshiba's FST black picture tube with a black level expander (which helps keep the black areas of the picture truly black) and a glass comb filter providing 700 lines of resolution. What separates this combo from others in the larger screen sizes is that it includes two tuners—most units available only have one tuner. While for smaller sets one tuner is fine, for larger models it puts you at a technological disadvantage: You cannot watch one program and tape another. Toshiba understands that this model will find its way to the living room as the main set in the house. Because it has two tuners, it will allow you to utilize picture-in-picture without an additional video source. This combo sports a 181-channel tuner that allows programming of six events over a one-month period. The CV32G68 offers an innovative on-screen analog clock system for programming through the turning of one knob; conventional on-screen programming is also available. The 46-button remote will control all functions of the combo. This unit also includes a rear A/V input for the attachment of other video components, such as a laser disc player or a DVD player. The set features trilingual on-screen menus and displays along with EDS (or XDS), bass/treble/balance controls for its ten watts of audio power, auto head cleaner, and a 180-minute sleep timer. The CV32G68 includes parental channel lock, which allows parents to lock out four channels.

Specifications: height, $30\frac{5}{16}$"; width, $37\frac{19}{64}$"; depth, $23\frac{1}{32}$"; weight, 118 lbs.
Warranty: 1 year, parts and labor; 2 years, picture tube
Manufacturer's Suggested Retail Price: $1,699
Approximate Low Price: $1,600

Panasonic PV-M2058

✓BEST BUY

The Panasonic PV-M2058 is a TV/VCR combo that combines a 20-inch stereo TV and a four-head mono VHS VCR. Utilizing Panasonic's PanaBlack picture tube technology coupled with black level expansion circuitry for enhanced contrast, picture quality is excellent. On its own, this combo unit stands among the best 20-inch sets. The set's tuner is capable of receiving 181 channels and you can program up to eight events over a one-month period. The VCR provides slow motion and high-speed search. The stereo portion of the TV is rated at 1.5 watts per channel from front-firing speakers. Programming could not be easier thanks to Panasonic's proprietary 42-button universal remote. Besides controlling both the TV and VCR, the universal remote will also control most cable boxes. Convenience features include auto clock set (with 24-hour program back-up) that will automatically keep the correct time. A time signal is continuously being broadcast by your local PBS station and received via a special extended data service chip. Even with power failures, the VCR will always come back to the right time. A 24-hour backup program memory is also included to save your future timed tapings. Other features found on the PV-M2058 include a real-time counter, on/off sleep timer, trilingual on-screen icon displays and menus, commercial skip (that advances the tape one minute), VCR lock, earphone jack, and a front A/V input. New features added include a built-in FM radio making it a convenient main TV for apartment dwellers.

Specifications: height, 19⅞"; width, 20¼"; depth, 19"; weight, N/A
Warranty: 90 days, labor; 1 year, parts (limited)
Manufacturer's Suggested Retail Price: $449
Approximate Low Price: $399

Samsung CXD1942

Recommended

The Samsung CXD1942 is a TV/VCR combo that marries a 19-inch TV with a two-head VHS VCR. Offering improved contrast, the set's picture quality is quite good. Colors are vibrant.

While resolution is only about 330 lines for the TV and 240 for the VCR, it is more than adequate for this unit. The VCR utilizes two video heads that allow you to do slow motion and frame advance. Its 181-channel tuner features auto programming, allowing you to record six events over a one-month period via its on-screen programmer. Housed in a redesigned black cabinet, the CXD1942 includes front A/V inputs for easy attachment of a camcorder or video game system. Other features include a real time counter, earphone jack, variable sleep timer, and trilingual on-screen displays. If power is interrupted for less than 40 seconds, the clock and all programming will remain intact. The unified remote controls all functions on both the VCR and TV, including ejecting the tape via the remote. This set is easy and intuitive to use, and is an ideal combo for a bedroom.

Specifications: height, 18⅞"; width, 19"; depth, 17¾"; weight, 48 lbs. 8 oz.
Warranty: 90 days, labor; 1 year, parts; 2 years, picture tube
Manufacturer's Suggested Retail Price: $329
Approximate Low Price: not available

Sony KV-20VS40 Double Feature

Recommended

The SONY KV-20VS40 combines a 20-inch stereo TV and a four-head hi-fi VCR. While slightly larger than the standard 20-inch set, this set offers good performance and value. Picture quality is excellent, thanks to its Trinitron picture tube, which includes Dynamic Picture Circuitry (for better contrast and detail). Recorded images are quite good at both the slowest and fastest speeds. Its 181-channel tuner features auto programming, plus you can record six events over a one-month period via its on-screen programmer. The set includes two front-firing stereo speakers rated at 1.5 watts each situated under the screen and featuring matrix surround sound. Housed in a black cabinet, the set includes front A/V jacks providing for the easy attachment of a camcorder or video game system. The set's unified remote controls all TV and VCR functions. Since this is a four-head model, it includes slow motion and frame advance; other features include digital auto tracking, auto repeat, quick start mechanism, and bilingual on-screen displays (English and Spanish). Included with this combo is auto clock set that sets the clock as soon as the 20VS40 is plugged in and receives a signal. It also features a parental control/tamper-proof mechanism that locks out or limits channels and times.

Specifications: height, $20\frac{3}{8}$"; width, $19\frac{15}{16}$"; depth, $18\frac{3}{4}$"; weight, 57 lbs.
Warranty: 90 days, labor; 1 year, parts; 2 years, picture tube
Manufacturer's Suggested Retail Price: $600
Approximate Low Price: $579

RCA T13080BC

Budget Buy

The RCA T13080BC is a smartly styled 13-inch TV/VCR combo that is housed in a black cabinet and designed to be taken anywhere. This set includes a cigarette lighter adapter so that it can be used in the car or RV. It has the capability to receive 181 channels. The set features a high contrast dark-tint picture tube. Images are quite good for a 13-inch TV. The two-head mono VHS deck has an auto head cleaner and will tape up to eight events over a one-year period. Resolution is about 240 lines for the TV and 220 for the VCR. Like the combo itself, the 36-button "Nite Glo" remote is illuminated and ergonomically designed. The set also features trilingual displays, on-screen clock, sleep timer, and alarm timer plus both front (for the attachment of games or a camcorder) and rear A/V jacks.

Specifications: height, 15"; width, $15\frac{1}{8}$"; depth, $16\frac{1}{2}$"; weight, 35 lbs.
Warranty: 90 days, labor; 1 year, parts
Manufacturer's Suggested Retail Price: $449
Approximate Low Price: not available

DIGITAL SATELLITE SYSTEMS (DSS)

JVC HM-DSR100DU

Recommended

JVC is the only manufacturer offering a D-VHS (Digital VHS) and an EchoStar DTH (direct-to-home) DISH Network satellite system that is completely integrated. D-VHS records superior video images over standard VHS. It's especially useful in recording digital images off a satellite system. On the VCR side, the HM-DSR100DU is a full-featured hi-fi VCR with eight video heads that can use both D-VHS tapes and regular VHS tapes. The unit features a one-year timer to tape up to eight of your favorite programs off the DISH Network. It also features HQ circuitry with digital, chrominance, and luminance noise reduction. Other features include digital AV tracking, on-screen color menus, tape position indicator, auto daylight savings time, index search, repeat playback, and a real-time counter. What separates this D-VHS VCR from all others is the built-in DISH Network DBS (direct broadcast satellite) tuner. The 2D comb filter helps deliver sparkling images. A 32-bit microprocessor allows for quick access to the electronic program guide (EPG), which offers one-button recording of DISH Network channels. Other satellite features include the 18-inch satellite dish with dual LNB, which allows for the attachment of a second DISH Network receiver. A V-chip for parental control is also included. A UHF/IR universal remote is included to control both TV and/or cable box as well. Part of the DISH Network tuner includes Local Link, which allows for seamless integration with the program guide of local program listings along with DISH Network Top 40 or Top 50 packages. You can also get an optional smaller second dish (through Echostar) to receive your local channels. (Check with the DISH Network to see if the city you live in is part of the local channel package beamed from one of its satellites.) The DSR100DU is Dolby Digital compatible, allowing you to tape and playback signals in Dolby Digital (as long as the receiver is attached to a Dolby Digital decoder or an A/V receiver with one built in). This is a new videocassette recorder combined with a satellite receiver with the capability of receiving HDTV signals along with Dolby Digital sound. That's a hard combination to beat.

Warranty: 90 days, labor; 1 year parts
Manufacturer's Suggested Retail Price: $1,000
Approximate Low Price: not available

EchoStar 5000

Budget Buy

The EchoStar 5000 is the top-of-the-line DISH Network receiver and features a 32-bit microprocessor for quick channel and EPG (electronic program guide) response. The unit includes two A/V outputs, one S-video output and three inputs (one for the DISH Network dish and one for your rooftop antenna cable). It has a universal remote that can control up to four components, and a ten-event timer. While not offering as many channels as DSS, the DISH Network offers more than 200 programming services. This service offers a monthly subscription of either the Top 40 or Top 50 channels of integrated programming (which includes many of the same channels as DirecTV and USSB combined) plus music channels. It also offers pay-per-view movies. The system includes Local Link, which allows you to easily scroll between satellite and off-air channels on the EPG. EchoStar also offers local channels. If you live in a city that can receive local signals, you need to buy a smaller second dish, which makes a great alternative to a rooftop antenna, or Lifeline service from your local cable operator. While there is a small monthly charge to receive local signals (along with local advertising), its digital images are crystal-clear and free of interference. You will also be able to receive local HDTV signals (if you have an HDTV decoder and/or an HDTV TV set) via the EchoStar 5000.

Specifications: height, 2½"; width, 14½"; depth, 9¾"; weight, 8 lbs.
Warranty: 90 days, labor; 1 year, parts
Manufacturer's Suggested Retail Price: $449
Approximate Low Price: $400

UNIVERSAL REMOTE CONTROLS

RCA NiteGlo RCU4GLW

✓BEST BUY

Ergonomically designed with raised clear keys and black labels, the NiteGlo RCU4GLW features 32 keys laid out into distinct sections. It is capable of controlling four devices: TV, VCR, cable box, and second VCR/cable. The function keys are situated across the top with VCR transport keys. The keypad is in the middle of the remote. The bottom of the remote is shoehorn-shaped for easy resting in the palm of either a left-handed or a right-handed person. Because of this design, your thumb automatically rests on the circular channel/volume up/down keys, which are laid out as cursor-type keys. Below those keys you'll find the power button, followed by a light-bulb key on the bottom. The light-bulb button activates the NiteGlo feature, which illuminates all of the keys. Powered by four AAA batteries, the NiteGlo RCU4GLW allows you to program codes easily. Within its manual, you will find extensive product category lists of virtually every brand of TV, VCR, and cable box. A new feature found on this remote is a surf button, which allows you to scan through your channels on any of the controlled devices automatically.

Warranty: 90 days
Manufacturer's Suggested Retail Price: $25
Approximate Low Price: $19

Rotel RR990 Universal Remote

Recommended

While somewhat expensive, Rotel's RR990 offers a backlit LCD touchpad screen divided into three distinct areas. The top section contains five function buttons that are always visible, and five hidden confirmation indicators that alert the user to various operating states on a "need to know" basis. The larger center panel is devoted to individual control panels, which change upon the component selected. Three different views are available: complete, basic, and custom. The bottom of the screen contains selectors for eight different system components including DSS and DVD. As you customize screens to fit your particular needs, macro programming is also possible.

Warranty: 5 years
Manufacturer's Suggested Retail Price: $200
Approximate Low Price: $200

Sole Control SC-555

Recommended

The Sole Control SC-555 is part of a new breed of aftermarket remotes capable of controlling up to six devices. Ergonomically designed with raised keys placed within different groupings, it will stand up on your coffee table. The SC-555 utilizes 39 easy-to-read, spongy keys on a black background. The layout is uncluttered. Within a few minutes, six component codes can be stored in memory. Write the codes down on the supplied label that attaches to the back of the unit. The SC-555 has no memory backup. You'll have to rekey the codes each time you change batteries. As with many universal remotes, it is powered by four AAA batteries. An added bonus is the audio and video macro keys that store several functions together. Simply press one key to turn on several components.

Warranty: 1 year
Manufacturer's Suggested Retail Price: $30
Approximate Low Price: $24

VCRS, DVD, AND LASER DISC PLAYERS

More than twenty years ago, videocassette recorders (VCRs) were a rare and exotic commodity found in only a handful of consumer households. Today, they are a basic component found in most home entertainment systems, reaching more than 89 percent of all households in the U.S. And even though other technologies are fast becoming common, VCRs still hold their position as the machine of choice, largely because they are the one technology that allows consumers to record programs unattended.

LASER DISC (LD) PLAYERS

Laser disc players provide excellent picture and sound for home video; however, they do not record. The list of movies available on laser disc is extensive; virtually all films are now released on laser disc. Many are released in special editions that include added footage, interviews with actors and directors, and additional material not previously available on the videocassette version.

Prices of discs are generally competitive with videotapes, but are far less subject to mechanical failure and wear than tapes. The imminent death of laser discs has been rumored for many years, but the quality and economy of the format should ensure its place in the market for the next several years. However, virtually all manufacturers have discontinued their laser disc player in response to the introduction of Digital Video Disc (DVD). Pioneer is one of the few brands that continues to manufacture DVD/LD models.

DIGITAL VIDEO DISC (DVD)

DVD (Digital Video Disc or Digital Versatile Disc) is almost two years old, with sales close to 400,000 in the last year alone. DVD's superb digital audio and video quality has made it a formidable successor to VCRs and laser discs. Besides playing movies from a five-inch disc, it will also play CDs. Player prices start at approximately $400 for a basic unit and $600 for a more fully-featured model. Close to a dozen manufacturers have DVD players available. Purchasing a disc a DVD costs about $25 per movie.

DVDs also hold promise for the computer industry. As the successor to CD- ROM, it will be known as DVD-ROM. The storage capacity is phenomenal. Data that now needs several discs will be held on one disc. For example, the complete Encyclopaedia Britannica—all 26, or so, volumes—along with sound and video clips relating to each entry, could be stored on one disc.

BUYING TIPS

Buying video components from a specialty dealer usually eliminates hassles and confusion. Specialists do not necessarily charge a higher price than the mass-market superstores, but if they do, they often make it up to you in service. In our experience, home entertainment specialty dealers display a wider selection of equipment in a space more suitable for viewing. They also pride themselves on good, in-store service departments.

However, if you know exactly what you want, you'll be perfectly satisfied with most of the national chain superstores. Keep in mind that superstores often use select models during promotions, selling them at lower prices. Sometimes these models are discontinued or about to be discontinued and the manufacturer wants to unload them. Since there's minimal change from one model year to the next, buying last year's model can be a good value.

BEST BUYS '99

Our Best Buy, Recommended, and Budget Buy VCRs, laser disc players, and DVD players follow. Within each category, items are listed by quality; the item we consider the best of the Best Buys is first, followed by our second choice, and so on. A Budget Buy describes a less-expensive product of respectable quality that perhaps sacrifices some of the performance and/or convenience features of a Best Buy or Recommended product. Remember that a Best Buy, Recommended, or Budget Buy designation only applies to the model listed—it does not necessarily apply to other models made by the same manufacturer or to an entire product line.

VCRs

VHS VCRs continue to be the preferred format for consumers, largely due to the wide range of movies and other programming available for either purchase or rental. Eventually the future may shift to digital with the introduction of Digital VHS (D-VHS) to record digital images from digital sources (DSS and EchoStar/JVC) and DVC (Digital videocassette—an entirely digital format). HDTV will also play a part in this digital revolution, but not until the end of the decade. VHS, as we know it, will continue to dominate the market well into the next century.

VCR FORMATS

The most common format for the video cassette recorders is VHS, which uses half-inch tape in a cassette shell roughly the size of a paperback book. Hi-8mm is a totally digital format that is technically dazzling and uses a much smaller cassette while producing markedly superior pictures and sound. Regular 8mm tape offers digital images, but does not match the technology of Hi-8mm decks. It should be noted, however, that there are only a handful of 8mm and Hi-8mm machines available, since both formats are primarily used in camcorder applications. You can find combination 8mm/Hi-8mm and VHS decks available from a couple of manufacturers that facilitate editing.

Beta, while in many ways superior to VHS, has virtually disappeared from the marketplace. Sony continues to sell one consumer deck as a replacement model for its installed based (approximately nine million plus) of "betaphiles."

S-VHS VCRs are VHS machines that separate luminance and chrominance signals to give a more detailed image with better definition. Thanks to a lack of prerecorded software, S-VHS never really caught on with the masses, and it continues to represent about one to two percent of total VCR sales. However, with the introduction of DSS (Digital Satellite System) and EchoStar, we finally have a medium suited for making S-VHS recordings. Obviously, for the almost eight million people who have already purchased satellite systems, S-VHS decks make a good choice for replacing their VCR—they will provide them with the best recorded image currently available.

CHOOSING TAPES

If you are going to record on a tape only once or twice, and only occasionally play it back, standard-grade tapes are perfectly fine. However, if you plan to record and play back the same tape many times, use a high-grade tape. We recommend that you use brand-name tapes; many of the less costly, no-name tapes are made so poorly that they can quickly cause extensive, expensive damage to the heads of your VCR. Most people buy T-120 tapes that record two hours at the fastest speed and six hours at the slowest speed. The longest tape presently available is a T-210 tape, which records 10½-hours at the slowest speed.

CHOOSING A VCR

Shopping for a VCR can be a confusing or even intimidating experience. With so many features available in so many different combinations, it can be difficult to make solid comparisons among available machines. Since not every consumer needs or wants every feature, it is important to understand what is available and to know what you want.

FEATURES AND TERMINOLOGY

Auto Clock Set: This noteworthy feature is found on most brands of VCRs. These models set their own clock thanks to a time signal being sent from your local PBS station. This means you never have to set the clock initially or worry if there is a blackout or a brownout. Once power is restored, the VCR will display the right time.

Commercial Advance: New decks include commercial zapper circuitry that senses the beginning and end of commercials. It records the entire program including commercials. Upon playback, it will automatically fast forward through the commercials and go back to the play mode when the program resumes. This is different from commercial skip, which allows you to view other channels and then return you to the station you were watching after a preset time of 30, 60, 90, or 120 seconds.

Editing Features: Unless you actually plan on editing your camcorder tapes and making duplicates, you will not need a VCR with sophisticated editing features such as assemble editing, insert editing, or video dubbing. These features can add up to $100 to the cost of the model, and only make the machine more difficult and intimidating to use.

Hi-Fi Sound: If you want the best quality sound from your prerecorded movies, you'll need hi-fi. If you're thinking about home theater, you'll definitely need a hi-fi VCR. Hi-fi stands for high fidelity or high quality sound. It is true stereo—not the low-fi sound that was available on VCRs several years ago. Prices for hi-fi VCRs range from approximately $300 to $600. If you are in the market for a VCR, hi-fi is the one upgrade feature that you should consider. All movies and videos are now released with hi-fi soundtracks (encoded with Dolby Surround) as standard.

Index Search: Many VCRs record an electronic index code at the beginning of each recording. To scan your recordings on a tape, press index search. The VCR then stops at each index mark, and plays back a few seconds of the recording. Some VCRs even let you go directly to a specific index mark and start playback.

Jog/Shuttle Control: These special-effect tape advance features allow you to control the speed at which a tape is viewed. Shuttle control allows you to search forward or backward through a tape at a range of fast and slow speeds. Jog control allows you to move the tape forward or backward frame by frame.

Programmability: If you are buying a VCR primarily to record television broadcasts, ease of programming is an important consideration. Except for video cassette players, all VCRs can be programmed to record at least one program. The most rudimentary programming scheme uses a built-in clock timer that you set to start and stop within a 24-hour period. More elaborate programming allows you to record several different programs on different channels for a period of 28 days or more. Other program operations let you record the same program every day or every week. Many VCRs now include VCR Plus+, a simple method of programming by entering a number listed in your channel guide or many newspapers' television guides. Some VCR Plus+ models will also change channels on your cable box via a mouse or blaster, or an infrared transmitter located on the top of the VCR. The inventor of VCR Plus+ is introducing Guide Plus+ Gold, which, if included in your TV, will provide "free" TV listings and one-button programming.

Tape Speeds: Virtually all VCRs let you choose among two or three different recording speeds. Playback speed is automatically set, and even VCRs that record in only two speeds play back on all three speeds. The slow speed allows more recording time on the tape, but the faster speed produces a better quality recording. Since many people record at the slowest speeds, some manufacturers have developed special video heads (19-micron heads) for improved picture quality for recording/playback at the slowest speeds.

Universal Remotes: Many models now feature preprogrammed universal remotes with the ability to control a TV, cable box, and satellite system. A unified remote will control the same brand of TV as your VCR.

Video Heads: To record and play back a tape, you only need two video heads. Additional heads are used for special effects such as slow motion, freeze-frame, and on-screen search. Many manufacturers are tweaking their heads to improve picture quality.

VHS VCRs

Toshiba M784

✓BEST BUY

The full-featured Toshiba M784 is a six-head hi-fi VCR that produces some of the finest images available on a handful of VHS decks today. It records pristine images at its slowest speeds, rivaling images recorded at its fastest speed, and provides steady, natural colors with fine detail. Its new 19-micron heads, largely responsible for superb video resolution, are coupled with the V3 Pro Drum chassis, which features a preamp integrated into the heads that reduces video noise. To further improve picture quality, this VCR includes color signal enhancement (CSE), which makes colors more robust and distinct by reducing color bleed. To further enhance its recorded images, this VCR also includes dynamic noise reduction (DNR) circuitry. DNR cleans up the images on tape including video noise, snow, and dropouts. Equipped with a 181-channel tuner and capable of recording six events over a one-month period, the M784 includes a 46-button universal remote that controls your TV, DSS (all brands), and cable box. To facilitate programming, the VCR includes VCR Plus+ with cable-box control and easy-to-use on-screen graphics and programming. The VCR's transport keys become cursor keys for programming. Other features include a jog shuttle dial on the front of the unit, front A/V jacks, auto speed select, auto head cleaner, and a trilingual on-screen display. As with other hi-fi VCRs, the sound quality is excellent, ranking it among the best available. Toshiba has also added auto clock set, which will continue displaying the correct time even if there has been a power failure.

Specifications: height, 3⅝"; width, 16¹⁵⁄₁₆"; depth, 12½"; weight, 10 lbs.
Warranty: 1 year, parts and labor
Manufacturer's Suggested Retail Price: $500
Approximate Low Price: $399

RCA VR692HF

Recommended

The RCA VR692HF is one of the latest generation of a relatively new breed of four-head hi-fi VCRs. One of its innovative features is Commercial Advance, which enables you to "zap out" unwanted commercials by touching one key on the VCR's remote. Upon playback, the VCR senses those index marks and quickly fast-forwards to the end of the segment. You have the choice of having a blue screen displayed or the actual commercials in fast-forward. Picture quality is on par with comparable VCRs. The VR692HF features a 181-channel tuner capable of recording eight events over a one-year period. Being DSS compatible, the tuner can record up to channel 999. A new feature found on this and several RCA VCRs is ShowSaver 24 Memory Protection, which retains all of your programming in the event of a power failure. Other impressive features include auto clock set with auto daylight savings time, VCR Plus+ with cable box, All Picture Control (which optimizes picture quality based on a specific tape), front A/V jacks, child protection system, and XDS Broadcast Data Service (which, if broadcast, offers Station ID and Program Information). Another feature is Movie Advance, which quickly bypasses previews of coming attractions found on most prerecorded tapes. To complete the package, RCA supplies an illuminated, 46-button universal remote that will control a second RCA video component and RCA audio equipment.

Specifications: height, 3$\frac{5}{8}$"; width, 15"; depth, 12"; weight, 9 lbs. 8 oz.
Warranty: 90 days, labor; 1 year parts
Manufacturer's Suggested Retail Price: $329
Approximate Low Price: $249

JVC HR-VP650U

Budget Buy

The JVC HR-VP650U is a top-of-the-line four-head hi-fi VCR that includes some useful convenience features. This unit produces clean, crisp images that are free from smear from both off-air taping and playback of prerecorded videos, thanks to its oval-cut video heads. This model includes 19-micron video heads that provide optimum video resolution when recording at the slowest speed. This set also has Dual-Quick Set, or Plug and Play, which means the VCR has auto clock set (with the auto daylight savings time feature) combined with auto tuner set. Consequently, the VCR's channels are automatically tuned and the clock is set to the correct time. To further improve its sound reproduction, the HR-VP650U includes an audio-switching noise reduction system. You can record up to eight programs over a one-year period and receive up to 181 cable channels. The set also includes VCR Plus+ with a cable-box controller. Other features include auto picture control (which optimizes the inserted tape for either recording or playback) and Instant ReView (which will turn on the VCR and rewind it to the last segment taped). The set is packaged with a newly designed universal remote, which includes a shuttle-plus dial with cursor keys at the bottom. The easy-to-use remote will also control a TV, cable box, and a satellite system. A new feature added this year is Movie Advance, which skips previews of coming attractions and goes directly to the feature.

Specifications: height, $3\frac{3}{4}$"; width, $14\frac{3}{16}$"; depth, $10\frac{7}{8}$"; weight, 10 lbs.
Warranty: 90 days, labor; 1 year, parts
Manufacturer's Suggested Retail Price: $250
Approximate Low Price: $230

Samsung VR-8808

Budget Buy

Samsung's VR-8808 four-head hi-fi VCR offers several desirable features at an economical price. Like many VCRs on the market today, the VR-8808 features the easy-to-use VCR Plus+ on-screen programmer. Just press the VCR Plus+ on the remote, then key in the number found in either your local newspaper or *TV Guide* to tape a program. There is also a Skip Search button on the remote, which will advance the tape in 30-second increments at the touch of a button. Picture quality for this VCR is quite good on both prerecorded videos and taped programs. To improve picture quality, the VR-8808 uses 26-micron heads for better playback at slower speeds. The auto clock set feature instantly sets the time; it searches for the time signal in the Vertical Blanking Interval of your TV (the bar you see if your picture rolls), which carries Station ID and Program Title Display (if being broadcast). Even with blackouts, brownouts, or daylight savings time changes, you'll never have to set the VCR's clock. It also has a six-hour memory backup feature that will save your programming. The VCR allows you to program up to eight events over a one-month period from its 181-channel tuner. The universal remote is sophisticated and easy to use. Other features include an auto head cleaner and a tamperproof mechanism to keep prying fingers out of the VCR. The VCR also includes trilingual on-screen menus and displays.

Specifications: height, 3½"; width, 15¾"; depth, 12½"; weight, 8 lbs. 12 oz.
Warranty: 90 days, labor; 1 year, parts
Manufacturer's Suggested Retail Price: $239
Approximate Low Price: $219

DIGITAL VIDEO DISC (DVD) PLAYERS

Digital video disc (DVD) is a small five-inch disc that will hold a 133-minute movie on one side of the disc, without having to turn it over. Reportedly, 90 percent of all the movies released run 133 minutes or less. Depending on the company that is releasing the film, many discs are dual-layered so that discs containing longer films will not have to be turned over. Each disc, however, clearly states if it is dual-layered.

QUALITY

Touted as the future of home video, DVD has a far superior picture (500 lines of resolution or better) than either Digital Satellite System (approximately 480 lines of resolution), laser disc (425 lines of resolution), S-VHS (400 lines of resolution), or VHS (240 lines of resolution) formats. Besides playing movies, DVD players will also play CDs. Audio is of digital quality, and comparable or superior to CDs. Most discs include Dolby Digital soundtracks that also play back Dolby Pro Logic. You can watch movies in pan-and-scan (action is centered on one image, while information on both sides of the screen is cut off) and letterbox on regular TV and anamorphic on wide-screen TVs. All discs offer several language/subtitle versions. You can invoke parental control, which will convert an R-rated movie into a PG-13 version, with certain footage or scenes simply not played.

DVD AND DIVX

A formidable challenge for DVD is DIVX, which stands for Digital Video Express. DIVX is the other type of DVD player that has caused a lot of confusion and speculation. While a DIVX player may look like a DVD player, and plays discs that look similar, it is an entirely different type of player. DIVX is a specialized rental form of DVD. DIVX players include special circuitry that decodes and "unlocks" DIVX discs. Players are currently sold only at both Circuit City and The Good Guys chain stores.

Instead of paying approximately $25 to buy a DVD movie, DIVX offers a special rental of $4.50 for 50 hours play. Prior to playing any discs on the machine, you must set up a credit card account with DIVX. You'll also need a telephone outlet for the DIVX player as it needs to be in constant contact with DIVX Central, which will "unlock" your movie for viewing. At the end of the initial viewing period, you can either throw the disc away, keep it for future viewing (paying an additional rental fee), or purchase it. There are a two ways to purchase the disc: There is a "Silver" plan, which allows unlimited play within your own home but you cannot play the disc on someone else's DIVX machine without paying an additional rental. Some discs, however, can be made "Gold," which means you can buy it for unlimited viewings on any DIVX machine.

It should be noted, however, that DIVX players play both DVD and DIVX discs, as opposed to DVD players, which cannot play DIVX discs. Also unlike DVD players, DIVX players include a built-in modem; thus you'll need to install another phone jack so you can have your DIVX always attached to it.

FEATURES AND TERMINOLOGY

Audio and Video (Inputs/Outputs): Normally there are more audio outputs than video outputs. More video outputs (and their audio counterparts) are desirable because they allow you more versatility in signal switching of multiple VCR, laser disc, and DVD players. Depending on how you hook up your A/V system, either the TV or your A/V receiver can be used for video switching.

Chapter Numbers: These numbers are recorded on the discs and are used to indicate sections or chapters (almost like track numbers on CDs).

Component Video (Inputs/Outputs): Also called Color Difference or ColorStream, component video is the newest input and output to date. It provides images that are far superior to S-VHS. Most high-end DVD players include component video outputs, which will also be included on most HDTV set-top boxes. Many TV manufacturers are now including these inputs on their mid- to upper-line TVs. Component video provides 500 lines of resolution or better.

Dolby Digital: This is the next step beyond Dolby Pro Logic, offering 5.1 channels of sound. The player has outputs for the sound audio technique called Dolby Surround Digital, or Dolby AC-3. The rear channel is now stereo, along with a separate channel (the .1) for the subwoofer. This gives the director and sound engineer the ability to localize sound to a specific area or speaker, providing you full stereo surround.

Jog/Shuttle Control: These special-effect tape advance features allow you to control the speed at which a tape is viewed. Shuttle control allows you to search forward or backward through a tape at a range of fast and slow speeds. Jog control allows you to move the tape forward or backward, frame by frame.

Parental Lockout or Channel Block: Designed to help parents manage their children's viewing time, this feature is available on all DVD players. Simply access the on-screen menu system and you can set specific viewing levels for the player. You can override these controls by punching in a personalized code.

S-Video (Inputs/Outputs): Many components besides S-VHS VCRs now include S-video jacks. S-video offers better picture quality than standard video inputs. While increasing resolution, it helps color reproduction and reduces jitter at scene transitions. On many televisions, you will find as many S-video inputs as you have standard video inputs. To get the most out of your video source, you should use an S-video jack for the highest resolution.

Universal Remotes: Many models now feature preprogrammed universal remotes with the ability to control TVs and cable boxes. Some are equipped to control satellite systems. A unified remote will control the same brand of TV as your DVD.

RCA RC5510P

✓ BEST BUY

The RCA RC5510P is a superb example of DVD. This model is DTS (Digital Theater System) compatible, which means that it will pass a DTS 5.1 surround sound signal through a DTS decoder for translation into spectacular sound. This player also includes a built-in Dolby Digital Surround decoder. Simply attach it to a Dolby Digital-ready A/V receiver or processor to enjoy the benefits of 5.1 audio. RCA supplies a preprogrammed universal remote that will also control a TV, RCA-DSS, VCR, RCA audio equipment, and cable box. All keys on the remote are color-coded and divided into sections. Its ergonomical design makes it easy to use. Outputs include one S-video, two composite video, one AC-3 digital audio, and two pairs of analog audio. For the budget-minded, you can attach the RC5510P to RCA's 3798 A/V receiver, which is 5.1-ready, for an economical home theater package.

Specifications: height, 2⅘"; width, 15½"; depth, 11½"; weight, 9 lbs.
Warranty: 1 year, parts and labor
Manufacturer's Suggested Retail Price: $599
Approximate Low Price: $599

Toshiba SD-3108

✓ BEST BUY

The Toshiba SD-3108 is yet another excellent example of a DVD player, producing some of the most striking video images of any in its class. It comes equipped with a backlit universal remote, which includes a jog dial that will also control a TV and cable box. It is DTS (Digital Theater System) compatible, ensuring sensational sound. For users who do not have a full-blown home theater setup, the SD-3108 includes built-in Spatializer circuitry that will enhance your sound in a two speaker playback situation. Outputs include one S-video, one composite video, one AC-3 digital audio, two pairs of analog audio, one digital coax, one digital optical, and one component video. An innovative feature found on this year's model is Zoom, which allows you to blow up a particular scene. Also included with the SD-3108 is a certificate from netflix.com for three free DVD rentals.

Specifications: height, 3 3/16"; width, 17"; depth, 12 1/8"; weight, 7 lbs. 8 oz.
Warranty: 90 days, labor; 1 year, parts
Manufacturer's Suggested Retail Price: $800
Approximate Low Price: $650

Sony DVP-S500D

Recommended

The DVP-S500D includes all of the desirable features now considered standard on a DVD player. First and foremost, this player features a dual discrete optical pickup—one for DVD and one for CD—which enables stable and accurate playback of both types of discs. The DVP-S500D features digital-to-analog (D/A) converters for optimum playback of all types of discs. A built-in Dolby Digital decoder is also included, which allows you to attach this player to a Dolby Digital-ready A/V receiver. A built-in circuit automatically looks for the Dolby Digital signal to output. A feature included here (but not found on most other players) is Speaker Set-Up and Adjustment, which includes balance, subwoofer levels, and test tones that maximize surround sound. If you don't have rear speakers, the DVP-S500D includes Digital Cinema Sound, which uses Virtual Enhanced Surround, offering the illusion of rear speakers. Besides including two S-video and two composite video outputs, the DVP-S500D features component video outputs for optimal video images (as long as they are attached to a television with component video inputs). Other outputs include both optical and coaxial digital. This player comes with a universal remote that controls other brands of TVs and selected Sony A/V equipment. A jog/shuttle ring is situated at the bottom for slow motion or frame-by-frame advance. Like many other Sony products available, this model includes S-Link. If you press the power or play button on the DVP-S500D, S-Link will turn on your Sony TV, your Sony A/V receiver, and switch everything to the proper inputs.

Specifications: height, 3¼"; width, 17"; depth, 12⅝"; weight, 8 lbs. 6 oz.
Warranty: 1 year, parts and labor
Manufacturer's Suggested Retail Price: $700
Approximate Low Price: $545

Pioneer DV-505

Budget Buy

Pioneer, the first to introduce laser disc players and longtime advocate of optical technology, offers a terrific entry-level DVD player. This player features digital-to-analog (D/A) converters for excellent image and sound reproduction. The DV-505 features a dual optical pickup—one for DVDs and one for CDs—for proper sound optimization. Like other DVD players on the market, the DV-500 offers multiple aspect ratios, multiangle, multiple languages, multiaudio, and parental lockout. This model also includes its Heads-Up remote. Designed to fit in your hand easily, it offers top-mounted cursor keys for easy control. There are two audio outputs, one S-video output, one video output, two Dolby Digital outputs (one coaxial and one optical), and one optical digital output. Overall, the DV-500 is a solid performer that is easy to use. A welcome addition to anyone's budding home theater.

Specifications: height, 4⅛"; width, 16 9/16"; depth, 11 13/16"; weight, 6 lbs. 6 oz.
Warranty: 90 days, labor; 1 year, parts
Manufacturer's Suggested Retail Price: $635
Approximate Low Price: $499

LASER DISC PLAYERS

A laser disc is an optical medium for playing video and digital audio recording. Pits cut in the disc are read by a laser beam. Because information can be read from the discs without any physical contact, the acrylic-coated discs will virtually last forever. Laser discs also produce excellent image quality with ordinary hookups to your television set. They are capable of producing superb images, with nearly twice the horizontal resolution of standard videotapes when used with TVs that have S-video connections.

WHAT IT OFFERS

Most laser disc players are combination players, meaning they play multiple types of discs from 5-inch CDs through 12-inch laser discs. Many models today provide a separate drawer for CD-only playback. These models utilize a CD Direct input that operates the drawer and disconnects the video circuitry for less interference.

Many laser disc players offer dual-sided play, which automatically turns the disc over. This process takes about 12 seconds. The unit will either display a blue screen or freeze the last frame of the video until the next scene starts.

Because laser disc is primarily a medium for people who love movies, many discs are available in letterboxed versions. Letterboxing places black bars at the top and bottom of the screen, retaining the original aspect ratio the director intended. On videocassette, for example, most movies are panned-and-scanned. This means that the action is centered on one image and information on the left and right sides of the screen is cut off.

FEATURES AND TERMINOLOGY

Chapter Numbers: These numbers are recorded on the discs and are used to indicate sections or chapters (almost like track numbers on CDs).

Digital Time Base Correction: Time base correction helps reduce jitter at the edges and corners of the picture.

Dolby Digital-Ready: This is the next step beyond Dolby Pro Logic, offering 5.1 channels of sound. The rear channel is now stereo, along with a separate channel (the .1) for the subwoofer. This gives the director and sound engineer the ability to localize sound to a specific area or speaker, providing you full stereo surround.

Random Access: All laser disc players have the ability to provide random access, allowing you to locate a particular spot on the disc.

Theater Mode: Several seconds are cut from the turnover time of a disc by skipping over side B's table of contents. It will also dim the front panel's illumination.

Types of Discs: There are two types of laser discs: CAV (constant angular velocity) and CLV (constant linear velocity). CAV discs spin at a constant speed of 1,800 rpm, with a playing time of 30 minutes per side. CLV discs spin at speeds ranging from 1,800 rpm for the inner tracks to 600 rpm for outer tracks. This permits a playing time of 60 minutes per side.

Pioneer CLD-D606

✓BEST BUY

The Pioneer CLD-D606 is one of the last laser-disc-only players available. Picture and product design are excellent. It offers many advanced and useful features including a 3D digital comb filter and dual-sided disc play. Capable of displaying 425 lines of resolution, it produces crisp images with little video noise. It also includes standard features such as a digital time base corrector (which eliminates noise and jitter from the picture) and video enhancement circuitry. A handy feature included on this model is CD Direct. This means there is a separate drawer in the middle of the laser disc drawer to play your CDs. The easy-to-use remote features a jog/shuttle dial at the bottom of the remote. Outputs include two S-video, one Dolby Digital, and one digital optical for maximum home theater fidelity. For straight Dolby Pro Logic sound, standard audio outputs are also included. The front panel is easy to read and provides all of the information needed, including a calendarlike grid that displays the track/chapter currently playing.

Specifications: height, 5 3/16"; width, 16 9/16";depth, 15 15/16": weight, 14 lbs. 8 oz.
Warranty: 1 year, parts and labor.
Manufacturer's Suggested Retail Price: $760
Approximate Low Price: $600

Pioneer Elite DVL-91

Recommended

Pioneer's DVL-91 player is an exceptional combination unit that plays both laser discs and digital video discs (DVD). Using Pioneer's 10-bit video digital-to-analog converter, picture quality is superb compared to standard DVD players. To achieve quality sound, the player uses a 20-bit digital-to-analog conversion system capable of decoding DVD stereo audio tracks. The player has separate trays for LDs and CD/DVDs. Like most upscale LD players, the DVL-91 has a dual-sided play mechanism. The DVL-91 includes a Heads-Up remote control and video graphic user interface (GUI), which resembles the company's new PTV and A/V receiver remotes. The player includes two S-video outputs, one component video output, and two digital audio outputs: one optical and one coaxial (for either AC-3 or DTS). The unit also includes Variable Digital Noise Reduction for improved picture clarity. Other enhancement features include Pioneer's Legato Link circuitry, which restores high frequencies filtered out of the digital signal during recording. Housed in black cabinetry, this player is among the best and most versatile DVD players around, offering the added bonus of playing your laser discs. While somewhat expensive, it is a powerhouse that combines state-of-the-art video technology of both DVD and laser disc.

Specifications: height, 5 1/2"; width, 16 9/16"; depth, 18 1/4"; weight, 19 lbs. 3 oz.
Warranty: 2 years, parts and labor
Manufacturer's Suggested Retail Price: $1,800
Approximate Low Price: $1,700

CAMCORDERS

The camcorder, which combines a video camera and a videocassette recorder in one unit, records live action on tape for near-instantaneous playback. Even the least expensive camcorders incorporate a variety of useful features with satisfactory performance. As the sales boom of the late 1980s faded, prices for basic models fell, reaching new lows in 1997. Sony, Panasonic, JVC, Sharp, Canon, and Hitachi manufacture nearly all camcorders on the market, no matter what brand name is on the unit. Thus, you might be able to save a few dollars by comparing two similar (sometimes identical) models sold under different brand names.

ZOOM LENSES

Manufacturers use increasingly longer (more powerful) zoom lenses as enticements to buy more expensive models. In reality, they serve little purpose. An 8-power zoom lense is about the maximum necessary for steady shooting with a compact handheld model, and a 12-power lens is the maximum for shoulder-supported full-size models or those with effective electronic image stabilization. However, virtually all models sold today come with a 16- or 18-power zoom as standard. Only if you have firm support, such as with a monopod or tripod, can you effectively use a zoom lens greater than 12-power. Digital zoom, in which the camcorder electronically magnifies the picture, causes graininess and picture distortion, making it nearly useless for serious shooting. Despite this fact, there are models with high magnifications upward to 200-power.

VIEWFINDERS

Many models now come with color LCD viewfinders, which have improved somewhat since they were first introduced several years ago. While it's nice to see what you're shooting in color, these viewfinders are usually dimmer and lower in resolution than their black-and-white counterparts. Manufacturers have, however, improved the pixel count and beefed up the brightness levels. If you opt for a color viewfinder, choose a model with at least 100,000 (or 100K) pixels, preferably more. A color viewfinder adds about $100 to the camcorder's cost, which is somewhat excessive to the benefit derived.

A recent feature that replaces the viewfinder on some camcorders is a 2.5- to 4-inch color LCD screen. This allows shooting from a variety of positions without holding the camcorder directly to your eye. It's also convenient for playback away from a TV set. The drawback is that the LCD screen may wash out in bright sunlight. Sony, RCA, Panasonic, and JVC offer the screen as a "stealth" option that folds into the camcorder body while you continue shooting using the standard black-and-white viewfinder.

BUYING TIPS

When shopping for a camcorder, understand that picture quality between models in similar categories varies only slightly, but the feel and operational ease differ substantially. When shopping for a camcorder, try it on for comfort and ease of use.

CAMCORDER FORMATS

The market share among the three different camcorder (8mm, VHS, and VHS-C) formats has somewhat stabilized. Both 8mm and VHS-C continue to do well, but full-size VHS continues to decrease in popularity. DVC, the newest format, has grown about five percent in the last year.

The VHS and 8mm formats are electronically compatible. This allows you to connect your 8mm camcorder to your VHS VCR and copy your 8mm videos onto VHS tape. Front-panel input jacks for this purpose are becoming nearly standard on VHS decks. Input jacks have previously been placed on the back panels. You can also connect your 8mm camcorder directly to your TV for viewing as well. Many TVs also sport front A/V jacks just for this purpose.

Digital Video (DV): These camcorders, introduced a couple of years ago, offer superior audio and video quality. While somewhat pricey, DV offers the highest quality currently available. With cassettes slightly larger in size than a matchbox, these camcorders digitally record and process information. This means that there is virtually no loss of picture quality after dubbing to another format or your computer. These camcorders use a 570,000-pixel, ⅓-inch CCD image sensor to create high quality recordings. PCM digital audio offers equally superior digital audio, which is several notches above VHS hi-fi. The standard DV cassette uses metal tape and records for 60 minutes. Power is provided by lithium batteries that are slightly larger than AA batteries and have no battery "memory effect."

8mm: The cassettes for the 8mm format are roughly the size of audiocassettes, though slightly thicker, and they use ⅓-inch-wide tape, which is narrower than the ½-inch VHS video format. By using metal tape to increase recording density, 8mm tapes reproduce an image comparable to VHS or slightly better. Camcorders that use this format are compact and lightweight, with many models weighing less than 1½ pounds. A standard 8mm camcorder records up to 2½ hours on a single tape in SP. Many models offer both SP and LP recording capability.

Hi-band 8mm (Hi8): This format offers the same resolution as S-VHS (about 400 lines), but Hi8 records with slightly less color noise, making the picture quality subtly better than S-VHS's. Standard 8mm tape will record and playback on Hi8 machines, but tapes recorded on Hi8 will not playback on conventional 8mm machines. Hi8 camcorders require special tape formulations: a premium metal evaporated tape (Hi8-ME) and the improved metal particle tape (Hi8-MP). Both are more expensive than standard VHS tape. Hi8-ME offers superior performance, but it is difficult to manufacture, costs appreciably more, and is more difficult to find. New Hi8-MP formulations narrow the performance gap and work as well for everyday shooting. Hi8 camcorders, like S-VHS, include S-video jacks for maximum signal transfer quality to a TV or an S-VHS VCR. However, most of the Hi8 advantage can still be realized through ordinary cables.

VHS: This format has the longest recording capacity of all formats. VHS can record up to 10½ hours on a T-210 tape using the slow, extended play (EP) speed; however, picture and sound quality noticeably degrade. The bulky size of the VHS cassette with its ½-inch-wide tape requires a relatively large, often heavy camcorder. Full-size VHS is the only format that can be played back directly in home VHS VCRs. Camcorders without the hi-fi option record low-fidelity audio.

VHS-C: This format is a variation of the VHS format that uses cassettes about one-third of the size of regular VHS cassettes. The signals recorded on VHS-C are fully compatible with full-size VHS. This allows VHS-C cassettes to record and play back on any VHS VCR when placed in an adapter supplied with nearly all VHS-C camcorders. VHS-C tapes record for a maximum of 40 minutes at the standard play (SP) and two hours at the low quality extended play (EP) speed. Like full-size camcorders, VHS-C camcorders without the hi-fi option record low-fidelity audio.

Super VHS (S-VHS): This format uses a specially formulated, much more expensive tape along with superior electronics. This tape records up to 400 lines of resolution—close to laser disc in video quality—and far outperforms conventional VHS (240 lines). It also substantially improves the video quality of the slow EP speed, making it more acceptable for ordinary recording.

FEATURES AND TERMINOLOGY

Aperture Designation: This refers to the maximum opening of the iris—in other words, to the greatest amount of light that can be admitted. The designation is given as an f-stop rating, such as f/1.6. The smaller the f-stop number the larger the aperture and the more light that will pass through the lens. In all camcorders, the iris automatically adjusts. Some camcorders offer a manual adjustment as well.

Autofocus: This feature focuses the lens and keeps it focused even as the distance between the camcorder and the subject changes. Some camcorders also permit manual focusing. Each manufacturer uses a proprietary autofocus system with varying degrees of speed and accuracy. Although most companies employ some form of computerized through-the-lens (TTL) system, the simpler infrared system sometimes works better. Be sure to try out the autofocus system when evaluating the camcorder.

Automatic (or Continuous) White Balance: This keeps the color of the video image true to life under varying lighting conditions, from outdoor to indoor and fluorescent to incandescent. An inaccurate white balance can result in a picture that is too pink or too blue.

Character Generators: These allow you to add the time, date, titles, and other written information to the images that you are recording.

Fade In/Fade Out: This feature automatically fades the image from, or to, a black (or white) screen.

Flying Erase Head: This is mounted on the spinning video head drum rather than in a stationary position along the tape path. Because it spins with the other heads, a flying erase head allows you to make smooth transitions when you stop and start the tape between scenes, eliminating noise bursts. The flying erase head is particularly desirable if you want better quality in edited tapes.

Image Stabilization: This is a generic term for reducing unwanted camcorder motion caused by shakes and jitters. It has become a standard feature in recent years. Some companies use a digital electronic system that slightly fuzzes the picture to reduce the unwanted motion. Others compensate by rapidly moving the lens, calling it optical image stabilization. Having reviewed a large number of camcorders, we question the overall benefit of this feature. Effectiveness of image stabilization will vary from brand to brand, however.

Imager (or Imaging Device): This solid-state device collects light and transforms it into an electrical signal. A high-speed shutter alters the method that the camcorder uses to collect light from its CCD (charged-coupled) imaging device. This results in the equivalent of allowing less light into the camcorder. A high-speed shutter permits operation at speeds up to 1/40,000 of a second. Most camcorders on the market today have a shutter range from 1/60 to 1/4,000 of a second, which is adequate for most people. Unless you plan to shoot sporting events, a high-speed shutter is probably not an essential feature.

Lux: This refers to a unit of measurement that gauges the amount of light falling on a photo subject. Many camcorders have a low-light rating of around 10 lux, which is similar to the amount of light cast on an image about 12 feet from one 60-watt lightbulb. Although sensitive camcorders can deliver a picture at 1 lux, you are most likely to get a good image with 80 lux. The best color and depth of field require several hundred lux. For many years, manufacturers have played a lux war game with each claiming the lowest lux level with no real standard in place for measuring lux. There is now a standard in place—EIA-639. New literature will state lux as "measured by the EIA standard." This will mean that brand A's 3 lux will be equivalent to brand B's 3 lux if they both state their lux "as measured by the EIA standard." Minimum illumination tells you the minimum amount of light, stated in lux, necessary to record a clear picture.

Pixel: Short for "picture element," a pixel is one of the tiny points (or dots) that make up a video image. The higher the pixel count, the more detailed the image. But because the size and type of imaging devices vary, comparing pixel counts between different devices doesn't always determine which can yield the most detailed image.

Program Auto Exposure (or Program AE): This feature offers different modes of preprogrammed exposures depending on your shooting and lighting conditions. These modes alter the shutter, iris, and white balance to different settings; for example, snow, twilight, sepia, and sports (high-speed shutter). Usually found on a dial located on the side of the camcorders, these settings can easily be changed to suit your lighting or special effects needs.

Resolution: This is the ability to produce fine detail in a video picture. It is usually measured in horizontal lines. Vertical resolution, less frequently used, is a more stringent measure. A good video monitor produces more than 500 lines. Television broadcasts have about 340 lines, and DSS more than 450. Conventional VHS reproduces 240 lines and 8mm close to 300.

Superimposer: A superimposer is a digital memory function that can store images or titles. At the push of a button, you can superimpose the stored image over the picture currently being recorded.

BEST BUYS '99

Our Best Buy, Recommended, and Budget Buy camcorders follow. Within each category, camcorders are listed by quality; the item we consider the best of the Best Buys is first, followed by our second choice, and so on. Remember that a Best Buy, Recommended, or Budget Buy designation only applies to the model listed—it does not necessarily apply to other models made by the same manufacturer or to an entire product line.

8MM CAMCORDERS

Sony CCD-TR87

BEST BUY

The Sony CCD-TR87 represents one of the best combinations of features in a reasonably priced 8mm camcorder. It uses a ¼-inch, 270,000-pixel CCD imager to record sparkling pictures. Although this model features a 64-power digital zoom, the 16-power optical zoom is more than sufficient under normal shooting conditions. The camcorder has the ability to shoot video down to 0.7 lux. The six-mode programmed auto exposure is helpful in extreme lighting situations. The TR87 uses an f/1.4-2.7 lens with a focal range of 4.1-65.6mm. The filter diameter is 37 millimeters. Sporting one of the better color viewfinders, this camcorder has a precision color LCD with 113,000 pixels. To improve brightness, Sony employs its Solar Window to allow additional light into the LCD via a special top-mounted viewfinder "window." The TR87 uses "no memory effect" batteries, which means that the batteries will retain a full charge even if you recharge them before they are fully run down. You can also use AA batteries if you find that you've run out of standard battery power. As with many 8mm camcorders, you can tape at two speeds: SP and LP. The TR87 features Sony's quick-record system, which can start recording in one-third of a second and has the ability to record five-second snippets for fast-paced videos automatically. You can also record the date and time on your videos, plus eight preprogrammed titles from the built-in clock/calendar and character generator. Also included is a nine-button remote for easy playback of your videos. A wireless attachment system called LaserLink attaches to your television with an optional adapter.

Specifications: height, 4¼"; width, 4¼"; depth, 7⅝"; weight, 1 lb. 7 oz. (without tape and battery)
Warranty: 90 days, labor; 1 year, parts
Manufacturer's Suggested Retail Price: $599
Approximate Low Price: $499

Sony CCD-TRV85

Recommended

A 3½-inch color LCD viewing screen folds out from the left side of this impressive 8mm camcorder. When folded in, it becomes part of the camcorder body, allowing you to bypass the use of the LCD screen in bright sunlight by using the standard top-mounted black-and-white viewfinder. This system surpasses the Sharp ViewCams, in which the LCD is permanently affixed to the camcorder body. The Sony screen pivots and tilts, and when folded out, reveals a speaker and secondary camcorder controls. The screen permits the camcorder to function as a mini-monitor, enabling you to view prerecorded videos or previously shot footage. It also has a dial to adjust the brightness for use while shooting a video. A set of zoom keys is located at the front of the camcorder. The high cost of the LCD causes this camcorder to fall within the Recommended range rather than the Best Buy. Although the TRV85 is a standard 8mm, rather than Hi8, it has maximum conventional resolution. It features a ¼-inch, 470,000-pixel CCD imager that is also used on Sony's Hi8 models. It uses five video heads. Operationally, the TRV85 is equivalent to Sony's full-featured TR series models, with digital picture effects and fades, digital noise reduction, SteadyShot optical image stabilization, 72-power digital, and Sony's virtually instantaneous quick record system. The high pixel count of the CCD allows using the digital effects with pleasing results. The TRV85 has a low light sensitivity of 0.7 lux and uses an f/1.4-3.0mm lens with a focal length of 4.1-73.8mm. A six-mode programmed auto exposure optimizes the camcorder for a range of shooting conditions such as sports, portrait, and night. Like other camcorders in the 8mm format, it has a flying erase head for seamless edits, it can record at two speeds, and it comes with the necessary jacks for editing. It also includes six preprogrammed titles in memory and a nine-button remote. A built-in speaker is also included. Besides the standard battery, it also uses AA batteries. LaserLink, a new feature from Sony, allows wireless hookup to your TV with an optional wireless receiver.

Specifications: height, 3"; width, 4⅓"; depth, 8"; weight, 2 lbs. 12 oz. (without tape and battery)
Warranty: 90 days, labor; 1 year, parts
Manufacturer's Suggested Retail Price: $1,099
Approximate Low Price: not available

RCA ProV730

Budget Buy

The RCA ProV730 is part of RCA's PROVIEW line of 8mm camcorders. It offers several compelling features at a reasonable price, including a three-inch color LCD display panel (112,320 pixels) that folds out of the left side of the camcorder. Camcorders with color LCD displays allow users to watch the action on larger screens instead of the tiny ½-inch black-and-white viewfinder. The camcorder uses a standard lithium battery to power the unit (allowing 120 minutes of use on one charge). The ¼-inch, 250,000-pixel CCD imager is coupled with a 16-power zoom. It includes an f/1.4-2.6 lens with a focal range of 4.0-64mm. Like most camcorders, date and time, tape remaining, battery, and zoom gauges are displayed within the viewfinder. Also included is a full-function remote. The camcorder features a built-in lens cover.

The ProV730 includes a flying erase head for seamless edits. Other convenience features include Scene Select AE recording dial with nine recording modes, eight Quick Titles, one-page titler, manual exposure control, and an automatic head cleaning system.

Specifications: height, 4½"; width, 4⅛"; depth, 9⁷⁄₁₆"; weight, 5 lbs.
Warranty: 90 days, labor; 1 year, parts
Manufacturer's Suggested Retail Price: $599
Approximate Low Price: $450

FULL-SIZE VHS CAMCORDERS

RCA CC4371

✓BEST BUY

The RCA CC4371 is a full-size VHS camcorder that takes good videos with a minimum of fuss and bother with its full-range autofocus system. It is the first full-size VHS camcorder to include a three-inch color LCD monitor. Its 32:1 Zoom Plus system coupled with a ¼-inch, 250,000-pixel CCD imager and its full-size video heads need as little as one lux to record a picture. Conventional zoom is 16:1, and then doubles digitally to 32:1. RCA has fully automated the camcorder with programmed automatic exposure and automatic white balance for ease of use. It includes a two-line titler to record captions on your videos, and it will also record the date and time. An added bonus is electronic image stabilization. For convenience, the ½-inch black-and-white electric viewfinder tilts and slides so you can position the camcorder more comfortably (for either left- or right-eye viewing). Included is audio/video dubbing, which is handy for replacing either the audio or video portions of one of your tapes. New this year is a color enhancement light that helps provide illumination in low lighting conditions. Program auto exposure (AE) is also included, as well as digital signal processing for more accurate colors. Digital special effects are also included. It provides all of the features needed to take good videos at a reasonable price.

Specifications: height, 8⅜"; width, 4¾"; depth, 13⅛"; weight, 4 lbs. 9 oz. (without tape and battery)
Warranty: 90 days, labor; 1 year, parts
Manufacturer's Suggested Retail Price: $699
Approximate Low Price: not available

Panasonic PV-950-B

Recommended

The Panasonic PV-950-B full-size VHS camcorder addresses most of the awkwardness of the full-size format. The centrally-positioned handgrip and the viewfinder that flips from one side to the other suits both left-handers and right-handers. Thus, it has earned the name of "SwitchHitter." Its slim width also makes this camcorder more manageable. Acknowledging that you won't dangle it from your neck like a compact model, Panasonic supplies an attache-style carrying case. The PV-950-B's ⅓-inch, 270,000-pixel CCD coupled with a 14-power dual-speed zoom requires a minimum of 1-lux illumination. A color viewfinder (116,150 pixels) is included for ease of use, as well as color enhancement light. Automatic operation assures the best videos in most shooting situations. As with all of Panasonic's full-size models, this camcorder clock/calendar comes preset—all you have to do is switch it to your time zone. The date and time will automatically record on the tape if you desire. The bookmark search finds the end of the previous recording, eliminating gaps and overlaps before new recordings, even if you remove and reinsert a tape. A flying erase head eliminates glitches when you stop and start recording, which is particularly useful in editing. It comes with a standard two-hour battery.

Specifications: height, 8¼"; width, 3⅜"; depth, 15"; weight, 4 lbs. 2 oz. (without tape and battery)
Warranty: 90 days, labor; 1 year, parts
Manufacturer's Suggested Retail Price: $800
Approximate Low Price: $600

COMPACT VHS (VHS-C) CAMCORDERS

RCA Small Wonder CC6371

✓BEST BUY

The RCA CC6371 is an excellent example of a full-featured VHS-C camcorder. Its four video heads provide nice images and it includes many useful features, such as flying erase heads. The CC6371 features a ¼-inch, 250,000-pixel count CCD imager with a 22-power zoom. It utilizes a fast f/1.6 lens with a focal range of 3.8-83.6mm. Instead of a color viewfinder, this model sports a three-inch color LCD monitor. At the front of the camcorder is a color enhancement light with three settings: off, auto, and on. Instead of a dangling lens cover, the CC6371 has a built-in lens cover that you manually open and close. Programmed auto exposure, which is controlled via a dial on the left-hand side of the camcorder, has nine modes. The fairly complete menu is displayed within the viewfinder so that you can make appropriate adjustments to the camcorder based on shooting conditions. A one-page titler is included with eight separate titles. Other features include variable high-speed shutter, edit search, and VCR controls. Audio is mono, and like most VHS-C camcorders, it's just passable. This is a simple VHS-C camcorder with all the right features for a fledgling videographer that doesn't want or need a lot of fancy extras.

Specifications: height, 4⅝"; width, 4⅝"; depth, 9⁹⁄₁₆"; weight, 2 lbs. 5 oz. without tape and battery.
Warranty: 90 days, labor; 1 year, parts
Manufacturer's Suggested Retail Price: $699
Approximate Low Price: not available

Panasonic PV-A208

Budget Buy

Although the PV-A208 represents the economical end of Panasonic's VHS-C Palmcorder line, it performs the same as the considerably more expensive models. This palmcorder is quite compact and uses a full-size video head drum, the same kind found in a home VCR. The PV-A208 includes all the essential features for shooting good videos, plus it is easy to use. The $\frac{1}{4}$-inch, 270,000-pixel CCD image sensor provides good pictures and has a low-light sensitivity of 1.4 lux. The 23-power optical autofocus zoom lens can be operated in four speed steps from 2 to 16 seconds. There is also a two-second Quick Zoom feature. The model includes a bright $\frac{1}{2}$-inch color viewfinder with 116,150 pixels. The high-speed shutter has a range of $\frac{1}{10,000}$ to $\frac{1}{100}$ second. Not only will the PV-A208 automatically date- and time-stamp your videos but the clock toggles between daylight and standard time on the appropriate day. The automatic fade works by simply pushing the fade button before starting or stopping a recording. For smoother edits, a flying erase head eliminates video noise when starting and stopping recording. Graphical tape and battery gauges in the viewfinder, rather than numbers, show tape remaining and battery-charge levels. An auto titler is built in with greetings for ten specific holidays. A record indicator light on the record button reduces the chance of accidentally leaving the recorder running. This camcorder now comes with a color-enhancement light. With the PV-A208, you have everything in your hands to shoot great videos at a great price.

Specifications: height, $4\frac{5}{8}$"; width, 4"; depth, 7"; weight, 1 lb. 14 oz. (without tape and battery)
Warranty: 90 days, carry-in service; 1 year, parts
Manufacturer's Suggested Retail Price: $500
Approximate Low Price: $430

DIGITAL VIDEO (DV) CAMCORDERS

JVC GR-DVL9000 CyberCam

✓BEST BUY

The JVC GR-DVL9000 is a high-band digital video camcorder that features exceptional resolution (500×480 lines). While compact in size, its picture quality is superior to either Super VHS-C or Hi8mm. This lightweight camcorder is equipped with battery, tape, and hand strap. Besides shooting normal video, the

DVL9000 also allows you to take digital still pictures. Within the snapshot mode, one 60-minute DV cassette will hold 5,400 stills. Digital enhancement extends the 10-power optical zoom to 40-power digital and 200-power digital. Going to the 200-power digital zoom affords no loss of picture quality. The high resolution improves the performance of the digital image stabilization, which can easily discriminate between deliberate movement and unwanted panning and tilting. The DVL9000 utilizes a ⅓-inch, 380,000-pixel progressive scan CCD image sensor. PCM digital stereo audio offers two digital audio recording modes. Coupled with a built-in high-quality stereo microphone, this model provides exceptional audio performance. The DVL900 uses an f/1.2 lens with a focal range of 5.0-50mm, plus a filter diameter of 58mm. You have two ways to view the action: either the rear-mounted 0.55-inch color viewfinder or the four-inch color LCD that flips out from the left side. All on-screen menus and displays can be seen and accessed within the viewfinder or through the LCD monitor. There are eight different effects that can be utilized on the program auto exposure mode along with 18 different scene transitions. With its built-in random assemble editor and 24-button multibrand remote, you can create your own home movies. You can also reposition scenes already taped to highlight different aspects of the shot. These changes and special effects will then be added to the copy being made on a separate VCR. The camcorder utilizes an optional lithium battery that allows you to tape for 100 minutes.

Specifications: height, 3 7/16"; width, 3 7/16"; depth, 5 3/4"; weight, 1 lb. 8 oz.
Warranty: 90 days, labor; 1 year, parts
Manufacturer's Suggested Retail Price: $2,800
Approximate Low Price: $2,100

Canon Optura

Recommended

Canon has introduced the first hybrid digital video camcorder with a 35mm SLR camera design. The Optura offers several new and innovative features not found on either DV camcorders or digital cameras. While being able to capture full motion audio and video digitally, the Optura can also captures digital still images. Using Canon's progressive scan movie mode, this model records high resolution still images of moving subjects at a rate of 30 frames per second, which is three times faster than the motor drive on a 35mm camera. The Progressive Scan CCD image sensor reaches 360,000 pixels in a single scan to capture a full frame every 1⁄60 of a second. Complementing the Progressive Scan CCD are the RGB primary color filters, which allow the CCD to achieve color resolution comparable to three CCD systems. The Optura employs a 14:1 optical zoom and a 35:1 digital zoom as well as optical image stabilization. The photo mode turns the hybrid DV camcorder into virtual digital SLR camera by using its auto mode to set exposure and shutter speeds automatically. Each digital image is recorded for approximately six seconds on the tape. Canon has also incorporated its FlexiZone autofocus image control system, which brings any part of the frame into focus. There are five programmed auto exposure modes, PCM stereo, digital fades, self timer, SP/LP recording, date code, time code, and a lithium battery. In addition to its color viewfinder, the Optura also features a two-inch LCD screen.

Specifications: height, 4 3⁄16″; width, 5 7⁄16″; depth, 5 1⁄4″; weight, 2 lbs.
Warranty: 1 year (limited)
Manufacturer's Suggested Retail Price: $2,699
Approximate Low Price: $1,800

STEREO COMPONENTS

Home music systems, as separate entities from radios and record players, arrived about 50 years ago. Originally they were the domain of hobbyists and serious audiophiles only. Since that time, however, home music systems have evolved from complicated and costly to accessible and affordable. In the process, performance has also dramatically improved, making today's stereo components an exceptional bargain.

HOME THEATER SYSTEMS

Purists think of stereo components as strictly for music, but the rest of us also enjoy the delights of the home theater experience. With the right components you can re-create the movie theater experience at home. In fact, even on a reasonable budget you can enjoy better sound at home than at the local multiplex movie theaters. The recipe is simple: Start with a 32-inch (or larger screen) TV and add a quality sound source, such as a hi-fi VCR or DVD player. Combine these with a multichannel receiver equipped with Dolby Pro Logic (or the newer, more impressive Dolby Digital) and five speakers (you may also want to add a subwoofer for low frequency effects). Wire it together in an hour or less and get ready to challenge the local movie house for sonic supremacy.

Nearly all manufacturers now design the majority of their audio components to be used in home theater systems. All but the most basic audio receiver switch video sources, and many display their settings on your TV screen. Generally, the more money you spend the more versatility you'll have. Most companies market complete home theater packages, either assembled from existing components or as custom designed systems, often at a discount over separate components. The system typically includes a five-channel AM/FM receiver (with Dolby Pro Logic or Dolby Digital), the necessary five speakers, and perhaps an optional powered subwoofer. Ideally, the system should include a matched trio of speakers for the left, center, and right front channels, plus another pair of matched speakers for the left and right surround channels. The surround speakers don't necessarily have to be as large as the front ones, but they should sound similar, even if they sacrifice some bass. (In Dolby Pro Logic the two surround speakers reproduce the same mono signal, while in Dolby Digital they are stereo.) Try to include a subwoofer, as it provides the "oomph" for music and the boom and bang for movies.

In the past year Dolby Digital surround sound rapidly overtook its predecessor, Dolby Pro Logic. Originally called AC-3 when introduced in 1996, Dolby Digital provides a dramatic upgrade in sound quality and realism over the analog Pro Logic. Initially, receivers and processors featuring Dolby Digital were so expensive they could not be included here. However, with dramatic price decreases we can include several high-performance and moderately-priced receivers and processors.

While you still pay a significant premium for Dolby Digital, we feel it's justified. However, be aware that even if you own a Dolby Digital receiver, you can only enjoy its benefits if you have Dolby Digital sources such as DVD and laser disc players. Nonetheless, Dolby Digital receivers also include Pro Logic, so you still can enjoy surround sound from VHS tapes, satellite, stereo TV broadcasts, and DVDs lacking Dolby Digital soundtracks. Direct-to-home satellite systems (such as DSS and Primestar) and the new digital television systems (DTV and HDTV) provide extremely high quality audio, and offer further incentives to consider home theater. All these innovations—plus the ever improving audio quality of CDs and MiniDisc—justify a good stereo component system now more than ever.

QUALITY AND COST

Over the past 50 years, technology continued to raise the performance level of audio and video components while lowering the prices. For example, the first CD players introduced just 16 years ago cost $1,000. Now you can enjoy a far better sounding player for about $125.

The dramatic fluctuations in the exchange rate between the dollar and the Japanese yen have forced Japanese companies to increase productivity through automation or by manufacturing off-shore in countries with cheaper labor costs. This has caused a subtle decline in the quality of some gear. When the yen increased in value against the dollar, companies eliminated features or kept the same models in the line for two or three years. At the time of writing, the value of the dollar has dramatically increased over the yen, making for better values in 1999 than ever before.

CHOOSING YOUR COMPONENTS

In this book we offer Best Buy, Recommended, and Budget Buy ratings as guideposts to a satisfying sound system. Most important, however, use your ears. Bring your favorite CDs to the store. You should always make an effort to listen before you purchase any audio components. Remember, speakers will always sound different in your home than they do in the store. Room acoustics determine the sound of speakers as much as the speakers themselves.

Buying stereo components instead of a prepackaged or all-in-one system lets you upgrade your equipment at any time without discarding the entire system. Keep this in mind as you observe the present pace of technology. If you can't afford all the components you want or the quality of components you desire, begin with a good multichannel receiver (or stereo receiver if you only plan to listen to music), a pair of speakers that offer optional matching center and surrounds, and a budget CD or DVD player (since DVD players also play CDs without compromise). This setup will serenade you with high-fidelity AM/FM stereo radio, play prerecorded music, and work with your TV and VCR as a basic home theater system. Later you can add an audio recording/reproducing system such as cassette or MiniDisc (MD).

BUYING TIPS

Buying components from a specialty dealer usually eliminates hassles and confusion. Specialists do not necessarily charge a higher price than the mass-market superstores; but if they do, they often make it up to you in service.

In our experience, home entertainment specialty dealers display a wider selection of equipment in a space more suitable for listening. They also pride themselves on good, in-store service departments. But if you know exactly what you want and feel confident about installing it, you'll be perfectly satisfied with most of the national chain superstores.

Superstores often use select models during promotions, selling them at a lower prices. Sometimes these models are discontinued or about to be discontinued and the manufacturer wants to unload them. Since there's minimal change from one model year to the next, buying last year's model can be a good value. Just be careful of the "bait-and-switch," where you ask for the advertised model and the salesperson attempts to sell you a different and usually more expensive model.

Many people express concerns about obsolescence. Unlike the computer industry, audio and video maintain their currency for many years, often decades. Today some people play CDs through the receivers and speakers they purchased during the 1970s. LPs enjoyed a 35-year run, and CDs, now in their 16th year, continue going strong. Generally it takes a decade for a new technology to surpass an old one, so you can expect a minimum of 10 years, or a possible maximum of 20 or more years, before applying the word obsolete to most audio equipment.

WARRANTIES

Extended warranties reward the dealer with almost pure profit. The big superstores promote extended warranties as a means to increase profit margins on discontinued equipment. Most audio equipment will long outlive the extended warranty. If equipment fails, it's usually in the first few weeks, well inside of the manufacturer's warranty. Leave nonmechanical equipment, such as a receiver, powered up continuously for the first few weeks you own it. Also, use your tape player or CD player extensively during its first few weeks. If the equipment does not fail by then, it probably will not die before the end of its natural life expectancy. Over the past few years, many extended warranty firms failed before the equipment they insured, leaving buyers holding a worthless piece of paper.

PRECAUTIONS

Purchase a surge protector. Jolts of electricity quickly fry integrated circuits, unlike the rugged tube equipment of the early days. A lightning strike two miles from your home can possibly zap your equipment. Most power companies regularly send unexpected jolts down the line as they switch loads or suffer equipment failures. A good surge protector costs between $20 and $50; however, you can spend as much as $200 for a deluxe six-outlet model that protects outdoor antenna cable, cable company cable, and phone lines. The better models come with free insurance policies. Consider a quality surge protector essential to the longevity of your home theater system.

Never ground your equipment to anything but the third hole of your electrical outlet. If you ground your system to water pipes, the earth, or anything else, it could act as a magnet for lightning or electrical faults and not only blow out your gear but possibly set your home on fire.

Avoid placing speakers too close to a television unless they are specifically designed for this kind of placement with magnetic shielding. The magnetic field of regular speakers can distort the TV picture, and permanently damage the picture tube.

Keep all your equipment well ventilated. Heat causes premature equipment failure. Never obstruct ventilation slots or holes, and if you stack components, try to leave at least one inch of breathing room between them. A small, quiet cooling fan mounted near your components may extend their life expectancy.

When making connections, removing or installing components, or swapping speakers, always turn the power off. You can blow out your speakers from plugging cables in and out with the power on. Just one strand of speaker wire touching the adjacent terminal can blow the receiver's fuse(s), or in rarer cases, the entire power output section of the receiver.

Heed the instruction manuals' warnings about no user-serviceable parts inside. Most components consist of a power supply and a board full of chips and transistors permanently soldered in place. You cannot diagnose or replace anything by poking around inside because you may cause more damage or give yourself a nasty electrical shock.

BEST BUYS '99

Our Best Buy, Recommended, and Budget Buy stereo components are listed below. Products within each category are listed according to quality. The best of the Best Buys is listed first, followed by our second choice, and so on. A Best Buy, Recommended, or Budget Buy designation only applies to the model listed—it does not necessarily apply to other models made by the same manufacturer or to an entire product line.

SPEAKERS

More than 365 speaker companies flood the market with multiple models, from those constructed in garages to those constructed in large factories. Every few years someone announces a radical new speaker technology, but generally, the tried-and-true speaker designs offer the best sound for the money. Because speakers are material and labor intensive (rather than technology intensive), their prices typically do not decline like other audio components. While discerning the differences among electronic components taxes your concentration, you can relax and still tell speakers apart. Always insist on the right to return speakers that fail to meet your expectations.

CHOOSING THE RIGHT SPEAKERS

Because speakers are so integral to sound, they retain a respected position when choosing stereo components. Like choosing a favorite singer, judging speakers is a subjective task. Speakers will determine your choice of receiver, since some speakers require more power than others, and some receivers and speakers make a better match than others. Thus, the advice of friends, reviews, and the recommendations here should serve only as a starting point. Take care in choosing speakers by spending ample time listening.

Spend some time positioning your speakers. Speakers dramatically interact with room acoustics. What sounded stunning in the store may sound tinny, muddy, or boomy at home. You can alter this slightly by where you place them in your room—even a few inches closer to or further from a wall can make a difference. The speakers should form a triangle with your normal listening position. The front of the speakers should always be precisely in the same plane, although they may be angled slightly inward. Taking the time to experiment will reward you in the long run.

The size of the speaker enclosure and the number of speakers inside it (woofers, midranges, tweeters) do not always correlate with sound quality. Always look for solid, dense, well-made cabinetry. We base our speaker ratings on the quality of construction, reputation, and listening tests.

HOME THEATER SPEAKERS

Home theater speakers share many of the desirable attributes of the stereo speaker pair, except there are five placed appropriately around the room. You can enjoy fairly small speakers when you include a subwoofer in the system to reproduce deep bass.

Home theater makes its own demands. First, all of the speakers should sound the same, even if some are larger or smaller than others. This is called "timbre matching," which means the speakers should have the same tonal quality and balance, even if some of the speakers reproduce more extended frequency response than others. The surround speakers may be smaller, but should retain the same sonic characteristics as the rest of the system. One quick way to determine if the speakers are timbre-matched is to listen to the applause from a live recording. No one speaker should draw attention to itself with a different sound quality. It's also best to buy the entire home theater system speakers from a single manufacturer.

Traditionally, and in most of our listings, the surround speakers are smaller than the left and right front speakers. Dolby Digital now sends a greater amount of bass to the surround channels, so future home theater speaker systems may include somewhat larger surround channels. Since many people refuse to let speakers dominate their rooms, it is unlikely they would want surround speakers that match the front speakers in size.

Most of the companies we recommend magnetically shield the three front channel speakers. Many people usually place them in close proximity to a TV screen. Speakers normally generate powerful magnetic fields that can distort the TV picture if they are not shielded. Incidentally, the magnetic fields of unshielded speakers can also mildly erase magnetic tapes, so don't place tapes near the speakers.

Place the center channel speaker either directly above or below the TV screen. The surround speakers generally should be placed high on a side wall, not necessarily on the rear wall behind you. The surrounds should be above and just slightly behind where you sit. Try not to point them directly at your ears, since you don't want to localize the sound as coming from the speakers. As with stereo speakers, experimenting with the placement of four of the five home theater speakers (the center channel offers limited options, although you can tilt it up or down) can pay off in the long run.

FEATURES AND TERMINOLOGY

Power and Ratings: Different speakers take advantage of different physical properties to produce sound. For example, large floor-standing speakers can reproduce throbbing sound levels with as little as 20 watts of power, whereas compact bookshelf models often require twice that much power to reproduce the same sound level, if they can play that loudly. Too much power can damage speakers, but speaker ratings and amplifier ratings don't always tell the whole story. Speakers rated at 100 watts maximum may safely be powered by a 300-watt amplifier, but if you force all 300 watts into the speaker, the sound will cause you pain and damage the speakers. Too little power can also damage a speaker. If you try to play a low-powered amplifier too loudly it can distort the sound waves, and this distortion can destroy a speaker.

Construction Quality: The crossover network consists of resistors, capacitors, and coils that divide the incoming sound from the receiver into appropriate frequency ranges, ensuring that the bass goes to the woofer and the treble to the tweeter. You cannot tell the actual sound or construction quality of a speaker system just by the size of its components and the material from which they are manufactured. An 8-inch woofer sometimes reproduces better bass than a 12-inch woofer, and paper occasionally surpasses space-age plastics and metals in the quality of a speaker cone and the sound it reproduces. The thickness, materials, and construction of the speaker enclosure, or cabinet, can influence the system's sound as much as the drivers. When shopping for speakers, keep an eye out for a solid, rigid enclosure that shows minimal resonance when you rap your knuckles on it.

High-Efficiency Ported Systems: Also known as ducted or reflex systems, these highly-sensitive (sensitivity has replaced the term efficiency when referring to how much sound a speaker produces from a given amount of power) systems are common among large speakers. Ported systems often require less power from the amplifier (or amplifier section of your receiver) to produce a given level of sound when compared to acoustic suspension speakers. Ported speakers take advantage of the port's resonance to amplify the bass frequencies acoustically.

Acoustic Suspension Speakers: Sometimes referred to as air-suspension speakers, acoustic suspension speakers are most common among bookshelf-size speakers. A tightly-sealed enclosure forces the speaker to fight the air within. This causes them to be less sensitive to power than most ported speakers, therefore requiring more amplifier power to produce a given level of sound. A well-designed acoustic suspension system reproduces superb, tightly controlled bass.

Speaker Impedance: Speaker impedances are commonly listed from 4 to 8 ohms, with some ranging from 2 to 16 ohms. This is a technical description of the amount of inductive resistance the speaker offers to the flow of electrical signals. Under normal circumstances, impedance bears no relation to sound quality, but many receivers need a minimum of 4 ohms to work properly. A good receiver may work with 2 ohms, but other receivers or amplifiers will automatically shut off or blow a fuse. If you intend to use two pairs of speakers in parallel from the same terminals, choose speakers rated at least 8 ohms. Also note that speaker impedance ratings are nominal, meaning that a speaker may actually fall below its rated impedance at some frequencies.

Woofers, Tweeters, and Other Speaker Elements: The woofer is the largest speaker component (or driver). It reproduces bass notes and often the lower midrange sounds as well. The tweeter is the smallest component and reproduces higher sounds (treble and upper midrange). The tweeter is the most fragile component because of its fine wires and is the most prone to failure. Many speaker systems include one or more midrange speaker components that reproduce the range of sound between the woofer and the tweeter—the range of the human voice. A midrange component is not essential for good sound, although most larger systems include them.

STEREO SPEAKERS

B&W DM305

BEST BUY

The stylishly slender B&W DM305 columns—just under a yard tall—reproduce crisp, clean, wide-range sound while making minimal demands on floor space and your receiver/amplifier. The DM305 occupies less than one square foot of floor space. Its high sensitivity produces ample sound from just a few watts. The innards include a 6½-inch woofer/midrange mounted in a reinforced cast-steel chassis and a 1-inch soft-dome tweeter. B&W mounts the tweeter in a novel internal damping mechanism coupled with a low-diffraction face. (What all this means is that the sound waves head directly for your ears and don't bounce around the front of the speaker.) B&W's Prism System sets these speakers apart from the pack. The system uses plastic wedges to diffuse, or break up, sound waves, which then pass through an absorptive layer. You can see and feel the indentations of the wedges on the rear of the cabinet. The sound that spills from the DM305 is spectacularly clean; you'll hear every nuance and detail of sound. The speakers also provide solid bass. B&W offers the sonically matched CC3 center-channel speaker, should you decide to use the DM305 in a home theater system.

Specifications: height, 33⅛"; width, 8½"; depth, 12⅛"; weight, 24 lbs. each
Warranty: 5 years, parts and labor
Manufacturer's Suggested Retail Price: $450 (per pair)
Approximate Low Price: $450

NHT SuperOne

BEST BUY

The NHT SuperOne is not a misnomer. It ranks as the Mighty Mouse of speakers, producing a super sound from a compact size. NHT began by manufacturing small speakers, and though it now builds floor towers, it keeps returning to small speakers to see just how good it can make them. This two-way acoustic suspension speaker uses a 6½-inch woofer with a 1-inch fluid-cooled soft-dome tweeter. NHT magnetically shields the speaker for use near video equipment. Its natural tonal balance will even please demanding listeners. Small speakers generally produce a good stereo image because of their small baffles. The SuperOnes excel in this important attribute. The voices and instruments sound like they're playing not only between the speakers but in front of and behind them. To achieve their impressive bass, the SuperOnes sacrifice some sensitivity, requiring a minimum of 25 watts, but they'll accept plenty of high power (up to 150 watts per channel). NHT offers the SuperOne in high gloss black or white laminate. The company also designed custom stands and wall brackets for these speakers, although you can use any appropriate stand.

Specifications: height, 11⅗"; width, 7¼"; depth, 8½"; weight, 10 lbs. each
Warranty: 1 year, parts and labor
Manufacturer's Suggested Retail Price: $375 (per pair)
Approximate Low Price: $350

B&W CDM 2SE

Recommended

The B&W CDM 2SE bookshelf speakers pack a punch from their small package. B&W upgraded this model from the original CDM 2 without increasing the price, incorporating advances originally pioneered in B&W's more expensive 800 series. For example, the 6½- inch midrange/woofer contained in this two-way system uses a woven Kevlar cone, which radiates sound waves with near-ideal stiffness for accuracy and low distortion. Similarly, the 1-inch tweeter uses a metal alloy formulated for accurate high-frequency reproduction without coloring the sound. Removing the stylish contoured grille, with its acoustically beneficial shape, reveals a well-finished front baffle. B&W surrounds the tweeter with eccentric diffraction rings, which reduce the effect of the baffle on the high frequencies. This produces a cleaner, more accurate sound. Lifting the surprisingly heavy speakers quickly convinces you that these are no ordinary small speakers. The enclosure, covered in real wood veneer in black or red ash, is very dense. This non-resonant design reduces box vibrations, which muddy the sound. The quality of the sound makes the speakers' small size almost irrelevant. You will need at least 30 watts per channel of amplifier power. The CDM 2SE can be placed on a shelf or on a stand. The improved "SE" model sounds subtly better than the original. These speakers are ideal for uncompromised sound in tight places.

Specifications: height, 12¼"; width, 8⅝"; depth, 9½"; weight, 15 lbs. 6 oz. each
Warranty: 5 years, parts and labor
Manufacturer's Suggested Retail Price: $800 (per pair)
Approximate Low Price: $800

Bose 201, Series IV

Budget Buy

The Bose 201, Series IV, represents a further upgrade of the best-selling 201. Bose sells a lot of 201s because, like Henry Ford, it perfected mass production without sacrificing quality. Bose sells these speakers in mirror-image pairs. The 2-inch fluid-cooled tweeters are angled from a corner of the enclosure to cover a broader listening area. This radiates high frequencies (and allows the sound to be enjoyed) over a wider area. A 6½-inch woofer in the ported enclosure provides satisfying bass with as little as 10 watts of power. The 201, Series IV, reproduces appealing sound at an affordable price. Injection-molded plastic end caps, foam grilles, and a black or rosewood vinyl finish provide a contemporary look.

Specifications: height, 9½"; width, 15⅛"; depth, 6¾"; weight, 9 lbs. each
Warranty: 5 years, parts and labor (transferable)
Manufacturer's Suggested Retail Price: $198 (per pair)
Approximate Low Price: $198

HOME THEATER SPEAKERS

Atlantic Technology System 4.5

✓ BEST BUY

The Atlantic Technology System 4.5 home theater speaker system combines elegance with good sound. Atlantic Technology entered the home theater speaker arena long before many of its competitors, allowing the company to perfect its product over several generations. The 4.5 is a deluxe system at an entry level price. All the speakers except the subwoofer come in a gloss black finish. Their small size simplifies placement. The front left and right speakers contain a pair of 3½-inch midrange drivers and a 1-inch silk dome fluid-cooled tweeter. The center channel speaker is virtually the same, except it contains a variable high frequency level control for added clarity. It also rests on an adjustable mounting platform, enabling you to angle the speaker toward the listening area. The dipole surround speakers radiate in two directions, which enhances realism when properly placed. The woofer/subwoofer, with a gloss black top, contains a powerful 150 watt signal sensing amplifier that automatically detects the audio signal and powers up. This system delivers smashing movie sound. There's plenty of punch for the action scenes and plenty of clarity for dialog.

Warranty: 5 years, parts and labor
Manufacturer's Suggested Retail Price: \$1,596
Approximate Low Price: not available

Bose Acoustimass 10 Series II

Recommended

The Bose Acoustimass 10 Series II is the ideal home theater speaker system for those without the space for home theater, and for those unwilling to sacrifice decor for sound. Five magnetically shielded pairs of tiny speaker cubes, each housing a 2½-inch speaker, provide the front and surround channels. A compact woofer/subwoofer (called the bass module) reproduces the bass. Bose employs its proprietary Acoustimass design using three 5¼-inch drivers inside the box to achieve surprising bass. The bass module separates the sound, sending the mid and high frequencies to the cubes. Since bass is omnidirectional, the module can be placed almost anywhere in the room or even in the basement firing upward through a grate in the floor. You can twist each pair of cubes to vary the spaciousness of the sound. If you aim one cube at the wall, it creates reflected sound, which broadens the sound field. The cubes come in black or white, and Bose offers optional wall-mounting brackets, table stands, and floor stands. When used with a good quality receiver or amplifier, the sound will impress you with breadth, depth, and balance.

Warranty: 5 years (transferable)
Manufacturer's Suggested Retail Price: \$1,099
Approximate Low Price: \$900

Cambridge SoundWorks Ensemble IV Home Theater

Budget Buy

Henry Kloss designed the Cambridge SoundWorks Ensemble IV Home Theater speaker system for those on a budget. Kloss, long behind some of the best-known names in speakers, started this company to offer good sound at bargain prices. He succeeds with the Ensemble IV. Since the system is designed with a sound-shaping circuit for each custom full-range speaker used in the five satellites, it allows the tiny cube satellites to sound larger and louder than much bigger speakers, while remaining true to the music or movie soundtrack. The compact woofer admittedly will not rattle the windows during a James Bond movie, but it provides enough punch to keep you in the action. The system comes finished in modest basic black. This little system provides a real taste of what home theater is all about without a second mortgage.

Warranty: 10 years, limited parts and labor
Manufacturer's Suggested Retail Price: $250
Approximate Low Price: not available

SUBWOOFERS

While there's no specific agreement on the definition of a subwoofer (many companies refer to the woofer as the subwoofer), most experts agree that it must produce full sound levels below 50 hertz and descend to at least 30 hertz while still producing a significant sound level. For reference, the lowest male bass voice sings at about 80 hertz, and the lowest note on a grand piano is about 27 hertz (some organs go as low as 20 hertz, which you feel more than hear). Most subwoofers begin at 80 hertz (although most allow you to select 120 hertz as their cutoff point). That means subwoofers do not, and should not, radiate sound above these frequencies.

CHOOSING A SUBWOOFER

While the size of the speaker driver in a subwoofer may hint at its effectiveness, larger is not automatically better. Sophisticated enclosure designs, the design of the driver, and electronic sleight-of-ear in the amplifier will allow a 10-inch subwoofer to sound as good as a 12- or even 15-inch model.

Bass is omnidirectional, which means you cannot tell where the sound comes from. For example, hearing bass in mono does not dilute the stereo or surround effect. You can hide the subwoofer from view and still experience its bass. We say "experience," because low bass is felt as much as it is heard. Bass also requires prodigious amounts of energy and can rattle room surfaces and contents. The one thing that should not rattle is the subwoofer itself. You should look for subwoofers with an amplifier that produces a minimum of 100 watts. Subwoofers should also be placed a considerable distance from the main speakers.

Velodyne CT-120

✓BEST BUY

In the audio world, Velodyne is synonymous with subwoofer. The CT-120 represents one of Velodyne's most affordable subwoofers. The CT-120 uses a 12-inch woofer with a reinforced fiber cone, powered by a 120-watt amplifier that is able to produce 270 watts of peak power. Special circuits prevent distortion and speaker damage. The CT-120 has plenty of boost down to 25 hertz with excellent accuracy. You can adjust the speaker's upper frequency limit and phase, and also bypass the speaker's internal crossover if your receiver has a subwoofer output. The speaker turns on automatically when it senses a signal from your system.

Specifications: height, 18"; width, 15"; depth, 18¾"; weight, 60 lbs.
Warranty: 2 years, parts and labor
Manufacturer's Suggested Retail Price: $599
Approximate Low Price: $599

Sunfire True Subwoofer Mk II

Recommended

Bob Carver, creator of the modestly titled True Subwoofer, always brings amazing technology and impressive performance to whatever product he designs. For the Mk II, he couples one of his proprietary design super-high efficiency amplifiers—which produces a jaw-dropping, house-shaking, 2,700 watts—to what initially appears as a pair of humble 10-inch woofers. However, these are no ordinary woofers. They have large voice coils that can move in and out 2½ inches, moving cones that displace 235 cubic inches of air—almost two or three times that of an average 15-inch woofer. Carver builds all this power and technology into a box less than one foot square. This subwoofer reproduces frequencies as low as 18 hertz. You can also adjust its upper frequency limit. This subwoofer rapidly responds to bass signals and accurately reproduces them. While it has a warranty, there is no warranty for your furnishings or structure of your home when you play this speaker loudly. It's finished in black anodized metal and black lacquer.

Specifications: height, 11"; width, 11"; depth 11"; weight, 48 lbs.
Warranty: 2 years, parts and labor
Manufacturer's Suggested Retail Price: $1,299
Approximate Low Price: $1,299

HEADPHONES

Like speakers, headphones are best judged according to how they sound. The general criteria for good headphone performance include a full bass response with accurate tonal definition and balance from the midrange frequencies up to the highest frequencies.

A comfortable headset is also an important consideration. Weight and fit should be carefully considered. There are three basic designs for headphones. Circumaural phones cover your entire outer ear and block out all external sound. Supra-aural phones do not completely block out external sound. Open-air phones rest lightly against the outer ear and usually have a foam pad that separates the actual phone from your head. This allows almost all outside sounds to be heard while you're wearing them. As a general rule, circumaural phones provide the most bass, whereas open-air phones usually provide the least bass.

NOISE-CANCELING HEADPHONES

This new technology enhances the pleasure of headphone listening. Extremely small microphones inside the headphones pick up ambient noise and feed it to a special amplifier in a small box or bulge in the headphone cord. This amplifier changes the phase of the noise and turns it into "antinoise," which is sent back to the earpiece. When the noise and antinoise meet, they cancel out, reducing the ambient noise that you hear. This reduces distractions and allows playing music at a lower volume, which protects your hearing. The phones can also be used to just reduce noise without listening to music, such as when flying on airplanes.

We strongly recommend against using noise-canceling phones when cycling, jogging, or in any activity where you must hear warnings. Noise-canceling phones range from large, elaborate, effective $1,200 models designed for pilots to ineffective $100 models. We've chosen models that meet our criteria for suitable headphones with the added bonus of noise cancellation.

Grado Labs SR60

✓BEST BUY

The SR60, praised by audio enthusiasts, easily compares with phones costing ten times as much. The large foam pads sit on the ear without sealing out external sound. The six-foot uncoiled cord is sturdier than most other phones. Grado also supplies a gold-plated ¼-inch plug adapter, so you can use them with home stereo components. Their high sensitivity works with the lowest output headphone stereos and makes even weak portables sound their best. These phones sound exquisite with clear crisp treble, deep authoritative bass, and transparent vocals. Although larger and heavier (7 ounces) than most phones, they are fairly comfortable. These are the kind of headphones you wear by choice, not necessity. Grado is a small company and the SR60 may be difficult to locate. However, the company has been in business many years and nationally distributes its products.

Warranty: 1 year, parts and labor
Manufacturer's Suggested Retail Price: $70
Approximate Low Price: $70

Sony MDR-65

✓BEST BUY

The lightweight, open-air-design MDR-65 headphones rest comfortably on the ear with their soft ear pads on gimbal-mounted ear cups. The wide molded headband with its gentle cushion further adds to the comfort of these phones. At only 2½ ounces, they feel like they're floating on your head. When it comes to sound, however, the MDR-65 is a heavyweight, with full, well-balanced sound from midsized diaphragms using powerful neodymium magnets. For convenience, a sturdy, nearly 6½-feet-long, single cord (rather than the cumbersome yoke design) connects the phones to your stereo. The MDR-65 can be used with either a personal stereo or home components, because the gold-plated miniplug comes with a screw-on adapter for standard ¼-inch jacks.

Warranty: 1 year (exchange)
Manufacturer's Suggested Retail Price: $40
Approximate Low Price: $30

Koss QZ2000 Quiet Zone

Recommended

Koss begins with its very good PortaPro noise-canceling headphones as the basis for the QZ2000 Quiet Zone. The comfortable, medium-density foam earpieces rest directly on the ear, supported by a single metal headband. The earpieces also pivot freely in their mounts. The physical design only modestly blocks external noise, but the active noise cancellation dramatically reduces noise between 30 hertz and 1,000 hertz (the area of most annoying noise, such as aircraft or bus engines). The titanium nitride coating on the headphone diaphragms aids in reproducing crisp, clear high frequencies when listening to music. A small black box, about half the size of a pack of cigarettes, contains the electronic circuitry for noise cancellation. A green LED indicates the active noise cancellation is on; a red LED warns of weak batteries. The QZ2000 operates on a pair of AA batteries that last for 60 hours or more. The 2⅘-ounce phones completely collapse for carrying in the supplied vinyl pouch. While we consider the noise cancellation a desirable feature, it adds about $100 to the cost of the basic PortaPro headphones.

Warranty: 1 year, parts and labor
Manufacturer's Suggested Retail Price: $200
Approximate Low Price: $160

Sony MDR-NC10

Recommended

Sony combines both passive and active noise cancellation in these 1⅗-ounce headphones. The in-the-ear design eliminates a headband. Unlike similar designs, these phones use a soft rubber bulb that easily contours itself to the ear and comfortably stays put. In the process, it effectively blocks noise. A bulge in the headphone cord—a bit larger than a package of chewing gum—contains all the circuitry and a single AAA battery, which lasts more than 80 hours. The bulge contains a push button that controls noise cancellation. A red LED indicates the battery is good. The MDR-NC10 are the only phones without an external ear seal, which provides a great degree of noise cancellation. These phones are so light you will forget you are wearing them. However, we rate them slightly below the Koss QZ2000 because the frequency response is not quite as smooth, and some people might find them mildly uncomfortable.

Warranty: 90 days, labor; 1 year, parts
Manufacturer's Suggested Retail Price: $200
Approximate Low Price: $180

STEREO RECEIVERS

Originally conceived as a space and cost-saving combination of a radio tuner and stereo preamplifier/power amplifiers, today's receiver usually includes five amplifiers instead of two, digital signal processing (DSP) to alter and enhance the sound, and Dolby Pro Logic and/or Dolby Digital surround sound decoders for home theater. (All Dolby Digital receivers contain Pro Logic.) Yet the package remains the same size, or smaller, than it was back at the receiver's conception about 40 years ago.

Preamplifiers were originally created to amplify the weak signal from a phonograph cartridge. Today, the universality of CD, as well as production cost-cutting, has resulted in some receivers without the phono stage of the preamp. If you still play vinyl, be sure to select a receiver with a phono input. The power amplifier provides the muscle that pumps up the electrical signal to power the speakers.

To fully enjoy the home theater effect, the power of each of the front channels must be the same, and the surround channels should each have at least half of the front-channel power. (We occasionally make an exception to this rule if the receiver is otherwise exemplary in performance.)

Video producers encode surround channels on stereo hi-fi VHS tapes, laser discs, DVDs, and many TV and satellite broadcasts. Surround sound processors can also extract ambience from many music sources, such as CDs, which may pleasantly enhance the sound.

TECHNOLOGY

Digital signal processing (DSP), increasingly common in even the lowest cost receivers, lets you make subtle or major changes to the sound with a minimum of distortion. You can use DSP to simulate the sound of different listening environments, from jazz clubs to arenas, because it can add echoes and reverberation to the sound. DSP also can spread two-channel sound among five speakers or simulate surround sound from only two speakers, although it is never as effective or impressive as having a true multichannel home system.

Dolby Labs, the company that set the standards for noise reduction, also dictates surround sound decoding with its analog Pro Logic and Dolby Digital. On the latest generation of laser discs and DVDs, Dolby upgraded surround sound with its new digital system. Dolby Digital normally provides five discrete channels, plus a low-frequency effects channel, commonly called the subwoofer channel. Retrieving four channels from two in the Pro Logic analog matrix system requires considerable electronic fudging, which can compromise sound quality, while the discrete Dolby Digital system involves fewer compromises. Pro Logic, virtually standard on all but the most basic receivers, adds only a few dollars in cost plus the expense of the extra internal power amplifiers. Dolby Digital adds about 20 percent extra.

FEATURES

Manufacturers fill most receivers with far more features than any normal listener needs or will ever use. Fortunately, these features add little to the price. When shopping, don't let dozens of buttons and flashing lights beguile you. Radio station presets offer great convenience. Some receivers go overboard with 40, although most cities don't have that many radio stations. Once again, it costs the manufacturer no more to include 40 presets than 20. We list the most essential features in our reviews.

The sonic differences between receivers vary, but tend to be slight when compared with speakers. It is best that you use your ears and listen and compare. We don't discuss sound extensively in our receiver reviews because of the slight differences and the lack of good subjective terms for these differences.

TWO-CHANNEL STEREO RECEIVERS

Stereo (two-channel) receivers face extinction as sure as the 8-track. Generally audiophiles who want a dedicated music system purchase separate preamplifiers, power amplifiers, and tuners rather than receivers. Manufacturers learned how to build receivers with five channels of amplification for a little more than what it cost to build a receiver with two channels. (They also realized that if you bought the five channel receiver, they could sell you five, more profitable, speakers.) Remember that even a multichannel home theater receiver can play just two stereo channels.

If you simply want a music system, the stereo receivers we list offer a remarkable value. They come without a plethora of unnecessary features and deliver solid, basic performance.

Sony STR-DE310

✓BEST BUY

The STR-DE310 represents the last two-channel receiver in Sony's product line, and like its predecessors, it represents an exceptional value. The STR-DE310 produces 100 watts per channel using discrete output transistors rather than integrated circuits. To keep the noise level low, separate transformers power the audio sections and the blue fluorescent display. The five inputs no longer include a phono input; however, you can buy a stand-alone phono preamp if you still have a turntable, and plug that into one of the high level inputs. The high-quality, frequency-synthesized tuner in this model matches, in most respects, the tuners in Sony's most expensive receivers. Direct-access tuning makes tuning a snap. Just tap in the radio station's frequency on the front panel's numeric keypad of the supplied Sony audio/video system remote. Direct-access or the auto-set feature enables you to preset as many as 30 stations. The use of knobs—a large one for volume and smaller ones for bass, treble, and balance—simplify operation. Sony also includes a headphone jack for private listening and a bass boost to compensate for loss of bass at low-listening levels.

Warranty: 2 years
Manufacturer's Suggested Retail Price: $220
Approximate Low Price: $160

Technics SA-EX110

Budget Buy

It's difficult to classify the Technics SA-EX110 as a Best Buy or Budget Buy. It has a bargain price, but a slightly higher distortion level than the Sony STR-DE310. Its five inputs still include a phono input, and the lone video input is strictly for audio from a video source. Its styling resembles the Sony STR-DE310, with a large volume knob and smaller knobs for bass, treble, and balance. The understated front panel (with its red and amber fluorescent display) contains a minimum of confusing clutter. However, direct-access tuning is only available from the supplied remote control, which is designed to control any Technics/Panasonic audio/video component; it also enables you to preset 30 radio stations. Technics' proprietary Class H+ amplifier circuitry provides a generous 100 watts, with some reserve for musical peaks. The modular design also simplifies servicing should it ever be necessary. The Quartz synthesized FM tuner delivers a respectable performance. Technics also includes a headphone jack for private listening. The design of the SA-EX110 places performance above frills.

Warranty: 1 year, parts and labor
Manufacturer's Suggested Retail Price: $180
Approximate Low Price: $150

DOLBY PRO LOGIC RECEIVERS

Dolby Pro Logic receivers currently dominate the receiver market—they've never been more affordable. Within a couple of years they may be as rare as two-channel stereo models are today, thanks to the arrival of the superior Dolby Digital. All of the Pro Logic receivers we list are upgradable to Dolby Digital with an external adapter. Do not buy a receiver that lacks the requisite audio inputs on the rear panel for connecting an adapter.

Sony STR-DE425

BEST BUY

The STR-DE425 is an affordable way to get into home theater. Think of this five-channel home theater receiver as Sony's two-channel stereo receiver on steroids. Its six inputs include a phono input. The audio/video inputs switch video as well as audio. This receiver produces 100 watts per channel for all three front channels, and splits 100 watts for each of the two rear channels. In addition to Dolby Pro Logic, there's a trio of digital signal processing enhancements for movies or music—arena, theater, and hall—which synthesize the ambience characteristics of those spaces. Six discrete audio inputs make this receiver Dolby Digital-ready. You can adjust audio input balance using built-in sequential test tones for proper Pro Logic operation, and adjust the delay times for the surround channels to suit your room and listening position. The frequency-synthesized tuner is the same as the tuners used in

Sony's most expensive receivers. Direct-access tuning makes tuning a snap. Just tap in the radio station's frequency on the front panel's numeric keypad or use the glow-in-the-dark keys on the supplied Sony audio/video system remote. Direct-access or the auto-set feature speeds up the setting of 30 possible station presets. The use of knobs—a large one for volume and smaller ones for bass, treble, and balance—simplify operation. A switchable bass boost compensates for bass loss when listening at low levels.

Warranty: 2 years, parts and labor
Manufacturer's Suggested Retail Price: $300
Approximate Low Price: $250

Yamaha R-V703

Recommended

The Yamaha R-V703 Pro Logic surround sound receiver provides ample features for the price, although its wattage is somewhat lower (especially on the surround channels) than our Best Buy units. However, the overall quality is first-rate and distortion levels are quite low. The R-V703 produces 80 watts for each of the three front channels, and 20 watts for each of the two surround channels. Along with Dolby Pro Logic and Yamaha's "enhanced" Pro Logic, Yamaha adds several acoustic environments and special effects, such as concert hall, rock concert, stadium, disco, as well as mono movie and concert video. Mono movie opens up the sound of older movies and gives them greater depth. The R-V703 contains six discrete inputs for Dolby Digital and other multichannel adapters. There are four audio and three audio/video inputs. The tuner offers 40 radio station presets. Yamaha provides a universal remote control with color-coded keys for easy operation. Although lower in power, the Yamaha weighs slightly more than other similar models. While this is not necessarily an indication of quality, in the case of this Yamaha, it indicates a solidly-built receiver.

Warranty: 2 years, parts and labor
Manufacturer's Suggested Retail Price: $400
Approximate Low Price: $350

DOLBY DIGITAL RECEIVERS

Dolby Digital receivers provide equal power on all five channels. There are probably fewer sonic differences between Dolby Digital decoders than Pro Logic decoders. Since manufacturers endow their best models with Dolby Digital we find most Dolby Digital receivers deliver excellent sound.

Dolby decided the original name of Dolby Digital—AC-3 (for audio coding, third generation)—lacked sex appeal. The system reproduces six channels, but not all of them are equal; thus you may see the nomenclature Dolby Digital 5.1. Technically, the .1 is designated the "low frequency effects" (LFE) channel, which means it is not a full-range channel and only carries the lowest frequencies intended for the subwoofer. Although you will appreciate the benefits of a subwoofer, it is not necessary to fully enjoy the five other channels of the Dolby Digital system. Those channels also contain plenty of bass, so you won't miss all the thrills and chills.

Sony STR-DE825

✓BEST BUY

Sony loads the STR-DE825 Dolby Digital surround sound receiver with sound and features. All five channels deliver 100 watts to 8-ohm or 4-ohm speakers. Sony uses both 24-bit and 32-bit digital signal processing (DSP) to offer a whopping 20 acoustic environments. The 32-bit DSP power enables Sony's proprietary Digital Cinema Sound system to optimize the movie theater experience for the home, based on measurements and knowledge gleaned from its Sony Pictures Studios in Hollywood. The Dolby Digital processing offers all the adjustments inherent in the system, including the ability to match bass output to your speakers. To input the Dolby Digital from your DVD player (or other forthcoming Dolby Digital sources, such as Digital TV), there are both optical and coaxial digital inputs. This is an important feature, as some DVD players only have one or the other. There are dual subwoofer outputs and a special surround output for the optional wireless surround speakers. The rest of this receiver, such as the phono preamplifier and tuner, is identical to Sony's basic surround-sound models. There are 30 radio station presets, and you can direct-access tune by using the numeric keypad on the front panel or the remote control. The two-way preprogrammed universal remote contains an LCD screen that duplicates some of the information from the front panel LED display. You can group stations by any musical category you desire and see that particular category displayed on the remote. The surface layer of the remote is simple, logical, and easy to use. The lower layer contains the lesser used (and more confusing) controls. You'll have fun using the STR-DE825, as well as listening to it.

Warranty: 1 year, parts and labor
Manufacturer's Suggested Retail Price: $600
Approximate Low Price: $500

Kenwood VR-209

Budget Buy

Considering the newness of Dolby Digital technology, and the cost of implementing it, the Kenwood VR-209 is a true Budget Buy model in this category. The receiver includes Dolby Pro Logic as well as Dolby Digital. It produces 100 watts for each of the five channels. Price doesn't limit flexibility. The VR-209 comes with seven analog audio inputs, three analog audio outputs, three composite video inputs, one composite video output, and coaxial and optical digital inputs. The styling is conducive to this flexibility. There's a large volume knob, and a pair of smaller knobs: One selects the input (just like in the old days of input selector knobs) and one is a multicontrol that cycles through functions and settings. For example, pressing "sound" turns the knob sequentially into a bass or treble control. This leaves the front panel uncluttered, with only 16 well-spaced, intuitively-sized buttons plus the power switch. The source-direct feature allows bypassing the tone controls and parts of the preamplifier for the cleanest sound. You can dim the bright, clear fluorescent front panel. The tuner is equipped with 40 radio station presets. Kenwood supplies an exceptionally well-designed, pleasure-to-use, universal remote control with the receiver, as well.

Warranty: 2 years, parts and labor
Manufacturer's Suggested Retail Price: $399
Approximate Low Price: $380

COMPACT DISC PLAYERS

The compact disc rapidly evolved from a technological novelty to a fact of life. In less than two decades, it vanquished the analog phonograph record and the cassette to become our primary way of buying music. A small clique of audiophiles still worship the LP, but now most CDs surpass the sound quality of LPs and analog tapes. Most obviously, the laser-scanned CD eliminates the annoying noise and hiss of analog recordings, not to mention the clicks and pops of vinyl records. If you hear hiss on some CDs, it originates from the analog master tape recording (some CDs originate from analog masters, although most are now digitally mastered). Inaudible distortion and flat (uniform) frequency response contribute to CD's popularity, along with the disc's incredible convenience and ease of use. Furthermore, CDs contribute no wow or flutter (distracting speed variations and inaccuracies that cause a wavering of pitch) to the sound.

CD changers dominate the market, far overshadowing sales of single-disc players. Unlike LP changers, CD changers play without compromise and they cause no additional wear to the discs. Since changers sell for only a small premium over single-disc players there is little reason not to choose a changer. Only in the audiophile realm do single-disc players hold their own.

CAROUSEL CD CHANGERS

Carousel CD changers load discs on a large tray and rotate them into playing position. The mechanism lifts the disc from the tray and places it on a turntable inside the unit where the laser scans it. This permits the tray to rotate while the disc plays, allowing you to change discs. All carousels hold five discs, except for those from Onkyo, which hold six. There are minimal differences between models. They compete on how fast they can change discs, but the differences between brands are not much more than one second or two. The original carousel changers used a hinged lid that you lifted to access the CDs. This prevented stacking the changer beneath other components. Contemporary models all use a drawer system. Carousel changers, introduced about a decade ago, prove impressively reliable.

MEGA CD CHANGERS

A recent development in the CD market, mega-changers store anywhere from 50 to 200 discs. Increasingly, manufacturers allow you to daisy-chain two or three changers creating mammoth 600 disc changers. Change time from one disc to another on the opposite side of the changer takes about ten seconds; some changers operate faster than others.

Nearly all models reserve one slot for impromptu disc loading, so that you don't have to unload one disc to listen to a new one. Manufacturers allow you to categorize discs loaded in the mega-changer by music type or family member or both. Many also provide notebooks or albums for storing the CD booklets. Many now display CD text, or allow you to enter your own titles and artists.

SINGLE-PLAY CD PLAYERS

Sony CDP-XA20ES

✓BEST BUY

The Sony CDP-XA20ES single-play CD player strongly resembles Sony's most expensive player in basic technology and features at one quarter the price. The difference is that the CDP-XA20ES is not as ruggedly built and does not use the same hand-selected parts. You lose more status than sound. The fixed-pickup laser tracking keeps the laser stationary while the disc moves beneath it on a motor-driven sled. This reduces vibration and increases stability, resulting in fewer digital errors. The CDP-XA20ES employs eight advanced current-pulse digital-to-analog converters, which, when their outputs add together, cancel distortion. The 8x-oversampling, three-stage, feed-forward digital filter with 20-bit outputs greatly reduces noise and further reduces distortion. All this is mounted on a rigid frame-and-bean design chassis to resist vibration and shock. One interesting new feature is a knob, which Sony calls a jog dial, that you twist or spin to select tracks. You'll also find the rest of the features you'd expect on a pricey CD player, including the 12-key direct-access supplied remote. You can program 24 tracks, aided by the 15-track music calendar on the fluorescent display. There are six play modes and eight repeat modes, along with computerized time-editing and peak search for optimal cassette recordings. Digital outputs enable flawless recordings to MiniDisc or CD recorders. Sony also includes a front-panel headphone jack with a volume control.

Warranty: 5 years, parts and labor
Manufacturer's Suggested Retail Price: $700
Approximate Low Price: $700

Technics SL-PG480A

Budget Buy

Just because the Technics SL-PG480A rates as a Budget Buy doesn't mean you sacrifice sound or performance. It could just have been as easily rated as a Best Buy. If the SL-PG480A runs true to previous Technics models, it should also last an impressively long time for a budget model. Technics uses its recently upgraded MASH single-bit digital-to-analog converter technology (now called S-Advanced MASH Class A) for low distortion and noise. It also employs its amazingly effective digital servo, which keeps the laser focused on the disc (even on imperfect or warped discs), reducing digital and tracking errors. The player includes a peak level search for setting tape levels. You can program as many as 20 tracks, and the player will automatically cue for taping. The multifunction fluorescent display shows track numbers and various timings. The unit includes expected random and repeat play functions as well as a full-function remote control.

Warranty: 1 year, parts and labor
Manufacturer's Suggested Retail Price: $150
Approximate Low Price: $130

CAROUSEL CD CHANGERS

Technics SL-PD888

✓BEST BUY

The Technics SL-PD888 five-disc carousel CD changer continues an unbroken string of well-made, surprisingly durable CD players. Technics was one of the innovators of carousel changers and has refined it to near perfection. It has taken out cost without noticeable compromises in performance. Its Bidirectional Quick Disc Rotation change time from one disc to another is a quick seven seconds. It complements the player's lightning-fast ability to skip from the first to the last track on a disc. You can swap four discs while one plays. An easy-to-read disc location display clearly shows the discs that are loaded and which disc is playing. Technics provides a plethora of playing choices, including full random play, single-disc random play, or a spiral play that plays all the first tracks from each disc, followed by the second, third, fourth, and so on. You can even program the changer to delete tracks in the random mode. Similarly, the repeat mode can repeat individual tracks, discs, or programmed sequences. The Edit Guide and Synchro Edit features compute optimum track arrangement for taping. The ID scan mode samples the loudest, and presumably more recognizable, portion of each track. Direct disc/track access keys, logically arranged on the front panel and the wireless remote, make 32-track programming from any or all of the loaded discs easy. Technics backs up all these features with good sound from its proprietary MASH single-bit digital-to-analog converters. Its advanced digital servo accurately controls the laser pickup for low digital errors. This feature and a decent suspension allow the player to resist minor shocks and vibration.

Warranty: 1 year, parts and labor
Manufacturer's Suggested Retail Price: $180
Approximate Low Price: $170

Onkyo DX-C540

✓BEST BUY

When Onkyo was designing the DX-C540 carousel changer, they wisely decided if five discs are good then six discs are even better. This carousel changer handles six discs as easily as players that change five discs. In the process, the single-bit digital-to-analog converters with 8x-oversampling digital filters provide natural sounding music. You can change five discs while the sixth plays. You can program 40 tracks from among the six discs, assisted by a 20-track music calendar on the fluorescent display. The "drawer-under" layout keeps the player's highly legible, four-mode display visible while changing discs. You can also select one of the six repeat modes or random-shuffle play. The Next Selection control permits choosing the next track to be played without interrupting the track currently playing. Playing or programming tracks is easy with the direct disc and track access buttons on the front panel and supplied remote. The player's Music File will remember your favorite tracks on up to 202 discs. Not only will the peak-level search find the loudest portion of the disc for setting record levels, but it will repeat the segment for six seconds until you complete the level setting. Regardless of features, this Onkyo changer sounds superb.

Warranty: 1 year, parts and labor
Manufacturer's Suggested Retail Price: $320
Approximate Low Price: $260

Denon DCM-360

Recommended

We chose the Denon DCM-360 five-disc carousel CD changer for its solid construction and performance. It includes fewer features and a higher price than competing models, thus lowering it to a Recommended choice. This changer uses Denon's proprietary Alpha digital-to-analog converter with a 20-bit 8x-oversampling digital filter. This arrangement produces clear, clean sound with an impressive 100 decibel signal-to-noise ratio. Denon's digital servo keeps the laser focused on the disc even when playing imperfect discs or when the player experiences minor shock and vibration. Denon offers three-mode random play and five-way repeat. If you're throwing a party, you play music all night in the player's continuous play mode. A digital attenuator (volume control) allows you to connect the DCM-360 directly to a power amplifier if you desire maximum sound quality. The blue fluorescent display provides disc, track, and timing information. Denon keeps the button count to ten on the front panel. Direct disc and track access are available from the supplied remote control.

Warranty: 1 year
Manufacturer's Suggested Retail Price: $319
Approximate Low Price: $290

Technics SL-PD788

Budget Buy

The Technics SL-PD788 five-disc carousel changer is basically the same as the Best Buy SL-PD888 without a few of the features such as the edit guide taping convenience and ID scan. Bidirectional Quick Disc Rotation reduces change time from one disc to another to about seven seconds. It complements the player's lightning-fast ability to skip from the first to last track on a disc. You can swap four discs while one plays. An easy-to-read disc location display clearly shows which discs are loaded and which is playing. Technics provides a plethora of playing choices, including full random play, single-disc random play, or a spiral play that plays all the first tracks from each disc, followed by the second, third, fourth, and so on. You can even program the changer to delete tracks in the random mode. Similarly, the repeat mode can repeat individual tracks, discs, or programmed sequences. You can program 32 tracks on this changer. Technics backs up the features with good sound from its proprietary MASH single-bit digital-to-analog converters. Its advanced digital servo accurately controls the laser pickup for low digital errors. This feature and a decent suspension allow the player to resist minor shocks and vibration. The only inconvenience that drops this from a Best Buy to Budget Buy rating is the noticable lack of a remote control, which is necessary for direct track access.

Warranty: 1 year, parts and labor
Manufacturer's Suggested Retail Price: $160
Approximate Low Price: $140

MEGA CD CHANGERS

Technics SL-MC6

BEST BUY

The Technics SL-MC6 110-disc changer can rocket from one disc to any other disc in 11 seconds or less. The SL-MC6s optical detection system scans the disc compartments every time you turn the power on, memorizing empty slots, thus reducing change time. The front panel flips down, revealing the CD slots, so you can replace or rearrange any of the other discs while one is playing. A single-play slot allows you to insert and play a CD without finding an empty storage slot or needing to remove a disc. The player displays CD text if the record company encoded it on the disc. You can also store your own titles by entering them with a convenient telephone-style ten-key pad. You can electronically group discs into one of 14 musical categories, such as rock, jazz, country, or even romantic. A disc can also be in more than one category. You can program up to 32 tracks, even while a disc is playing. There's random play from a single disc or all the discs within a group, a repeat play of a track or disc, and ID scan, which plays the loudest and most recognizable passage from each song on a disc. Technics backs up these features with good sound from its proprietary MASH single-bit digital-to-analog converters and noise shaping digital filters. Its advanced digital servo accurately controls the laser pickup for low digital errors. This feature and a decent suspension allow the player to resist minor shocks and vibration. The SL-MC6 comes with a 27-key full-function remote control and an attractive portfolio to hold the booklets from the jewel boxes.

Warranty: 1 year, parts and labor
Manufacturer's Suggested Retail Price: $300
Approximate Low Price: $250

Sony CDP-CX240

Recommended

The Sony CDP-CX240 changes 200 discs and can be teamed with a second CD changer for even greater capacity. The CDP-CX240 uses Sony's proprietary Hybrid Pulse digital-to-analog converter with an 8x-oversampling digital filter on a single IC chip for shorter signal paths. Sony also adds its Direct Digital Sync circuitry to minimize a digital phenomenon known as jitter, which subtly muddies sound. It uses the sum of four converters to cancel out distortion. You can organize your discs into eight groups by category using Custom File. The Custom File Memo displays CD titles that you can enter from the supplied full-function remote or any PC keyboard—use of a real keyboard truly makes this feature practical. The player stores up to 400 disc titles or memos. It also displays CD text if the record company encoded it on the disc. The fluorescent display uses a dot matrix for greater resolution and clearer lettering. The player will remember 32 of your favorite hits, as well as allow you to program 32 tracks. Instead of number keys, you can use the jog dial on the front panel to expedite programming and finding your favorite disc or track.

Warranty: 1 year, parts and labor
Manufacturer's Suggested Retail Price: $480
Approximate Low Price: $350

Technics SL-MC70

Budget Buy

The Technics SL-MC70 60-disc changer is similar to our Best Buy SL-MC6, less 50 discs. It sounds the same, even though Technics removed a few features. It can still zip from one disc to any other disc in 11 seconds or less, and the player's optical detection system scans the disc compartments every time you turn the power on, memorizing empty slots, thus reducing change time. The front panel flips down, revealing the CD slots, and you can replace or rearrange any of the other discs while a disc is playing. A single-play slot allows inserting and playing a CD without finding an empty storage slot or removing a disc. You can electronically group discs into one of 14 musical categories, such as rock, jazz, country, and dance. A disc can also be in more than one category. You can program up to 32 tracks, even while a disc is playing. There's random play from a single disc or all the discs within a group, repeat play of a track or disc, and ID scan, which plays the loudest and most recognizable passage from each song on a disc. Technics backs up these features with good sound from its proprietary MASH single-bit digital-to-analog converters and noise-shaping digital filters. Its advanced digital servo accurately controls the laser pickup for fewer digital errors. This feature and a decent suspension allow the player to resist minor shocks and vibration. The SL-MC70 comes with a 27-key full-function remote and an attractive portfolio to hold the booklets from the jewel boxes. The price makes this mega-changer a remarkable bargain.

Warranty: 1 year, parts and labor
Manufacturer's Suggested Retail Price: $230
Approximate Low Price: $180

CASSETTE DECKS

Cassettes could whimsically be called "the people's format." They are cheap, easy to use, and universal. Since being introduced by Philips in the early 1960s as a low fidelity dictation medium, cassettes matured into a true high fidelity contender by the 1980s, thanks to Dolby noise reduction and improved tape formulations.

However, the ever-increasing portability of CD, along with the newer digital MiniDisc format, pose formidable challenges to the cassette. Manufacturers noting decreased interest in cassette decks released the fewest new models last year since the format took off in the 1980s, and the new models that did arrive contained fewer features, such as the Dolby S noise reduction.

SINGLE-TRANSPORT CASSETTE DECKS

We list single cassette decks solely for people serious about recording. We chose decks that offer the maximum fidelity and flexibility. There remain a few ultimate single decks with prices over

$1,000, but we cannot justify this in the age of digital recording. The decks listed here make great recordings at a reasonable price and have the features that help you get the most from your recordings. Dolby B and C noise reduction and HX-Pro headroom extension are mandatory, and Dolby S is preferred for serious recording. Decks should have at least two motors. Real-time tape counters that show you how much actual tape time you've been recording or how much time is left on the tape is a desirable feature. All decks should smoothly and assuredly handle tape and never jam.

DUAL-TRANSPORT CASSETTE DECKS

Dual-transport cassette decks became the rage a decade ago when people began duplicating tapes, and nearly eclipsed single-transport cassette decks. They offered a bargain since each transport could share common parts, making the cost only one-third to one-half more than a single deck. A good dual-transport deck should have many of the same features as a good single deck. In addition it should have auto-reverse on both transports. We think that dual-transport decks should offer the added utility of being able to record as well as play on both transports. This permits over three hours of virtually uninterrupted recording, or making two copies of a third source (such as a CD) simultaneously. Many of the decks we list include this feature. All dual-transport decks can high-speed copy tapes in half the normal playing time. However, even on the best decks, high-speed copies lose more fidelity than copies made at standard speed.

Before you shop for a single- or dual-transport cassette deck for your stereo system, read through the following brief explanation of major specifications.

TAPES

Always buy brand-name tapes. The brands we recommend include Fuji, JVC, Maxell, Sony, and TDK. Some companies add a bit more zing to the treble with certain tapes, such as TDK tapes that end in an X (SA-X) or Maxell tapes that end in an S (UD-XLIIS).

FEATURES AND TERMINOLOGY

Frequency Response: Frequency response is sometimes improved at the expense of distortion and signal-to-noise ratio. But achieving the true hi-fi range of 20 to 20,000 hertz may not mean the overall quality is better, since most humans (especially as they get older) cannot hear much above 15,000 hertz and few instruments other than a grand pipe organ produce tones that go much below 30 hertz. When comparing the frequency responses of two different machines, be sure the response of each machine is accompanied by a tolerance, usually stated as plus or minus a certain number of decibels (dB); otherwise the frequency response statement is meaningless.

Distortion: Distortion is quoted by tape deck manufacturers at a -20 dB recording level, which is lower than the level at which most people record. (A few specs quote a more realistic 0 dB level.) Many manufacturers advise recording peaks as high as +5 dB.

Signal-to-Noise Ratio (S/N): S/N ratios often use the -20 dB recording level as a reference. Choose a deck with better-than-60 dB S/N ratio when the Dolby noise reduction is switched off. To enjoy the best sound from the tape deck you have selected, use the brand and type of tape recommended by the manufacturer, or have a technician adjust the machine for your favorite type of tape. Avoid bargain-brand tapes—not only will they lower sound quality, they can potentially damage the machine.

Wow and Flutter: A measurement of tape-speed fluctuation, wow and flutter is usually listed as a percentage, followed by the acronym WRMS. For example, a wow-and-flutter specification might read 1/10% WRMS. Look for the lowest percentage available within your budget limitations.

Bias, Equalization, and Level-Setting Adjustments: These adjustments are not available on all cassette decks; however, some tape decks offer fine-tuning controls that allow you to adjust for slight differences in the bias of recording tapes. Other decks control adjustments with microprocessor chips. These circuits test the tape and adjust for the optimum bias, equalization, and sensitivity to provide the best performance from a tape.

3-Head Cassette Decks: These decks have one head for erasing, one for recording, and a third for playback. This arrangement provides the same sort of rapid off-the-tape monitoring capability found on professional open-reel machines. Using a separate head for each function also improves performance by permitting the use of specialized heads for record and play.

Noise Reduction Systems: Even with the very best cassette tape used in a superior cassette recorder, you will probably notice some tape hiss, or noise, when playing back your recordings. Hiss, which occurs where the human ear is most sensitive (in the upper midrange and treble), is especially noticeable during playback of softer musical passages. Although several noise-reduction technologies competed during the cassette's early days, Dolby noise reduction proved the most viable. Different levels of noise reduction from Dolby Laboratories are now standard on all cassette decks. Dolby A is a very expensive professional noise-reduction system not used in consumer cassette decks.

Dolby B reduces high-frequency (treble) noise by 5 to 10 decibels; this is equivalent to perceiving about a 50 percent reduction in high-frequency noise. Tapes recorded in Dolby B can be played back on non-Dolby players with only a slight sonic aberration.

Dolby C reduces both midrange and high-frequency noise by about 10 decibels, but it sounds as if it reduced noise twice as much as Dolby B. It also slightly lowers distortion on high-frequency peaks. While Dolby C-encoded tapes can be played back with some success using Dolby B, they sound unpleasant when played back on machines lacking any Dolby decoding.

Dolby S reduces noise throughout the audible range and as much as 20 decibels in high frequencies. It also significantly reduces distortion. Dolby S is the consumer version of the Dolby SR professional noise-reduction system. Dolby requires a basic standard of quality for cassette decks equipped with Dolby S. Tapes recorded on these decks approach digital sound quality, with dramatically low noise and distortion. Dolby S cannot eliminate speed variations such as wow and flutter. Dolby S tapes can be played back through Dolby B or C with reasonable success. Although its full benefits won't be realized, the sound quality is acceptable.

Dolby HX-Pro is a headroom expansion (HX) system that, unlike noise-reduction systems, is single-ended. That means it works only during recording and needs no decoding on playback. Dolby HX-Pro adjusts the recording current, or bias, to allow higher levels of high frequencies on the tape, while lowering distortion. A by-product of this is a subtle reduction of noise. A cassette deck with HX-Pro will greatly assist your efforts to make superior tape recordings. It is now becoming standard on all but the least expensive models.

SINGLE-TRANSPORT CASSETTE DECKS

Denon DRM-650S

BEST BUY

The Denon DRM-650S single-transport cassette deck combines the features we demand from a single deck at a surprisingly affordable price. In addition to the expected Dolby B and C noise reduction and HX-Pro headroom extension, the deck includes the less common Dolby S, which enables recording with a wide dynamic range and impressively low noise. You can play back tapes recorded with Dolby S on machines with Dolby B, but you lose the benefits of Dolby S. At the press of a button, Denon's automatic tape tuning adjusts the deck's electronics to the specific tape on which you plan to record. The dual-motor, microprocessor controlled, full-logic mechanism handles tapes smoothly and assuredly. The DRM-650S includes music search, memory stop, and the ability to return automatically to where you started recording if you make a mistake and want to record over. Wide fluorescent recording level indicators along with a large record-level knob aid setting levels. You can also dim the display if it becomes distracting. A timer switch, a disappearing feature on most decks, allows making unattended recordings with an external timer. The unit features a headphone jack with volume control for private listening.

Warranty: 1 year
Manufacturer's Suggested Retail Price: $300
Approximate Low Price: $300

Sony TC-KE500S

Recommended

The Sony TC-KE500S is a high performance, full-featured single-transport cassette deck. The triple-head design permits tape monitoring while recording, and it also permits optimization of the heads for maximum fidelity. Not only does the deck have Dolby B and C noise reduction and HX-Pro headroom extension, but it includes the less common Dolby S, which enables recording with wide dynamic range and impressively low noise. You can playback tapes recorded with Dolby S on machines with Dolby B, but you lose the benefits of Dolby S. You can manually adjust the bias for the type of tape you're using. The dual-motor transport with full-logic controls features high-speed fast-forward and rewind. Sony keeps the cassette rigidly seated with a ceramic cassette holder and damps vibrations with its cassette stabilizer. The real-time tape counter displays minutes and seconds. Some of Sony's earliest products were tape machines, and it continues to produce a superior product.

Warranty: 1 year, parts and labor
Manufacturer's Suggested Retail Price: $360
Approximate Low Price: $260

DUAL-TRANSPORT CASSETTE DECKS

Sony TC-WE825S

✓BEST BUY

The Sony TC-WE825S incorporates Dolby S noise reduction in addition to the standard Dolby B and C and HX-Pro headroom extension. The deck also includes real-time tape counters, along with pitch control and Sony's high-speed winding mechanism. Unlike Sony's single deck, this deck has an auto-calibrate feature, which allows tuning the electronics to match a specific tape you're using. The dual auto-reverse decks record and play on both transports, enabling sequential and parallel recording. They use two motors and two heads in each transport for good fidelity and smooth, steady tape handling. Full-logic, feather-touch controls provide easy operation. An auto-record level control optimizes levels for lowest noise and distortion. You can program the deck to play songs in any order you choose using the RMS Track Programming feature. The deck also includes a headphone jack for private listening.

Warranty: 1 year, parts and labor
Manufacturer's Suggested Retail Price: $300
Approximate Low Price: $250

Onkyo TA-RW544

Recommended

The Onkyo TA-RW544 dual-transport cassette deck delivers solid performance with all essential features. Since both auto-reverse decks record and play, you can make serial and parallel recordings. The deck comes with Dolby B and C noise reduction and HX-Pro headroom extension. The TA-RW544 uses four motors and handles tape swiftly and smoothly. The electronic counter is part of the fluorescent display, but it does not indicate real time. Although the headphone jack lacks a volume control, and you are unable to custom tune the electronics to the tape, the TA-RW544 produces a good sounding cassette tape and operates with ease.

Warranty: 1 year, parts and labor
Manufacturer's Suggested Retail Price: $350
Approximate Low Price: $299

JVC TD-W254BK

Budget Buy

The JVC TD-W254BK offers good value in an auto-reverse, dual-transport deck: one transport records and plays, while the second only plays. Both decks auto-reverse, allowing for over three hours of uninterrupted playing time. The TD-W254BK includes Dolby B and C noise reduction and HX-Pro. The two decks share six motors, one of which operates the mechanism that automatically opens and closes the doors. High-speed dubbing lets you copy tapes in half the normal time. A blue-and-red fluorescent display shows recording levels, the numeric tape counter, and the operating mode. Full-logic controls provide simple, reliable operation. JVC even includes a headphone jack for private listening. This deck has the same basic performance specifications as JVC's most expensive double-deck; only the features, such as the lack of custom tape calibration, differ.

Warranty: 1 year, parts and labor
Manufacturer's Suggested Retail Price: $190
Approximate Low Price: $170

MINIDISC DECKS

Last year dozens of new MiniDisc (MD) models from nearly a dozen companies appeared on the market, perhaps an indicator that MD's time has arrived. For a number of years only Sony and Sharp marketed MD in the U.S. Ahead of its time when introduced seven years ago, MD may yet become a successful format.

Many critics, and subsequently most of the public, leapt to the conclusion that Sony intended MD to replace CD. It took awhile for Sony to realize MD was the ideal replacement for the cassette, not the CD. The MD is to the CD what the cassette was to the LP: a highly portable, recordable medium.

HOW IT WORKS

This innovative technology digitally records (and rerecords) up to 74 minutes in stereo (the same amount as what's stored on a CD) on a 2½-inch disc encased in a protective caddy like a computer diskette. The player uses a laser and a magnetic head, similar to a tape head, to record on the disc. MD is as easy, if not easier, to use than CD, with nearly instant access to desired tracks, and programming capability. Recordable MDs perform some of the same tricks as computer diskettes, permitting nonsequential recording on any blank space on the disc. You can also reorder selections on the MD without rerecording or programming, as well as electronically label discs and tracks.

All MD players use a "shock-resistant memory" to perform their computerlike functions and improve portability. These memory chips store from 10 to 40 seconds of sound. Shake or jar the player and the music just keeps playing. This makes MD a more effective portable medium than CD.

THE FUTURE OF MD

Because of initially high prices and failure to understand the format, minuscule MD sales nearly doomed its existence. However, the Japanese public now enthusiastically embraces MD, making it wildly successful in its homeland. Europeans also are showing interest. Many broadcasters in the U.S. have replaced tape cartridge machines with MD. This increasing success has resulted in falling prices for the players and discs, and holds some hope for acceptance of the format here.

Sony MDS-JE520

✓BEST BUY

Sony leaves few features off its MDS-JE520, yet it sells at an exceptionally low price for a MiniDisc deck. To insure its sound quality surpasses analog tape and rivals CD, Sony uses its latest Hybrid Pulse digital-to-analog converter and the newest generation of the ATRAC compression algorithm, so the sound quality is comparable with CD. Sony also uses a 20-bit analog-to-digital converter for recording. The deck has two optical digital inputs and one optical digital output, along with the standard analog inputs and outputs. It even uses a sampling rate converter, so it will accept the direct digital output of CD or DAT. The MDS-JE520 includes all the features only available in an MD format, such as the ability to combine, divide, move, and selectively erase tracks. Sony uses the MD memory to give you a six-second reprieve if you hear a song on the radio you want to tape. Assuming the deck is on, you can start recording six seconds into the song, and still capture the whole song on disc. You electronically enter your own CD and song titles on a two-line display by scrolling through the alphabet using the jog dial. The same jog dial assists in automatic music search, letting you skip forward or back to your favorite tracks. Not only does this deck record up to the normal 74-minute maximum in stereo, but it will record up to 148 minutes in mono. A timer switch enables unattended recording or play when used with an external timer. Sony includes a headphone jack and a remote control.

Warranty: 1 year, parts and labor
Manufacturer's Suggested Retail Price: $360
Approximate Low Price: $300

Pioneer MJ-D707

✓BEST BUY

Pioneer applies many of its advances in digital audio technology to MiniDisc with the MJ-D707. The company uses its digital noise reduction circuitry and digital FLEX (frequency level expander) to restore the sparkle to recordings of less-than-perfect sources. Pioneer employs 20-bit digital-to-analog and analog-to-digital converters as well as an automatic threshold control circuit that restores incoming digital signals to their original form. The built-in sampling rate converter accepts all digital signals, such as those from CD and DAT. When recording analog sources, you can invoke the automatic level control to maintain an even level when recording from different sources. The MJ-D707 has an optical digital input and output, as well as standard analog inputs and outputs. This deck records up to the normal 74-minute maximum in stereo, and will record up to 148 minutes in mono. Pioneer includes all the innovative features of MD, such as being able to combine, divide, move, and selectively erase tracks, as well as electronically label the disc and tracks.

Warranty: 1 year, parts and labor
Manufacturer's Suggested Retail Price: $399
Approximate Low Price: $380

Denon DMD-1000

Recommended

Denon stresses its digital expertise with the DMD-1000. The company uses its proprietary Enhanced Dual-Bit Delta Sigma 20-bit analog-to-digital converters in the recording stage, and its Advanced Super Linear Converter for digital-to-analog in playback. Other enhancements include both optical and coaxial digital inputs, an optical digital output, and the standard analog inputs and outputs. The sampling rate converter enables recording from any digital source, such as CD or DAT. Denon also employs its Disc Recovery function, which salvages most of the recording time normally lost when an MD is edited and rerecorded. The DMD-1000 includes standard MD features such as combining, dividing, moving, and selectively erasing tracks. Should you be in a rush to record, you can set the deck to begin recording as soon as you insert a disc. Denon allows you to label discs and tracks electronically. You can record the standard 74 minutes in stereo or 148 minutes in mono, and you can program 25 tracks or select random or repeat modes.

Warranty: 1 year
Manufacturer's Suggested Retail Price: $599
Approximate Low Price: $599

STEREO SYSTEMS

Sometimes you just can't decide among the assortment of stereo components available and would rather purchase your sound system as a single package. Most manufacturers market a wide array of complete systems in an equally wide range of prices. The packaged system, once called a "rack system" because it came in a rack inside of a cabinet, now comes in many monikers. Many still come in a cabinet. The advantage of a single-brand system is that you know the manufacturer designed all the components to work optimally together, and this often represents a good value. (However, some manufacturers cut corners on these systems in ways not always evident, reducing the actual value.) Usually the systems come prewired, or require minimal wiring, making installation and setup a breeze. For people who desire music and/or movie surround sound without electronic involvement, these systems offer a satisfying alternative.

COMPLETE HOME THEATER SYSTEMS

Buying a packaged system won't eliminate all decisions, however. You will still need to decide which components you want as part of your stereo system, as the choices will vary. For example, none of today's systems come with a turntable, but a few offer it as an option. Multiple CD changers now occupy the space originally given to single disc players on all but the entry level systems. A great convenience feature, the wireless remote control, comes with most systems. Logic connections between components simplify operation. For example, the system will automatically switch from radio to CD when you load a CD, or from CD to radio when you tap a preset on the tuner. Most systems interconnect the CD player and cassette deck (or MiniDisc deck) to simplify recording CDs. Many even calculate CD and tape length and then optimally arrange tracks for the best use of tape.

Complete home theater systems can magnify the speaker problem by five, but many times home theater systems come with perfectly acceptable speakers. Buying a complete system reduces the complexity of home theater and frequently lowers the cost of admission. Complete home theater systems are becoming increasingly common and may replace basic stereo systems in a year or two.

MINI-/MIDI-SYSTEMS

Originally, big, imposing rack systems owned the lion's share of the stereo system market. In the past few years, mini-/midi-systems have proven that small is beautiful as they steadily outsell the larger systems. In return, manufacturers offer a wider array of small systems. The best of these small systems reproduce surprisingly big sound and easily stand tall against many of the full-size systems. As a bonus, these compact systems often include more features than larger systems, such as clock/timers that can turn them into deluxe clock radios.

Speakers are the weakest link in stereo system packages, especially with the full-size models. Good speakers often elude electronics manufacturers, but some companies specially engineer good speakers for their stylish mini-/midi-systems. By custom-matching the electronics and the speakers, manufacturers improve the sound of these compact systems. Bass enhancement circuits compensate for the space-saving speakers, enabling them to deliver a satisfying amount of bass. Although you rarely have an option with mini-/midi-systems, occasionally you might be able to convince a dealer to allow you to substitute speakers in a full-size system. If that's not possible, consider buying better speakers in the future.

CHOOSING YOUR SYSTEM

In this book we offer Best Buy, Recommended, and Budget Buy ratings as guideposts to a satisfying sound system. We look for the same features in a mini-/midi-system as we do in our full-size systems, although we make allowances for single-transport cassette decks and CD changers that change a limited number of discs, or play only a single disc, in the interest of size and space. Compact systems also tend to make more compromises, such as including cassette decks without any noise reduction. Mini-/midi-systems restrict swapping or upgrading components, and most include only a single additional input.

Most important, however, use your ears. Bring your favorite CDs to the store. You should always make an effort to listen before you purchase any stereo system. Remember, speakers will always sound different in your home than they do in the store. Room acoustics determine the sound of speakers as much as the speakers themselves.

BUYING TIPS

Buying a system from a specialty dealer usually eliminates hassles and confusion. Specialists do not necessarily charge a higher price than the mass-market superstores; but if they do, they often make it up to you in service. In our experience, home entertainment specialty dealers display a wider selection of equipment in a space more suitable for listening. They also pride themselves on good, in-store service departments. But if you know exactly what you want and feel confident about installing it, you'll be perfectly satisfied with most of the national chain superstores.

Superstores often use select models during promotions, selling them at a lower prices. Sometimes these models are discontinued or about to be discontinued and the manufacturer wants to unload them. Since there's minimal change from one model year to the next, buying last year's model can be a good value. Just be careful of the "bait-and-switch," where you ask for the advertised model and the sales person attempts to sell you a different and usually more expensive model.

BEST BUYS '99

Our Best Buy, Recommended, and Budget Buy stereo systems are listed below. Products within each category are listed according to quality. The best of the Best Buys is listed first, followed by our second choice, and so on. A Best Buy, Recommended, or Budget Buy designation only applies to the model listed—it does not necessarily apply to other models made by the same manufacturer or to an entire product line.

HOME THEATER SYSTEMS

Bose Lifestyle 12

✓BEST BUY

The Bose Lifestyle 12 is so elegant, so easy to install, and so sonically pleasing that we list it as a Best Buy regardless of its high price. The system includes a good AM/FM stereo tuner and a CD player. Bose also includes a surround-sound decoder, built-in amplifiers, and five pairs of its nifty cube speakers. The sleek, brushed-aluminum music center is smaller than most coffee-table books. A modest fluorescent display and a few buttons occupy a long oval cutout along the top front left. Bose expects you to operate the system from the white, uncluttered, finger-friendly remote control. The Lifestyle remote works via radio waves rather than the infrared light used by most remotes. This means you can conceal the music center or even operate it from another room. This system gives you big sound for playing music, which is demonstrated by a superb-fidelity CD sampler provided by Bose. But it's the speakers that represent the penultimate refinement of a concept Bose innovated about a decade ago. The woofer uses Bose's Acoustimass design for thundering bass from a relatively small enclosure. This bass module is about the size of a carry-on suitcase, and it includes all the power amplifiers as well as bass and treble controls. Because of the innovative amplifier and speaker designs, Bose does not rate the system's power. The five pairs of speaker cubes can be placed on a shelf (the center channel on top of the TV) or can be attached to optional stands or wall brackets with the built-in threaded adapters. Each cube of the pair twists, so they can be aimed at right angles or even opposite directions. Aiming one of the cubes toward you and the other at the wall creates a more spacious sound and improves the effect of the surround channels. You can set up the complete system in less than an hour, even if you consider yourself technologically impaired. All the color-coded wires terminate in plugs or tinned leads that easily slide into spring-clip speaker inputs—you won't even need a screwdriver. Bose uses its own VideoStage surround decoding system rather than the industry standard Dolby Pro Logic. While not identical to Pro Logic, VideoStage works admirably. Bose also markets an advanced version of this system, called the Lifestyle 20. This version reduces the size of the speaker cubes about 50 percent and incorporates a five-disc changer in place of the single CD player, making the music center slightly larger.

Warranty: 1 year (limited)
Manufacturer's Suggested Retail Price: $2,000
Approximate Low Price: $2,000

Sony R-5800

BEST BUY

The Sony R-5800 full-size system stands tall, about 40 inches. It includes the TC-WR681 dual-transport tape deck and the CDP-CX681 200-disc changer. It is a complete Dolby Pro Logic surround system and is Dolby Digital-ready, meaning there are discrete audio inputs for all five channels on the back of the receiver. The STR-SE581 receiver produces 100 watts for each of the three front channels and 50 watts for each of the two surround channels. The main front speakers include a 12-inch woofer made from a special material that Sony claims improves bass response and lowers distortion. It also includes digital signal processing for re-creating various acoustic environments such as movie theater or concert hall. The tuner section stores 30 radio station presets. The dual-transport auto-reverse cassette deck records and plays on one transport, while the second only plays. Both transports include Dolby B noise reduction and the recording transport uses HX-Pro headroom extension. Full-logic, feather-touch controls simplify operation and provide smooth tape handling. The CD changer allows you to divide the 200 discs by music type or family member. The jog shuttle on the front panel expedites programming and finding your favorite disc/track. You can also use the supplied full-function universal remote control if you prefer the glow-in-the-dark number keys. You can program 32 tracks, and choose among three play and two repeat modes. Sony houses the system in a black, wood-grain cabinet .

Warranty: 1 year, parts and labor
Manufacturer's Suggested Retail Price: $1,200
Approximate Low Price: $1,000

Denon D-850

Recommended

The Denon D-850 offers a fair degree of luxury at a modest power level of 35 watts per channel for the three front channels and 15 watts split between the two rear speakers. Denon packages this home theater system in two chassis: One contains the receiver (tuner, amplifier, control functions), and the other contains the dual-transport auto-reverse cassette deck and three-CD carousel changer. The D-850 incorporates Dolby Pro Logic surround sound for all five speakers, along with digital signal processing that creates hall and studio acoustic environments. You can bypass the tone controls and other preamplifier stages with the source direct setting. A three-mode preset EQ tailors the sound to what Denon considers best for pop, rock, and classic. You can preset 32 radio stations on the tuner, and you can manually enter station call letters for the display. The D-850 also comes with Radio Data System (RDS), which means if the station transmits the RDS signal, the station's format and call letters will be automatically displayed. The CD player allows you to program up to 32 tracks. Both cassette transports include Dolby B noise reduction. One transport records and plays, while the second only plays. Denon includes music search and an electronic tape counter. This system sounds quite good, and should accommodate listeners with limited space. The D-850 comes complete with the supplied 55-key universal remote control.

Warranty: 1 year
Manufacturer's Suggested Retail Price: $799
Approximate Low Price: $699

Onkyo PTS-505

Budget Buy

Onkyo calls its PTS-505 a "personal theater system" because it combines the flexibility and compactness of a stereo mini-system with the surround capabilities of a theater system. Since the electronics form a single block, you need only connect the video sound source (such as the audio outputs from your hi-fi VCR) and your speakers. For strictly audio pleasure, the PTS-505 incorporates a ten-disc CD changer, dual-transport auto-reverse cassette with Dolby B noise reduction, and an AM/FM stereo tuner with 30 presets. It adds theater thrills with Dolby Pro Logic, a center-channel speaker, and surround speakers. The center channel receives a scant 20 watts and the surround speakers receive a meager 10 watts each, compared to the 50 watts of the two stereo channels. While it's better to pump the same power all the way around, we make an exception for all this in a box that barely measures 11×8 inches. The Dynamic Theater Expander enlivens soundtracks with an extra shot of bass and treble, working with five preset equalization curves to tailor the sound for cinema, action, drama, sports, and live events. The tricolor fluorescent display and two-color illuminated control keys add to the attractiveness of the unit and simplify operation. The speakers are fairly small but sound quite good. The PTS-505 comes with remote control.

Warranty: 1 year, parts and labor
Manufacturer's Suggested Retail Price: $699
Approximate Low Price: $500

Technics SC-S2050

Budget Buy

Technics builds its SC-S2050 around the SA-G68 five-channel receiver, balancing an equal 70 watts to all channels with a Dolby Pro Logic decoder. The system even comes with a pair of video inputs, so you're all set to connect your VCR, DVD, or TV. You can preset 30 stations on the tuner. Beneath the receiver is a seven-band stereo graphic equalizer with enough red-and-green LEDs to show you the effects of your adjustments. Below the equalizer, Technics installs an auto-reverse, dual-transport RS-TR180 cassette deck. Both transports have Dolby B noise reduction, and one plays and records while the second only plays. The deck gently power-ejects cassettes and includes an electronic tape counter. The automatic record-level control is a recording convenience. Finally, there's the SL-MC59 60+1 disc mega CD changer. You can load a single disc without removing one of the 60 discs. Like all Technics CD changers, this unit changes discs with impressively high speed. Loading is also remarkably easy with the slide-out loader carriage. Technics offers 14 different subject groups in which to divide your CDs, and supplies a notebook for filing the CD booklets. You can program up to 32 tracks. The system offers a standard array of random and repeat modes as well. Technics magnetically shields the speakers: The left and right front channel SB-A28 three-way speakers have 12-inch woofers and special tweeters that widely disperse the sound. The center and surround speakers are substantially smaller, conventional boxes. Technics also supplies a universal remote control.

Warranty: 1 year, parts and labor
Manufacturer's Suggested Retail Price: $800
Approximate Low Price: $680

MINI-/MIDI-SYSTEMS

JVC UX-C30WT

BEST BUY

The JVC UX-C30WT packs ample sound with plenty of flexibility into a compact package. It combines a three-CD changer, AM/FM stereo tuner, cassette deck, amplifiers, and matching speakers in either a dark gray or white unit that fits easily on a kitchen counter. We particularly like the concept of the changer, which loads each CD in a separate drawer, providing instant accessibility to each disc. You can program 20 tracks from any or all of the discs, or you can have the player randomly play from any or all the discs. The digitally-synthesized tuner has 30 presets (15 AM/15 FM) that you can manually set or the tuner can automatically set. The single auto-reverse cassette deck has full-logic electronic controls and Dolby B noise reduction, and it works in conjunction with the CD changer to record CDs. The amplifier section produces 12 watts per channel, which is a lot of power from such a small unit, and has preset equalizations for beat, pop, clear, and live. The custom-matched speakers reproduce impressive sound. There's also an auxiliary input, for such components as a hi-fi VCR. The fluorescent display includes a clock/timer for auto shut-off in the sleep mode and wake-up. JVC supplies a full-function remote control.

Warranty: 1 year, parts and labor
Manufacturer's Suggested Retail Price: $330
Approximate Low Price: $280

Yamaha GX-50

✓BEST BUY

Yamaha has made a name for itself by manufacturing some of the finest sounding mini-systems available. Its GX-50 continues this tradition, offering greater wattage than previous models, but at a lower price. The futuristic styling of the GX-50 doesn't distract from its outstanding performance, either. Even though the controls might seem intimidating at first, they are logically laid out with different sizes and shapes. The single package of electronics includes a 45-watt-per-channel amplifier and Yamaha's proprietary Active Servo Technology, which makes small speakers sound large and natural. Playing through the amplifier is a dual-transport, auto-reverse cassette deck with Dolby B noise reduction. The deck is able to relay-play for almost four hours of uninterrupted music. A timer enables you to record from the AM/FM stereo digitally synthesized tuner, which has 40 station presets and direct access tuning. There's a three-CD changer, which permits swapping two of the discs while a third plays. The GX-50 includes a five-band graphic equalizer with a spectrum analyzer to facilitate its use; it also includes preset equalizations for various types of music. Furthermore, you can select from the digital signal processor sound fields for arena, club, or studio ambience. The timer also allows you to use the mini-system as an elaborate alarm clock. The three-way speakers contain a super tweeter for exceptional extended treble. This is probably the best sounding mini-system available in its size and price range.

Warranty: 1 year, parts and labor
Manufacturer's Suggested Retail Price: $499
Approximate Low Price: $399

Sony LBT-D390

Recommended

The Sony LBT-D390 midi-system bristles with features and power. Since you will pay a bit more for this loaded system, it receives a Recommended rather than a Best Buy rating. It consists of a receiver/equalizer, a five-disc CD changer, and an auto-reverse, dual-transport cassette deck. The amplifier produces an impressive 100 watts per channel, which is a lot of power for a midi-system. The three-way speakers contain 6¾-inch woofers, 2½-inch tweeters, and a ¾-inch super tweeter. Sony presets ten equalization settings, and you can memorize five of your own on the five-band equalizer with three-band spectrum analyzer; the latter puts on quite a light show. Sony also includes its Dynamic Bass Feed Back circuit to compensate for lack of bass at low listening levels. If you like dance music, the "groove effect" will set your heart pounding. The Matrix Surround Sound provides the illusion of sound coming from all around when you sit in the right position. It expands the sound field, even if it doesn't actually surround you. You can preset 20 FM and 10 AM stations on the tuner. You can program 32 tracks on the CD player and you can exchange four discs while the fifth plays. The CD player also includes time-edit to optimize taping and synchronizes with the cassette deck for one-button recording. The jog/shuttle dial speeds up and simplifies programming your favorite tracks. You control the cassette deck by touching the full-logic, feature-touch controls. The deck plays on both transports and records on one, offering Dolby B noise reduction on both. A clock/timer permits using the system as an elegant clock radio. Sony supplies a full-function remote control, a microphone input, and a karaoke function

Warranty: 1 year, parts and labor
Manufacturer's Suggested Retail Price: $480
Approximate Low Price: $430

Aiwa NSX-A303

Budget Buy

If you can live without Dolby noise reduction and auto-reverse on your cassette deck, the Aiwa NSX-A303 represents a marvelous value. The otherwise full-featured mini-system includes a three-disc CD changer, a dual-transport cassette deck, and a pre-set graphic equalizer coupled with an eight-band spectrum analyzer that shows relative frequency levels (and puts on quite a light show). The amplifier produces 30 watts per channel into two-way magnetically shielded speakers. The equalizer comes with rock, pop, and classic settings, and there's a switchable super bass boost. You can program 32 radio station presets on the tuner. The clock/timer function allows you to use this system as a clock radio. A jog dial speeds up and simplifies programming, as well as allowing you to program 20 tracks on the CD changer. The full-logic, feather-touch-controlled cassette deck plays on both transports and records on one. Even at this price, Aiwa supplies a full-function remote control. This compact system packs plenty of sound.

Warranty: 1 year, parts and labor (limited)
Manufacturer's Suggested Retail Price: $250
Approximate Low Price: $219

PERSONAL STEREOS

Personal stereos have changed the face of civilization as we know it. All around the world, people live in a private world of stereo headphones. Whether you have a stereo headphone, radio, tape player, or CD player, you can thank Sony for their unlikely invention of the Walkman almost two decades ago. (People often mistakenly call all personal stereos by Sony's trademarked name of Walkman, which has become almost generic for a category alternately known as headphone stereos or personal portables.) Sony still offers the widest variety of personal stereos on the market. The company—and its competitors—began a revolution in the music industry, raising cassettes above records, FM above AM, and now CD above all.

FEATURES

In an effort to hold prices, many features (such as auto-reverse and Dolby B noise reduction) continue migrating to top-of-the-line models. The major brands compete with models of diminishing differentiation. Only modest differences in sound quality and a feature or two separate them. However, factors such as construction quality and battery life continue to give some models the edge.

Among personal stereos, some popular radio features include liquid crystal displays and synthesized tuning with preset buttons; tape features can include auto-reverse, Dolby, automatic music search (AMS), and recording ability; and general frills are graphic equalizers (for fine tuning frequency response), bass boost circuits, water resistance (sport models), and rechargeable batteries. Beware: Features can sometimes be marketing ploys more than performance enhancements. However, you may find auto-reverse and preset station buttons offer great convenience.

BUYING TIPS

Recognizable brand names generally deliver the best sound and most dependable operation. However, even among models within a single brand, the least expensive and most expensive unit might come from different factories—or even different countries.

Under ideal conditions, many portable stereos perform alike. The true test comes in motion and heavy usage. Shake the player in the store while you listen for tape skewing (variations in frequency response and clarity) and wow-and-flutter (warbling or off-speed sound). Gently shake and lightly tap CD players to determine stability. See if memory-equipped "shock-resistant" CD players live up to their billing. If they do, remember that shock-resistant memory circuits reduce battery life and add considerably to cost.

RADIO RECEPTION

The critical test of FM reception occurs in big cities, where the unit may overload from nearby transmitters. The signal bouncing between tall buildings creates a condition (called "multipath") that further distorts reception. In contrast, the signal might be too weak in the far suburbs. A stereo/mono switch or local/distant switch helps in these situations. Some FM models use automatic stereo/mono blending to smooth out the rapid and distorting change between stereo and mono in difficult reception areas. The length of the headphone cord determines the quality of FM reception, since the cord usually doubles as the FM antenna. A few inches of cord, more or less than the ideal 31 inches, makes a significant difference.

CLOCK RADIOS

Today, nearly all clock radios use digital LED displays or LCDs, and you can set the wake-up time and the sleep timer to the minute. Sizes range from a VHS tape to a boom box and prices range from $10 to $350. Many models offer two alarms—a great convenience when each member of a couple arises at a different time. You also have a choice of mono or stereo sound. More deluxe models may even contain an auxiliary input for a tape or CD player.

Some desirable features include automatic display dimming when you turn out the light. (Most people don't want their clock radio to double as a night-light.) Bidirectional alarm/clock set buttons save time and frustration. If you zip past the desired setting you don't have to scroll through 24 hours to return to the right spot.

Unfortunately, this feature usually only appears on more expensive models. Budget models use mostly mechanical switches, while more expensive models tend toward electronic switches. You may find the electronic switches last longer and are easier to use. However, you can rarely set an electronic volume control when the radio is off. (You might desire to do this if your partner is asleep and you want to make sure the radio is loud enough to awaken you in the morning.)

We consider a battery backup essential to keep the clock circuitry running and sound the alarm if it is set. The backup doesn't need to keep the clock display illuminated, but it should prevent you from oversleeping or having to reset the clock.

BEST BUYS '99

Our Best Buy, Recommended, and Budget Buy personal stereo systems and clock radios are listed below. Products within each category are listed according to quality. The best of the Best Buys is listed first, followed by our second choice, and so on. A Best Buy, Recommended, or Budget Buy designation only applies to the model listed—it does not necessarily apply to other models made by the same manufacturer or to an entire product line.

PORTABLE CD PLAYERS

Sony D-E301

BEST BUY

The Sony D-E301 portable compact disc player became an even better buy when Sony lowered its price. It combines all the features and performance you need for music on the go. Ten seconds of electronic shock protection coupled with an improved mechanical suspension make this player suitable for most activities. At the center of the D-E301 is the LCD screen, which displays tracks, timing, mode, and battery condition. On the right are the major function controls for play/pause/stop and skip/scan, and on the left are smaller buttons that select functions not used as often such as turning the electronic shock protection (ESP) on and off. With the ESP off, the D-E301 plays for 12 hours on two AA batteries. It will also recharge an optional rechargeable battery pack. The unit has ten playback modes (such as random and repeat) and you can program 22 tracks. Sony's automatic volume limiter system (AVLS) protects your hearing, and its Mega Bass feature pumps up the bass. The player's one-bit digital-to-analog converter and related audio circuitry deliver superb sound quality. Sony provides decent on-the-ear headphones supported by a medium-width plastic headband.

Specifications: height, 1⅛"; width, 5¼"; depth, 6¼"; weight, 8.8 oz. (without batteries)
Warranty: 90 days, labor; 1 year, parts
Manufacturer's Suggested Retail Price: $120
Approximate Low Price: $89

Sony D-E705

Recommended

The D-E705 Discman's performance matches its elegant appearance. The sleek, ultra-slim design immediately catches the eye. While slightly more expensive, it will not disappoint. Sony downsized the controls to complement the look, making the buttons a bit small for the average finger. Above the eight identical buttons is a larger than usual LCD screen that displays tracks, timings, mode, and battery condition. Sony builds in 20 seconds of electronic shock protection (ESP) in its newest Steadysound technology. With the ESP off, the D-E705 plays for about 20 hours on a pair of AA batteries (it will also accept rechargeable batteries). Steadysound ESP keeps the D-E705 playing through all but the worst shock and vibration. The unit has ten playback modes (such as random and repeat) and you can program 22 tracks. Sony's automatic volume limiter system protects your hearing, and its Mega Bass feature pumps up the bass. The player's one-bit digital-to-analog converter and related audio circuitry deliver exceptional sound quality. There's even an optical digital output for copying CDs to a MiniDisc recorder. Sony supplies great sounding on-the-ear headphones with a remote control built into the cord. It also includes an AC adapter and a carrying case.

Specifications: height, 15⁄16"; width, 5 3⁄16"; depth, 5 1⁄2"; weight, 7 oz. (without batteries)
Warranty: 90 days, labor; 1 year, parts
Manufacturer's Suggested Retail Price: $200
Approximate Low Price: $170

Aiwa XP-570

Budget Buy

The Aiwa XP-570 portable CD player optimally combines features and performance at an economical price. Its most innovative feature is the XP-570's ten-second Electronic Anti-Shock System Plus (EASS Plus) memory coupled with mechanical shock absorption that makes the XP-570 far more shock-resistant than last year's model. The dynamic super linear bass circuit (DSL) satisfies bass-hungry listeners. The LCD screen displays tracks, timings, and battery life. The XP-570 even offers two-way repeat play. The simple, easy-to-use player comes with an AC adapter. The light, on-the-ear headphones, suspended with a plastic band, are comfortable and provide good sound.

Specifications: height, 13/16"; width, 5¾"; depth, 6¼"; weight, 9 oz. (without batteries)
Warranty: 90 days, parts; 1 year, labor
Manufacturer's Suggested Retail Price: $80
Approximate Low Price: $69

PERSONAL RADIO-CASSETTE PLAYERS

Panasonic RQ-E30V

✓BEST BUY

The full-featured Panasonic RQ-E30V exemplifies good value in a personal radio-cassette player. Panasonic portables have shown excellent durability over the years and continue to do so with the RQ-E30V. Its auto-reverse mechanism incorporates a digitally-synthesized tuner and five AM and five FM radio presets. A local/distance switch helps optimize reception. The LCD screen displays station and preset numbers as well as tape mode and battery condition. Five mechanical buttons along the spine control tape function, two large silver buttons on either side of the LCD control main radio functions. The XBS Extra Bass System boosts the low frequencies for bass lovers, enhancing this unit's already superior sound. The RQ-E30V can operate as long as 24 hours on a single AA battery, making it a most economical unit. Panasonic supplies a detachable belt-clip, rechargeable battery, and comfortable on-the-ear headphones.

Specifications: height, 3¼"; width, 4⅜"; depth, 1 5/32"; weight, 5.9 oz.
Warranty: 1 year, parts and labor
Manufacturer's Suggested Retail Price: $55
Approximate Low Price: $49

Sony WM-FX451

Recommended

The Sony WM-FX451 personal radio-cassette player offers ample features and great performance at a modest price without unnecessary frills. It has an exceptional 24-hour battery life in tape playback—33 hours in the radio mode—and operates on a pair of alkaline batteries. Its auto-reverse mechanism automatically shuts off after playing both sides of a tape. The digitally-synthesized tuner stores 15 FM and 5 AM radio presets in its memory. When the small LCD screen isn't showing radio frequency/preset, it shows the time. The mechanical controls for tape operation are placed along the top spine. A local/distance switch helps optimize FM reception for both near and distant stations. Sony's automatic volume limiter system (AVLS) protects your hearing. Superb-sounding, on-the-ear headphones are also provided.

Specifications: height, $4\frac{3}{8}$"; width, $3\frac{3}{8}$"; depth, $1\frac{3}{8}$"; weight, 8.2 oz.
Warranty: 90 days, labor; 1 year, parts
Manufacturer's Suggested Retail Price: $60
Approximate Low Price: $55

Aiwa HS-TX481

Budget Buy

The Aiwa HS-TX481 combines an impressive number of features with an economical price. The unit plays for up to 18 hours on a single pair of AA batteries. Its digitally-synthesized tuner stores 30 radio presets. The cassette's auto-reverse automatically stops after playing both sides. The mechanical tape control buttons are conveniently located on the top spine of the unit. The LCD screen not only displays radio frequency and preset numbers but other player functions as well. A sleep timer turns off the unit after a preset time. The Super Bass circuit should satisfy most bass lovers. Aiwa supplies decent on-the-ear headphones, comfortably supported by a plastic band.

Specifications: height, $3\frac{1}{2}$"; width, $4\frac{1}{2}$"; depth, $1\frac{1}{2}$"; weight, 6.3 oz. (without batteries)
Warranty: 90 days, parts; 1 year, labor
Manufacturer's Suggested Retail Price: $45
Approximate Low Price: $40

PERSONAL RADIO-CASSETTE PLAYER/RECORDERS

Aiwa HS-JS385

Recommended

The HS-JS385 personal radio-cassette player/recorder will satisfy anyone who wants to record classes or meetings—and, of course, listen to music—with or without headphones. When listening without headphones, a special "stereo wide" circuit enhances the stereo effect from the built-in stereo speakers. This unit also includes a built-in microphone. The HS-JS385 uses a conventional analog tuner with an easy-to-read, slide-rule dial. The cue and review function helps you transcribe recordings. There is a large window, which allows viewing the tape so you can estimate how much recording time is left, and a battery-life indicator. The HS-JS385 operates up to 22 hours on a pair of AA batteries. Aiwa supplies on-the-ear headphones suspended by a plastic band. Aside from the features, the HS-JS385 has decent sound and operates reliably.

Specifications: height, 3 7/16"; width, 4 1/2"; depth, 1 7/16"; weight, 6.5 oz. (without batteries)
Warranty: 90 days, parts; 1 year, labor
Manufacturer's Suggested Retail Price: $100
Approximate Low Price: $89

Panasonic RQ-A161

Budget Buy

The Panasonic RQ-A161 offers no frills, but it provides admirable and dependable operation. The built-in microphone on the front of the unit records in mono, but you can plug in an external stereo mike to record in stereo. The conventional AM/FM-stereo radio's horizontal tuning dial, which runs along the top front of the unit, is spread out enough to make tuning relatively easy. A local/distant switch optimizes FM reception for the listening location. The tape player is auto-reverse in the playback mode and auto-stop in the record mode. An LED doubles as both a recording indicator and a battery "good" indicator. Battery life is significantly less than a Sony—plan on about 10-12 playback hours from a pair of AA batteries. Panasonic's shell-lock case works like a car door lock. It keeps the case tightly sealed, protecting the tape and the mechanism. The sturdy mechanical tape function switches reduce the chance of accidental operation. Panasonic includes its "eXtra Bass System" (XBS) for listeners who desire ample low frequencies. The comfortable on-the-ear headphones, which are supported by a wide plastic headband, deliver satisfying bass. The RQ-A161 also comes with a belt clip.

Specifications: height, $4\frac{13}{16}$"; width, $3\frac{11}{16}$"; depth, $1\frac{11}{16}$"; weight, 6.8 oz. (without batteries)
Warranty: 1 year, parts and labor
Manufacturer's Suggested Retail Price: $75
Approximate Low Price: $69

PERSONAL CASSETTE PLAYERS

Sony WM-EX162

BEST BUY

The handsome Sony WM-EX162 is blissfully simple, yet still delivers satisfying music. We believe someone buying a personal stereo in this category is looking for economy with good performance, and the WM-EX162 fits the bill. One desirabe attribute is its 16-hour battery life on a pair of AA batteries. (A decade ago only the most expensive models offered this kind of playing time.) This unit shuts off automatically at the end of the tape side. It includes a switch that activates the Mega Bass for bass hungry listeners and Sony's automatic volume limiter system (AVLS) to protect your hearing. The WM-EX162 comes with a belt-clip and decent-sounding on-the-ear headphones, which are supported by a comfortable, wide plastic headband.

Specifications: height, $4\frac{3}{8}$"; width, $3\frac{1}{2}$"; depth, $1\frac{3}{8}$"; weight, 4.5 oz.

Warranty: 90 days, labor; 1 year, parts
Manufacturer's Suggested Retail Price: $27
Approximate Low Price: $20

Aiwa HS-PX387

Recommended

The Aiwa HS-PX387 offers a deluxe alternative if you want a tape-only personal cassette player. Above all, this player offers great sound. It includes Dolby B noise reduction and a multi-sound processor, which allows fine tuning the sound to your taste. For additional flexibility, the headphone cord contains a remote control, complementing the unit's full-logic, easy-to-use controls. The HS-PX387 includes auto-reverse and a music search feature, which will find and play up to five songs. It will also play for up to 30 hours on a single AA battery. You can even view the tape through a large window. Aiwa supplies good sounding on-the-ear headphones supported by a plastic headband.

Specifications: height, 3 1/8"; width, 4 3/8"; depth, 13/16"; weight, 4.8 oz. (without battery)
Warranty: 90 days, parts; 1 year, labor
Manufacturer's Suggested Retail Price: $120
Approximate Low Price: $99

Panasonic RQ-P35

Budget Buy

The economical RQ-P35 personal stereo cassette player is a durable, no-frills unit that plays your tapes with satisfying fidelity. The only feature is automatic stop at the end of the tape and the XBS Extra Bass System. It gives you music on the go without a major investment in the player or batteries. The RQ-P35 delivers roughly 14 hours from a pair of AA batteries. Panasonic supplies a detachable belt-clip and a pair of comfortable on-the-ear headphones.

Specifications: height, 4 7/16"; width, 3 7/16"; depth, 1 1/4"; weight, 4.6 oz.

Warranty: 1 year, parts and labor
Manufacturer's Suggested Retail Price: $25
Approximate Low Price: $20

PERSONAL HEADSET RADIOS

Sony SRF-H2

✓BEST BUY

The Sony SRF-H2 AM/FM stereo headset radio stays where it belongs—on your head—because of its double headband. You won't mind the tenacity, because it's extremely lightweight and has reasonably comfortable on-the-ear cushions. A flexible short-whip antenna resists breaking, yet it pulls in stations loud and clear. The reflective yellow tip on the antenna is a safety feature that increases visibility, which is especially useful when jogging at night. The SRF-H2 has a local/distant switch for optimizing FM reception. The unit operates for about 74 hours on a single AAA alkaline battery (about 25 hours on a regular battery).

Specifications: weight, 4.2 oz.
Warranty: 1 year, parts and labor
Manufacturer's Suggested Retail Price: $30
Approximate Low Price: $30

Aiwa HR-SP75

Recommended

The Aiwa HR-SP75 stays firmly on your head because of its wide dual headbands—it's perfect for joggers. Aiwa places this model in its Cross Trainer Series because it is meant to take a pounding in heavy outdoor use. Its AM/FM digitally-synthesized tuner automatically programs 20 station presets (10 AM/10 FM). You tune by touching a button on one of the ear cups. There is an LCD that helps with tuning, which also serves as an exercise monitor that shows calories/distance. The super bass circuit pumps up the bass if you desire maximum bass, adding to the wide range of quality sound the headphone can reproduce.

Specifcations: weight, 6.7 oz. (without battery)
Warranty: 90 days, parts; 1 years, labor
Manufacturer's Suggested Retail Price: $60
Approximate Low Price: not available

PERSONAL RADIOS

Sony SRF-85

✓BEST BUY

Although this sports-model radio carries a premium price for its bright yellow water-resistant case, we think it's convenient to own at least one all-purpose, nearly indestructible radio that brings in good reception. The SRF-85 includes Sony's Automatic Volume Limiter System to protect your hearing and improve audibility in noisy environments. The ultra-light, in-the-ear headphones make sense for this kind of radio. If your ear canal is shaped right, they may stay put better than the over-the-ear kind when you're active. A belt clip and swiveling armband/handgrip keep the SRF-85 glued to you whether you're relaxing or jogging. You won't break your budget on batteries because it operates on a single AA battery. The SRF-85 uses mechanical tuning, which we prefer because the feather-touch buttons of the digital models can accidentally activate when you put the radio in a pocket or purse.

Specifications: height, 3⅞"; width, 2⅝"; depth, 3 1/32"; weight, 3.4 oz.
Warranty: 1 year, parts and labor
Manufacturer's Suggested Retail Price: $35
Approximate Low Price: $30

Sony SRF-49

Budget Buy

The Sony SRF-49 AM/FM stereo personal radio brings in reasonably good reception under most conditions. The large tuning wheel—with a fairly long slide-rule dial across its front—is easy to use. A local/distant switch optimizes FM reception. The lightweight, on-the-ear headphones are supported by a wide, comfortable plastic band. Sony also supplies a belt clip, but this radio is easily pocketable. It operates on a single AA battery.

Specifications: height, 3¾"; width, 2½"; depth, 11/16"; weight, 2.3 oz. (without battery)
Warranty: 90 days, labor; 1 year, parts
Manufacturer's Suggested Retail Price: $18
Approximate Low Price: $17

PERSONAL MINIDISC PLAYERS

Sony MZ-E40

Recommended

The Sony MZ-E40 MiniDisc personal player finally brings the cost of MD playback down from the stratosphere. The player offers nearly all of the benefits of MD: a ten-second shock-resistant memory for stable playback; virtually instant random access; and an LCD (however small) that shows disc and song title, track number, battery life, and play mode. All the controls, including the volume, are touch buttons. The MZ-E40 plays four hours from a pair of AA batteries, and Sony offers an optional rechargeable battery that charges within the unit. This handsomely designed player sounds very good, certainly better than the best cassette portables (although no better than a CD portable). Sony supplies comfortable on-the-ear headphones, an AC power adapter, and a carrying case.

Specifications: height, 15/16"; width, 5"; depth, 3"; weight, 6 oz. (without batteries)
Warranty: 90 days, labor; 1 year, parts
Manufacturer's Suggested Retail Price: $200
Approximate Low Price: $200

Sharp MD-S301

Recommended

The Sharp MD-S301 is one of the smallest MiniDisc players on the market, and one of the easiest to use. Rather than opening up the unit to insert a disc, you discretely slide it in through a hinged door; thus, you need less space to operate the player. The headphone cord includes a handy remote control and display, so you need never touch the main controls. The remote looks like a backlit digital watch, with tiny controls more appropriate for a watch than a disc player. The display shows all the same MD information as the larger displays, such as track titles and numbers. In the ten-second buffer mode, you should be able to jog without ever hearing an interruption of your music. Sharp supplies light, comfortable on-the-ear headphones, which provide great sound. The rechargeable batteries last about six hours after a three-hour charge (using the included AC adapter/battery charger).

Specifications: height, 1″; width, 3 7/16″; depth, 3 1/4″; weight, 7 oz. (including rechargeable battery)
Warranty: 90 days, parts and labor
Manufacturer's Suggested Retail Price: $350
Approximate Low Price: $280

BOOM BOXES

BOOM BOXES WITH CDs

RCA RP-7998

✔BEST BUY

The RCA RP-7998 superbly-designed boom box includes an ample amount of features. This rugged heavy-duty model is splash proof and features a high-impact plastic cabinet with rubberized controls. Operating this unit is almost effortless. RCA places all controls in middle of the cabinet for easy access. Superb sound emanates from twin four-inch dynamic front-mounted speakers. There is a four-position Graphic Equalizer with settings for rock, vocal, and jazz. They do add some ambience to the music selection. The drawer-loading single-play CD player features a 16-bit digital-to-analog converter. It has continuous 20-track play with repeat and random-play functions. The top-mounted single-play cassette deck includes auto-stop. The RP-7998 also features a digitally-synthesized tuner with ten station presets. It is easy to tune in and memorize stations. An AC adapter, which plugs into the wall, or six D batteries power the RP-7998. The unit also offers a large, easy-to-read LCD. While this unit may not have all of the fancy features of other boom boxes, this rugged "go anywhere" model is perfect for the beach, cabin, or bedroom.

Specifications: height, $7\frac{7}{8}$"; width, $20\frac{7}{8}$"; depth, $9\frac{7}{8}$"; weight, 12 lbs.
Warranty: 1 year, parts and labor.
Manufacturer's Suggested Retail Price: $125
Approximate Low Price: not available

Aiwa CSD-MD5

✓BEST BUY

If you want pleasing sound and versatility from a boom box, the CSD-MD5 is just the ticket. This stylish boom box produces great sound, offering all the features of a portable stereo system with a CD player and a MiniDisc deck. Sound is of prime importance on this model, which pumps a solid eight watts per channel from its two bass reflex speakers. These speakers provide "Q-Sound," which is a psycho-acoustic effect that makes the sound appear larger than it is. And the sound that emanates from this boom box certainly sounds much larger—as if it's coming from an upscale rack or mini-system. The single-play CD player features a one-bit digital-to-analog converter. It has continuous 20-track play with repeat function options. The single-play MD deck will also play 20-tracks. Unlike the CD player, the MD player records from either the CD or the AM/FM tuner. The CSD-MD5 also features a digitally-synthesized tuner with 30 station presets (either AM or FM). It is easy to tune and memorize stations. A large top-mounted LCD screen is easy to read and includes a music calendar. A simple remote controls playback and repeat commands. Power is provided via the AC adapter. This attractive boom box is at home either on a shelf or at the beach.

Specifications: height, 6 13/16"; width, 21 3/16"; depth, 9 7/8"; weight, 12 lbs. 10 oz. (without batteries)
Warranty: 90 days, parts; 1 year, labor (limited)
Manufacturer's Suggested Retail Price: $525
Approximate Low Price: $500

Panasonic RX-DS28

Recommended

Panasonic's RX-DS28 is a basic boom box with a single-disc compact disc player. What this unit lacks in features, it makes up for in excellent sound. There is a four-position graphic equalizer with settings for XBS/Clear/Soft/Vocal. This model also features an acoustic separator cabinet with bass reflex ports. There are two four-inch, front-mounted speakers. It includes Power Blaster circuitry called XBS (extra bass system) for high-powered sound. The front-open CD player includes a one-bit digital-to-analog converter. You can program 24 tracks for random-access programming and repeat play. The RX-DS28 also features a digitally-synthesized tuner with ten FM and ten AM station presets for drift-free reception. It is easy to tune and memorize stations. The top-mounted cassette deck features soft-touch controls, auto-stop, pause control, and a soft eject system. This unit also includes a front-mounted LCD display and a sleep function. A basic remote allows you to adjust volume, tune in radio stations, and operate the CD player. Eight D batteries power the RX-DS28 for easy on-the-go play or you can use the AC power cord for at-home play.

Specifications: height, 5 3/4"; width, 19 53/64"; depth, 10 23/64"; weight, 8 5/6 lbs. (without batteries)
Warranty: 1 year, parts and labor
Manufacturer's Suggested Retail Price: $130
Approximate Low Price: not available

Sony CFD-980 "Sports"

Recommended

First and foremost, Sony's appealing CFD-980 provides excellent sound from its top-mounted compact disc player. It includes the MegaBass system for improved bass and surround sound for added ambiance. Each speaker enclosure includes a four-inch, full-range speaker. The CD player features twin digital-to-analog converters and a four-way disc repeat mode: single track, all tracks, 20 track RMS (random music search), and shuffle play. It also has 20 Track programmability. An excellent bonus is the ten-second electronic-shock protection (ESP) circuitry. The top-mounted single stereo cassette deck allows direct recording from either CD or tuner. It also includes auto-stop and synchronized CD/cassette dubbing, which starts the CD as soon as you press record on the cassette. The digital tuner provides ten AM and ten FM presets. The front panel sports a clean and uncluttered design. There is an LCD screen located directly in upper center section of the unit that includes a ten-track music calendar. Convenience features include a built-in clock with a 120-minute sleep timer, which also can be set to wake you up. Besides operating on either AC power or eight D batteries, this model features adapters for both car and boat.

Specifications: height, 6⅜"; width, 17⅛"; depth, 9½"; weight, 8 lbs. 5 oz.
Warranty: 90 days, labor; 1 year, parts
Manufacturer's Suggested Retail Price: $220
Approximate Low Price: $180

Sharp QT-CD121

Budget Buy

Sharp's QT-CD121 is your basic boom box that offers playback of either a single CD or single cassette at a reasonable price with few frills. This model features two front-mounted, four-inch full-range speakers rated at two watts per channel. The sound quality is quite good. For more bass, X-Bass circuitry is included so that you can pump up the volume. There is also simulated surround sound circuitry to enhance the sound even more. The CD player is top-mounted and the cassette deck loads from the front.

What may be a bit confusing at first is that the CD controls are located on the front of the cassette, and the cassette functions are found on the top of the box in front of the CD player. The CD door lifts up with your finger instead of pressing an "open" button. The changer uses a 16-bit linear digital-to-analog converter. The QT-CD121 includes an analog tuner with a rotary dial for easy tuning. While locking in a station is not digital, the analog tuner is able to capture most stations easily. An LCD screen is located front and center. The center front-loading cassette deck features basic controls, including pause and auto-stop. Eight D batteries power the QT-CD121 for easy on-the-go play. For at-home play, an AC power cord is included. A headphone jack is also included for private listening.

Specifications: height, 6 1/16"; width, 18 15/16"; depth, 10"; weight, 7 lbs. 3 oz. (without batteries)
Warranty: 90 days, parts and labor
Manufacturer's Suggested Retail Price: $80
Approximate Low Price: $70

BOOM BOXES WITHOUT CDs

Philips/Magnavox AQ7050

✓BEST BUY

The Philips/Magnavox AQ7050 is a compact portable stereo with big boom-box sound. The pleasing sound quality comes from the dynamic bass boost (DBB) to provide added depth. The dual four-inch full-range speaker system provides excellent sound reproduction. This model features a dual cassette deck that allows you to record from either AM or FM or dub from another tape. Deck 1 includes auto-reverse and Deck 2 features auto-record level control, high-speed dubbing, and one-touch recording. This model features an electronic tape speed control that monitors specific tape functions. AM and FM stereo tuning is accomplished via a rotary analog dial. The unit is powered by six D batteries or an included AC power cord.

Specifications: height, 6"; width, 17½"; depth, 6⅕"; weight, 4 lbs. 10 oz. (without batteries)
Warranty: 90 days, free exchange
Manufacturer's Suggested Retail Price: $40
Approximate Low Price: $40

Aiwa CS-P6

Recommended

The Aiwa CS-P6 is a simply elegant portable stereo system that features a single cassette deck. The play/record tape system gives this model lots of flexibility. An analog tuner with AM (featuring AM Wide) and FM bands is also included. All controls (including tape transport) are top-mounted for ease of use. Otherwise, there are two full-range speakers to pump the sound. The carrying handle is arched-shaped making the portable cassette player more visually appealing. The unit is powered by four AA batteries or an included AC power cord. For a small and easy-to-carry portable stereo, sound quality is quite good. A built-in microphone and a headphone jack are included as well.

Specifications: height, 3⅝"; width, 10⅞"; depth, 2 5/16"; weight, 1 lb. 7 oz. (without batteries)
Warranty: 90 days, parts; 1 year, labor (limited)
Manufacturer's Suggested Retail Price: $50
Approximate Low Price: $40

CLOCK RADIOS

Panasonic RC-6099

✓BEST BUY

Panasonic understands the essence of a clock radio, and it shows in the RC-6099. A bright green, dimmable clock display and lighted linear radio dial make the radio easy to use under any lighting condition. Rather than jarring you awake, the radio wake-up mode gently increases the volume. An earphone jack permits late-night listening without disturbing your spouse, but should you fall asleep with the earphone in, the buzzer alarm will still function. The radio has two alarms with indicators on the display. It has the usual sleep timer and snooze functions found on nearly all clock radios. You can easily set the clock and alarm times with the forward, back, and fast buttons that provide a choice of speed in either direction. A battery backup keeps the clock running and sounds the alarm in case of a power failure, and an indicator shows when the power has failed. A mechanical rotary volume control lets you set the volume with the radio off. A three-inch speaker provides good (although not outstanding) sound quality. If this radio continues the Panasonic tradition, it will operate nearly forever. The RC-6099 comes in a compact black or white cabinet.

Specifications: height, 2⅜"; width, 9⅛"; depth, 6 1/16"
Warranty: 1 year, parts and labor
Manufacturer's Suggested Retail Price: $35
Approximate Low Price: $30

Proton RS-330

✓BEST BUY

Proton originated the concept of a high-fidelity clock radio. It uses a relatively large five-inch speaker with a four-watt amplifier for extremely pleasing sound quality. The low-key black styling, with a black knit grille, doesn't draw attention to this clock radio. We particularly like the photo cell that automatically adjusts the brightness of the large clock display to the room lighting. You can manually adjust brightness to your taste, as well. In the dark, the clock remains just bright enough to read without becoming a night-light. The digitally-synthesized tuner has 12 AM and 12 FM station presets. The RS-330 includes dual alarms, awakening you to either radio or buzzer. The radio volume gently fades up, so as not to shock you awake. Sleep timer and snooze alarm are standard. The front-panel control buttons are backlit so you can see them in a dark room. A capacitor, rather than a battery, maintains time and alarm settings in the event of a power failure. It will not sound the alarm and may not keep the settings for as long as a battery, but it should work fine during most normal power outages. Setting the time and alarm is easy with forward and backward buttons. Proton lays out the controls logically for ease of operation, using manual knobs for volume and "loudness" (which balances the frequency response for volume level, providing a richer sound at low levels). There are terminals for external radio antennas, and a headphone jack.

Specifications: height, 6"; width, 11½"; depth, 3¼"
Warranty: 1 year, parts and labor
Manufacturer's Suggested Retail Price: $150
Approximate Low Price: $150

Sony ICF-C233

Recommended

The Sony ICF-C233 clock radio offers easy placement with its thin wedge-shaped design and overall compact size. It is one of the few clock radios to use a backlit LCD display, which is easy to read but not quite as bright in the dark as some of the LED and fluorescent displays. Sony offers digitally-synthesized tuning (unusual for a model at this price) that permits five radio station presets, and you can set time and alarm forward or backward. A capacitor, rather than a backup battery, powers the clock through brief power outages. However, it will not sound the alarm in the event of a longer power loss. It includes the usual sleep timer/snooze functions and offers dual alarms. Sony builds the ICF-C233 in black, white, or green.

Specifications: height, 2"; width, 7⅝"; depth, 5¾"
Warranty: 1 year, parts and labor
Manufacturer's Suggested Retail Price: $40
Approximate Low Price: $30

Sony ICF-C390

Budget Buy

The Sony ICF-C390 is a very basic clock radio, yet it includes the features we feel necessary, as well as reliable performance and acceptable sound. The small AM/FM clock radio has a large red LED display and will display the date at the touch of a button. It has manual tuning with a linear dial and includes dual alarms. The ICF-C390 is one of the least expensive clock radios with forward and backward time and alarm setting. It also comes with the usual snooze/sleep timer functions. A battery backup maintains time and sounds the alarm during extended power outages. The small 2½-inch speaker reproduces thin sound, but it should suffice if you only use this radio for awakening. Sony offers the ICF-C390 in black or white. There are cheaper clock radios, but they lack features, and in many cases, reliability.

Specifications: height, 1⅞"; width, 8⅝"; depth, 6⅛"
Warranty: 1 year, parts and labor
Manufacturer's Suggested Retail Price: $23
Approximate Low Price: $20

CAMERAS

A trip to the camera store can be bewildering to someone unfamiliar with cameras. Row upon row of gleaming chrome and shiny black cameras, of all different sizes and prices. How do you choose? The process isn't hard if you first determine exactly what you want to do with the camera.

Before buying a camera, first determine the types of photos you'll be taking and the degree of personal involvement you wish to have in the process. Shop for a camera that will best suit your needs. Even some less expensive cameras provide sophisticated systems to automate your photograpy.

TYPES OF CAMERAS

Single Lens Reflex (SLR) Cameras: With this type of camera, you are looking through the same lens that will form the image on the film; this is the most precise method of viewing available. Most SLR cameras feature interchangeable lenses, and this is one of the reasons to consider an SLR. Lens choices range from wide angle and telephoto to a wide variety of zooms and close-up or "macro" lenses. The major brands of SLRs also have extensive accessory systems that allow you to tackle almost any photographic task. Whether it's special lenses and flash units for close-ups of tiny insects, an intervalometer for recording a time-lapse series of a flower opening up, or a high-speed motor drive that permits taking up to ten pictures per second for fast-action series, the SLR is the most versatile and adaptable form of camera. Another variation, the ZLR (zoom lens reflex), has a permanently attached zoom lens. While slightly less versatile, it is a good choice for traveling because it avoids a lot of separate components that may get lost or stolen.

Viewfinder Cameras: With this type of camera, you view scenes through an optical window adjacent to the lens. This method is not as precise as an SLR, but is fine for everything except close-ups. All cameras reviewed here other than SLRs fall into this general category. Within this category are five subtypes of cameras:

Autofocus Viewfinder Cameras: This type of camera, as the name implies, automatically focuses the lens for you for maximum sharpness in your photo.

Fixed-focus Viewfinder Cameras: The lenses on this class of camera are set at the factory for a distance that will deliver the greatest range of sharp focus on objects from just a few feet from the camera to distant landscapes. This type of lens is found mostly on economy models.

Rangefinder Cameras: This type uses manual focusing to bring a split image in the viewfinder together as one image. Today these are only available as expensive professional models.

Single-use Viewfinder Cameras: Also referred to as "disposable" cameras, these are merely inexpensive fixed-focus cameras, usually featuring a plastic lens that is preloaded with film. When you're finished taking pictures, you drop the entire camera off for processing. They are great for use in environments that would damage a good camera, such as at the beach, in the rain, and even underwater with some models. The results are surprisingly good for album-size prints.

Instant-print Cameras: Polaroid is the only brand available in the U.S. They use only Polaroid film, which is more costly per print than with 35mm or APS cameras. However, there's no denying the appeal of having a fully-developed color or black-and-white print in hand in a matter of seconds or minutes. Polaroid cameras have been popular party-goers for decades, and probably will be for the foreseeable future.

FEATURES AND TERMINOLOGY

Lens Aperture: Also commonly referred to as the "f-stop," this is a mathematical ratio of the size of the lens opening relative to the focal length of the lens. Lens designations are most often expressed by the focal length in millimeters and the maximum aperture (largest opening), such as a 50mm f/2.8 lens. The f-stop is usually marked on the lens. This is important because the larger the lens opening, the more light can get through. A lens that lets a lot of light through (referred to as a "fast" lens) allows you to take pictures in dimmer light without using a flash. This type of lens also lets you use faster shutter speeds in all light conditions (for better action-stopping photos). Faster lenses are more expensive, though. F-stops run in a sequence that may seem backward when you first encounter it, but all you need to remember is the smaller the number the more light gets through. For example, a lens with a maximum aperture of f/2 lets more light through than a lens of f/5.6.

Lenses: In different camera formats, what is called the "normal lens" will be different. This "normal lens" approximates the angle of view seen by the human eye. For a standard 35mm camera, this is a lens of about 45mm focal length. Lenses with shorter focal length than the normal lens are referred to as telephoto. A zoom lens is a lens that can vary its focal length, which varies the angle of view as well as the magnification. There has been some confusion concerning focal length now that the new Advanced Photo System (APS) cameras have been introduced. These new cameras use a film that is only 24mm wide, as opposed to the standard 35mm. This smaller film means the "normal lens" is also smaller, so a "normal lens" for an APS camera is about a 28mm lens.

Focal Plane Shutters: Most commonly found in 35mm SLRs, this type of shutter consists of either a cloth curtain or metal blades located just in front of the film. They allow you to change lenses without fogging the film.

Leaf Shutters: Most commonly used in the popular "point-and-shoot" cameras, these are located within the body of the lens. They are found in cameras without interchangeable lenses.

Exposure Compensation: This is a means of overriding a camera's automatic film speed setting, allowing you to modify the exposure for tricky lighting conditions, such as backlighting or for special effects. Not available on economy models.

Viewfinder Display: When looking through the viewfinder, most cameras provide some degree of exposure information. This can be as basic as red or green lights, with their obvious implications, or a sophisticated LED or LCD readout of shutter speed, aperture, flash status, and other information.

Film Speed: The more sensitive to light a type of film is, the "faster" it is said to be. This rating is expressed by ISO (International Standards Organization), followed by a number, such as ISO 100. This example is considered to be a medium-speed film; ISO 400 is a fast film and ISO 25 is a slow film. Fast films allow you to take pictures in lower light levels or set higher shutter speeds to freeze fast action. Slower films are sharper, important if you regularly have enlargements made. Slower films also have better color saturation. Picture quality will be best with films of ISO 200 or less, as a grainy appearance increases with film speed.

Hot Shoe: This is a fitting on the camera that will accept an accesory flash unit without the need for a connecting cord. Most camera makers today offer dedicated—or proprietary—hot shoes when they have such a fitting. A dedicated hot shoe requires a flash made by the camera maker, or made specifically for that brand of camera, for proper operation.

Self-timer: This is a timer within the camera that allows you to get into the picture with the camera mounted on a tripod; ten seconds is the usual delay before the shutter fires. Some cameras have an infrared remote control that lets you fire the camera at any time after you've gotten into position in front of the camera.

Daylight Fill-flash: In bright sunlight, the sunlit and shadow sides of a person's face vary greatly in brightness. Our eyes compensate for the disparity, but film does not, resulting in inky-black shadows. You can overcome this contrast difference by firing the camera's flash unit, which brightens the shadows for a more pleasing rendition. You can manually adjust the flash intensity on some cameras, or have the camera deal with it for you (see Auto Fill-Flash).

Auto Fill-flash: This is an automatic flash mode on the camera that decides when and if daylight fill-flash is needed and the amount of flash light to deliver.

Red-eye Reduction Mode: We've all seen photos of people or animals with glowing red eyes. This occurs under dim lighting conditions when the pupils of the eyes are wide open. Light from a flash is reflected off the back of the eyeball and back to the camera lens, resulting in the "red-eye" appearance. A camera's red-eye reduction feature fires several short, rapid bursts of light before the actual exposure is made. This closes the pupils down somewhat and reduces the red-eye phenomenon. Note that the term is "reduction," not necessarily elimination. The effect is worse when subjects are staring directly at the camera; if you can photograph them at a slight angle it will help.

BUYING TIPS

If a camera that is featured here appeals to you but is a bit too expensive, or perhaps lacks a particular feature you're looking for, keep in mind that there is often a companion model just above or below the one reviewed. It may save you money by deleting an unnecessary feature.

Cameras are carried by several types of retail stores. You may have to shop around to find the exact model you're looking for. Calling ahead can save time. The discount stores often have good prices if they have what you want. Camera specialty stores will have more knowledgeable help, and are often the only place to find some of the more upscale camera models, though you will generally pay a little more. Look for sales and manufacturer rebates.

BEST BUYS '99

Our Best Buy, Recommended, and Budget Buy cameras are reviewed below. Products within each category are rated according to overall quality. The best of the Best Buys is listed first, followed by our second choice, and so on. A Best Buy, Recommended, or Budget Buy designation only applies to the model listed—it does not necessarily apply to other models made by the same manufacturer or to an entire product line.

35MM MANUAL-FOCUS SLR CAMERAS

The 35mm SLR (single-lens reflex) camera is probably the most widely used professional camera. Manual-focus SLR cameras are particularly suitable for amateur photographers who want focus and exposure controls to master the images they create.

Nikon FM2N

✔BEST BUY

Popular as both a serious camera for amateurs and a "backup" camera for pros, the Nikon FM2N offers every feature necessary for quality photography without meaningless frills. The sturdy die-cast metal body has a "heft" that feels good in your hands and provides the durability necessary to cope with active outdoor photography. The shutter features aluminum alloy curtains and a top speed of 1/4,000 second. The top flash sychronization speed of 1/250 second is important when using daylight fill-flash, which enables you to easily balance the flash exposure with the background exposure. Its fully-manual exposure control has the widest range of film speed settings—from ISO 12 to ISO 6400—in its class. A fail-safe switch turns the meter off after 30 seconds, preventing draining of the meter batteries. A three-point LED display in the viewfinder indicates whether the exposure is over, under, or correct. Film advance is manually controlled with a thumb lever that incorporates four ball-bearing clusters for smooth action. If you use long telephoto or extreme macro lenses, you will appreciate the FM2N's interchangeable focusing screens.

Warranty: 1 year
Manufacturer's Suggested Retail Price: $745
Approximate Low Price: $540

Contax Aria

Recommended

Contax has long been known for making some of the finest professional 35mm SLRs in existence, and Aria is an excellent example. The smallest Contax SLR camera ever made, the Aria combines value, versatility, and ease of use in its lightweight camera body. This entry-level manual-focus SLR camera has a built-in motor drive that transports the film at three frames per second in continuous mode. Its versatile metering system offers three exposure modes—center-weighted, evaluative, spot—to accommodate all types of photography. Other standard Contax features include custom functions, automatic exposure bracketing, and auto exposure lock. Top shutter speed is 1⁄4,000 second with flash synchronization at 1⁄125 second. An optional D-9 Data Back adds multifunction capabilities and can imprint exposure and dating information. Keeping the Aria buyer in mind, Contax has also introduced a new, lightweight Zeiss Vario-Sonnar 28-70mm zoom lens, which features a mode for easy close-ups.

Warranty: 3 years
Manufacturer's Suggested Retail Price: $849
Approximate Low Price: $589

Pentax ZX-M

Recommended

The Pentax ZX-M is a compact, lightweight, manual-focus model that offers a surprising degree of flexibility for the price. Included is an array of exposure controls designed to handle a wide variety of photographic applications. The electronically controlled, focal-plane shutter has a top speed of 1⁄2,000 second. Flash synchronizaton is at 1⁄100 second or slower. The viewfinder's LCD data panel shows all relevant exposure information, including the frame counter, and the illuminated display automatically varies intensity according to brightness level. A built-in motor advances film up to two frames per second; advance to frame one when loading and film rewind are also automatic. Other features include a meter memory lock button and a 12-second self-timer. You can also manually set the film speed if you prefer pictures lighter or darker than "normal." An optional data back is available as well as three auto flash units. The ZX-M accepts a full line of excellent SMC Pentax lenses, both manual and autofocus versions.

Warranty: 1 year
Manufacturer's Suggested Retail Price: $280
Approximate Low Price: $160

Vivitar V4000

Budget Buy

Vivitar understands that many people simply want to take better photos without spending a small fortune on unnecessary technical features and adjustments. The V4000 nicely fits the bill. Taking good pictures has never been this easy. First load the film and set the shutter speed high enough to avoid camera shake (1/125 second or higher, depending on lighting conditions). Then simply zoom the lens to frame the scene to your liking, focus, turn the aperture ring until you get the green signal in the viewfinder, and press the shutter release. The V4000 is packaged as a kit, complete with a 35-70mm f/3.5-4.8, close-focusing zoom lens. This range is all that is required for quality pictures. The viewfinder features a split-image focusing screen, and a three-LED exposure display (red under/over, green correct) monitors the center-weighted averaging system. The vertical travel, metal focal-plane shutter has a top speed of 1/2,000 second and a flash synchronization at 1/225 second. Film advance is manual via thumb lever and film is rewound by using the traditional crank. The meter is the only feature that requires batteries.

Warranty: 1 year
Manufacturer's Suggested Retail Price: $299
Approximate Low Price: $230

35MM AUTOFOCUS SLR CAMERAS

When autofocus SLRs first appeared, most professionals shunned them. Today it's hard to find a pro without one. Improved accuracy and reliability are the main reasons for their popularity.

FEATURES

Today's sophisticated, motor-driven autofocus SLR tracks fast-moving subjects much more quickly and precisely than by doing it manually. In a programmed-auto mode, these cameras are nearly as simple to operate as a point-and-shoot camera, with the advantage of having interchangeable lenses. However, most photographers who invest in these cameras do so to take advantage of their wide-ranging capabilities, plus their versatile lens and accessory systems.

Adaptable to any task from the family vacation to involved scientific-industrial imaging, this class of camera can be configured for any photographic task from sky diving to scuba diving. Most of the better models allow you to turn off the autofocus and auto exposure facilities when creative manual control is desired or necessary. All but the top-end pro models now have built-in, pop-up flash units. While no substitute for a more powerful and versatile shoe-mount unit, they are great for informal shots. These cameras place no limits on your picture-taking possibilities.

Minolta Maxxum XTsi

✓ BEST BUY

One of the most compact models in its category, the Minolta Maxxum XTsi is a fashionable, user-friendly camera. A combination of eyepiece and handgrip sensors automatically activate auto exposure and auto focus. It even includes an eye-start function that turns the camera on by just putting it up to your eye. There are four exposure settings, including manual. The metering system includes a 14-segment pattern for bright lighting and spot-metering for more difficult lighting. For various camera settings, the Maxxum XTsi offers five program selections: portrait, landscape, close-up, sports, and night portrait/night view. The electronically controlled shutter has speeds from 1/4,000 second to 30 seconds. The built-in, pop-up flash covers lenses as wide as 28mm. Flash synchronization is at 1/125 second. High-speed flash synchronization up to 1/4,000 second is possible with Minolta's 5400HS dedicated flash unit. A built-in motor drive provides auto-film loading and auto rewind. Exposure information appears in the viewfinder and the

LCD data panel on top of the camera. Other features include a slow-shutter flash for balancing flash with low ambient lighting; a ten-second self-timer; panorama format via internal mask; a remote-control terminal including access to ten custom functions; and a three-stage battery check indicator. The Maxxum XTsi is a terrific SLR camera that should satisfy the demands of most photographers.

Warranty: 1 year
Manufacturer's Suggested Retail Price: $880
Approximate Low Price: $500

Canon EOS Elan IIE

Recommended

The Canon EOS Elan IIE is a handsome camera, complete with impressive styling and a sophisticated autofocus system. When you look into the viewfinder, three autofocus areas are clearly marked. After a simple calibration procedure, the camera actually tracks your eye movement and turns on the autofocus for the specific area in which you are looking. This system is simple and quick to learn, and it works well in all sorts of situations for horizontal and vertical photos. The camera's large command dial controls ten exposure modes, including portrait, landscape, close-up, and sports. The six-zone advanced light-metering system is linked to the autofocus, so that the exposure emphasis is on the point of focus, thus ensuring optimal exposure. For advanced users, the camera also offers partial (semispot) and center-weighted metering. The EOS Elan IIE features a variety of custom functions that can be set to the user's preference, such as manual film-speed, multiple exposures, and automatic exposure bracketing.

Warranty: 1 year
Manufacturer's Suggested Retail Price: $750
Approximate Low Price: $600

Nikon N50

Budget Buy

The Nikon N50 is a competent performer at an affordable price. An N50 body and a mid-range zoom lens, selected from the huge array of Nikkor lenses available, are all that the casual photographer may ever need. The Nikon N50 is a great camera for anyone who doesn't want to have to "learn photography" but just wants to take good pictures. For the ultimate in "hands-off" SLR photography, just set the N50 to "simple" mode; the camera automatically focuses and sets the exposure controls. The N50 uses a dot-matrix LCD panel that displays user-friendly graphic symbols for different photography. After you gain familiarity with the Simple Mode programs, you can explore the picture possibilities of the four Advanced Mode programs: Sport, Silhouette, Night Scene, and Motion Effect. The N50's six-segment 3D matrix metering improves your batting average with tricky lighting conditions. Shutter speeds range from 1/2,000 to 30 seconds, and extra-long time exposures are also possible. A built-in drive motor advances the film up to one frame per second and automatically rewinds the film. The built-in, pop-up flash covers lenses as wide as 35mm; an accessory Nikon Speedlite can be added for greater power and range. If user-friendly automation appeals to you, the N50 could be your camera.

Warranty: 1 year
Manufacturer's Suggested Retail Price: $420 (body only)
Approximate Low Price: $300

35MM AUTOFOCUS CAMERAS

The 35mm leaf-shutter autofocus (AF) camera is popular because it makes it easy to shoot high-quality 35mm film. An AF camera does more than automatically focus the lens. It also loads the film, advances it after each exposure, and rewinds it at the end of the roll.

FEATURES

Many AF cameras come with a sophisticted meter that activates a built-in flash in difficult lighting situations, such as backlighting, to produce a lighting balance between the subject and the background. Dual-lens cameras have both a normal and a moderate telephoto lens. Others have a zoom lens that gives you a variety of focal lengths. Many now have special red-eye reduction features. The ultracompact design trend has come to zoom cameras, and the panorama format has come to the autofocus field.

Minolta Weathermatic Dual 35

✓BEST BUY

Most people put their cameras away when the weather turns unfavorable, and in so doing, miss a lot of great picture opportunities. The waterproof Minolta Weathermatic Dual 35 frees you from any concerns about ruining your camera in the rain, in the snow, or at the beach. In fact, the camera is usable underwater down to 16 feet, so you can take pictures from a fish-eye view in the pool or while snorkeling in the ocean. The "Dual" designation refers to the camera's lens. By means of a built-in micro motor, you can choose either a 35mm f/3.5 focal length or change it to a 50mm f/5.6 configuration. The Weathermatic is autofocus above water, focusing from 2½ feet to as far as the eye can see. Underwater, the camera operates in a "focus-free" mode, automatically setting either lens for picture-taking within a range of approximately 4-12 feet (water's index of refraction is greater than that of air, so objects underwater appear closer than they actually are). An underwater close-up button sets the lenses for a range of 1.7-4.3 feet with the 35mm lens and 2-3.3 feet for the 50mm. Film speed range is ISO 100-1000 (ISO 400 or 800 is great for rainy days or underwater). Exposure metering is subject-weighted. Film loading, advance, and rewind are automatic. The built-in flash fires automatically in low light and the shutter button locks while the flash is recharging. The camera can be powered either by a 6V lithium battery pack or four readily available AAA batteries. The high-visibility body floats, a nice feature if you should drop it in the water. This is an all-around fun camera.

Warranty: 1 year
Manufacturer's Suggested Retail Price: $351
Approximate Low Price: $200

Olympus LT Zoom 105

Recommended

While most cameras are mainly clunky black boxes, the burgundy covering and bright chrome trim of the Olympus LT Zoom 105 immediately set it apart. At the heart of the camera is a 38-105mm f/4.5-8.9 zoom lens, providing from mild wide-angle to medium telephoto coverage and focusing down to two feet. The zoom is motor driven, via a control lever next to the shutter release button. With the camera turned off, the lens retracts into the body and is protected with a swing-up lens cover that's hinged beneath the lens. The sophisticated, programmed automatic exposure control features three-zone light metering, switchable to spot measurement for tricky lighting conditions. Film loading, advance, and rewind are automatic. The built-in, pop-up flash automatically activates in low light and offers red-eye reduction. Other features include forced fill-flash, night scene capability (in conjunction with a slow shutter speed, with the camera mounted on a tripod, and the optional accessory infrared remote unit), and a flash-ready signal that appears in the viewfinder. In the various mode, flash and exposure counter data are displayed in an LCD panel on top of the camera. A Quartz date feature adds the date to your photos when desired. The viewfinder can be adjusted to your vision via a dial to the left of the finder window. A 12-second self-timer is provided and the panoramic mode is selectable. As a bonus, the LT Zoom 105 is classified as weatherproof, which means swimming pool splashes or light rain won't hurt it (not for underwater use).

Warranty: 1 year
Manufacturer's Suggested Retail Price: $455
Approximate Low Price: $280

Rollei Prego 115

Recommended

The Rollei name has been appearing on cameras for over 75 years. It is simple enough for a beginner to use with confidence, yet has many manual overrides and creative options available when you're ready for them. The 38-115mm f/3.9-10.8

power zoom lens delivers the high degree of sharpness necessary for first-class enlargements and autofocuses down to 1.6 feet. Many picture-taking modes are provided, including intelligent exposure, portrait, landscape (infinity), snap shooting (fixed-focus override), and double exposure. The several operating modes of the built-in flash, which automatically activate in low light, include forced fill-flash in daylight, slow speed synchronization for night shots, and red-eye reduction. Film loading, advance, and rewind are automatic. A data imprinting feature can put the time and date in your pictures or you can personalize your photos by adding your choice of seven different messages. An infrared remote control accessory can release the shutter and zoom the lens from up to 20 feet away. A double self-timer offers a brief two-second setting for taking pictures with a tripod-mounted camera, without having to use a remote shutter release to avoid jarring the camera. Camera power is supplied by a 3V lithium battery. The camera turns off automatically if inactive for three minutes, preventing unnecessary battery drain.

Warranty: 3 years
Manufacturer's Suggested Retail Price: $299
Approximate Low Price: $299

Fuji Discovery 270 Zoom

Budget Buy

The Fuji Discovery 270 Zoom offers every feature necessary to capture quality photographs, while remaining user-friendly and easy on your budget. Ten minutes with the instruction manual will have you up and running. The 35-70mm zoom lens covers the most beneficial range from wide-angle to moderate telephoto in a camera of this type. The built-in lens cover also serves as a shutter lock when closed, preventing accidentally wasting film. The most innovative feature on this camera is its method of film loading. After dropping in the film and closing the back of the camera, the camera winds the entire roll of film out of the film cassette. After you take a picture, each exposed frame is wound back into the cassette. What does this accomplish? First, it protects exposed film frames from being lost if someone accidentally opens the camera before the film is finished and rewound. Second, instead of showing how many pictures you've taken, the Discovery 270 starts at the number of exposures and counts down, telling you how many pictures you have left. A lot of buyers will find this approach more logical. Other features include built-in, auto-firing flash with red-eye reduction mode, electronic self-timer with ten-second delay, zoom optical viewfinder, and panorama mode. One lithium battery provides power for approximately 300 pictures.

Warranty: 1 year
Manufacturer's Suggested Retail Price: $210
Approximate Low Price: $130

35MM COMPACT CAMERAS

The 35mm compact is a relatively inexpensive camera with a fixed lens. Many 35mm compact cameras are point-and-shoot cameras with simple exposure systems designed for color negative film. Some compacts are more versatile and take high-quality photographs; these cameras demand more input from the photographer than point-and-shoot and auto-focus compacts, but they often produce superb results.

Konica Big Mini VX BM-701

✓BEST BUY

The Konica Big Mini VX is proof that you don't have to spend a fortune to get a camera capable of taking good quality pictures. The autofocusing (down to 3.5 feet) 29mm f/4 lens is all glass. A focus-lock feature allows you to keep off-center subjects in focus. Acceptable film speeds are ISO 100, 200, and 400. An LCD data panel on top of the camera displays exposure counter, flash modes, and battery check. The built-in flash automatically activates in low light, has a red-eye reduction mode, and can be forced in daylight to fill shadows of a subject framed against a bright background. Film advance and rewind are automatic. The Big Mini's power supply is one 3V lithium battery. This exceptional lightweight camera also includes a panorama mode.

Warranty: 1 year
Manufacturer's Suggested Retail Price: $155
Approximate Low Price: $100

Argus 3D Stereo

Recommended

As the model designation implies, the Argus 3D Stereo camera produces color prints that are three-dimensional when viewed in either of two Argus hand viewers. The camera uses a mirror system to take two pictures simultaneously, each separated by the average distance between a person's eyes and putting them side-by-side on a single frame of standard 35mm color print film. The film requires no special processing; each 4×6-inch print has the two stereo images on it. The camera is focus-free, from 2.5 feet to infinity. A built-in electronic flash pops up at the push of a button on the back of the camera and requires two AA batteries. The camera comes as a kit, with a case and either two mini viewers or one maxi viewer. Extra viewers are available separately. This camera is a fun show-and-tell item. The Argus 3D Stereo camera may be difficult to find locally; if so, you can call Argus at (847) 297-8900 for the nearest dealer.

Warranty: 1 year
Manufacturer's Suggested Retail Price: $80 (with one maxi-viewer)
Approximate Low Price: $80

Minolta AF-Big Finder

Budget Buy

Just because you don't have a lot to spend on a camera, or if you simply want a no-fuss, no-frills camera, you don't have to settle for an inferior no-name model. The Minolta AF-Big Finder offers a 34mm f/4.5, all-glass lens, with autofocusing down to 4.3 feet. The camera automatically sets the film speed for films of ISO 100, 200, and 400. The built-in flash automatically fires when needed and has a red-eye reduction feature. Film loading, advance, and rewind are automatic. A 12-second self-timer signals its engagement via a warning light on the front of the camera. The camera is powered by two AA batteries. A date-back model is also available, which requires an additional 3V lithium battery. The extra-large viewfinder will especially appeal to anyone with far-sighted vision problems. The AF-Big Finder is quite a bit of camera for very little money.

Warranty: 1 year
Manufacturer's Suggested Retail Price: $74
Approximate Low Price: $60

24MM ADVANCED PHOTO SYSTEM (APS) CAMERAS

The Advanced Photo System (APS), developed by a number of international camera and film manufacturers, has been in existence for about three years now. It is designed around a smaller size film and cassette, which at first glance resembles a 35mm film cassette. However, the APS film employs an impressive array of new technologies, all with the ultimate purpose of giving you better pictures and more ways of putting them to use in your daily life.

FEATURES

Film loading couldn't be simpler; just drop the cassette into the camera and close the film chamber. The camera automatically winds the film to the first frame, eliminating the bothersome threading of 35mm film leader. The film features a clear magnetic coating, similar to audio recording tape but optically transparent, which records exposure and format selection data from the camera. This information is in turn read by the processing machinery at the film lab, resulting in more precise adjustments of color and density during the printing stage.

Depending on the camera model, a variety of information, such as date, time, exposure data, or special titles and messages, can be imprinted on the back of your prints. You can choose from three different formats, including panoramic. The format choice is indicated on the film, so if you change your mind later, you can have any picture printed in any format at a later date. Your film is returned with an index print, containing small thumbnail images of every picture on the roll, making filing and negative selection a breeze.

Some cameras also allow you to switch film types in midroll, such as from color to black-and-white. Upon reloading the partially exposed cassette, the camera remembers where you left off and automatically advances the film to that frame. Some companies even offer APS scanners that let you view your pictures on a TV or import them into your computer to incorporate them into various kinds of documents. These options offer more user control over the end product than any other film-based camera system. APS prints cost a little more to process than 35mm, but your options are limited only by your imagination.

Pentax efina

✓BEST BUY

The Pentax efina is an effective blend of the best of what the APS format has to offer. It is compact, lightweight, stylish, and capable. The 24-48mm f/4.5-8.0 zoom lens, which is protected by a sliding cover and focuses down to 2.1 feet, spans a useful wide-to-normal focal length range. The way a camera fits your hands has a lot to do with how easy it is to take pictures with. If the controls aren't logically located, the camera will be difficult to use, with your fingers always ending up somewhere that they shouldn't (in front of the lens), making it necessary to remove the camera from your eye constantly and hunt for the controls. The efina fits all but the largest hands comfortably, with your index finger falling naturally on the shutter release button and your thumb resting on the power zoom control of the lens. A short leftward movement of your thumb accesses the picture format selector lever, making it simple to see what a picture would look like in the various format shapes before you take the picture. Film loading, advance, and rewind are automatic. A date and title imprinting feature prints your choice of date or 31 prerecorded titles; the titles can be rendered in 12 different languages. The versatile exposure and flash system meets any challenge. The flash automatically comes on in low light, and red-eye reduction and slow-shutter modes can be used for flash-lit foreground subjects (perfect for evening shots combined with a colorfully lighted background). The efina includes a ten-second self-timer and two accessory remote controls.

Warranty: 1 year
Manufacturer's Suggested Retail Price: $350
Approximate Low Price: $230

Canon EOS IX

Recommended

If you are intrigued with the many interesting features of the APS system, but want the versatility and lens selection of a 35mm SLR, then Canon's EOS IX is for you. There are only a few interchangeable-lens SLRs in the APS format, and most of them have special lenses made specifically for those cameras. The EOS IX uses the same lens mount as Canon's entire line of EOS 35mm SLRs. The camera's high-tech profile and satin stainless-steel-clad body make it an eye-catching stand-out among cameras. It fits your hands well and its controls are logically and conveniently located. The wide three-point autofocus is quick and precise, and accommodates off-center subjects. An autofocus mode tracks subjects moving toward or away from the camera, ensuring sharp focus. Exposure measurement is via a sophisticated six-zone evaluative system that handles a wide range of lighting conditions. Another system integrates the six-zone metering with the TTL flash metering and autofocus, delivering balanced exposures that elude lesser cameras. A command dial sets your choice of five Creative Zone modes, which favor particular aperture and shutter speed combinations according to the type of subject. Simple preprogrammed modes help beginners shoot with confidence. Full manual exposure control and focus are also included. The pop-up flash can be augmented with a more powerful shoe-mount unit when desired. Daylight fill-flash is even possible. From simple drop-in film loading and midroll film change capability to the range of professional lenses and accessories, the Canon EOS IX places no restrictions on photography.

Warranty: 1 year
Manufacturer's Suggested Retail Price: $750 (body only)
Approximate Low Price: $550

Kodak Advantix 5800 MRX Zoom

Recommended

The 5800 MRX is Kodak's top-of-the-line APS model. Its distinctive styling sets it apart from cameras with features and capabilities that let it perform as impressively as it looks. A wide-range f/5.6-15.3 zoom lens covers 26-130mm, giving the photographer a choice of compositions from wide-angle to telephoto. It auto-focuses down to 2.5 feet. As with several of the more advanced APS cameras, the 5800 MRX allows you to switch films in midroll. It rewinds the exposed film back into the cassette, then advances the film to where you left off when you reload the roll into the camera. This feature allows you to switch from color to black-and-white film, switch from slow speed to high speed film for nighttime use, or dedicate a roll of film to one subject. The camera's LCD data panel displays "battery low," and helpful advice such as "move back" (when you're closer than the lens can focus). A red light near the viewfinder window alerts you when the LCD panel is displaying a warning. The camera not only has a preprogrammed library of messages (Thanksgiving, Christmas, Birthday) and captions for imprinting on the back of your pictures, it lets you create your own titles via a fast-access scroll system. The messages can be imprinted on random frames or on the entire roll of film. Messages can be displayed in English, French, German, Spanish, or Japanese. The built-in, pop-up flash has a red-eye reduction feature. The 5800 MRX is packaged complete with case, camera strap, remote control unit, batteries, and three rolls of film.

Warranty: 1 year
Manufacturer's Suggested Retail Price: $549
Approximate Low Price: $470

Canon ELPH Jr.

Budget Buy

The Canon ELPH Jr. is a commendable combination of features, price, small size, and light weight. This is a camera that slips easily into pocket or purse as a constant picture-taking companion. The lens is a 26mm f/2.8, which focuses as close as 1.5 feet. It retracts into the camera behind a protective cover when power is switched off. You can choose the standard three different picture formats via a lever just to the right of the viewfinder window. Information seen in the viewfinder includes a close-up frame and a green "OK-to-shoot" signal. There is also an LCD data panel atop the camera. Film loading, advance, and rewind are automatic. Film speeds accepted are ISO 25-10,000. The built-in flash has red-eye reduction and slow synchronization for combining a flash-illuminated foreground subject at night with colorful background lighting. A time/date imprint feature prints this information on the back or front of your photos. There's a ten-second self-timer, which can be activated with the shutter button or via an optional infrared remote control unit from up to 16 feet away. The Canon ELPH Jr. is proof that sophisticated technology comes in small, reasonably priced packages.

Warranty: 1 year
Manufacturer's Suggested Retail Price: $270
Approximate Low Price: $170

INSTANT-PRINT CAMERAS

Instant-print cameras are only available from Polaroid in the United States. Consumer models produce color prints that self-develop within a few minutes. Although the cost per print is higher than with 35mm and APS, these cameras offer the advantage of providing immediate gratification for those who can't wait to see the pictures they've taken.

Polaroid Spectra AF

✓BEST BUY

The Polaroid Spectra AF is the best choice for those who enjoy the instant gratification of having a fully-developed color print in hand almost immediately after taking the picture. It uses Polaroid Spectra film only, which yields pictures that measure $3\frac{5}{8} \times 2\frac{7}{8}$ inches. The lens, which focuses as close as two feet, autofocuses via Polaroid's sonar rangefinder system. The autofocus can be switched off when shooting through glass windows. Exposure is automatic, with the flash automatically activating when the camera determines a need for it. There is an electronic viewfinder display, as well as a data panel on the rear of the camera. Focus confirmation and self-timer countdown are indicated with an audible signal, which also alerts you when the camera is out of film. The flash is effective up to 15 feet and an indicator in the viewfinder will signal if you're too far away for proper flash exposure.

Warranty: 5 years
Manufacturer's Suggested Retail Price: $99
Approximate Low Price: $95

Polaroid OneStep Autofocus Restyle

Budget Buy

Polaroid's popular OneStep Autofocus has been updated and given a facelift, thereby earning the "restyle" designation. The rounded, ergonomic design is more comfortable to hold, and the camera exterior is now finished in an attractive midnight blue. It is a great camera for those looking for an economical, yet capable instant-print camera. It is designed to use Polaroid 600-series film, for pictures in both color and black-and-white. This film has a special drawable matte surface that accepts pen, pencil, and markers, for those with artistic urges. A close-up lens comes into play automatically when needed. The flash normally fires all the time, providing 100 percent of the illumination indoors and fill-flash outdoors to lighten shadows for portraits. The autofocus/autoexposure technology features special "ready-response" circuitry. As the shutter release button is pressed, the flash emits a brief "rangefinding beam." This beam enables the camera's photometer to analyze the scene before firing the flash burst to actually take the picture. The OneStep Autofocus Restyle is quite a lot of Polaroid for little money.

Warranty: 1 year
Manufacturer's Suggested Retail Price: $50
Approximate Low Price: $40

DIGITAL-STILL CAMERAS

A few years ago, you had only two choices in digital still cameras: good quality and extremely expensive or reasonably priced but poor picture quality. Today, consumer digital cameras offer a favorable combination of quality, versatility, and affordability. It is simple to import your pictures into your computer for use with computer graphics. You can take a picture, and within minutes, can be sending it to friends, relatives, or business associates. You can also view your pictures on a TV, or print them out as regular photos with either a special printer or via your color inkjet printer.

QUALITY

Instead of film, images are captured by a charged-coupled device (CCD), then stored on one of various removable magnetic storage media, usually referred to as a "card." Unlike film, the exact number of pictures obtainable per card can vary considerably, depending on the resolution and degree of compression chosen. The higher quality (resolution) desired, the fewer pictures per card.

While digital cameras share many similarities with film cameras, there are some terms specific to digital. Before making a purchase, decide if you will use a digital camera in conjunction with your computer and be sure of the camera's compatibility with your computer's operating system. Adapters are also available.

FEATURES AND TERMINOLOGY

CCD: A charge-coupled device, often referred to as a "chip," is the light-sensitive device that captures the image when you press the shutter release.

Storage Media: A magnetic equivalent of film, this is usually referred to as a "card" that stores the pictures as they are taken.

Spare cards can be carried, like spare rolls of film. Unwanted pictures can be erased, freeing up space for new pictures. Some examples of these cards include PCMCIA (types I and II), CompactFlash, and SmartMedia.

Compression: A means of storing a greater number of images on a given card size or disk. Compression is a trade-off of quality for storage space. Uncompressed images are the highest quality, but severely limit the number of pictures per card. Many cameras let you choose the degree of compression applied.

Equivalent Focal Length: Since a CCD is much smaller than a frame of 35mm film, and therefore requires lenses of much shorter focal length to produce the same coverage (magnification) as a lens on a 35mm camera, manufacturers usually specify what the equivalent lens would be on a 35mm.

Sony Digital Mavica MVC-FD71

✓BEST BUY

The Sony Digital Mavica MVC-FD71 qualifies as a Best Buy based on user-friendliness, as well as the ease with which its images can be incorporated into many applications. The camera uses 3.5-inch floppy disks as its image storage media, the same used in your personal computer. This allows you to take your pictures, then remove the floppy from the camera and insert it directly into your computer, without the need for any auxiliary cables or equipment. Once in the computer, you can view the pictures on your monitor; incorporate them into letters, presentations, and other documents; or email the images to friends or relatives. The universal JPEG compression format is used, making the camera compatible with Windows systems. A copy feature lets you save images in the camera's temporary memory. A Progressive Scan CCD enhances picture clarity. A bit-map mode allows saving images in a noncompressed format, for even sharper images; the cost is less pictures per disk. You can view and play back images on the 2.5-inch color LCD screen. You can also apply special effects such as monotone, sepia, negative art, and pastel. Resolution is 640×480 pixels in 24-bit color. Forty images can be stored on a floppy in standard compression format and 20 images can be stored in fine format. You can automatically or manually focus and expose. Flash is built-in. Power is supplied by a rechargeable lithium-ion battery, good for up to 1,000 shots in fine mode (that's 50 floppies).

Warranty: 90 days, labor; 1 year, parts
Manufacturer's Suggested Retail Price: $799
Approximate Low Price: $700

Kodak DC200

Budget Buy

A great combination of styling, performance, and affordability, the Kodak DC200 appeals to a wide audience. It is compatible with Windows systems, and a Macintosh connection kit is available as an accessory. The focus-free lens is equivalent to a 39mm lens on a 35mm camera and focuses as close as 27 inches. Image resolution is 640×480 in standard mode and 1,152×864 in high resolution mode. This camera includes three image quality settings: good, better, and best. You can store images on compact flash cards. The number of images per card varies up to 60, depending on the chosen resolution and quality setting and the size (capacity) of the card. A 1.8-inch color LCD on the back of the camera permits review and edit functions. You can even erase unsatisfactory pictures. It also displays indicators for battery level, resolution setting, number of pictures remaining, flash mode, and self-timer. The built-in flash fires automatically when needed and is effective to about 9.8 feet. The DC200 is powered by four AA batteries or an optional AC adapter. The user can select either JPEG or FLASHPIX finished file formats, and a video-out capability lets you view your pictures on a TV. The camera includes Kodak Picture Easy 2.0 software, which provides a quick route from camera to computer and allows even novice computer users to make basic corrections, email, and print their pictures.

Warranty: 1 year
Manufacturer's Suggested Retail Price: $499
Approximate Low Price: $480

TELEPHONES AND ANSWERING MACHINES

Telephones are getting smarter, smaller, more streamlined, and more stylish. Even tabletop, corded phones have a futuristic cell-phone look. Basic corded phones offer some of the same capabilities that high-priced, multi-featured models had just a few years ago. The good news is you can ignore more features you don't need and choose a phone for the features that make your life easier.

CORDLESS TELEPHONES

Cordless phones have also evolved. They are now much clearer, more secure, and operate at longer distances than before. Since the Federal Communications Commission authorized the use of 25 different channels in the frequency range used by cordless telephones, the quality of reception on these units has dramatically increased. When shopping for one of these convenient phones, check how long the battery remains charged. If it needs to be recharged frequently, the convenience is greatly diminished.

Another important feature is the pager. When you page (send a tone) from the base of the handset, you can find a misplaced handset quickly. Also, these phones come with an intercom feature, which allows you to talk from the phone to the base.

CELLULAR TELEPHONES

As cellular phones become more popular and an integral part of our lives, we're having to learn new cellular technologies, as they are introduced with dizzying speed. Cell phones used to be classified by size, but adapters and other accessories now make the difference between a lightweight slim phone and a car phone plugged into the cigarette lighter.

The first cellular phones were analog, with different rate plans that probably included a free or low-cost phone. Then carriers began offering the more advanced digital service. The latest technology—digital PCS cellular—sounds less like a radio. Instead, the sound may have a slightly mechanical quality. The digital signal can carry much more information than the analog signal can, so the carrier can offer extras such as caller ID, pagerlike messaging, and call forwarding. PCS phones cost a bit more, and they are usually not offered free with a service commitment, but their built-in security means eavesdroppers are much less likely to monitor your calls. So far, analog networks still cover more ground than PCS networks, but the gap is closing.

ANSWERING MACHINES

Answering machines come with many features developed for your convenience. With the addition of digital technology, answering machines can become a high-tech communications center right in your home. Phone company options such as caller ID and call waiting have also had an impact on telephones and answering machines; getting units that help these services can be an important part of the buyer's decision.

FEATURES AND TERMINOLOGY

Caller ID/Call Waiting: A supplement to caller ID service, which lets users see who is calling without having to interrupt the current call.

Caller ID Memory/Log: This feature remembers the last calls made to your phone. Some phones can also move stored numbers into permanent speed-dial memory.

Flash: This sends a brief signal that duplicates a quick press of the telephone's switch hook—without the chance of accidental disconnection. Flash is useful if you subscribe to optional phone-company services such as call waiting and conference calling.

Hearing-aid Compatible: These phones are designed to provide normal conversation for people who wear hearing aids. Most phones are hearing-aid compatible.

Hold: Retains the call, but both parties are on mute.

Last-number Redial: A common feature. A press of this key dials the last number called on the specific phone you're using.

Mute: The mute key stops transmission of sound. The other party cannot hear noises at your end of the conversation while the mute key is pressed.

900-MHz: 900-MHz technology, commonly used with cordless phones, is more secure, provides clearer communication, and has better range than traditional 47-MHz. The 900-MHz phones come in three varieties: analog (good range but poor security); digital (better clarity, range, and security, but can be blocked by obstructions); and Digital Spread Spectrum, or DSS, (best clarity, range, and security).

Speakerphone: A microphone and a speaker are built into the phone, so you can have a conversation without picking up the handset.

Speed-dialing memory: Most phones have some type of speed-dialing memory; higher-end phones have keys set aside just for speed dialing. These memory keys usually have enough space for 16 or 24 digits each, and are designed to hold phone numbers frequently dialed. Some phones also allow programming pauses—you would use this if you must dial 9 to access an outside line.

Three-way Conference: Found on several two-line phones, this allows the user to connect a second user through the speakerphone using the second line, thus enabling a three-way conversation with the caller on the other end of the line.

BEST BUYS '99

Our Best Buy, Recommended, and Budget Buy telephones and answering machines follow. Within each category, the unit we consider the best of the Best Buys is listed first, followed by our second choice, and so on. Remember that a Best Buy, Recommended, or Budget Buy designation only applies to the model listed—it does not necessarily apply to other models made by the same manufacturer or to an entire product line.

FEATURE TELEPHONES

BellSouth 8830

✓BEST BUY

BellSouth offers a handy bedside phone. This combination of options is perfect for the nightstand: a phone with a clock, an alarm, caller ID, and a night-light. Digital-clock numerals are almost a half-inch tall and the alarm is a buzzer. To shut it off, you must press one of the four buttons on the phone's base. The illuminated caller ID is about ¼-inch tall. The calling phone number and time and date of the call are half the size of the name; these all appear at the same time as you scroll through up to 32 calls. The 8830 stores ten numbers in a speed-dial memory (and it has flash and redial keys). BellSouth also offers the BP-200PL, which has three alarms and a snooze feature. The BP-200PL stores 13 speed-dial numbers, but it does not include caller ID.

Warranty: 1 year (limited)
Manufacturer's Suggested Retail Price: $50
Approximate Low Price: $40

BellSouth 8862X

Recommended

With a generous amount of memory (the unit stores 75 names and numbers or 99 numbers only), the 8862X is a serious caller ID speakerphone. Many units that allow you to return a caller ID call assume that you want to call the last seven digits, unless it is not your area code. This assumption can cause problems in places with multiple area codes. The 8862X provides no less than three keys to streamline your callback. Press one key for the last seven digits, another for one plus the last ten digits, and the third for ten digits only. You can quickly store caller ID information in one of the three Auto Memory keys or one of the 15 speed dial memory locations. (You can also manually store numbers of up to 32 digits each in these locations.) The phone has mute, flash, and redial keys.

Warranty: 1 year (limited)
Manufacturer's Suggested Retail Price: $70
Approximate Low Price: $60

Lucent Technology 135

Budget Buy

In a world where a telephone keypad often doubles as a way to enter your account number or punch in your selection from a series of menus, the Design Line Memory Telephone 135 provides a regular phone keypad that doubles as a dozen stylish, sculpted data-entry keys. What's more, the buttons have a snappy, positive feel like miniatures of those on a good computer keyboard, quite unlike the mushy keys on some other phones. The Design Line 135 offers few extras: nine-number memory of up to 24 digits each for speed dialing, flash and redial keys, and a set of two volume buttons next to the keypad to change the receiver's volume during a call.

Warranty: 1 year (limited)
Manufacturer's Suggested Retail Price: $25
Approximate Low Price: $20

General Electric 2-926

Budget Buy

General Electric's 2-926 is a basic phone with a few additional features and a caller ID display. The legible screen to the right of the handset makes information on the call's origin hard to miss. At little more than the cost of a stand-alone caller ID box, this telephone can't help but make the most of your caller ID investment. It provides the caller's name, time and date of call, and call sequence number in approximately ¼-inch letters and numbers. The caller's phone number, if provided by the telephone company, appears at the touch of a key. An indicator light flashes when unreviewed caller ID information is available. The usual display shows how many new and total caller ID entries the phone has stored. It holds 95 names and numbers. Extras not related to caller ID include 12 speed-dial memory locations for phone numbers of up to 16 digits each. This phone also has flash and redial keys.

Warranty: 1 year (limited)
Manufacturer's Suggested Retail Price: $40
Approximate Low Price: $40

CORDLESS PHONES

25-CHANNEL MODELS

Casio PhoneMate CP-760

✓BEST BUY

With two telephone lines becoming the norm in many households, a telephone such as the Casio PhoneMate 760 becomes less of a luxury and more of a necessity. Although slightly more expensive than many 25-channel cordless phones, the CP-760 justifies its price tag with a bright informational display built into the handset that shows who is calling on either of two lines (caller ID service from local phone company is required). The CP-760 holds the last 75 incoming calls in memory; to return a call, just access this phone book and press a button. You can save as many as 20 of the temporary numbers into the telephone's permanent auto-dial memory. The CP-760 also features a speakerphone and "on hold" controls (which takes the caller off hold if you pick up on an extension).

Warranty: 1 year
Manufacturer's Suggested Retail Price: $110
Approximate Low Price: $110

Panasonic KX-TCC106-B

Recommended

Now that caller ID support is carried nationwide, telephones that make use of this feature are gaining in popularity. This no-frills 25-channel cordless telephone is equipped with an easy-to-read backlit LCD in the handset that clearly displays the number and name of the person calling. In addition, telephone customers who subscribe to caller ID with Visual Call Waiting (where available) can see the name and number of an incoming call even when the phone is in use. Speed dial and an illuminated keypad make the phone easy to use, and a 21-day battery standby time means you can keep the phone nearby, wherever you are in the house.

Warranty: 1 year
Manufacturer's Suggested Retail Price: $90
Approximate Low Price: $90

900-MHz MODELS

Casio PhoneMate CP-820

✓BEST BUY

The Casio CP-820 is an excellent DSS 900-MHz cordless phone. This phone's most innovative feature is Casio's "Modem Monitor" technology, which combats line corruption. For example, if the student around your house is researching the Internet or your spouse is retrieving email, their connection is protected if someone else in the house unknowingly picks up the phone. The CP-820 scans the line, distinguishes between a voice call and a data transmission, and secures the modem connection until the user can hang up the phone. A flashing light warns phone users that the line is in use. Other features include a 20-number memory, a flash button for call-waiting subscribers, and a range of almost 4,000 feet from the base.

Warranty: 1 year
Manufacturer's Suggested Retail Price: $100
Approximate Low Price: $100

Philips CL8740

Recommended

There's no point in having a cordless phone if you have to retreat to the base to get access to advanced features such as caller ID. That's not a problem with the CL8740, however, which builds its informative display into the handset. The phone's caller

ID features, when enabled through a local phone company, can store 99 names and numbers. Although it does not use digital spread spectrum technology, the 900-MHz CL8740 provides good security and enough power to penetrate interior house walls, so you can carry it from room to room without losing your connection.

Warranty: 1 year
Manufacturer's Suggested Retail Price: $199
Approximate Low Price: $150

CELLULAR PHONES

We do not list prices for cellular phones because most phones are included with the cost of installation. Installation costs and service commitments vary.

Motorola StarTAC 3000

✔BEST BUY

Lightweight, versatile, feature-rich, and smartly engineered, the StarTAC 3000 is a popular pick with analog service providers. Without any optional equipment, the lightweight 3000 is comfortable to carry in a suit-jacket pocket or a purse. An illuminated keypad makes it easy to answer or to dial in dim light. A 20-number auto-dial phone book keeps important numbers at hand and dials with a single button. The 3000 supports many optional service features available from digital phone networks including programmable call timers for tracking usage and budgeting package minutes, selectable rings and tone to distinguish calls, voice mail alert, caller ID, and data/fax support. The 3000 provides 60 minutes of talk time and up to 14 hours of standby time.

Warranty: 1 year

Nokia 252

✔BEST BUY

Because many consumers outside of major cities are still waiting for the digital networks that work with PCS digital cellular phones, this easy-to-carry, easy-to-use analog cellular phone from Nokia sets the pace. You'll get more than you might expect from this model. Caller ID support, voice mail alert, and one-button speed dialing are just a few of the features that make the 252 a Best Buy. With almost two hours of talk time from a single charge (30 hours of standby time) and a contoured design that fits comfortably in the hand, the 252 will go anywhere. Nokia offers the 252 in a variety of colors. If you're on the go, then go with a little style and take the 252 along for the ride.

Warranty: 1 year

Ericsson KF 688

Recommended

Until mobile digital networks are as common as analog cellular networks, people who depend on mobile communications will need a phone that effortlessly slips between both kinds of signals. The KF 688 supports digital and analog networks. Although the KF 688 is heavier than some other cellular phones, it provides a number of essential features. One of the most convenient is the flip-open answer and disconnect—just open the phone to take a call or close it to hang up. The phone can act as a pager, and it will even dial numbers embedded in incoming messages. A 200-entry alpha-numeric phone book, redial for the last 40 numbers, and a 40-number caller ID memory make for excellent storage. Depending on the battery and network used, the KF 688 has between 45 minutes and 2½ hours of talk time and from 15 to 57 hours of standby time.

Warranty: 1 year

Ericsson AF 778

Recommended

This version of Ericcson's popular 738 model adds several features to keep up with the demands of mobile phone customers. Most notable is caller ID support, which will display the name and number of the caller on the small, easy-to-read backlit LCD screen. The 778 also remembers the last ten numbers processed through caller ID, and allows one-button redial so one can easily stay in contact. In addition, the 778 holds up to 99 numbers (up to 32 digits each) and can log two separate credit card numbers. Voice mail capabilities include a handy Message Waiting indicator. The lightweight AF 778 is also easy to carry. And with 90 minutes of talk time and 24 hours of standby time, it's just right for a day away from home.

Warranty: 1 year

ANSWERING MACHINES

Answering machines have become as indispensable as videocassette recorders around the house. Picking a good answering machine for your needs isn't hard; you just need to pay attention to the features each offers. Obviously, the machine must have something to record on, either a cassette tape or memory chips. A cassette model is portable and usually less expensive. A digital model is simple to operate and usually allows you to delete messages selectively, instead of having to keep all messages or erase them.

FEATURES AND TERMINOLOGY

Call Intercept: The answering machine stops working when you pick up the phone. This can work from the phone connected to the answering machine or it can work from an extension phone.

Individual Voice Mailboxes: Callers can press a number to store their message in a mailbox separate from other voice mailboxes.

Remote Features: These provide a way to listen to messages, fast-forward, erase messages, and otherwise control the machine from any touch-tone telephone.

Time/Date Stamp: The machine records the time and the day of the message.

Toll Saver: The machine answers on the second ring if there are new messages, or the fourth or fifth ring if there are no new messages. This feature allows you to check if you have new messages from a pay phone before paying the toll.

Sony SPP-A945

✓BEST BUY

Don't worry about trying to find your way through the array of features on this answering system. The A945 literally talks you through each step, with voice-guided instructions. The tapeless message center supplies three password-protected mailboxes. You always know if new messages are waiting, thanks to the bright, easy-to-read digital counter and the audible beeps. The 20-number speed-dialing memory keeps your most important contacts right at your fingertips, and the phone's battery protects messages in case of power failure. In addition to the 900-MHz portable telephone that is supplied with its own keypad, the message center also has a dialing keypad as well as a speakerphone. The speakerphone allows the handset and the answering system base unit to act as a two-station intercom—perfect for locating your phone.

Warranty: 1 year, parts and labor
Manufacturer's Suggested Retail Price: $190
Approximate Low Price: $170

Philips CL8750

Recommended

The CL8750 is a combination cordless phone and digital answering system. It provides four distinct mailboxes, which can either separate work calls from personal calls or be used for individual members of the family. The tapeless digital message system is good for 22 minutes of recording time—ample time for saving important calls. Battery backup retains messages in memory in case of a power outage. A digital readout shows how many messages are waiting, which is much more informative than a simple blinking light. Add to the mix a speakerphone and a 900-MHz cordless phone, and you have more than just an answering machine: You have a versatile and well-balanced communications center that's compact and easy to use.

Warranty: 1 year
Manufacturer's Suggested Retail Price: $150
Approximate Low Price: $150

Casio Phonemate TC-540

Recommended

Busy families will appreciate the multiuser features of this tapeless answering system. Three different voice mailboxes allow you to record and receive separate and distinct messages. Messages (14 minutes of recording time) can even be forwarded from one mailbox to another. When you're pressed for time, you can speed through messages or slow down the playback for hard-to-understand callers. If your phone company offers distinctive rings, each mailbox can be set to a different number (an excellent way to handle home office messages). Also included is a 25-channel cordless phone, which provides portability while talking, and a speakerphone.

Warranty: 1 year, parts and labor
Manufacturer's Suggested Retail Price: $70
Approximate Low Price: $70

Casio PhoneMate TA-111

Budget Buy

An answering machine can go a long way with just the basics. In the case of the TA-111, extras like tapeless recording and remote operations won't strain the family budget. The TA-111 provides ten minutes of recording time on a digital chip. Each message is indexed with time and date. A indicator light flashes when new messages are awaiting retrieval. For added convenience, users can dial in from remote locations, punch in an access code, then pick up messages or record different greetings and announcements. The TA-111 is smart enough to stop recording when you pick up an extension somewhere else in the house. This economical recording machine has all you need for managing your home communications.

Warranty: 1 year
Manufacturer's Suggested Retail Price: $25
Approximate Low Price: $25

COMPUTERS

As much as computers seem to change every year, one fact remains constant: Prices drop as technology rises. For the past few years, an entry-level PC has run about $1,200. A good, midrange system brings the price up to about $1,700. A top-of-the-line system with all the bells and whistles is just over $2,700. And even when prices stabilize, as they do from time to time, the technology inside the box gets better. That means today's $1,500 PC often outperforms last year's $3,000 unit. We have to pay a price to keep up with the amazing progress we continue to see in the PC market, but it's a price that pays off in the long run. Technologies that looked like science fiction a decade ago beckon to us from catalogs and store windows.

PCs continue to grow more powerful and more loaded with standard features. So don't worry about what's looming over the horizon, because today's PCs already offer power and versatility.

BUYING TIPS

All this progress can make a PC purchase an intimidating prospect, especially if it's your first computer. But with the design of today's PCs, obsolescence isn't nearly as great a concern as it used to be. Video cards, CD-ROM drives, and other components can be upgraded with better equipment as it comes on the market. Pentium processors can be replaced with faster chips from Intel and its competitors. Hot new technologies, such as DVD drives, are only a credit card and a screwdriver away.

Whether you're looking for a family computer, a business system, a portable companion, or a game machine that blows Nintendo 64 off the map, it's a great time to be buying a new PC. Even entry-level PCs now ship with fast Pentium processors, plenty of RAM, CD-ROM drives, and sound cards. Midrange machines with large monitors and 3D graphics that would have required a $20,000 workstation a few years ago are still under the magic $2,000 mark. And with the addition of a simple modem, millions of pieces of information on the Internet are only a mouse-click away—all for an insignificant monthly fee.

NOTEBOOK PCS

Notebook PCs are undergoing a similar revolution. CD-ROM drives and sound chips, options found only on the most expensive notebooks a year or two ago, are standard on all but the least expensive units today. Not only are powerful notebooks easier on the wallet, they're easier on your back as well. The latest trend is modular notebooks that put the CD-ROM drive and extra battery in a "slice" that clips on to the bottom of the unit. When you need access to your word processor, spreadsheet, and email, detach the slice and just bring along a four-pound lightweight. When you need full multimedia capabilities, take the whole thing on the road.

FEATURES AND TERMINOLOGY

Although computers have become much easier to use over the years, a basic understanding of computer terms is useful.

Bytes: RAM and ROM are measured in bytes, which are made up of bits. A bit (binary digit) is the smallest unit of data. Its value is either one or zero. A byte is a group of bits, usually eight, that stands for one character (it could be a letter, number, or symbol) and is treated as a unit of data. A kilobyte (KB) is roughly 1,000 bytes, while a megabyte (MB) is about a million bytes. A gigabyte (GB) equals 1,000MB. With more RAM, a computer can run powerful programs faster. You can increase the amount of RAM by adding chips or expansion cards.

Central Processing Unit (CPU): Often referred to as a microprocessor, this is a computer's "brain." Like car engines, CPUs run at different speeds, usually measured in megahertz (MHz). The CPU and the computer's software-based operating system regulate the flow of data between the computer's internal components, as well as between the computer and its printer, monitor, or other peripherals.

Disk Drive: A disk drive transfers data and programs back and forth between a disk and RAM. There are different sizes of floppy drives and hard-disk drives. The disk drives differ in diameter (usually 5.25 or 3.5 inches) and height (there are full-height, ½-height, and even ⅓-height drives). Disk drives also differ in the average speed at which they randomly access data from the disk. This access time is measured in milliseconds (ms). A good hard drive should have an access speed of between 10ms and 15ms.

Motherboard: The CPU, RAM, ROM, connecting circuits, and other parts are found on the main circuit board, called the mother board. This board often has slots for expansion cards, which are circuit boards that increase a computer's functions, speed, or memory.

Mouse/Trackball: The CPU usually receives data from an input device such as a disk drive or keyboard; sometimes data will come from a mouse or trackball. A mouse is a small device that you move around on a desktop or a pad to move the cursor or on-screen pointer. The buttons on a mouse allow you to access on-screen functions. Trackballs also have buttons, but instead of moving the mouse on a level surface, you merely spin the trackball in its socket to position the cursor.

Operating Systems: Today's IBM-compatible personal computers available in stores use the Windows 98 operating system. Some clearance or older models may sport Windows 95, which differs little from the 1998 version. Other operating systems include System 8.1 for Macintosh computers and OS/2, an operating system designed and sold by IBM which, like Windows and System 8.1, uses icons and folders and other graphical elements to represent computer commands.

Peripherals: Besides the basic components of a CPU, RAM, and a disk drive, a personal computer uses other devices to display or relay information. The most essential of these external devices are a monitor, a printer, and a modem. Always figure in the cost of these components when shopping. Almost all computers come as a package, with these three devices and others included in the final price, but savvy buyers can mix and match these components to lower the price or to gain more power for their dollar.

RAM/ROM: The CPU manipulates data and software programs in random-access memory (RAM). When the computer is turned off, RAM loses its contents. Another type of memory, read-only memory

(ROM) retains its contents even when the power is off (a small lithium battery in the computer keeps ROM alive). ROM stores essential information about the PC that must be kept intact, such as the clock and the list of components inside the computer (the size of the hard disk, for example, or the amount of memory). ROM can be found in all kinds of devices, from computers to modems to microwave ovens. RAM, on the other hand, is confined to those devices that have to make quick and complicated calculations: your computer, your printer, the video card that sends signals to the computer monitor, and so on. Printers, for example, use internal RAM buffers to store data received from the computer. These buffers allow you to use the computer even when it's sending documents to the printer.

Storage: Programs and data can be saved to magnetic disks. As a rule, today's computers ship with a standard-size 3.5-inch floppy disk drive, which accommodates 1.44MB diskettes (referring to the amount of data a diskette can store) that can be inserted and ejected as needed, and which are housed in a plastic casing. Hard disks, by comparison, are normally fixed in place and provide a much bigger storage area—literally thousands of times bigger than floppy diskettes. Hard disks work at high speeds, so they can load software into RAM more quickly and make programs run much faster than floppies can. This makes them suitable for storing your programs and working files, while diskettes are used for storing copies of your information or for files you don't need very often.

When shopping for diskettes, avoid the inexpensive, no-name variety. Considering the value of information that could be lost if a disk fails, buying poorly made disks save you nothing and could end up costing you in the long run.

THE RATINGS

At the end of each review, you'll find a rating based on a scale of 1 (worst) to 10 (best).

Documentation: This rating judges whether or not the manuals and on-line help are effective and well organized.

Expandability: This rating (for computer systems) is determined by the availability of and capacity for add-ons or peripherals. Portable computers are given an expandability rating because most of them have provisions for adding more memory, a fax/modem, or other peripherals.

Ease of Use: This rating (for peripherals) is based on the efficiency of setup and operation of the product.

Overall Value: This rating compares the product's price to its performance, ease of use, and features. Accordingly, an overpriced item will not have a high overall rating, even if it is an excellent product.

Performance: This rating tells how well the product performs its various functions. Keep in mind that the performance ratings of different items can't always be fairly compared unless the products are similar.

BEST BUYS '99

Our Best Buy, Recommended, and Budget Buy computer systems and peripherals are listed below. Products within each category are listed according to quality. The best of the Best Buys is listed first, followed by our second choice, and so on. A Best Buy, Recommended, or Budget Buy designation only applies to the model listed—it does not necessarily apply to other models made by the same manufacturer or to an entire product line.

We have tried to provide accurate prices in this chapter. However, the release of new products, the withdrawal of older products, and strong competition in certain markets cause prices to change constantly. To complicate matters further, the availability of dynamic RAM (DRAM) chips (the kind supplied with computers and peripherals) often varies, which can cause price fluctuations. This means that the retail and low prices in this chapter might differ from what you find at your local store. Be sure to contact several dealers and compare their prices.

HOME & SMALL OFFICE COMPUTERS

Dell Dimension XPS D333

✓BEST BUY

A well-designed, high-quality PC, the Dimension XPS D333 incorporates a fast 333MHz Pentium II CPU with 512K Level 2 cache and 64MB of fast RAM (the upper limit is 384MB). Dell didn't skimp on the hard drive, either—it's a hefty 8.4GB unit, one of the larger ones provided with this class of system. The XPS D333 is outfitted with a DVD drive instead of CD-ROM. This means the system can be used for a variety of multimedia tasks, including business presentations, game playing, and even serving as a home entertainment center. Of course, the XPS D333 can perform the mundane tasks, too, such as word processing and personal finances. Graphics on the XPS D333 are powered by an STB Velocity 128 video card in an AGP slot. One of Dell's 1200HS 19-inch monitors makes a great companion to the system, as does the optional Turtle Beach Montego A3D 64 Voice PCI sound card. Dell also supplies Altec Lansing ACS-495 speakers, a three-piece set of two bookshelf speakers and a subwoofer that produces excellent bass response. Although you don't get a large software collection with this system, you'll get plenty of productivity power from the Microsoft Office 97 Small Business Edition package and protection with the McAfee VirusScan program. The XPS D333, however, lacks the kind of expansion capability you get with other high-end machines. With only two open PCI slots, you'll need to be careful about what you add to the system in the future, though the system is so well configured to start with. Dell's Dimension XPS D333 is a bit more expensive than some similarly-configured personal computers, but the level of quality and the unit's three-year warranty (with the first year of service on-site) commands a bit of a premium.

Specifications: operating system, Windows 95; RAM (std/max), 64MB/384MB; CPU/MHz—Intel Pentium II/333MHz, 512K Level 2 cache; floppy drives, one 3.5-inch 1.44MB; hard drive, 8.4GB Ultra ATA IDE; CD-ROM, DVD drive; storage bays—two open 5.25-inch bays, one open 3.5-inch bay; expansion slots, two open PCI

slots; ports—one serial, one parallel, mouse/keyboard, headphone, microphone, two USB; monitor, 19-inch Dell 1200HS; software included—Windows 95, MS Office 97 Small Business Edition with Encarta 98.
Ratings: overall value, 9; performance, 9; expandability, 6; documentation, 8
Warranty: 1 year, on-site labor; 3 years, parts
Manufacturer's Suggested Retail Price: $2,453
Approximate Low Price: $2,317

Compaq Presario 4860

✓BEST BUY

The Presario 4860, with its JBL speakers, FX700 multimedia monitor, and attractive charcoal case, desperately wants to be part of the typical high-end stereo system. But inside the box beats the heart of a powerful computer. The 4860 uses a Pentium II CPU running at 333MHz, the fastest available at the time of testing. Supplementing the CPU is 512K of Level 2 cache and 64MB of RAM, sufficient even for the most robust computer software. Other top-flight components include a huge 8GB hard disk, plus the popular ATI RAGE Pro 3D graphics accelerator chipset with DVD decoder circuitry. The built-in DVD can play movies on the excellent 17-inch monitor or be connected to a TV for viewing on the big screen; the DVD drive also handles standard CD-ROM as well as compact discs. The FX700 monitor has a 16-inch viewable area. Easy-to-use buttons and controls on the monitor, as with those on the computer case, can be used to start programs and control the CD player. A built-in microphone can work as part of a speakerphone system, thanks to the 48609s 56K modem. Built-in multimedia features, such as the ability to capture video as still pictures, make the 4860 a standout machine. And features such as USB ports, five open expansion slots, and enough open bays make it easy to add another hard disk, a CD-ROM recorder, or a removable media drive. The Presario 4860 offers a great hardware setup and a nice software selection at an affordable price.

Specifications: operating system, Windows 95; RAM (std/max), 64MB/384MB; CPU/MHz—Intel Pentium II/333MHz, 512K Level 2 cache; floppy drives, one 3.5-inch; hard drive, 8GB Ultra ATA IDE; CD-ROM, DVD drive and decoder; storage bays—two 5.25 external, one open hard disk mounting bracket; expansion slots, five; ports—one serial, one parallel, joystick/MIDI, headphone/speaker-out, microphone-in, line-in/out, 2 USB; monitor, Compaq FX700 17-inch multimedia; software included—Windows 95, Quicken Basic 98, Microsoft Bookshelf 98, Microsoft Encarta 98, Microsoft Money 98, MotoRacer, Incoming, Wing Commander (DVD Interactive version), Video Phone, U-Lead iPhoto Express, Microsoft Works 4.5, Colordesk, Intel Video Capture Utility, Selective QuickRestore CD.
Ratings: overall value, 8; performance, 10; expandability, 8; documentation, 8
Warranty: 90 days, on-site; 1 year, parts and labor
Manufacturer's Suggested Retail Price: $3,098
Approximate Low Price: $2,400

Apple Power Macintosh G3

Recommended

There are similarities and substantial differences between the G3 and IBM-compatible computers running Windows 95 or 98. Comparing performance is tricky, as the G3 runs different software than a Windows-based PC. Roughly speaking, the 233MHz CPU in the G3 performs as well as a 266MHz Pentium II system. The G3 comes in several models with CPU speeds up to 300MHz, either as desktop or mini tower configurations. Hard-drive sizes and monitors can all be ordered in different styles and sizes, as can other computing accessories. Excellent graphics power is controlled with an ATI 3D Rage II+ video chipset backed up with 2MB of video memory (which can be increased) to display millions of colors. Upgrading and maintaining the G3 is simple. The case opens up like the hood of a car to provide access to the inside for memory upgrades. If your computing needs include networking, you won't have to add that capability—it's built into the G3 (as it is in every Macintosh laptop and desktop machine). The G3 does have available to it all of the essential programs a buyer needs for home, school, and work. Buyers with specific computing needs should check first to see if the necessary software applications are available in a Mac version. (There are both hardware and software products that will let a Macintosh run Windows 95 software.) The Macintosh G3 boasts a superior design in use and performance. But while it still has a lot to offer the home user, the system's primary market remains those professional publishing and graphics arts designers with a large investment in software.

Specifications: operating system, Mac OS 8; RAM (std/max), 32MB/192MB; CPU/MHz, PowerPC G3/233MHz; floppy drives, one 3.5-inch 1.44MB and 800K; hard drive, 4GB IDE; CD-ROM, 24X; storage bays, two 3.5-inch; expansion slots, three PCI; ports—one modem/LocalTalk, one printer/LocalTalk, sound output, sound input, SCSI, Apple Desktop Bus (Apple Desktop Bus), 10BASE-T Ethernet; monitor, multiple-scan 15-inch display; software included—Macintosh OS 8 operating system.
Ratings: overall value, 7; performance, 9; expandability, 7; documentation, 10
Warranty: 1 year, parts and labor
Manufacturer's Suggested Retail Price: $2,098
Approximate Low Price: $2,098

BUSINESS/HI-POWERED COMPUTERS

Gateway 2000 Enterprise E-3200 333

✓BEST BUY

Gateway sells a lot of its PCs to computer enthusiasts and first-time purchasers who respond to its clever advertising. But a large part of Gateway's business is business. The strictly-business Enterprise series from Gateway comes in several configurations, from a technical graphics workstation to this powerhouse executive desktop system. The E-3200 comes in a midtower case fitted with a small switch that is triggered when the side panel is opened to record the event. It then passes the information on to the network administrator, which is responsible for maintaining computers in a large company environment. The system's roomy interior includes three open 5.25-inch drive bays, an open 3.5-inch bay, four empty expansion slots, and two USB ports. The motherboard can accommodate up to 384MB of RAM (our review system had 128MB). While 128MB seems excessive, it's not so large when considering the programs and networking software a machine such as this usually runs. Our review system had an ATI 3D Rage Pro video card with 8MB of video RAM plugged into the AGP slot to power the system's 17-inch EV700 monitor—a good quality unit. Other video setups are available, as are a host of multimedia, storage, and printing options. The pre-installed network interface card and Intel LANDesk software handle all of the networking chores for the E-3200 (a modem is not standard equipment, as this system uses the network to access the Internet). Performance and expandability make this Gateway a good choice for buyers with company-wide responsibility for purchasing or maintaining networks and technical gear.

Specifications: operating system, Windows 95; RAM (std/max), 128MB/384MB; CPU/MHz—Intel Pentium II/333MHz, 512K Level 2 cache; floppy drives, one 3.5-inch 1.44MB; hard drive, 10GB Smart II Ultra ATA IDE; CD-ROM, 13X min/32X max; storage bays—three open 5.25-inch, one open 3.5-inch, two open hard disk mounting brackets; expansion slots—three PCI, one ISA, one PCI/ISA, and one AGP; ports—serial, parallel, VGA, PS/2 keyboard/mouse port, microphone, headphone, line-in, game port/MIDI, 2 USB ports, RJ-45 network port; monitor, 17-inch EV700; software included—Windows 95, Intel LANDesk Client Manager software.

Ratings: overall value, 7; performance, 9; expandability, 7; documentation, 10

Warranty: 3 years, parts and labor
Manufacturer's Suggested Retail Price: $1,909
Approximate Low Price: not available

Compaq DeskPro 4000

Recommended

Compaq maintains two PC model lines: the Presario, for home and small-business, and DeskPro, a corporate workstation series built for easy maintenance. The DeskPro 4000 uses a trim case that allows easy access to the inside. A switch inside the case can send a "case-open" message across the network to an administrator, if desired. Networking capability is built in, with two different network connectors on the rear panel. The DeskPro 4000 comes with Windows NT 4.0 Workstation as the operating system, though it can be ordered with Windows 98. Since it is a corporate-oriented system, the DeskPro is configured more as an applications system than a multimedia machine. Video capability is controlled by a Matrox MGA 1064/SG graphics accelerator with 2MB of video memory, suitable for most business users. The Compaq's V75 monitor is a high-quality 17-inch monitor; other models and sizes are available. There are a number of areas where the DeskPro seems sparse, especially when compared to units built for the consumer market. It comes with only 32MB of RAM, which is adequate enough in a network system running Windows NT. We recommend 48MB, and more likely 64MB of RAM. Corporate purchasing agents and information managers want ease of setup more than expandability and high-end multimedia. Those buyers will appreciate the Compaq design and reliability.

Specifications: operating system, Windows NT 4.0; RAM (std/max), 32MB/384MB; CPU/MHz, Intel Pentium II/333MHz, 512K Level 2 cache; floppy drives, one 3.5-inch 1.44MB; hard drive, 3.2GB Ultra ATA IDE; CD-ROM, 24X; storage bays, one open 5.25-inch; expansion slots—one open ISA, one open PCI (one shared, one open AGP); ports—two serial, one parallel, MIDI/headphone, microphone, line-out, line-in, two USB ports, one

RJ-45 network connector, one AUI network connector, one external Infrared transceiver connector; monitor, Compaq V75 17-inch; software included—Windows NT 4.0 Workstation, Insight Management Agents.

Ratings: overall value 7; performance 9; expandability 3; documentation 7

Warranty: 3 years, parts and labor

Manufacturer's Suggested Retail Price: $2,059

Approximate Low Price: $1,799

PORTABLE COMPUTER

Toshiba 480CDT

✓BEST BUY

Toshiba's 480CDT provides all of the power most computer owners are likely to need. A full slate of working tools, from a floppy disk drive to a CD-ROM drive and a stereo audio system, ensure that you can walk away from your desktop computer without an extended grieving period. Unlike the trackpad used in NEC's Versa 6230 and other portables, Toshiba uses an eraserhead mouse device, plus two buttons integrated into the broad palm rest. Most users will find the eraserhead pointer more accurate than a trackpad, but it takes some practice to become proficient if you're used to a standard desktop mouse. It's easy to expand the 480CDT's versatility using SelectBay modules or with the NoteDock III port replicator docking station. The SelectBay modules can house a CD-ROM drive, an optional floppy disk drive, a second battery, or a second hard disk. This unit ships with an external floppy disk drive, so it's possible to have the CD-ROM and the floppy disk drive installed at the same time. Performance in word processing, web browsing, spreadsheets, and other applications is sprightly, thanks to the P233 processor and 32MB of RAM. The local bus video controller is a disappointment, however, given that competing systems use the more robust PCI-type controller. If you plan on using your new portable to design sophisticated multimedia presentations, you'll do better with PCI-bus video. The optional built-in 33.6 fax/modem included with the review unit browses the Internet without a hitch, and handles email and faxing chores. The 480CDT makes a few tradeoffs in this otherwise attractive package. It can make a good choice if you don't work exclusively with multimedia presentations.

Specifications: operating system, Windows 95; RAM (std/max), 32MB/160MB; CPU/MHz, Intel 233 MMX with 256 level 2 cache; floppy drives, one 3.5-inch 1.44MB; hard drive, 3.8GB; storage bays—SelectBay swaps out CD-ROM for optional floppy drive, second battery, or second hard disk drive; PC card slots, two Type II or single Type III PCMCIA; ports—one serial, one parallel, PS/2, SVGA, IrDA, docking station connector, external floppy disk drive connector, microphone, headphone, RJ-11 modem jack, cellular phone jack, one USB, line in, line out; screen, 12.1-inch TFT color/64-bit VESA graphics accelerator with 2MB VRAM; software included—Toshiba Control Panel, magiCD, TranXit Battery; sound—16-bit Sound Blaster Pro compatible audio, built-in stereo speakers; CD-ROM, 10X CD-ROM.
Ratings: overall value 8; performance 9; ease of use 8; documentation 8
Warranty: 1 year, labor; 3 years, parts
Manufacturer's Suggested Retail Price: $2,699
Approximate Low Price: $2,699

DATA STORAGE DEVICES

Imagine your computer's hard drive as a cabinet where you store your books and papers. Eventually, you're going to fill up that cabinet. Unless you throw away some of your books and papers, you're going to have to buy a larger cabinet or add a second one. And just like the cabinet shelves in your own home, it seems no matter how much extra capacity you start out with, stuff will come along to fill up all the available space.

STORAGE CAPACITY

Today's newest hard drives have capacity undreamed of only a few years ago. And prices have fallen so rapidly that consumers can readily buy all the storage space they need by purchasing a big hard drive at the initial sale or by adding a hard disk later. A more flexible option is a removable storage drive. These devices aren't as fast as hard drives, but they offer virtually unlimited storage capacity. When you fill a cartridge, you simply eject it and pop in a new one.

Removable storage has grown so popular and so inexpensive that many computer manufacturers are including Zip drives as standard equipment. Also, 100MB floppy disk drives and 200MB floppy disk drives, which use special high-capacity diskettes, have also appeared on the market. One advantage of these new drives is that they work with older 1.44MB diskettes, so you can buy one with your new PC and never have to worry about adding equipment to access older files stored on older floppy diskettes. Removable storage cartridges have pushed aside tape drives as backup devices.

SyQuest SparQ

✓BEST BUY

SyQuest, once the leader in removable disk storage for personal computers, was hit hard by the success of Iomega's Zip drive. Now, SyQuest is back with an excellent product, the SparQ. It offers ten times the storage and almost twice the speed of a Zip drive—for almost the same price. The SparQ comes in two models: an internal model, which connects to the EIDE connector on your motherboard; and an external version, which attaches to the computer's printer port. The external version is best for casual users because it's easy to connect and get up and running. More experienced PC buffs who are comfortable with installing the EIDE drive may want to choose the internal SparQ, as it's quite a bit faster. The SparQ is great for storing data files, such as graphics and documents. Each SparQ cartridge stores one gigabyte of data (compared to 100MB for a Zip disc). Three-packs sell for under $100, making the SparQ media one of the least expensive storage options. The SparQ driver software is easy to install, but unfortunately uses files that come with the drive. That means you won't be able to utilize all the space on that disk, since you may need to reinstall the drivers someday. The Install cartridge also includes a number of bundled programs, including Serif DrawPlus, an art program; McAfee Webscan, a virus-scanner for Internet use; NovaStor NovaDisk SE, for backing up your hard drive to a SparQ disk; Howdy!, for making multimedia email postcards; and NetResults WebVCR, for downloading web pages to view offline. Several portable storage options are available for today's PC consumer. The SparQ is one of the best values, if you need to store away files no longer needed on your hard disk.

Specifications: available for IBM PCs and compatibles.
Ratings: overall value, 10; performance, 7; ease of use, 9; documentation, 7
Warranty: 1 year, drive; 5 years, cartridges
Manufacturer's Suggested Retail Price: $199
Approximate Low Price: $199

Iomega Zip Plus

Recommended

The Iomega Zip drive has become so popular that it's now standard equipment in many computers. Identical in appearance to the original Zip drive, the Zip Plus makes several useful improvements. This version includes both the traditional parallel and the high-performance SCSI interface, and buyers can move the drive between computers with either of those connections. Zip Plus's eject switch now doubles as a power button, so the drive isn't powered all the time as it was in the original Zip drive. Since the Zip installation software now comes on a CD, buyers are free to use the Zip disk that comes with the unit. Several other useful software programs come on the CD, including the Adobe PhotoDeluxe graphics editor; DataViz Web Buddy, which lets you store Internet sites on Zip disks for later perusal; Recordit, for recording music CDs or other audio; PictureWorks NetCard, for designing postcards to send over the Internet; and Digital Arts & Sciences' ImageAXS, a program for cataloging and accessing graphics files. You may wonder why you'd opt for the Zip when drives such as the SyQuest SparQ sell for about the same price and offer ten times more storage. If your disks will never leave your home or office, the Zip may not be the best choice. But if you need to exchange data with friends, the office, or printing centers, chances are you'll probably find Zip drives a better option.

Specifications: available for IBM PCs and compatibles, Macintoshes.
Ratings: overall value, 8; performance, 7; ease of use, 10; documentation, 10
Warranty: 1 year, drive; lifetime, disks
Manufacturer's Suggested Retail Price: $200
Approximate Low Price: $200

MONITORS

Many computer buyers don't give enough thought to the monitor when making a system purchase. Don't get distracted by processor speeds and CD-ROM specifications and forget the monitor. The display screen is equal to the CPU, RAM, and hard drive as one of the most important components in your computer system.

CHOOSING A MONITOR

The right monitor can make the difference between a pleasant computing experience and one scattered with eyestrain and headaches. When choosing a one, consider two factors before all others: size and resolution. You should consider 15 inches as an absolute minimum size. When viewing a monitor's size, make sure to check the viewable area specification. A 17-inch monitor may have a tube that gives 16 actual inches of viewable display, while a competing unit might have a tube with only a 15.3-inch diagonal measurement. That 0.7 inch can make a noticeable difference.

Resolution refers to the size of the items on the screen. For example, a resolution of 640×480 shows larger icons than a resolution of 800×600. As a rule, bigger monitors can display higher resolutions without sacrificing clarity, while smaller monitors work better at lower resolutions.

Another specification to consider is dot pitch, which measures a monitor's clarity. Screen pictures are composed of tiny dots. The dot pitch refers to the spaces between those dots. The smaller the number (the closer the dots), the crisper the display. A dot pitch of 0.28 should be considered an absolute maximum, with .26 or .25 optimal (but more costly).

Ask about the monitor's refresh rate, which measures how often the screen is updated each second. Most people don't detect any flickering of the screen at rates of 72Hz and higher. Monitor makers list the refresh rate as it relates to screen resolution.

BUYING TIPS

The best test of a monitor is your own eyes. Try a few different models at the store. Ask the sales clerk to set the monitor at different resolutions to find the most comfortable viewing size for you, then make sure the monitor will support a comfortable refresh rate at that resolution.

Sony Multiscan GDM-400PS

✓BEST BUY

For computer users who spend their time running standard business applications such as word processing, the most important feature in a monitor is a clear display that's easy on the eyes. But for some applications, such as page layout or computer-aided design, users benefit from a professional-level display such as the large-screen 19-inch Sony GDM-400PS. It costs more than a similarly-sized consumer monitor, but offers better performance for that premium. With monitors, better performance boils down to sharper images at higher resolutions. The Multiscan's Trinitron CRT has an aperture of .25mm. This measurement isn't directly comparable to the dot pitch that most conventional digital displays advertise, but for the size of the display, it's quite good. Sony claims a maximum pixel resolution of 1,600×1,200, but we preferred the slightly lower resolution of 1,240×1,024. Getting the best performance from a professional display such as this one is also highly dependent upon the video card in the PC. Our review was based on an ATI Rage Pro AGP card with 4MB of video RAM. This is a high-performance card, though not a professional-level one. The Sony display offers BNC inputs in addition to the standard DB-15 connector; some high-quality video controllers may be able to provide more stable output at the display's rated maximum resolution. The quality of this display is everything a buyer would expect from the Sony name. Images are geometrically perfect, even before making any adjustments. On-screen controls make it easy to customize the display to individual tastes, from the amount of screen used to the color temperature. Sony's Multiscan GDM-400PS is overkill for most consumer applications, but if you need razor-sharp images over a large display area, this high-end model is worth the price.

Specifications: available for IBM PCs and compatibles; Macintoshes.
Ratings: overall value, 9; performance, 10; ease of use, 10; documentation, 8
Warranty: 3 years, parts, labor, CRT
Manufacturer's Suggested Retail Price: $1,000
Approximate Low Price: $900

Princeton EO90

✓BEST BUY

Princeton has been producing PC displays for about as long as there have been PCs. So it's no surprise that the vendor's line of large-screen monitors performs well. The EO90 is a 19-inch model with an 18-inch viewable area and boasts a .26mm dot pitch for very fine details in a monitor of this size. The EO909s out-of-box performance was quite good—just the slightest bit of framing adjustment was required to use the entire display, which was easily corrected using the comprehensive set of on-screen digital controls. During testing, the monitor displayed a small amount of moiré pattern, but this was not evident when using the monitor with real-world applications. Comprehensive adjustment controls eliminate barreling, pincushion effects, and other geometric abnormalities, though none of these were observed during our review. Color temperature, rotation, and other settings can also be adjusted. The EO90 has a maximum pixel resolution of 1,600×1,200, although the manufacturer recommends 1,280×1,024 at 85Hz refresh rate for best performance. We agree that the lower setting gives a sharper image. Our tests showed that the corner focus was observably less sharp than the center focus. This is not uncommon in consumer-grade displays and is more pronounced at higher resolutions. Customers working with page layout or engineering design might want to spend more for better performance at the highest resolutions. But for just about any other business or home use, the Princeton 19-inch monitor is a winner.

Specifications: available for IBM PCs and compatibles; Macintoshes.
Ratings: overall value, 8; performance, 8; ease of use, 9; documentation, 8
Warranty: 3 years, parts, labor, CRT
Manufacturer's Suggested Retail Price: $999
Approximate Low Price: $600

NEC MultiSync A700

Recommended

NEC was the first monitor vendor to introduce multiscan frequency technology. The company's products have been so popular that its trademarked MultiSync description of that technology is often used generically, like the terms "Scotch tape" and "Xerox." The new "A" model lineup is a consumer-oriented monitor in 15- and 17-inch sizes. A similar, but somewhat more upscale, "E" line is also available. We tested the A700, an attractive 17-inch monitor very similar in size, appearance, and features to

NEC's popular XV7+, which the A700 and E700 models supersede. On paper, the MultiSync A700, even for a consumer-oriented model, has excellent specifications for a 17-inch display. It features a viewable diagonal of 15.6 inches and offers an Invar shadow-mask type display with a .28mm dot pitch. The maximum rated pixel resolution on the A700 is 1,280×1,024. NEC recommends that consumers use a pixel resolution of 1,024×768 for best image quality, and our testing determined this to be an accurate statement. Image quality, right out of the box was quite good. The display was centered and did not require any additional adjustment either vertically or horizontally. All adjustments are performed via a simple six-button set that's identical in function and format to previous NEC 17-inch models. An on-screen menu displays adjustments for brightness and contrast, size and position, geometry, and color adjustment as well as color temperature. NEC offers what it calls an AccuColor Control System. This fancy name actually means that you can simply shift the display between two color temperatures (7,500 and 9,600 degrees). For the price, the NEC MultiSync A700 offers good value for the average computer user. However, for buyers with software applications that demand accurate, high-resolution performance, a different kind of display might be a better choice.

Specifications: available for IBM PCs and compatibles; Macintoshes.
Ratings: overall value, 7; performance, 7; ease of use, 10; documentation, 8
Warranty: 3 years
Manufacturer's Suggested Retail Price: $429
Approximate Low Price: $420

MODEMS

It used to be that buying a modem was a confusing exercise, with technical terms like v.32bis and MNP5 to deal with. Much of the technical confusion is now gone, with features such as error correction and compression standard on practically all modems. Now the biggest concern is speed. You won't find anything slower than 28,800 bps, except at clearance sales. Today, that's the speed of choice for most people.

BUYING TIPS

The minimum speed on any modem you buy should be 28.8K. An inexpensive and smart compromise is the 33.6K modem. Be wary of modems that claim to double speeds by using two phone lines—such a set up normally requires two online accounts, an unjustified expense to most consumers. If you buy a brand new computer with a modem built in, chances are you will get a 56K modem. Ask the sales clerk if the modem supports the V.90 standard or if it can be modified to support the highest standard. If the answer is no, ask that the modem be substituted for a newer model at the same cost, or have the modem removed and subtracted from the purchase price, then buy a newer model yourself and have it installed.

Now that the international communications standard has been set for high-speed modems (called the V.90 standard, in modem sales literature), a 56K modem (56,700 bps) is the fastest modem you can buy for a personal computer using ordinary telephone lines. Before buying a modem at that speed, check the maximum speeds supported by your online service provider.

Global Village TelePort 56K Plus V.90 for Macintosh

✓BEST BUY

By design, one modem is pretty much the same as another. At least in theory. But in fact modems do differ in features, performance, and price. Global Village makes modems for IBM compatibles, but has earned its reputation with Macintosh-smart modems. Built specifically for the Mac, the TelePort 56K Plus is compact (5.5×3 inches) and differs from an IBM-compatible modem in two respects. First, the TelePort comes with a Macintosh-compatible cable for connecting to a personal computer (the Macintosh uses a round DIN-8 style plug, rather than the DB-9 or DB-25 connectors used on IBM compatibles). The second difference—and it's a major one—is the modem software. Along with an exceptional setup program that walks new owners through the TelePort installation, Global Village also supplies both major web browsers (Internet Explorer and Navigator), a great fax program, Apple's latest OS (8.1), and a personal information manager. The TelePort 56K Plus is a dual-mode modem that supports both K56 Flex and the V.90 standard (the industry agreement for 56K transmissions). It does not support the ×2 protocol (before buying any modem, always check with your Internet service provider to see which protocol support you need). When tested with America Online and Microsoft Network, both of which support K56Flex, the TelePort connected quickly and without quirks. Considering the excellent software bundle, the TelePort 56 makes a valuable connection. It's generally a better choice for many Mac users than a generic modem.

Specifications: available for Macintoshes, other models available for IBM PCs and compatibles.
Ratings: overall value, 9; performance, 8; ease of use, 10; documentation, 9
Warranty: 5 years
Manufacturer's Suggested Retail Price: $189
Approximate Low Price: $160

Diamond Multimedia SupraExpress 56e

Recommended

The small SupraExpress 56e (6×4 inches) is an external modem that comes in several models, ranging from the simple fax/modem to the more sophisticated voice mail/speakerphone/videophone model. Although inexpensive, the 56e doesn't cut too many corners. Unlike many external modems, the SupraExpress comes with a serial cable already attached. It sports an internal speaker and a few indicator lights that keep users informed of connection status. Curiously, the modem doesn't have a power switch. Once you attach and plug in the power supply, it's always on. The SupraExpress is V.80 compatible. V.80 is the international standard for video phones, and as these devices become more popular, you won't have to upgrade to a new modem to perform videoconferencing. Diamond includes a trial copy of VDO's videoconferencing software, as well as other software packages, on a CD-ROM with the 56e. (You will need additional equipment for videoconferencing, such as a camera and TV-capable video card.) Our tests showed the SupraExpress performing slightly poorer than other external PC modems we tested. With a connection to America Online, for example, transmission speeds averaged between 40 kbps and 45 kbps (not the 56 kbps we came to expect from other modems supporting the V.90 56K standard). Still, the low price and simple installation make the 56e worth considering.

Specifications: available for IBM PCs and compatibles; Macintoshes.

Ratings: overall value, 9; performance, 7; ease of use, 10; documentation, 8

Warranty: 5 years

Manufacturer's Suggested Retail Price: $130

Approximate Low Price: $120

PRINTERS

A couple of decades ago, futurists predicted that computers would usher in a paperless society. However, the overall effect of the computer revolution seems to be that a lot of us are using more paper than ever. Today's printers can create such amazing results that many computer users are printing everything from greeting cards to company newsletters. The best news for today's printer buyers is that even the least expensive, entry-level printers produce stunning results.

CHOOSING A PRINTER

The printer market has segmented primarily into two types of printers: color inkjets and black-and-white laser printers. The quality of a printer is measured by how many dots per inch (dpi) it can place on a page. The higher the number, the better the print quality. Today's inkjets support 360 or 720 dpi, and lasers achieve 600, 1,200, or more dpi.

If speed or top-notch printed text is what you seek, a laser printer is the tool of choice. Essentially, a laser printer is a photocopier with a microprocessor and RAM added to make it smarter. It prints using the same technology as the Xerox machine at your local library. Black-and-white laser printers are no longer expensive to purchase and maintain. Even inexpensive, entry-level printers now sport resolutions of 600 dpi, which is good enough for all but professional publishing applications.

The primary differences among consumer laser printers relate to image quality and speed. The quality of printed graphics can vary dramatically between different brands, which is why you should always look at a print sample with both text and graphics before making a final purchase decision.

PRINTER SPEED

Printer speed is rated in pages per minute (ppm), with 4, 6, and 8 ppm being common speeds. Be aware, however, that the ppm rating refers to the speed of the printer's drum ability to put toner on paper. Much of the time spent in printing actually occurs before that point, when the printer is creating the page image; some printers do this dramatically faster than others that have the same ppm rating. Also watch the amount of RAM built into the printer—less than 1MB of RAM may result in lower speeds or the inability of the printer to print a full-page image because the printer's "brain" is too small to hold all the necessary information.

COLOR PRINTERS

If you want to add a splash of color to your documents, there's an inkjet in your future. Color laser printers exist, but they're still priced in the stratosphere. The good news is that today's color inkjets rival lasers in black-and-white print quality, if not speed, and can print near-photographic-quality color images.

One primary difference between color printers is the number of print cartridges they require. Traditionally, the most inexpensive color printers hold only one cartridge; you must swap black and three-color cartridges, depending on the type of document you're printing. Two-cartridge printers simultaneously hold color and black cartridges. These not only have better print quality, but you may eventually save the money in cartridge costs, since single-cartridge printers must mix all three colors to create black when doing mixed color/monochrome documents.

Like all technology, this setup is changing. Customers were so dissatisfied with the single-cartridge model that almost every color inkjet sold today uses the dual-cartridge system. Inkjet printers that specialize in photo printing can even use special "photo cartridges," which provide six colors instead of the basic four colors used in most color ink jets. Those four colors—cyan, magenta, yellow, black—are the basis for the CMYK label you see on many color printers. Photo printers work by letting users pop out the black cartridge and pop in the photo cartridge (which usually carries three inks—black, light cyan, and light magenta). The six color process is superior to the four-color process when printing photos because it captures flesh tones and other subtle shades more accurately.

BUYING TIPS

When shopping for a printer, there's one last item to check that's very important: cost of supplies. Saving $100 on a printer initially, only to discover that it has twice the ink cost per page, doesn't pay off in the long run. Color ink jet cartridges sell in the $30-$35 range. Toner for laser printers goes for about $60. On a per-page basis, the cost of a laser printer runs about three cents per page, while a color ink jet can run from five to seven cents a page.

NEC SuperScript 1260

BEST BUY

Most laser printers under $1,000 can't keep up with the demands of a small office. They aren't fast enough or they don't easily support multiple users. But the NEC SuperScript 1260 proves the exception. The SuperScript 1260 is a big brother to the well-reviewed, but smaller, SuperScript 860. The 1260 retains much of what makes the 860 a great printer, then expands those capabilities to multiple users with an optional network card. Even without the network card, the 1260 is robust enough for any small office job. It prints at a remarkable speed of 12 pages per-minute. The 600 dots-per-inch resolution makes for crisp text and graphics. Although the 1260 only generates 124 levels of gray, the output looks good enough to be mistaken for 256 shades. The superb status monitor runs on the Windows desktop, allowing users to monitor and adjust almost every aspect of operation without leaving the desk. One can even use a Web browser to manage the printer—a clever way to control the printer in a workgroup environment. Paper capacity is somewhat limited (a 250-sheet tray and an 80-sheet multipurpose tray are standard), but a second paper tray can be added to increase the paper capacity to 830 sheets. The printer handles all weights of paper, plus legal-size paper, transparencies, and labels. One drawback, however, is the standard multipurpose tray only holds ten envelopes; customers should consider the cost of the optional 50-envelope bin into their buying decision. For buyers in a home office or small business, the 1260 is more than twice as valuable as an inexpensive $400 personal laser printer.

Specifications: available for IBM PCs and compatibles.
Ratings: overall value, 9; performance, 8; ease of use, 10; documentation, 8
Warranty: 1 year
Manufacturer's Suggested Retail Price: $699
Approximate Low Price: $699

Hewlett Packard LaserJet 1100

Recommended

Personal laser printers make small compromises to keep costs down, but those tradeoffs sometimes cost even more when you add up all the frustration. Slow printing and small paper trays are two of the biggest hidden costs. However, the Hewlett Packard LaserJet 1100 delivers a full suite of printer features at a price anyone can afford. Performance is more than adequate, with a resolution of 600 dots per inch and a speed of eight pages per minute; more expensive printers will print faster. The HP 1100 uses an "instant on" fusing assembly, so that warm-up times are minimal. Both text and graphics print well, with solid, sharp black characters and high-quality gray-scale images. The printer's space-efficient size is another plus, as is the 125-sheet vertical paper tray. An innovative design provides a vertical output tray, saving even more desk space. For printing heavier stock (such as transparencies or cardstock), a straight paper path can be used to avoid paper jams. The 6L also includes a second tray for feeding envelopes and single sheets so users don't have to remove the main tray. HP's new JetPath expansion technology allows users to add scanning and copying functions quickly and easily as their communication needs evolve. The Hewlett Packard 1100 is perfect for the one-person home office that needs sharp black text for professional looking correspondence; it also provides the right mix of speed, print quality and low operating costs.

Specifications: available for IBM PCs and compatibles.
Ratings: overall value, 8; performance, 8; ease of use, 9; documentation, 9
Warranty: 1 year, Express Exchange
Manufacturer's Suggested Retail Price: $399
Approximate Low Price: $399

HOME OFFICE PRODUCTS

The home office has become a fixture in many households as Americans continue to venture out on their own and more companies encourage flexible working arrangements. Home workers are demanding office machines capable of delivering solid performance at reasonable prices, and manufacturers are responding with products specifically designed for this key market. If you've held off buying new equipment because your old machines work just fine, you'll find that today's marketplace offers a wide range of products that offer greater convenience and quality, sometimes at a fraction of what you had paid for old equipment.

BUYING TIPS

Before purchasing office equipment, you must first decide on what are the best products to accomplish what you need done. Multifunction faxes, for example, can take the place of many pieces of equipment, but they may not be the answer for everyone. Second, what products best fit your office layout and budget? Maybe a sheet-fed scanner with a low resolution is fine for you, but a budding web site designer may need a more versatile flatbed with higher resolution.

Products in this category are priced competitively and are widely available at many specialty stores and national chain stores. Many can even be ordered over the Internet. It's also a good idea to watch your weekly newspaper for special offers as manufacturers often offer rebates at certain times of the year.

BEST BUYS '99

Our Best Buy, Recommended, and Budget Buy home office products are listed below. Products within each category are listed according to quality. The best of the Best Buys is listed first, followed by our second choice, and so on. A Best Buy, Recommended, or Budget Buy designation only applies to the model listed—it does not necessarily apply to other models made by the same manufacturer or to an entire product line.

DESKTOP COPIERS

Desktop photocopy machines may not be necessities in many home offices, but they are an important piece of equipment for anyone who regularly makes numerous copies of multiple-page documents. New models take advantage of technological advances to provide excellent copy quality and features once found on larger commercial machines. Prices are also coming down as these products face competition from multifunction fax machines and scanners.

TYPES OF COPIERS

Two types of desktop copiers are available: moving platen or fixed-platen. Less expensive machines often use a moving platen, which literally moves the item being copied over the copier lens. Moving-platen machines cannot reduce or enlarge, copy time is slower, and it's difficult to copy bulkier items such as books. Even though these machines are often smaller and lighter than fixed-platen copiers, they require more space due to their moving platen. They can also be more expensive to operate.

Although fixed-platen copiers offer more versatility and are slightly more expensive, they may also be a more economical choice in the long run. Many machines are now being offered with such features as automatic document feed, second paper trays, preset enlarge/reduction settings, and text/photo mode settings.

DRUM AND TONER CARTRIDGES

Toner cartridges comprise the major expense on photocopy machines. These cartridges contain a powdery, inklike material used to create copied images. Many copiers allow users to insert special toner cartridges for one-color copying in colors other than black. Some have combined cartridges, making it easier to change them but less cost effective since the drum (the element that transfers an image to paper) usually outlasts the toner. Most manufacturers have made drum and toner replacement much easier in recent years, eliminating many of the problems associated with this necessary part of copier maintenance. Still, if you're worried about spilling black toner, a copier with a combined cartridge may be the one for you. The quality of prints is measured in dots per inch (dpi). The higher the number, the finer the image resolution.

Xerox XC830

✓BEST BUY

The Xerox XC830 has many of the features of a commercial copier, yet is more affordable and sized to fit almost every home office. It features six preset reduction and enlargement settings, ranging from 70 to 141 percent; users also can enter other settings in one-percent increments. A quick-start feature allows copy jobs to start immediately once the machine warms up. The Xerox XC830 produces up to eight copies per minute and will make up to 100 copies of the same document. Copy quality is excellent in both text and photo modes. Although this machine lacks an automatic document feeder, its paper drawer is somewhat small in capacity at 100 sheets, and its bypass tray will only handle one sheet at a time. Xerox's customer support and maintenance program (which allows users to send the machine back for repair or exchange through any Mailboxes Etc.) and its three-year warranty make the XC830 a good choice for performance and price.

Specifications: height, 10"; width, 20"; depth, 18½"; weight, 41 lbs.
Warranty: 3 years
Manufacturer's Suggested Retail Price: $570
Approximate Low Price: $570

Hewlett Packard HP210

Recommended

The Hewlett Packard HP210 features many of the same controls and features as the XC830. It is as fast as the XC830 in the black-and-white mode, and its professional-quality color copies take up to ten seconds each. It can copy up to ten pages per minute in black-and-white and six pages per minute in color. Color reproduction is superb. It features broad reduction and enlargement settings, ranging from 50 to 400 percent. Its paper capacity is a generous 180 sheets, and its recommended copy volume is up to 1,500 per month. The HP210 is perfect for a small business that requires a lot of color copies. An optional automatic multidocument feeder is also available.

Specifications: height, 13½"; width, 22½"; depth, 18¼"; weight, 59 lbs.
Warranty: 1 year, parts and labor
Manufacturer's Suggested Retail Price: $999
Approximate Low Price: $799

Canon PC430

Budget Buy

The "mini" Canon PC430 is a worthy, economical choice for home office users who don't mind sacrificing a little quality and time for an unbeatable price. It can make copies on a wide variety of materials, such as stationery, transparencies, colored paper, and labels. It takes almost no time at all to warm up. Its paper tray holds a respectable 50 sheets, and copying is done on a moving copy board rather than the fixed-glass surface found on more expensive machines. It can copy up to four letter-sized pages per minute, but will not reduce or enlarge. The PC430 only will copy in black, but optional toner cartridges (brown, blue, red, or green) are available. Changing cartridges on the PC430 is simple with Canon's patented single cartridge system, which contains toner, drum, and development unit in one piece.

Specifications: height, 4⅛"; width, 16⅜"; depth, 15⅞"; weight, 18 lbs. 14 oz.
Warranty: 3 years, parts and labor
Manufacturer's Suggested Retail Price: $369
Approximate Low Price: $369

SCANNERS

Today's scanners pack versatility, quality, and performance into increasingly smaller machines. A scanner can substantially expand the capability of a computer system by allowing the direct transfer of graphics and printed text to the system.

TYPES OF SCANNERS

Most scanners on the market today are either flatbed or sheet-fed. Handheld scanners, the third type available, are becoming less popular as the others continue to come down in price. Flatbed scanners offer the most versatility and convenience. They can be used to scan thick objects, such as books, and portions of oversize objects, such as maps and charts. Sheet-fed scanners, which resemble portable printers, are convenient for scanning single sheets of paper and business cards but cannot be used with magazines or books unless the material to be scanned is torn out first.

FEATURES

Scanners generally come bundled with operating-system-specific software that controls the scans and adjusts scanned images. Many scanners now come with optical character recognition (OCR) software for scanning text. Communications software that allows faxing directly from the scanner is also included with many units. All use a light-sensitive charged-coupled device (CCD), which converts the scanned image to an electronic signal, which is then digitized and stored on the hard drive of your computer. Bits are used to describe the color and gray-scale images. The higher the number, the more colors or image depth of the machine.

Umax Astra 610

✓BEST BUY

Umax's Astra 610 is one of the easiest machines to use on the market. This color flatbed scanner offers 30-bit color depth, 10-bit gray-scale, and optical resolution of 300×600 dpi. It scans in a respectable 82 seconds; gray-scale takes about 20 seconds. The Astra 610 comes with all the necessary software to interface and operate with PCs or Macintosh computers. Bundled software includes Adobe PhotoDeluxe, Caere OmniPage LE for optical character recognition, and a copy utility that allows the machine to function as a copier. Because of its compact size, the 610 will only scan documents up to letter size.

Specifications: height, 16½"; width, 11⁹⁄₁₆"; depth, 3¹³⁄₁₆"; weight, 8 lbs. 9 oz.
Warranty: 1 year, parts and labor
Manufacturer's Suggested Retail Price: $109
Approximate Low Price: $100

Visioneer PaperPort Strobe

Recommended

If you primarily need a scanner for black-and-white documents, the Visioneer PaperPort Strobe is an excellent choice. This sheet-fed scanner takes up virtually no valuable desk space; it can conveniently sit behind a keyboard or on top of a computer monitor. The Strobe includes automatic application launch; just insert a piece of paper and Visioneer's PaperPort 5.0 software takes over. Another handy feature is automatic skew detection, which rejects any documents that aren't feeding smoothly. It delivers images in 24-bit color and 8-bit gray-scale; maximum resolution is 2,400×2,400 dpi for black and white, 300×600 dpi for color. At about four seconds for scanning a black-and-white text document, it's one of the fastest scanners on the market.

Specifications: height, 2¼"; width, 11"; depth, 2"; weight, 1 lb. 6 oz.
Warranty: 1 year, parts and labor
Manufacturer's Suggested Retail Price: $200
Approximate Low Price: $200

DESKTOP FAX MACHINES

An office mainstay, fax machines are the focus of much competition in the home office machine category. If you're prepared to pay $700 to $1,000, you can now buy a multifunction fax machine that can do it all—fax, copy, scan, print, answer the phone, even access images from a digital camera. You can even do it all in color.

Although multifunction machines are popular, they aren't the answer for everyone. As tempting as the multifunction machines are, they can have their drawbacks. If you already own a good scanner and you're using your phone company's answering equipment, you may not require a multifunction fax. If you receive faxes more than you send them, a simple plain-paper fax or a computer fax modem will be sufficient.

TYPES OF FAX MACHINES

Most fax machines today are plain-paper models. Thermal-paper faxes, which transfer images via heat to specially treated paper, are also still available. The ease and convenience of plain-paper faxes more than outweigh the hassles of dealing with thermal paper. Thermal paper tends to curl and will change color and fade over time. Plus recent price reductions have made plain-paper machines more affordable than ever. However, an advantage that thermal-paper faxes have over all plain-paper machines is that they don't need toner or ink cartridges to create images. If you really don't want the hassle of replacing ink or toner cartridges, a thermal-paper fax might be for you.

Brother MFC-7000FC

✓BEST BUY

Simply put, the Brother MFC-7000FC is amazing. It offers color capabilities on four of its six functions—printing, copying, scanning, and fax. It has 720×720 dpi output for crisp, high-quality copies and printing, and up to 1,200×1,200 dpi for clear scans. What also sets this machine apart is a message center that stores both voice and fax messages, a PC message center for storing messages on a hard drive, and a superb video capture function that allows the system to access video frames from a digital camera, VCR, TV, laser disc player, or camcorder. The well-chosen software bundle includes paper management and optical character recognition. It also includes three programs for creating documents ranging from business materials to greeting cards. Although you will need ink cartridges for the three colors for four-color printing, they are easy to change. The black cartridge will last for about 700 pages and the color cartridges for about 300 pages.

Specifications: height: 20⅛"; width, 18⅛"; depth, 11⅞"; weight, 22 lbs.
Warranty: 1 year, parts and labor
Manufacturer's Suggested Retail Price: $700
Approximate Low Price: $700

Panasonic KX-FM210

Recommended

The compact KX-FM210 multifunction fax machine includes six of the most requested office functions, making it ideal for the home office with limited space. Features that push this machine beyond the standard fax, copy, scan, and telephone include fax pager alert (which allows the unit to be programmed to call your pager when you receive a fax), paper save (which reduces the size of incoming faxes, allowing up to two pages on a single sheet), and extension line transfer (which allows the manual transfer of incoming fax calls from any touch-tone extension to the fax unit). However, what the Panasonic offers in features and price it loses in speed. Its top transmission speed is 9,600 bps, which is somewhat slower than comparable models. However, if the economical price and variety of features suffice, the KX-FM210 will fit the bill.

Specifications: height, 5⅞"; width, 14 7/16"; depth, 13 31/32"; weight, 11 lbs. 6 oz.
Warranty: 1 year, parts and labor
Manufacturer's Suggested Retail Price: $250
Approximate Low Price: $250

Sharp UX108

Budget Buy

The Sharp UX108 has no frills, no fancy bells, and no whistles—just a basic fax machine from one of the leading fax manufacturers. The UX108 features standard fax service including 30-number auto-dial, a ten-page automatic document feeder, and on-hook dialing. It transmits documents at approximately 15 seconds per page, slower than many plain-paper or multifunction fax machines but comparable to other thermal-paper fax machines. The UX108 accepts caller ID and distinctive-ring detection. There is also a special feature that allows blocking of unwanted faxes. If you just need a stand-alone fax machine, the UX108 is your best option.

Specifications: height, 5⅖"; width, 12⅒"; depth, 10"; weight, 6.2 lbs.
Warranty: 90 days, parts and labor
Manufacturer's Suggested Retail Price: $120
Approximate Low Price: $120

HANDHELD PERSONAL COMPUTERS (HPCs)

These small, powerful devices can pack substantial computing power and speed—rivaling desktop or laptop machines. If you're dedicated to these other systems and you don't spend a great deal of time away from your office, you may not need an HPC. However, if you're away from home on a consistent basis and you need portable computing support, an HPC can make your life a great deal easier.

FEATURES

Because HPCs are often used as supportive devices for other computers, it's important to choose products that offer easy data exchange between both systems. For this reason, many HPCs use Microsoft Windows applications specially designed for such devices. Those that don't, use built-in connectivity programs or docking devices for data transfer.

Memory is another important consideration when shopping for HPCs. More is better, especially if you need to store a large amount of text, spreadsheets, or to-do lists. Battery power is also a consideration. Color-screen HPCs will drain batteries faster than black-

and-white units. Be prepared to buy special battery packs, which will add some weight to the device.

HPCs, like electronic organizers, have screens that range from easy-to-read to difficult. Eyesight tends to fade as we age, and investing in a clear, easy-to-read screen can eliminate the frustration and headaches that can arise when trying to read these small screens. It's a good idea to test products in both full-light and low-light situations before you buy. Also be sure that the data-entry system is to your liking. They range from stylus and handwriting recognition to almost full-size keyboards.

Hewlett-Packard 620LX

✓BEST BUY

Although the 620LX is one of the more expensive handheld PCs on the market, it rates as a Best Buy because it offers an excellent combination of features and value. Software includes Windows CE 2.0 plus the standard Windows CE applications and Pocket Quicken ExpensAble. It comes with 16MB RAM, built-in speaker and microphone, voice memo recorder that allows recording without opening the unit, fax software, Internet access, data synchronization, and presentation capabilities through Microsoft Pocket PowerPoint. The bright and crisp color display on the 620LX's full-width, 640×240 pixel, 256-color backlit screen promises to dazzle. The 620LX also includes an ergonomically designed keyboard, with the keys angling up slightly from front to back, allowing for effortless typing.

Specifications: height, 1½"; width, 4⅛"; length, 7¾"; weight, 20.6 oz.
Warranty: 1 year, parts and labor
Manufacturer's Suggested Retail Price: $799
Approximate Low Price: $799

Psion Series 5

Recommended

The Psion Series 5 features great applications and one of the best keyboards available on a handheld PC. Onboard applications include a word processor, a spreadsheet, a sketch pad, and PIM (personal information management) applications. A built-in connectivity program allows information exchange between the Series 5 and PCs when running either Windows 95 or Windows NT. (There's also a Mac connectivity program available at additional cost.) A built-in microphone facilitates digital sound recording and an infrared IrDA port allows short-range printing and information transfer. It's 8MB of memory stores up to 2,000 pages of text, 40,000 appointments, or 20,000 database records. The keyboard, which slides forward when the Psion is opened, is similar to the size and feel of a standard PC keyboard. When you purchase the Psion Series 5, you'll receive free Lotus organizer premium software (while supplies last). Optional applications exclusive to the Psion's EPOC32 operating system are also available.

Specifications: height, 7/8"; width, 3 1/2"; length, 6 3/4"; weight, 12.5 oz.
Warranty: 1 year, parts and labor
Manufacturer's Suggested Retail Price: $549
Approximate Low Price: $499

3Com Palm Pilot Pro

Budget Buy

Small, reliable, and easy to use, the Palm Pilot is one of the most popular handheld computing devices on the market, even if it does lack a keyboard. Measuring slightly larger than a deck of playing cards, the Palm Pilot features a backlit LCD, six navigational keys, and a stylus for data entry. Touching any of the application icons displayed on the screen gives access to standard PIM (personal information management) software. An expense tracker and email client, which allow users to write, read, and delete messages, are also included. You will, however, need additional software and an external modem for transmission. The Palm Pilot Pro will store 4,000 addresses, 2,400 appointments, 750 tasks, and 100 email messages. A Palm III, with 2MG memory, infrared (IrDA) port for data transfer, flash memory, and 3Com's new desktop operating system, is also available for $100 more.

Specifications: height, 7⁄10"; width, 3 1⁄4"; length, 4 3⁄4"; weight, 6 oz.
Warranty: 1 year
Manufacturer's Suggested Retail Price: $300
Approximate Low Price: $300

ELECTRONIC ORGANIZERS

These small computers are an ideal way to keep track of information and schedules for anyone tired of carrying an appointment book or scheduler. Many electronic organizers are virtually indistinguishable from handheld personal computers (HPCs). For many buyers, the more limited capabilities of electronic organizers propel them towards their larger, more powerful counterparts, but there's still many reasons to pick an organizer over an HPC if you don't need a lot of bells and whistles and you don't want to spend a lot of money.

FEATURES

When shopping for an electronic organizer, try to find one with adequate memory (anything below 1MB can be more frustrating than helpful). Although cheaper units with limited memory may seem like bargains, it's a good idea to buy as much memory as you can afford for optimum storage and processing speed. Other features to look for include a well-spaced keyboard for data entry (if you intend to enter information away from home) and an easy-to-read display. Beyond that, most electronic organizers offer a pretty standard array of features, including calendar, to-do lists, expense logs, and telephone lists.

Sharp Wizard OZ650PC

✔BEST BUY

Sharp's Wizard series of electronic organizers has been popular since they were first introduced. The OZ650PC—a slim, pocket-size organizer—doesn't disappoint. It is smaller and lighter than similar products, but features a comfortable keyboard that lets you easily enter information. This powerful machine delivers superb organizing capabilities with its 1MB of memory, backlit-illuminated display, and IrDA infrared port for data transmission. It also includes impressive standard organizing utilities, including calendar, to-do list, expense log, telephone list, calculator, and clock. The 40-character/10-line display is easy to read. Sharp joined forces with Day-Timers, Inc., to include convenient Day-Timer Organizer software with this system. The OZ650PC also comes with IntelliSync software that allows easy, instantaneous data synchronization with the Day-Timer software.

Specifications: height, 3⅓"; width, 6"; depth, ¾"; weight, 7.2 oz.
Warranty: 1 year, parts and labor
Manufacturer's Suggested Retail Price: $200
Approximate Low Price: $169

Franklin Rex-3-DS PC Companion

Recommended

The lightweight, credit-card sized Franklin Rex makes looking up contacts, tasks, appointments, and short memos quick and easy. This tiny device is actually a Type II PC Card, offering on-the-go access to information stored on your PC. Just plug it into the appropriate slot on any notebook computer or use the Rex serial docking connection with a desktop PC serial port. The Rex's synchronization program then imports information from most common personal information manager (PIM) software, storing up to 3,000 items at a time. A small monochrome LCD screen displays about nine lines of information at a time, which is easily navigated with the Rex's well-spaced buttons. Unlike other organizers, data cannot be entered directly, but this is an ideal product for anyone wanting a small, portable organizer with plenty of storage capacity.

Specifications: height, ¼"; width, 2⅛"; length, 3⅜"; weight, 1.4 oz.
Warranty: 1 year (limited)
Manufacturer's Suggested Retail Price: $150
Approximate Low Price: $129

HOME FITNESS

Americans are increasingly concerned with good health and fitness, and this is a trend that will easily continue into the next century. With the vast array of home fitness equipment available, many of us are now able to find a few hours a week to lose weight and become more physically fit.

GETTING FIT

Home exercise equipment has such great appeal because it is often difficult to find time in our busy schedules to visit a health club or gym. If you are serious about getting fit or losing weight, home exercise equipment may be the solution. The key is to buy the best aerobic exercise equipment you can afford and use it on a regular basis. Many experts suggest that you should purchase a machine that you enjoy using and one that gets your heart rate up. (An increased heart rate is crucial for effective burning of calories.)

To be effective, though, exercise must be combined with a well-balanced diet. There are easily hundreds of food products and drinks that have been designed for this purpose. It is important to remember that you can eat healthy—and economically—from the basic food groups. Nutritionists agree that we should all cut down on our intake of fat and increase our intake of fruits and vegetables.

BUYING TIPS

It is important to shop wisely for home exercise equipment that you will use on a regular basis. Avoid trendy or cute equipment. Take the time to learn which machines will best help you accomplish your desired goals, whether it's a flatter stomach or bigger biceps. The best machine is one that you will use daily or at least several times a week. Each of the following categories have additional buying tips to help you choose a product that suits your exercise needs.

All home exercise equipment carries some type of warranty against defects in workmanship. The time period covered usually ranges from 90 days to the lifetime of the original purchaser. As a rule, extended warranties are indications of quality in-home exercise equipment.

BEST BUYS '99

Our Best Buy, Recommended, and Budget Buy home fitness products are listed below. Products within each category are listed according to quality. The best of the Best Buy's is listed first, followed by Recommended and Budget Buy. A Best Buy, Recommended, or Budget Buy rating only applies to the model listed; it does not necessarily apply to other models made by the same manufacturer or to an entire product line.

EXERCISE CYCLES

Exercise cycles continue to be popular for home use, and there are many on the market. Try as many as possible before making your final purchase decision. You should pick a unit that is comfortable to sit on and peddle. Foot straps are worthwhile features. Choose an exercise cycle that other family members can easily use. A wide variety of options are available for an additional cost—such as upright or recumbent design, advanced electronic controls and console, dual-drive belt/chain systems, dual-action capabilities—so you must decide which are best suited for your needs.

FEATURES

Standard features on all exercise cycles include a padded, adjustable seat, padded handle bars, adjustable resistance, and a console that provides current information on speed, distance, elapsed time, and preprogrammed workouts. Besides the standard upright models, several models offer upper-body workouts as well. The latest designs use recumbent seating, which supports your lower back with an upright lounge-chair seating style. Recumbent models also leave your hands and arms free to use weights for upper-body exercise while you peddle the cycle.

Lifecycle 5500HR

✓BEST BUY

The Lifecycle 5500HR is the home version of the health club exercise bike. The unit has an adjustable seat, peddle straps, and closed-cell urethane handle grips. Small front casters allow you to move the cycle easily around the home. A battery-powered electronic console provides elapsed time, total calories expended, calories burned per hour, total miles, pedal speed, and a workout summary. The 5500HR comes with seven workout programs: Fat Burn, Cardio, Hill, Random, Manual, Fit Test, and Race Mode. These programs are designed to provide you with a personalized workout based on your age and weight. The Fat Burn program, for example, runs you through an exercise program designed to burn calories.

Specifications: height, 55″; width, 23″; length, 46″; weight, 87 lbs.
Warranty: 3 years, electric and mechanical components
Manufacturer's Suggested Retail Price: $1,499
Approximate Low Price: $1,200

Schwinn Airdyne Evolution

Recommended

The Schwinn Airdyne Evolution is an updated version of one of the first exercise cycles to find its way into home use. This unit offers a patented synchronized arm-and-leg action, which operates with two steel handle bars (with PVC grips) that move back and forth as you peddle the bike. A fully enclosed fan provides resistance as well as a cooling effect for the user. A battery-powered display terminal offers a high contrast LCD screen that keeps track of time, distance, calories, level, and rpm. The Evolution comes with four workout programs: hills, intervals, summit, and manual. Each program is designed to give you a stimulating preprogrammed workout. The hills program, for example, shows your progression up and down a series of hills.

Specifications: height, 48″; width, 23½″; length, 52″; weight, 90 lbs.

Warranty: lifetime (limited to original owner)
Manufacturer's Suggested Retail Price: $699
Approximate Low Price: $650

Tunturi F250

Recommended

The quiet Tunturi F250 is an affordable, well-made recumbent stationary exercise bike. It is easy to adjust and can accommodate users of any height. The seat holds the user in an upright position, allowing the user to exercise prime mover muscles. An electronic control panel can be used to select from various programs including manual operation. Resistance is easily set by using push buttons, and the level of difficulty can also be adjusted. The F250 also includes five preset programs of varying duration.

Specifications: height, 45"; width, 23"; length, 35"; weight, 57 lbs.
Warranty: 2 years, parts; 10 years, structural components
Manufacturer's Suggested Retail Price: $699
Approximate Low Price: $650

ROWING MACHINES

Rowing provides a zero-impact, fluid type of exercise. Although rowing machines have fallen in popularity as new and more advanced types of home exercise equipment become available, there are still several good rowing machines on the market. The better models accurately reproduce the catch-and-pull motion of rowing and provide a true total-body exercise.

When shopping for a rowing machine, look for a smooth gliding seat and sturdy guide rail that is long enough for your legs. The unit should be able to accommodate both tall and short rowers. Air resistance models, which cool you as you work out, have been the most popular. Electronic features, such as a heart-rate monitor and magnetic resistance, add to the cost but may be worthwhile for your particular needs.

Concept II Model C

✓ BEST BUY

The Concept II Model C is a well-made flywheel/fan rowing machine that provides a lifetime of rowing exercise for the entire family. The wide, comfortable seat slides easily on a strong aluminum I-beam. The adjustable footrests are deep and flex naturally. The foot straps hold your feet firmly in place. A solid maple handle, covered with molded rubber grips, acts as the oar. The easy-to-read electronic monitor is centrally located and mounted on a movable arm. The monitor displays time for 500 meters, calories per hour, duration of workout, average stroke rate, heart rate (optional), total calories, on/off, and memory recall. In addition, there are three levels of operation—automatic, preset workout, recall—plus extra functions for advanced users. An optional computer interface for training, performance logging, and racing is available for an extra cost. The unit folds for storage and has built-in casters.

Specifications: height, 35"; width, 24"; length, 95"; weight, 61 lbs.
Warranty: 2 years, parts; 5 years, metal frame parts
Manufacturer's Suggested Retail Price: $725
Approximate Low Price: $725

Tunturi Air Rower R701

Recommended

The Tunturi Air Rower R701 is well designed and should provide decades of exercise for most users. The fan is covered by a fine mesh screen. The seat is stable and glides easily on the guide rail. This unit has foot pegs with straps and a large, well-padded oar. It comes with a small LCD readout monitor that indicates track load, tempo, calories, calories per minute, strokes, and time. Controls are simple: on/off, start/stop, reset, and mode. If storage space is a premium, the R701 conveniently folds for easy storage.

Specifications: height, 26"; width, 20"; length, 93"; weight, 72 lbs.
Warranty: 2 years, parts; 10 years, structural components

Manufacturer's Suggested Retail Price: $799
Approximate Low Price: $700

TREADMILLS

Treadmills are popular because they provide an indoor means for walking or running. This is a type of exercise that is not only worthwhile but enjoyable for most people. Basically, a treadmill consists of a wide belt that is stretched over a bed and around two or more rollers. Most units are powered by a motor, but some are powered by the user. Motor choices include AC or DC powered. An AC motor commonly runs at one continuous speed and relies on a transmission to regulate speed. A DC-powered unit uses variable voltage to regulate the speed at which the belt spins. If you plan on running more than walking, choose a treadmill with at least a 1½ horsepower motor.

FEATURES

Common features on all treadmills include a monitor that indicates belt speed (and any number of other factors such as heart rate, mph, distance covered), adjustable incline, handrails or levers, and easy-to-reach controls. Choose a model that has a wide belt and one that is long enough for your stride. Better units will also have some type of cushioning between the belt and bed, a feature that you will appreciate if you jog or run on the machine. Cost increasing features include advanced electronics and console, workout programs that automatically adjust speed and incline, health club construction, and a lifetime warranty.

PaceMaster Pro Plus HR

✓BEST BUY

The durable and quiet PaceMaster Pro Plus HR is a top-of-the-line treadmill with a price tag well below comparable models. It has a 2.3-horsepower motor that turns the belt from 0.7 to 11 mph. Grade can be adjusted from flat to a 15 percent incline. A Softstep deck cushions each step to reduce stress on ankles, feet, and back. Pro Plus HR includes three preset programs—Basic, Endurance, and Interval—with five levels of intensity for each. It also allows you to create up to four custom programs. The monitor indicates calorie burn, aerobic "points," and distance for any time, speed, and incline combination. You can also add an automatic warm up, cool down, or both to any workout. The Pro Plus HR also includes a heart rate control function, which varies the intensity of the workout to keep the user in his or her target training zone. The heart-rate control fastens around the chest and controls the speed of the moving belt and its incline. This unit will only operate with a special safety key in place.

Specifications: height, 50"; width, 28½"; length, 68"; weight, 185 lbs.
Warranty: 1 year, labor; 2 years, parts; 3 years, motor; lifetime, frame and fasteners
Manufacturer's Suggested Retail Price: $2,095
Approximate Low Price: $1,800

Star Trac TR901

Recommended

Star Trac has been supplying treadmills to fitness clubs for some time, and for several years the company has offered the reliable Star Trac TR901 for home use. It is a well-made unit with a variety of features that should provide years of dependable service. The deck has a polyethylene cushion to diminish foot-strike stress. Motor speed is monitored 430,000 times per minute for precise control. The TR901 has a heart rate monitor that keeps you in your training range by automatically adjusting speed and incline. The display contains visual clues to let you know where you are in your workout. The Track/Profile button allows you to switch between a running track profile and a graphic depiction of hills and valleys. There are 15 preset programs plus a manual program. Other controls include scan, stop/start, speed change, incline change, heart rate, and program selection. Additional indicators show your progress in variable-effort programs. Electronic readouts include speed, distance, elapsed time, and total calories. The TR901 also comes with a new "cool down" feature: When you have finished your workout, the unit automatically goes into a two-minute "cooling down" period instead of coming to an abrupt stop. This unit will only operate with a special safety key in place.

Specifications: height, 52"; width, 28½"; length, 69"; weight, 200 lbs.
Warranty: 1 year, labor; 3 year, parts (U.S. only); lifetime, frame
Manufacturer's Suggested Retail Price: $3,295
Approximate Low Price: $3,295

NordicTrack PowerTread 3000L

Recommended

The NordicTrack PowerTread 3000L is a rugged treadmill designed for serious home walking or running. Its three-horsepower motor turns the belt from 0 to 12 mph. Grade can also be adjusted from flat to a 12 percent incline. The full-stride deck (20"×60") can accommodate tall users and has an adjustable cushioning deck with a two-ply belt to reduce joint stress during use. When used with the included CardioSport transmitter, this unit will automatically adjust incline and speed to maintain optimal heart rate for your age and weight. Eight preprogrammed workouts can also be used, including three pulse-driven workouts that vary speed and incline. The 3000L maintains two memory profiles and has a quick-start button. Weight loss, fat burn, aerobic, and fitness test programs are also included. The easy-to-read display offers information on elapsed time, distance, incline, speed, pulse, and calories. Built-in accessories include a book holder and hand weights. For space-saving purposes, this unit folds for storage.

Specifications: height, 72¼"; width, 36"; length, 53"; weight, 260 lbs.
Warranty: 2 year (limited)
Manufacturer's Suggested Retail Price: $2,499
Approximate Low Price: $2,000

HOME GYMS

Home gyms have made enormous strides in recent years, and they are now more advanced then ever before. Many units offer many exercise options including rowing, leg curls, leg extensions, inner and outer thigh exercises, abdomen crunches, and pull-downs. Knowing what types of regular exercise you prefer will enable you to choose the best equipment.

Keep in mind that home gyms take up space, however, so you will require a space that measures at least 10×10 feet. Write down the dimensions of the room in which you plan to set up the gym and carry that information with you while shopping.

FEATURES

Quality construction is easy to spot in home gyms. The tube frame should be at least two-inches square, cables should be aircraft-grade and coated, pulleys should be easy to adjust (usually by setting a pin), benches and seats should be padded and covered with an easy-to-clean material, and the finish should be chrome or enamel. Cost increasing features or accessories include multistation capabilities, ease of switching from one exercise to another, additional weights, rubber bands, flexible rods (as add-on features), ease of resistance settings, and a lifetime warranty.

Vectra On-Line 1800

Recommended

The Vectra On-Line 1800 is a multi-station home gym equipped with many features found on machines in health clubs. Over 30 different exercises can be done on the On-Line 1800. The weight stack is 210 pounds, in 10-pound increments. The press station offers quick-lock press and ball bearings. The basic 235-pound plates are expandable up to 285 pounds. All pulleys are reinforced 4½-inch nylon with ball bearing hubs. The ⅛-inch aircraft-quality cables are internally lubricated and nylon coated, with a tensile strength rated at 2,000 pounds. Standard accessories include a lat bar, a curl bar, padded ankle straps, a D-handle, a padded abdomen strap, a squat attachment, weight stack guards, and a lat hold-down attachment. Optional equipment available includes cable-adapter clips, an accessory rack, a custom handle kit, and a 260-pound weight stack (instead of the standard 235-pound). This unit's high price puts it in the Recommended rather than the Best Buy category, but if you have the space and the cash, this home gym is worth considering.

Specifications: height, 73"; width, 96"; depth, 132"; weight, 677 lbs.
Warranty: 1 year, upholstery; 5 years, weight stacks and pulleys; 10 years, frame
Manufacturer's Suggested Retail Price: $4,300 (deluxe kit)
Approximate Low Price: $4,300

Soloflex 01097

Recommended

Soloflex has been around for 20 years and is probably the best-known home gym in the world. It offers anaerobic and aerobic exercises. Instead of actual weights, Soloflex utilizes weight straps, which resemble large rubber bands, in 2.5-, 5-, 10-, 25-, 50-, and 100-pound sizes. The user increases resistance simply by adding more weight straps. The straight weight bar has no grips, so it offers unlimited hand-spacing, much like a free-weight barbell. Optional iron plates can be added to the basic weight straps up to a 900-pound limit (400 pounds in straps, 500 pounds in plates). The barbell arm is designed to float so it overloads your weaker side with more exercise; this develops the weaker side faster until both sides are equal. Several optional accessories are available including a leg extension attachment and a butterfly attachment.

Specifications: height, 72"; width, 48"; depth, 48"; weight, 170 lbs.
Warranty: 30 days, money back guarantee; 5 years (limited)
Manufacturer's Suggested Retail Price: $1,195 (includes optional accessories)
Approximate Low Price: $1,195

STAIR CLIMBERS

Stair climbers are excellent machines for burning up calories and exercising the major muscle groups of the lower body. Add-on accessories for the upper body can provide a total body workout. An all-out workout on a stair climber can consume as much energy as you are capable of producing.

The best stair climbers keep your feet on an even plane with the floor at all times, allowing natural foot articulation. Some machines, however, prevent extreme foot flexion without keeping their steps completely horizontal.

When you shop for a stair climber, look for sturdy, padded handrails to aid balance, electronic programs to keep you interested, and easy-to-set resistance settings. A sturdy steel or aluminum frame is a must. Cost increasing features include advanced electronics and console, heart rate monitoring during exercise, automatic programming that changes resistance at preset intervals, and extended warranty coverage.

Tectrix Personal Climber

✔ BEST BUY

The Tectrix Personal Climber utilizes a patented cable drive system for smooth, quiet operation. A patented friction brake system allows consistent and precise speed control across a wide range of climbing speeds, from 10 to 150 feet per minute. This unit features three individual user profiles with 15 difficulty levels, plus a manual program with 39 difficulty levels. The self-leveling peddles operate independently, staying horizontal throughout all phases of the workout. The large surface of the pedals provides stable support. The monitor's LED display is easy to read and shows both progress and level of difficulty. The monitor registers the number of feet climbed per minute, the program in use, distance traveled, calories burned per hour, heart rate (with the optional transmitter accessory), and time remaining/elapsed or intervals.

Specifications: height, 59"; width, 31"; depth, 43"; weight, 151 lbs.

Warranty: 1 year, labor; 3 years, parts
Manufacturer's Suggested Retail Price: $2,295
Approximate Low Price: $2,000

Stairmaster 4000PT

Recommended

The rugged and dependable Stairmaster 4000PT is found in health clubs and homes everywhere. This climber features four-bar linkage on the pedal arms to keep the pedals parallel to the ground throughout the stroke. It also has comfortable, padded handrails and an electromagnetic brake that precisely controls pedal descent, from 26 to 138 steps per minute. The monitor charts elapsed time, step rate, cumulative work output, and instant/average power; it also produces a progress report. In addition to the one manual control setting, seven preprogrammed courses are also available. This climber offers 20 levels of difficulty as well as exercise periods from 1 to 60 minutes in duration. The 4000PT is a rugged, dependable machine.

Specifications: height, 58"; width, 32"; depth, 40½"; weight, 130 lbs.
Warranty: 3 years, parts
Manufacturer's Suggested Retail Price: $2,295
Approximate Low Price: $2,295

Tunturi C525i

Budget Buy

The economical Tunturi C525i is a suitable entry-level climber. It features independent foot action, easily adjustable resistance cylinders, and padded handlebars. The 12 preset resistance levels are adjusted by simply turning a dial. This unit has a carbon steel frame and a wide base for stability. A monitor charts elapsed time, steps per minute, calories per minute, and total calories burned. The padded handlebars are conveniently positioned.

Specifications: height, 56"; width, 26"; depth, 38"; weight, 79 lbs.

Warranty: 2 years, parts; 10 years, structural components
Manufacturer's Suggested Retail Price: $449
Approximate Low Price: $400

SKI MACHINES

Cross-country skiing provides total body fitness. The poling motion builds upper-body strength, the leg motion builds leg and lower-back strength, and combined motions add to a complete cardiovascular workout. Ski machines duplicate the total workout of cross-country skiing in a nonimpact manner that does not require snow.

There are two basic types of ski machines: independent leg motion and dependent leg motion. The former is harder to master but offers a better workout and a closer simulation of real cross-country skiing. Dependent models commonly cost more. Worthwhile features include an LCD (liquid crystal display) monitor with a variety of functions, a variable incline, and preset resistance settings. Most ski machines fold for storage and some have wheels for easy movement. Try several machines before making your final choice.

NordicTrack Classic Pro Skier 28601

✓BEST BUY

The Classic Pro Skier is a popular ski simulator from NordicTrack. It is constructed from oak and steel and features a single flywheel for resistance. Upper-body workouts are possible through the use of the arm-exercise assembly. Resistance for both arms and legs can be independently adjusted. Elevation can also be manually adjusted. An electronic workout monitor tracks personal fitness progress. This unit folds for convenient storage. Optional accessories include a book holder and a heart rate monitor.

Specifications: height, 88" (maximum); width, 36"; depth, 96"; weight, 53 lbs.
Warranty: 1 year, parts and labor (limited)
Manufacturer's Suggested Retail Price: $500
Approximate Low Price: $450

NordicTrack 900-T

Recommended

The NordicTrack 900-T is a top-of-the-line ski exerciser, built to last from black anodized aluminum components. The 900-T features an easy-to-learn training rail system and the patented flywheel and one-way clutch system of other NordicTrack ski machines. It has independent resistance for both upper and lower body exercise. It includes a pneumatic elevation tower that offers inclines from 2 to 10 degrees. The battery-powered electronic console indicates speed, distance, programmable time, and calories burned. The high price tag of this unit puts it in the Recommended rather than the Best Buy category.

Specifications: height, 12" plus user height; width, 24"; length, 84"; weight, 105 lbs.
Warranty: 1 year (limited)
Manufacturer's Suggested Retail Price: $2,499
Approximate Low Price: $2,000

TOTAL BODY MACHINES

Total body conditioning machines are a new concept in fitness. Although they resemble ski simulators and striders in use, these units allow you to perform a number of exercises at the same time—hence the name "total body machines." Prices are high but these machines offer no-impact, aerobic exercise and a terrific total body workout. In addition, these machines are complete; no cost increasing features or accessories are offered.

Reebok Body Mill

✓ BEST BUY

The Reebok Body Mill is designed to be used by all family members of all abilities. The unit resembles a ski machine—there are poles for both hands and the feet slide on skatelike pads. A padded waist belt holds the user from behind and a computer-controlled electromagnetic brake provides resistance. This unit will tone muscles in the chest, arms, back, hips, legs, and glutei. The frame and towers are welded, high-tensile-strength, aluminum extrusions, and the tower supports are welded structural steel. All bearings are factory lubricated and sealed, so they are virtually maintenance free. This machine comes with eight preprogrammed exercise options, from "walk in the park" to "Himalayan trek." In addition, up to five custom profiles can be created and stored in memory. A vacuum fluorescent display (VFD) monitor registers goal speed, actual speed, total distance, time remaining (or elapsed), energy expenditure (in calories per hour and watts), total calories, and heart rate. VFD and program instructions are available in English, German, Japanese, and Spanish.

Specifications: height, 60"; width, 29"; length, 85"; weight, 305 lbs.
Warranty: 2 years, parts and labor (limited)
Manufacturer's Suggested Retail Price: $4,995
Approximate Low Price: $4,500

Reebok Body Trec

✓BEST BUY

The Reebok Body Trec provides a total body workout for all family members, regardless of ability level. This unit resembles a walking or jogging machine. Your feet move in a natural elliptical motion, providing a no-impact workout for less stress on the joints. As you walk, your hands grasp poles that move in conjunction with your leg motion. This results in a smooth, fluid movement that tones arms, chest, back, hips, legs, and glutei. The unit can be operated in forward or in reverse. It is constructed of welded structural steel and requires no lubrication. Its eight preprogrammed exercise courses include Vail Pass, steady climb, and competition. The easy-to-read display registers calories burned, calories per hour, distance traveled, speed attained, and time remaining or elapsed. An optional heart rate monitor is also available.

Specifications: height, 64¼"; width, 29"; length, 65"; weight, 290 lbs.

Warranty: 2 years, parts and labor (limited)
Manufacturer's Suggested Retail Price: $3,595
Approximate Low Price: $3,000

ELLIPTICAL MACHINES

Elliptical machines are a relatively new product, resulting from the popularity of the commercial units found in health clubs. The term "elliptical" comes from the oblong pattern the pedals make when in motion. Elliptical machines—or cross-trainers, as they are sometimes called—combine the exercise motions of some of the most popular pieces of equipment—treadmill, stair climber, stationary bike, and ski machine—in one machine. The end product is a low impact machine that gives a great cardiovascular workout and works a wide range of lower body muscles.

Because elliptical machines can be adjusted, you can glide (in an elliptical motion) as you would on a ski machine or, with a simple adjustment of the pedals, get more of a stair-stepping or bike action. Your feet remain flat at all times within the pedals so there is no strain on back, hips, or joints.

All elliptical machines are not created equal and you should try out several models before purchasing. Inspect the welded parts, flywheel, resistance belt, and materials used for construction. A quality machine will be obvious. If you are serious about exercising with an elliptical machine, expect to pay at least $2,000 for a well-made unit. However, if you're just getting started and can do without all the bells and whistles, you'll pay a lot less. Features that can add to the cost of a home elliptical machine include electronic controls for adjusting the ramp, attachments for upper-body workouts, and solid construction for long life of the machine.

Precor EFX 5.21s

Recommended

The EFX 521s is the home version of the elliptical machine Precor introduced last year in health clubs across America. This full-featured elliptical machine provides a no-impact workout, so it can be used by anyone—even those with knee, ankle, hip, and back difficulties. It can also be operated in reverse to target muscles in your lower back, hips, hamstrings, and calves. The EFX 5.21s features an electronic console, which displays a variety of information including strides, strides per minute, calories, time, resistance, and ramp incline. In addition, 12 different programs are available with the touch of a finger. Eddy current resistance (the faster you go the greater the resistance) applies quiet, frictionless, resistance against the rotation of the flywheel. This is a well-made machine that will provide years of interesting exercise for the lower body.

Specifications: height, 63"; width, 30"; length, 76"; weight, 160 lbs.
Warranty: 1 year, labor; 3 years, parts; lifetime, frame
Manufacturer's Suggested Retail Price: $2,999
Approximate Low Price: $2,550

NordicTrack 910e Ellipse 33130

Budget Buy

The economical NordicTrack 910e Ellipse is a basic elliptical workout machine that features a total body workout with minimal impact on the user. It has dual rotation, adjustable pedal placement, a 14-pound flywheel, and drag strap resistance that is manually controlled by a knob. The single window, LCD console is nonprogrammable and indicates speed, time, and calories burned. Standard features include a book holder and water bottle holder. Perfect for the entry-level user.

Warranty: 1 year (limited)
Manufacturer's Suggested Retail Price: $400
Approximate Low Price: $300

HOME IMPROVEMENT

Maintaining a home—whether it be a house, condo, or apartment—can be a time-consuming and expensive task. First and foremost, a home must be kept safe from such threats as fire and carbon monoxide fumes. Also important is keeping up with repairs and maintenance. The products in this chapter can help you do both.

If you want additional information on the safety and effectiveness of these or any other units you may consider purchasing, you can consult public safety organizations such as the National Safety Council.

BEST BUYS '99

Our Best Buy, Recommended, and Budget Buy home improvement products are listed below. Products within each category are listed according to quality. The best of the Best Buys is listed first, followed by our second choice, and so on. A Best Buy, Recommended, or Budget Buy designation only applies to the model listed—it does not necessarily apply to other models made by the same manufacturer or to an entire product line.

SAFETY EQUIPMENT

Smoke alarms, carbon monoxide (CO) detectors, and fire extinguishers are important safety equipment that should exist in every home or apartment. Smoke alarms can provide an early warning of a fire in your home. CO detectors can also alert you and your family if this deadly gas is present. The proper use of a reliable fire extinguisher can save you thousands of dollars in damage by putting out a small fire quickly.

SMOKE DETECTORS

Fortunately, smoke alarms are present in most homes today. Because of a public awareness program ("Change the battery in your smoke alarm when you change your clock for daylight savings"), these devices have been credited with saving thousands of lives and millions of dollars in property damage. Some types of smoke alarms are wired directly into the electrical system of the home and have a battery backup system in the event of a power failure. These hardwired smoke alarms are now required by building codes in new construction in many parts of the country. Smoke alarms with a flashing strobe light—as well as an alarm—are also available and are a good choice for the hearing impaired.

Smoke alarms operate by one of two methods: ionization or photoelectricity. Ionization involves the use of a small, harmless amount of radioactive material that makes the air in an internal chamber conduct electricity. When smoke passes into this chamber, the flow of electricity is interrupted and the alarm is sounded. Ionization alarms are inexpensive (commonly under $20) and widely available. They pose no threat to your health or the environment. Photoelectric smoke detectors, like all photoelectric systems, shine a tiny beam of light toward a sensor. When smoke passes through this beam, it breaks the stream and the alarm is sounded. Some high-end units use both methods.

All smoke detectors reviewed in this section have a test button so you can check the condition of the battery and make certain the unit is working properly. One of the units can be checked by shining a flashlight at the button—a handy feature if the unit is located on a high ceiling or in a stairwell. (To test units without this feature, use a broom handle.) All smoke detectors "chirp" when the battery is low on power. Never ignore this sound or remove the battery to stop it—replace the battery immediately. Also, never paint a smoke alarm—paint can clog small holes and render the unit inoperable.

CARBON MONOXIDE DETECTORS

There is a growing awareness of carbon monoxide (CO) poisoning in America. This deadly gas can be present in the home as a result of incomplete combustion in any fuel-burning appliance, including fireplaces. Exposure to low levels of CO can cause flulike symptoms such as dizziness, headache, fatigue, nausea, confusion, and irritability. Prolonged exposure to higher levels of CO causes fainting and, in extreme cases, can lead to coma, brain damage, or death.

The best way to protect yourself and family from the dangers of CO is to make certain that all fuel-burning appliances are running properly, including kitchen ranges and ovens, furnaces, clothes dryers, water heaters, wood-burning stoves, fireplaces, and space heaters. Check the vent pipes on these appliances for obstructions or damage. (Local utility companies and suppliers of home heating fuel will usually check your appliances for free or for a minimal charge.) Be aware that automobile exhaust contains CO and can enter a home if a car is left running in an attached garage.

As a rule, a well-ventilated home with properly operating appliances should have minimum accumulations of CO. Keep in mind, however, if your home is tightly sealed against the weather (which is common during the heating season), the danger of CO accumulation increases. The only way to detect this colorless, odorless, deadly gas is to install a CO detector in the home. The Consumer Product Safety Commission (CPSC) recommends installing at least one carbon monoxide detector with an audible alarm near the sleeping area of the home. Most CO detectors resemble smoke alarms in appearance. Some units plug into an electrical outlet in the home and have a battery backup as well. Others are operated by a 9-volt battery.

FIRE EXTINGUISHERS

All fire extinguishers are rated by Underwriter's Laboratories, Inc. (UL) according to the types of fires they are designed to put out. There are three classes of fires. Class A fires involve paper, wood, cloth, rubber, and some plastics. Class B fires involve flammable liquids such as gasoline, paint thinner, grease, motor oil, and solvents. Class C fires are electrical in nature. As a rule, fire extinguishers rated A, B, and C are best for home use.

All fire extinguishers also receive a numeric rating, which indicates the size of the fire a particular unit is capable of fighting. For example, a 4-A rating means that the unit will put out twice as much Class A fire as a unit with a 2-A rating. There are no numeric ratings for C class (electrical) fires, because the C rating simply means that the extinguishing agent in the unit is not electrically conductive.

Check the dial gauge on your fire extinguisher monthly. The needle on the gauge indicates whether the unit is operable or in need of recharging. When required, have the unit recharged by a qualified professional. Recharging is required after every use, no matter how brief. Look in the Yellow Pages under "Fire Extinguishers."

SMOKE DETECTORS

First Alert 10 Year Lithium Power SA10YRB/C

BEST BUY

This is a top-of-the-line ionization smoke detector with an 85-decibel alarm horn. The unit has a clear plastic test button for testing the unit and a blue plastic button that silences the unit for about 15 minutes if it sounds accidentally because of nuisance smoke (cooking smoke in the kitchen, for example). The unit must be activated by turning a screw on the back before use. Its lithium batteries are permanently installed and cannot be replaced, so you must buy a new unit when the 10-year battery dies. The alarm will beep once a minute (for about 28 days) when the detector requires replacement. The unit comes with a plastic mounting bracket, mounting screws, and screw anchors. An informative booklet is also included.

Specifications: diameter, $5\frac{1}{4}$"; length, $6\frac{7}{8}$"; width $10\frac{1}{8}$"; depth, $2\frac{3}{4}$"; weight, 9 oz.
Warranty: 10 years (limited)
Manufacturer's Suggested Retail Price: $27
Approximate Low Price: not available

First Alert Double System SA301B/C

BEST BUY

The First Alert Double System is a high-quality, dual ionization-and-photoelectric smoke and fire detector. The unit has two test buttons and a 85-decibel alarm horn. One of the test buttons is clear plastic and flashes red about four times a minute to let you know the unit is working. The alarm will beep six times a minute (for about 28 days) when the battery requires replacement.

It comes with a 9-volt battery, mounting hardware (including screws and screw anchors), and a thorough instruction booklet. The battery is installed in the back of the unit.

Specifications: diameter, 5¼"; height, 5 11/16"; width 5¾"; depth, 2½"; weight, 11 oz.
Warranty: 10 years (limited)
Manufacturer's Suggested Retail Price: $25
Approximate Low Price: not available

First Alert Hall & Stairway SA150B/C

✓BEST BUY

The First Alert SA150B/C uses the ionization method of smoke detection and—as its name applies—is a good choice for stairs and hallways. The unit has a built-in "escape" light to illuminate the way through the dark. The light is activated at the same time as the alarm and the bulb is replaceable. A gold-colored test button can be activated either by pressing or by shining a flashlight from up to 15 feet away. The alarm horn sounds at an attention grabbing 85 decibels. The alarm will beep once a minute for about 28 days when the battery requires replacement. This unit requires two 9-volt batteries (which are included). Batteries are installed in the face of the unit after opening the hinged cover. The unit comes with an informative booklet and complete mounting hardware.

Specifications: diameter, 5¼"; height, 1 15/16"; width, 5¾"; depth, 1 15/16"; weight 8 oz.
Warranty: 10 years (limited)
Manufacturer's Suggested Retail Price: $25
Approximate Low Price: not available

Kidde Night Hawk Elite PE9N

✓BEST BUY

The Night Hawk Elite utilizes the photoelectric method of smoke detection and is especially effective at detecting smoldering fires in the home. This unit has a test button that verifies battery and alarm operation. It also includes a "hush" button that can be used to silence the alarm if it sounds accidentally because of nuisance smoke (cooking smoke in the kitchen, for example). The unit comes supplied with a 9-volt battery, mounting hardware (including screws and screw anchors), and an informative booklet.

Specifications: width, 7"; diameter, 2½"; height, 10½"; weight 1 lb.
Warranty: 5 years (limited)
Manufacturer's Suggested Retail Price: $25
Approximate Low Price: $20

CO DETECTORS

First Alert SC01

BEST BUY

The First Alert SC01 is the first unit in the industry to detect both smoke and elevated levels of CO. This smoke alarm uses the ionization method of smoke detection. When smoke is detected, three long beeps sound and a red colored flame indicator flashes. When elevated levels of CO are detected, a single on-and-off tone sounds with a flashing red dot pattern. A large test/silence button is located on the face of the unit. A green battery-indicator light flashes several times a minute to let you know the unit is operational. The unit "chirps" when the battery requires replacement. A yellow service light flashes when the unit should be replaced. This unit can be mounted on the ceiling or the wall. The unit is supplied with a 9-volt battery, mounting hardware (including screws and anchors), and an informative booklet.

Specifications: diameter 5¼"; height, 7¼"; width, 8½"; depth, 2⅛"; weight 11 oz.
Warranty: 5 years (limited)
Manufacturer's Suggested Retail Price: $52
Approximate Low Price: not available

First Alert FCD3

✓BEST BUY

The First Alert FCD3 CO detector is a top-of-the-line, 9-volt battery operated unit that can be placed or mounted anywhere in the home. To activate this unit, simply pull the factory seal tab to expose the internal sensor, which lasts for approximately five years. This detector has a test button that can also be used to silence the alarm. The green battery button flashes twice a minute to indicate the unit is operational. The alarm horn sounds at 85 decibels. This unit is supplied with mounting hardware and an informative booklet.

Specifications: height, 5⅝"; width, 8⅝"; depth, 2⅛"; weight 11 oz.
Warranty: 5 years (limited)
Manufacturer's Suggested Retail Price: $40
Approximate Low Price: not available

Enzone Air Zone II

✓BEST BUY

Designed to plug into any electrical outlet, the Enzone Air Zone II comes with an eight-foot power cord so the unit can be mounted at or about eye level (but no less than six inches from the ceiling). The manufacturer feels this location is more suitable for detecting CO levels than the standard outlet height. Since carbon monoxide is lighter than air, concentration will be greater close to the ceiling. The unit is equipped with a test/reset button, a green power-on light, a yellow warning light (for CO levels from 50 to 100 PPM), and red alarm light. A battery backup (which requires six AA batteries) is also included. The red light will blink and the alarm will chirp when batteries require replacement. The alarm horn sounds at 85 decibels. The Air Zone is supplied with an AC adapter and an informative booklet.

Specifications: height, 7"; width, 3"; depth, 1"; weight 1 lb.
Warranty: 5 years (limited)
Manufacturer's Suggested Retail Price: $40
Approximate Low Price: not available

FIRE EXTINGUISHERS

First Alert FE1A10GW

✓ BEST BUY

The First Alert FE1A10GW fire extinguisher is a dependable, multipurpose unit for fighting all types of small fires around the home. This lightweight fire extinguisher is powerful enough to douse all classes of fires. The unit has an ergonomic plastic handle/trigger, a pull ring, and an easy-to-read dial-type gauge that tells at a glance the charge condition. This unit has a quick release bracket for wall mounting and easy-to-read three-step instructions printed on the side. This extinguisher cannot be recharged.

Specifications: height, 15½"; diameter, 3"; weight, 3.6 lbs.; rating 1-A, 10-B:C
Warranty: 5 years (limited)
Manufacturer's Suggested Retail Price: $20
Approximate Low Price: $16

Kidde KHO-FA340

✓ BEST BUY

The Kidde KHO-FA340 is a good multipurpose unit for the home. While the unit is rated for fighting all classes of fires, it is especially useful for B:C class fires. It has plastic handles, a plastic break-away pull ring, a dial-type gauge for checking the charge condition, and a flexible hose. It is supplied with a plastic, U-shaped wall-mounting bracket that holds the unit just below the handles. Easy-to-read, three-step instructions are printed on the side of the unit.

Specifications: (packaging) width, 5.7"; height, 17"; diameter, 4.8"; weight, 9 lbs; Rating 2-A, 10-B:C
Warranty: 5 years (limited)
Manufacturer's Suggested Retail Price: $30
Approximate Low Price: $30

GARAGE DOOR OPENERS

Garage door openers offer both convenience and safety because they allow you to open and close your garage door while remaining in your vehicle. They are widely available in home centers and range in price from $130 to $350. Installation is usually not difficult but requires basic power and hand tools as well as do-it-yourself skills. Complete installation should take less than a day, and the work will be easier to accomplish with an extra pair of hands. Some units come complete with a guide rail, while others require that you purchase the appropriate size rail for your installation. This can add from $80 to $90 to the price.

SAFETY FEATURES

All new garage door openers are required to have several safety features to prevent injury. One feature automatically reverses door travel within two seconds after coming in contact with an obstruction. Another common safety feature is an electric eye that reverses door travel if anything gets in its path. The electric eye is mounted about 12 inches up from the floor on the door jamb.

REMOTE CONTROLS

Today, almost all garage door openers come with at least one remote control and a wall-mounted, doorbell-like button for operating the door from inside the garage. Advanced security features are standard on all high-end and many mid-priced units. Sears and Whistler, for example, offer remote controls that select a new access code from billions of combinations each time the unit is used, and that number is never repeated. Many types of accessories are also available to make opening and closing your garage door more convenient. These include keychain-size remote controls, exterior keypads, and exterior security lighting systems.

Sears Craftsman 53662

✓BEST BUY

If you're looking for a trustworthy, mid-priced garage door opener, this ½-horsepower chain-driven unit fits the bill. Safety features include an infrared sensor that stops and reverses door travel before making contact with an obstruction, a safety reverse that automatically reverses when door movement meets an object blocking its path, a 4½-minute light delay, a switch that locks out all handheld radio signals to prevent access while you are away, and an emergency release that allows manual door operation during power failure. A four-foot power cord plugs into a standard grounded outlet. A control console lets you operate the door from inside the garage. The unit comes with two remote control units that automatically choose a new entry code each time the door is opened. This unit can also be used with compact and keypad wireless controls, which are available at additional cost. An easy-to-use installation and maintenance manual is included, along with a 24-hour toll-free assistance number.

Warranty: 1 year; 5 years, motor; extended warranty available at additional cost
Manufacturer's Suggested Retail Price: $170
Approximate Low Price: $170

Whistler ST201

✓BEST BUY

The Whistler ST201 is a top-of-the-line chain-drive unit that features a ⅓-horsepower motor for dependable operation of garage doors up to 7½ feet high. This opener features Secure-Code, which chooses a new code each time the opener button is pressed. Each time one of 4.2 billion codes is automatically selected it is never repeated. This unit features five safety features: electronic instant reverse system, which automatically opens door if an obstruction is met during closing cycle; a Safe-T-Monitor, which electronically monitors the force-resistance of a door's closing cycle (when the force exceeds a safe limit, Safe-T-Monitor causes the door to reverse and open); an infrared reversing system, which stops and reverses a closing door when the infrared beam detects an object blocking its path; a Safe-T-Cycle System, which opens the door it hasn't closed completely in 23 seconds (a light also flashes when this system is activated); and Constant Contact to Close System, which causes the opener to accept a closing signal only from the wall button (the button must be held down through the entire closing cycle or the door will automatically open). This unit comes with one handheld, two-button transmitter; a lighted wall-mounted push button; and an informative installation booklet, along with a 24-hour, toll-free assistance number.

Warranty: 1 year parts; 5 years, motor
Manufacturer's Suggested Retail Price: $152
Approximate Low Price: $130

Sears Craftsman 53664

Recommended

The Sears Craftsman 53664 is a quiet and dependable ½-horsepower belt-drive unit. It features Sears' Motor Vibrations Isolation System, which reduces motor vibration and results in quieter operation, and has a steel-reinforced polyurethane drive belt. Standard safety features include an infrared safety reversing sensor, which stops the door and reverses door travel before making contact with an obstruction; safety reverse, which automatically reverses when it meets an obstacle blocking its path; a 4½-minute light delay; and an emergency release, which allows manual door operation during power failure. The four-foot power cord plugs into a standard grounded outlet. A control console allows for operation of the door from inside the garage. The unit comes with two remote control units for keyless entry system. Both remotes feature a "rolling code" security system that automatically chooses a new entry code—from a base of 100 billion codes—each time the door is opened. This unit can also be used with compact remote control, which is available at additional cost. An easy-to-use installation and maintenance manual is included, and a 24-hour toll free number should help with installation problems.

Warranty: 90 days, labor; 1 year, parts; 5 years, motor; extended warranty available at additional cost
Manufacturer's Suggested Retail Price: $220
Approximate Low Price: $220

Whistler ST401

Recommended

The Whistler ST401 is a chain-drive unit that includes a ½-horsepower motor for dependable operation of garage doors up to 7½ feet high. This unit features SecureCode, which chooses a new code each time the opener button is pressed. Each time one of 4.2 billion codes is automatically selected it is never repeated. This unit features five safety features: electronic instant reverse system, which automatically opens the door if an obstruction is met during closing cycle; a Safe-T-Monitor, which electronically monitors the force-resistance of a door's closing cycle (when the force exceeds a safe limit, Safe-T-Monitor causes the door to reverse and open); a Safe-T-Close infrared reversing system, which stops and reverses a closing door when the infrared beam detects an object in its path; a Safe-T-Cycle System, which opens the door if it has not closed completely in 23 seconds; and a Constant Contact to Close System, which causes the opener to accept a closing signal only from the wall button (the button must be held down through the entire closing cycle, or else the door will automatically open). This unit comes with a handheld transmitter, a lighted wall-mounted push button, and an informative installation booklet. A 24-hour, toll-free telephone number is available for questions about installation.

Warranty: 2 years, parts; 10 years, motor
Manufacturer's Suggested Retail Price: $160
Approximate Low Price: $150

POWER HAND TOOLS

There is a trend among consumers to purchase higher-priced power hand tools rather than less-expensive units. Extensive market studies by a leading manufacturer have shown that many more people are doing projects themselves rather than hiring a contractor for the work. As a result, sales for better-quality, higher-priced tools increase annually, while sales for lower-priced units remain relatively flat.

For example, a lower-priced drill is designed to provide decades of use for the average homeowner, who may use the drill for a total of ten hours per year. If that same homeowner decides to build a redwood deck, which may require the use of an electric drill for possibly six hours a day for several days, the drill will fail before the project is finished. It has been demonstrated that the current average consumer—who is most probably a "baby boomer"—will buy a higher-priced electric drill for several reasons. First, he or she usually has more disposable income. The second is that the old drill in the workshop or garage is just that—old. The third reason is that the consumer does not want to buy another drill as long as he or she lives and will usually purchase a mid-priced (or often a high-end) drill.

TYPES OF POWER TOOLS

Cordless Drills: These are increasing in popularity and are now offered in 9.6-, 12-, 14.4-, and 18-volt models. Cordless circular and reciprocating saws are also available in 14.4-, and 18-volt versions. Many units are offered in kit form that typically contains a drill (and a saw) two batteries, a charger, and a carrying case. While cordless tools are quite capable, their price tag is commonly two or three times as much as a similar corded unit.

Circular Saws and Jigsaws: These tools are handy for do-it-yourself projects, and there is a wide selection currently available. Improvements such as lightweight housings, no-mar bases, and quick-change blade features (on jigsaws) have all been introduced in the past year.

Random-orbit Finish Sanders: Several companies now offer random-orbit finish sanders for both homeowners and professionals. Most units include a dust collection canister. The Profile Sander (by Porter-Cable) is a handy detail sander with a variety of special heads for sanding irregular shapes. This is an ideal sander for furniture and molding refinishing. A belt sander is also a handy tool for larger sanding and shaping projects.

Routers: This is a handy power tool for a variety of home improvement projects. There is a wide selection of units available. Generally speaking, there are three basic types: two-handed routers, plunge routers, and one-handed or barrel routers. The basic two-handed router can be used for all routing tasks and is usually the lowest priced router on the market. Two-handed routers will have a horsepower rating of from 7/8 to 3 1/4. Plunge routers have advanced features and are more versatile for all types of woodworking. Horsepower ratings for plunge routers are from 1 1/2 to 3 1/4 horsepower. One-handed, or barrel routers, are primarily designed for trimming laminate material. They have a power rating in amps (from 3.8 to 5.6 amps) rather than horsepower. A router table will greatly increase the capabilities of both two-handed and plunge routers. All manufacturers offer a good selection of routers for both do-it-yourself projects and commercial applications.

ELECTRIC DRILLS

Skill Warrior 14.4 Volt Cordless Drill 2582-01

This Skill Warrior 14.4 volt cordless drill is an excellent choice for use around the home and shop. This lightweight drill/driver features a midhandle design with two gear ranges (0-400 and 400-1,200 rpm). It also has reversible and variable speed features plus a keyless chuck. The forward/reverse switch is located above the trigger. Four planetary gears deliver 175 inch/pounds of torque. This well-balanced cordless drill comes with two batteries, one-hour charger, and a plastic carrying case.

Specifications: 3/8″ keyless chuck; weight 9.5 lbs.
Warranty: 2 years
Manufacturer's Suggested Retail Price: $215
Approximate Low Price: not available

Black & Decker Firestorm 14.4 Cordless Drill HP532K-2

The Firestorm 14.4 is probably the most versatile for use around the home and shop. It features a 24-position clutch, two-speed gear box (high and low), variable speed (0-900 rpm), electronic brake, and an ergonomically balanced, midhandle design with a rubber comfort grip. The forward/reverse switch is conveniently located above the trigger. It has a one-handed keyless chuck with an automatic spindle lock for quick-changing of drill bits. This drill can reach up to 300 inch/pounds of torque, so it is powerful enough for almost any drilling/fastening task. The unit comes with a high-capacity battery and a three-hour charger.

Specifications: ⅜″ keyless chuck; weight 5.3 lbs.
Warranty: 2 years
Manufacturer's Suggested Retail Price: $129
Approximate Low Price: not available

Skil Classic Corded Drill 6245:44

Recommended

The Skil Classic is a good choice for a general purpose household drill. This unit features a 4-amp motor that is double insulated and has a 6-foot power cord. The chuck is keyed and the key is stored just below the handle on the power cord. This variable-speed drill (up to 2,500 rpm) has a reversing feature. A lock-on button is located on the bottom of the handle. A spirit level is located on the top of this drill and is an aid for drilling vertical holes. The Skil Classic comes with three steel, twist drill bits: 3/32, 3/16, and ¼ inch.

Specifications: ⅜″ keyless chuck; weight, 3.6 lbs.
Warranty: 2 years
Manufacturer's Suggested Retail Price: $38
Approximate Low Price: $38

ELECTRIC SANDERS

Black & Decker Mouse Sander/Polisher MS500K

✓BEST BUY

The Mouse Sander/Polisher is a versatile power tool for general sanding, polishing, and scrubbing. This palm-sized unit resembles a miniature iron (with V-shaped base). It includes velcro-backed sanding, polishing, and scrubbing pads, which attach or can be removed quickly—simply stick or peel off. The Mouse runs at 11,000 orbits per minute and features soft rubber grips, a one-finger on/off button, and an ergonomic design for comfort and control. The Mouse is sold in a storage case with 23 assorted polishing, sanding, and scrubbing accessories.

Specifications: pad, 3¾×½"; weight, 1 lb. 8 oz.
Warranty: 2 years
Manufacturer's Suggested Retail Price: $40
Approximate Low Price: not available

Porter-Cable Random Orbit Sander 333

Recommended

The Porter-Cable 333 sander features a palm-grip design that is especially comfortable for smaller hands. The 1.7 amp motor powers up to 12,000 orbits per minute. A pad-control feature prevents pad spin-up when the tool is lifted off the work. This sander uses five-hole hook-and-loop paper in six different grit sizes. An easy-to-empty dust-collection canister is located on the right side of the unit. Porter-Cable includes an accessory attachment that lets you hook-up to a shop-vac.

Specifications: pad diameter, 5"; weight, 3.5 lbs.
Warranty: 1 year
Manufacturer's Suggested Retail Price: $72
Approximate Low Price: $60

Porter-Cable Belt Sander 352vs

Recommended

The Porter-Cable 352vs is a professional grade belt sander that can easily accomplish the largest sanding project. This unit features a variable speed (850-1,300 square feet per minute), seven-amp motor (its speed is adjusted with a thumb wheel). The 352vs also features a lock-on trigger, a ten-foot two-prong power cord, and a dust collection bag. Belt-tracking is adjusted with an aligning knob on the left side of the unit. This sander can use a variety of different grit sanding belts.

Specifications: weight, 10.75 lbs.
Warranty: 1 year
Manufacturer's Suggested Retail Price: $198
Approximate Low Price: $165

CIRCULAR SAWS, JIGSAWS, AND SABRE SAWS

Skil Classic Skilsaw 5275:05

✓ BEST BUY

The Skil 5275:05 fills the need of the average do-it-yourselfer. This is a reasonably priced circular saw with a number of unique features that should provide years of service. The saw features a 2.5-horsepower, double-insulated motor with a six-foot power cord. There's a two-part trigger for safety. A blade-guard lifting mechanism is conveniently located close to the front handle. The depth-of-cut adjustment scale, located on the rear of the blade guard, is clearly marked in ¼-inch increments. The table can be adjusted for bevel cuts up to 45 degrees. A ripping guide/blade wrench can be stored in the base of the unit when not in use. An adjustable dust chute is located on the upper part of the blade guard and can be hooked up to a shop vac. An adjustable line-of-cut indicator can be adjusted for blade thickness. This saw comes with a sturdy 18-tooth carbide blade.

Specifications: blade size, 7¼"; weight, 10 lbs.
Warranty: 2 years
Manufacturer's Suggested Retail Price: $60
Approximate Low Price: $60

Black & Decker WoodHawk C2020K

Recommended

The WoodHawk 6½-inch circular saw is a lightweight, well-balanced saw that is suitable for home use. A small glass window, located in the upper part of the blade guard, provides a clear view of the cutting line. The front handle is a full-bail type, which is handy for steady balance and for making straight cuts. Despite a powerful 10-amp motor, this is one of the quietest saws we tested. Features include a wraparound bail handle, an adjustable dust chute (which can be attached to a shop vac), kerf indicator markings on the shoe, and a wider, more stable base.

Specifications: blade size, 6½"; weight, 8 lbs.
Warranty: 2 years
Manufacturer's Suggested Retail Price: $50
Approximate Low Price: $40

Skil Classic 4470:44

Recommended

The Skil Classic 4470:44 features dynamic vibration reduction, which greatly reduces most vibration normally produced by jigsaws. This saw features a 4-amp, double-insulated motor with a six-foot power cord. Other features include a five-position orbital cutting action; a four-position shaft lock for scroll cutting; a dial-type speed adjustment; and an anti-splinter position on the base. A clear plastic chip deflector slides up to permit blade changes. This saw also has a contoured trigger and lock-on feature. The base can be adjusted for bevel cutting, left or right. A dust chute on the rear of this saw can be connected to a shop-vac. This saw comes with a selection of blades and a plastic carrying case.

Specifications: blade speed, 800-3,200 rpm; weight, 4.1 lbs.
Warranty: 2 years
Manufacturer's Suggested Retail Price: $60
Approximate Low Price: $60

Sears Craftsman Circular Saw 10833

Recommended

The Sears Craftsman 10833 is a powerful saw for all types of home use. When used with two hands, the unit is well-balanced. There's a large one-stage trigger (without safety lock-out). The blade can be adjusted for both depth-of-cut and bevel cuts.

Blade wrench storage is in the rear of the base assembly. A unique length-of-cut scale, located to the right of the blade (on the base assembly), is handy for determining how far you have cut into the workpiece. The two-horsepower, double-insulated motor has a six-foot, two-prong power cord. The 10833 is equipped with a 20-tooth, 7¼-inch combination blade.

Specifications: blade speed, 5,000 rpm; blade size, 7¼"; weight, 9.75 lbs.
Warranty: 1 year
Manufacturer's Suggested Retail Price: $50
Approximate Low Price: $48

Sears Craftsman Orbital Action Sabre Saw 17228

Recommended

The Orbital Action sabre saw is a good choice for general home use. This unit comes with a number of unique features and accessories that make it versatile for most sabre saw projects. It has three orbital settings and one nonorbital setting. The base plate can be adjusted for bevel cuts. It has a variable speed (up to 3,000 scrolls per minute), one-part trigger with a lock-on feature. Blades are held in place with an allen head screw. The 17228 comes with a dust-free attachment that attaches to the base and one general purpose saw blade.

Specifications: weight, 4.5 lbs.
Warranty: 1 year
Manufacturer's Suggested Retail Price: $80
Approximate Low Price: $80

ROUTERS

Sears Craftsman Router 17506

Recommended

This two-horsepower router is a two-handed unit with ample power for most routing tasks. The 17506 has a ¼-inch collet size, and can be operated from 15,000 to 25,000 rpm by turning the variable-speed control dial. The depth of cut ranges from 0 to 1½ inches in 1/64-inch increments. The spiraling depth adjuster is accurate and easy to use. This unit also features a spindle lock for easy bit changes. (The wrench for bit changes is stored on top of the router.) The handle grips are quite comfortable, and there's a lock-on feature located on the trigger handle. The router has a built-in work light and clear plastic chip shield. A dust collection system greatly cuts down on cleanup. The unit is double-insulated and has a ten-foot power cord.

Specifications: collet size, ¼"; weight, 8.69 lbs.
Warranty: 1 year
Manufacturer's Suggested Retail Price: $100
Approximate Low Price: $100

Skil Classic Router 1845:44

Recommended

The Skil 1845:44 was recently introduced to complement the other tools in the Skil Classic Series. This plunge router has a number of worthwhile features that will appeal to the amateur woodworker. The soft-start, variable-speed motor is controlled with a thumb screw located on the top of the motor housing. The trigger is located on the right handle, and there is also a lock-on feature. A collet-lock feature makes changing router bits easy, and the collet wrench is stored in the top of the unit. A clear plastic chip deflection shield is located in the front base of the unit. This unit also features an adjustable depth-of-plunge gauge, fine-depth adjustment knob, and lever-lock that locks the router in the down position.

Specifications: collet size, ¼"; weight, 7.3 lbs
Warranty: 2 years
Manufacturer's Suggested Retail Price: $119
Approximate Low Price: $119

SNOW REMOVAL

Since snow throwers are such seasonal items, you can often save money buying one off-season. Since they are pretty basic machines (and new models are rarely introduced), your choices remain consistent from year to year. Gas-powered snow throwers are generally divided into three categories, based on their horsepower and clearing path width.

SMALL SNOW THROWERS

These single-stage throwers are generally auger-propelled, and have 20- to 22-inch clearing paths. Small snow throwers are for homeowners with relatively small spaces to clear. Despite their size, these machines are capable of handling heavier snows, including compacted driveway snow. The biting action of the auger blades help propel the machine. These are the simplest snow throwers to store because they are compact and lightweight.

LARGE AND MEDIUM SNOW THROWERS

If you live in the snowbelt and have an average-size walkway or driveway, a medium snow thrower should be adequate for just about any weather surprise. They're an excellent all-around choice—neither too big nor too expensive. These two-stage snow throwers are predominantly wheel-propelled. They also have a wider clearing path. If poorly maintained or stored outside, they can be hard to start under extremely cold conditions.

Large snow throwers are for serious duty. They're an excellent choice for homes with huge driveways or long lanes. These two-stage snow throwers are more than eight horsepower and are wheel-propelled.

FEATURES AND TERMINOLOGY

Nearly all snow throwers have Tecumseh Snow King engines, which are specially engineered for cold weather and wet conditions. Electric starters are either standard or optional on most units, and we recommend them.

Auger-propelled Snow Thrower: This type of unit has rotating rubber-edged auger blades that make contact with the ground surface, propelling the snow thrower forward as the blades dig into the snow. These machines are not very effective on gravel or uneven concrete or asphalt surfaces.

Discharge Chute: This is a partially- or fully-enclosed tube that guides snow up and out. The chute is usually rotated via a crank. An adjustable deflector at the top controls throwing distance. For safety, the machine must be turned off before attempting to dislodge clogged snow or debris in the auger enclosure or discharge tube.

Impeller: A bladed wheel located behind the auger that discharges the snow at high speed into the discharge chute.

Single-stage Thrower: This type of unit uses only an auger to collect and discharge snow.

Two-stage Thrower: This type of unit uses both an auger and an impeller for efficient snow collection and discharge.

BEST BUYS '99

Our Best Buy, Recommended, and Budget Buy snow throwers are listed below. Products within each category are listed according to quality. The best of the Best Buys is listed first, followed by our second choice, and so on. A Best Buy, Recommended, or Budget Buy designation only applies to the model listed—it does not apply to other models made by the same manufacturer or to an entire product line.

SMALL SNOW THROWERS

Toro CCR2400 R GTS

✓BEST BUY

If your driveway is two cars wide and three cars long, and snows are normally moderate, this is the machine for you. This single-stage thrower uses a four-horsepower, two-cycle engine that clears a path about 20 inches wide. Toro's patented "Power Curve" curved auger blade continues to be one of the most effective and efficient ones around. This machine scrapes surfaces clean, pitching snow 25 feet. The controls are conveniently centralized, and the chute crank is easy to access. Toro's "R-tek" snow engine is guaranteed to start; however, an electric start is available as an option.

Warranty: 2 years, full; 5 years, starting guarantee
Manufacturer's Suggested Retail Price: $550
Approximate Low Price: $499

John Deere TRS22

Recommended

The venerable TRS22 is one of only a handful of under-five-horsepower, wheel-propelled snow throwers around. It's an excellent choice if you want a small model that requires no help—other than steering—to make it throw with a vengeance. The TRS22 features six forward speeds and two reverse speeds. Its four-horsepower, four-cycle engine clears a 22-inch-wide path. A ten-inch auger coupled with a nine-inch impeller enable this machine to move serious snow. Although pricey, it is well built and extremely durable. An electric start is an optional attachment.

Warranty: 2 years, parts and labor
Manufacturer's Suggested Retail Price: $879
Approximate Low Price: $779

Yard Machines 140

Budget Buy

The economical Yard Machines 140 is a well-made, sound performer with an excellent single-stage auger design. It is built for easy access to the auger drive in the unlikely event that it needs adjustment. The three-horsepower, two-cycle engine can occasionally handle snow up to 11 inches deep, if you can help it along. It clears a path 21 inches wide, and includes a folding handle for convenient storage.

Warranty: 90 days (no-fault); 2 years (limited)
Manufacturer's Suggested Retail Price: $329
Approximate Low Price: $299

MEDIUM SNOW THROWERS

Troy-Bilt 42027

BEST BUY

The 42027 is a superb two-stage snow thrower with lots of power and cutting depth. It has a hefty 13-inch-diameter auger, can clear a 21-inch-wide path, and has an 18-inch auger housing to take on some serious snowfall. Construction is rugged on this machine, right down to a cast-iron auger gear housing. Controls are simple and straightforward. It features a six-horsepower, four-cycle engine with three forward speeds and one reverse. Optional accessories include an electric start and drift cutters.

Warranty: 2 years, engine; 3 years, unit
Manufacturer's Suggested Retail Price: $839
Approximate Low Price: $799

Ariens Suburban ST 524

Recommended

The ST 524 continues to be a winner because of its rugged design. The five-horsepower, four-cycle engine is coupled with Ariens' venerable (and well-liked) variable-speed drive system. This wheel-propelled machine can clear a 24-inch-wide path and will throw snow 35 feet. Options include an electric start, drift cutters, and a huge, effective snow brush.

Warranty: 5 years (limited)
Manufacturer's Suggested Retail Price: $1,049
Approximate Low Price: $999

Yard-Man E640F

Budget Buy

The low-profile, dependable, and economical E640F is an excellent choice for the budget-minded. Its big eight-horsepower, four-cycle engine clears a generous 26-inch path. It has a push-button electric start and easy-to-operate controls. It comes equipped with serrated edges on the auger blades, which improve clearing icy, hard-packed snow. A clutch lock allows single hand op eration while adjusting the chute. It has six forward and two reverse speeds for effective maneuvering.

Warranty: 90 days (no-fault); 2 years (Supreme Warranty)
Manufacturer's Suggested Retail Price: $769
Approximate Low Price: $699

LARGE SNOW THROWERS

Craftsman 88113

✓BEST BUY

New this year, the 88113 is a lot of snow thrower for the money. It's an effective performer and a real brute with its 18½-inch intake auger housing. The heavy-duty 11-horsepower, four-cycle engine clears a 30-inch path. With six forward travel speeds, two reverse speeds, exceptional comfort, and easy operation, the 88113 is destined to become a reasonably-priced winner. Outstanding features include a panel-mounted, easy-to-use remote chute adjuster and a headlight.

Warranty: 2 years, parts and labor
Manufacturer's Suggested Retail Price: $1,199
Approximate Low Price: $1,099

Noma Performance 627104X8

Recommended

The Performance 627104X8 is a feature-packed machine. Equipped with a ten-horsepower, four-cycle engine, this machine is ready to take on any amount of snowfall thrown at it. Features include a nonclogging chute, a headlight, a push-button electric start, single-hand control, and drift cutters. Its wide-track tires keep the unit stable. The 627104X8 clears a 27-inch path and operates with six forward and two reverse speeds. The fuel tank is located out in the open for easy, no-spill refueling.

Warranty: 2 years (limited)
Manufacturer's Suggested Retail Price: $1,099
Approximate Low Price: $898

LAWN CARE

The first self-propelled, walk-behind lawn mower (which was steam-powered) dates all the way back to 1893; the first gas engine mower appeared about 1920. Today, power equipment for lawns and gardens has become as important as washing machines and stoves are for homes. It is hard to find a home that does not own at least one lawn mower (and perhaps a string trimmer). With the ever-growing expansion of suburban sprawl and with more people buying or building homes on larger properties, the market for larger equipment has grown. At the same time, there is a steady demand for smaller gas models (as well as electric and battery-powered models) from people with modest-size lots.

LAWN MOWERS

Lawn mowers continue to evolve. For several years, dedicated mulching mowers were all the rage. But thanks to innovative deck and blade designs, nearly all lawn mowers can mulch, bag, or discharge without the inconvenience of changing blades. (Some of the parts for conversions may be optional, however.) Basically, the initial major buying decision is whether to purchase a push-type or a self-propelled model. There is a trend toward increased engine horsepower, particularly for self-propelled mowers, which are nudging up to 6.75 horsepower. You'll see more of both push and self-propelled models with high rear wheels because of their great performance on uneven terrain and in tall grass.

Choosing the right mower for your lot depends on the terrain, the amount of trees, fences, plantings, and so on. For small lots less than ¼-acre, corded electric and battery powered mowers are excellent choices. For ¼-acre lots, push-type gas mowers will suffice. Lastly, for lots up to ½-acre, self-propelled gas models are the best choices.

RIDING MOWERS AND LAWN TRACTORS

Riding mowers are generating greater interest as more people buy homes with larger lots. They are the ideal choice for reasonably level lots that are too large for walk-behind mowers. A rider may also be a better and more economical choice than a lawn tractor if you plan only to use it for mowing, and riding mower maneuverability is often better than that of a lawn tractor.

Lawn tractors also make up for a good share of lawn care products. The demand continues to grow for these machines, which offer more comfort and easy-operating features such as hydrostatic drives, cruise control, and tool-free adjustment.

STRING TRIMMERS AND BLOWER/VACS

These handy tools can handle most of the touch-up jobs around your lawn and garden. String trimmers use a spinning nylon line to cut grass, weeds, and light brush. Some trimmers have detachable power heads that can be quickly converted to drive other implements such as brush saws, edgers, mini-cultivators, blowers, and even snow throwers. These models can make good budget and space-saving sense by eliminating the need to buy and store an array of several complete individual units.

Blower/vacs are "must have" tools for keeping lawns and gardens tidy and reducing debris volume for efficient disposal, composting, or mulching purposes. There is not a great difference in performance (measured as "air speed" in the blower mode; "debris reduction ratio" in the vacuuming mode) between electric and gas-powered handheld models. Gas units have that "take anywhere" portability, but they usually weigh a bit more and are usually more expensive. An electric unit is less costly but is limited by its 100-feet maximum extension cord range.

All the dedicated blower/vacs reviewed here automatically chop up, mulch, or shred debris as it is sucked up and ejected into the collection bag in the vacuum mode.

BUYING TIPS

When purchasing lawn care equipment, it is important to remember that competition is stiff and there tends to be little price difference between stores. Watch for early spring or late fall sales for the best prices. If service and repair confidence as well as other dealer amenities are an important consideration, servicing dealers may be a better option. However, prices may be somewhat higher.

FEATURES AND TERMINOLOGY

Bump Feed: This feature allows you to advance the cutting string during operation, usually by bumping a cap on the cutter head against the ground.

Deck Leveling: This feature found on lawn tractors and riding mower decks allows the cutting blade(s) to be adjusted to cut parallel with the ground surface.

Hydrostatic Drive: This standard or optional feature can be found on many riding mowers and tractors, as well as a few self-propelled mowers. It provides smooth, shiftless propulsion by using hydraulic power.

Mulch Plug/Mulch Plate: These devices are used on many convertible mulching/discharge mower decks to plug or cover the discharge outlet in the shroud while in the mulch mode.

Power Takeoff (PTO): This is the power output shaft(s) found on tractors and riding mowers. It drives the mower blade(s) and sometimes optional attachments. Most are engaged and disengaged with electric clutches.

Turning Radius: A competitive measure of close-cutting and time-saving abilities of riding mowers and tractors. Turning radius is one-half the diameter of the uncut circle when mowing with the wheels turned the maximum amount.

BEST BUYS '99

Our Best Buy, Recommended, and Budget Buy lawn care products are listed below. Products within each category are listed according to quality. The best of the Best Buys is listed first, followed by Recommended and Budget Buy. A Best Buy, Recommended, or Budget Buy designation only applies to the model listed—it does not necessarily apply to other models made by the same manufacturer or to an entire product line.

LAWN MOWERS

GASOLINE-POWERED PUSH-TYPE MOWERS

Craftsman High-Wheel 38724

✓BEST BUY

If hand-mowing can be considered fun, it does not get much more fun than doing it with this decidedly gutsy six-horsepower, high-wheel mower. High wheelers offer superb maneuverability on uneven terrain and in tall grass—particularly important when you have to push. The 38724's mulch system easily converts to side discharge and bags with an optional catcher.

Specifications: width, 22" deck; weight, 81 lbs.
Warranty: 2 years
Manufacturer's Suggested Retail Price: $210
Approximate Low Price: $199

Lawn-Boy Silver Pro 10247

Recommended

Lawn-Boy's tradition of lightweight, reliable mowers is continued in its Silver Series 10247. Upgraded with a new DuraForce 6.5-horsepower two-cycle engine, the 10247 retains its offset wheels for great maneuverability, especially when mowing uneven terrains. The 10247 features tool-free conversion from mulch to side discharge, as well as to optional leaf bagging and leaf shredding. The handle conveniently folds for easy storage.

Specifications: width, 21" deck; weight, 67 lbs.
Warranty: 2 years
Manufacturer's Suggested Retail Price: $299
Approximate Low Price: $279

Yard Machines 084A

Budget Buy

Although the 084A is budget-priced, it has some quality features such as a deep, fully-baffled steel deck, nine-position fingertip height adjusters, a four-horsepower engine, and wide, eight-inch diameter wheels. Everything needed for mulching and side discharge is included, except the optional 1.6-bushel grass catcher bag. Its light weight makes this mower easy to maneuver, and the handle folds down for space-saving storage.

Specifications: width, 22" deck; weight, 65 lbs.
Warranty: 90 days (no-fault), 2 years (limited)
Manufacturer's Suggested Retail Price: $179
Approximate Low Price: $139

GASOLINE-POWERED SELF-PROPELLED MOWERS

Yard-Man 12A-999L401

✓BEST BUY

The 12A-999L401 is the ultimate in self-propelled mower maneuverability. Its secret is the lockable front caster wheels. You have to try such a mower to appreciate how it easily moves around flower beds, trees, and shrubs. When you're ready to mow inclines, the wheels quickly lock straight ahead. The six-horsepower Briggs & Stratton Industrial/Commercial engine provides plenty of power. The 12A-999L401's six-speed transmission allows you to match ground speed to your walking pace and to maximize mulching performance. No tools are needed to make mulching, discharge, or bag changes. The large 2.5-bushel grass catcher is easy to remove and replace thanks to a large handgrip.

Specifications: width, 21" deck; weight, 85 lbs.
Warranty: 90 days (no fault); 2 years (limited)
Manufacturer's Suggested Retail Price: $449
Approximate Low Price: $379

Craftsman 37756

Recommended

This mower provides many of the features you'd expect in a self-propelled mower. The 6.5-horsepower engine provides enough power to handle any moderate-size lawn easily. Using a combination of 14-inch rear wheels and geared front-wheel drive, the 37756 is exceptionally easy to maneuver. Its factory-installed EZ3 mulching system allows you to mulch, discharge (with optional deflector), or bag with the 2.4 bushel, lift-top rear catcher. Rounding off the package is its reliable Eager-1, one-pull starting system.

Specifications: width, 22" deck; weight, 83 lbs.
Warranty: 2 years
Manufacturer's Suggested Retail Price: $360
Approximate Low Price: $299

Murray Select 20656X8

Budget Buy

Murray made this self-propelled mower with convenience in mind. Because of front-wheel drive, an uncommon feature among comparable mowers, many will find the 20656X8 surprisingly easier to control. To prevent digging in, simply tip the mower up. You can also easily convert to mulch, bag, or discharge without the use of tools. The mulch plug is integrated so it cannot be inadvertently lost or damaged during changeover. It operates with a 5.5-horsepower engine and includes a seven-position height adjustment.

Specifications: width, 20" deck; weight, 101 lbs.
Warranty: 2 years
Manufacturer's Suggested Retail Price: $269
Approximate Low Price: $249

ELECTRIC MOWERS

Black & Decker CMM630

✓BEST BUY

The CMM630 takes this year's honor for the best corded mower in its class. This year's model is gutsy and easy to operate, thanks to Black & Decker's maneuverability enhancements. By adopting 7-inch front wheels and 14-inch rear wheels, the mower is virtually effortless to push and negotiate over uneven terrain. It mulches, side discharges, and side bags (with an optional bag). Its 12-volt built-in battery allows you to cut a ¼-acre lot on a single overnight charge.

Specifications: width, 18″ deck; weight, 65 lbs.
Warranty: 30 days, money back; 2 years, home use; 5 years, deck
Manufacturer's Suggested Retail Price: $325
Approximate Low Price: $284

Toro E120

Recommended

Toro's electric mower entry this year is the exceptional E120. With an innovative belt-drive reduction, the E120 has the cutting power of a five-horsepower gas mower. The 12-amp motor is almost silent, thanks to the acoustic foam baffling in the mower cover. The unusually lightweight mower includes a great cord lock and management system, a bumper that protects trees and shrubs, and turf-friendly tires that reduce scuffing. The E120 also includes a no-tools, three-position handle for transport and convenient storage.

Specifications: width, 18″ deck; weight, 38 lbs.
Warranty: 2 years
Manufacturer's Suggested Retail Price: $250
Approximate Low Price: $190

RIDING MOWERS

Yard Machines Yard Bug

✓ BEST BUY

Not only is Yard Bug one of the most charming riding mowers available, it is also one of the easiest to use and easiest to store. Its high-tech compact design allows it to fit through most gates and in sheds. It's powered by a quiet, 8.5-horsepower Briggs & Stratton engine that offers plenty of torque. Convenient fingertip and foot controls make it as simple as driving a car. The cutting width is great for small yards. The Yard Bug includes an ingenious internal grass catcher with a monitor that tells you when it needs to be emptied. The Yard Bug also includes a mulching kit, side discharge chute, and 2.5 bushel container.

Specifications: width, 27½" deck; weight, N/A
Warranty: 90 days (no fault); 2 years (limited)
Manufacturer's Suggested Retail Price: $999
Approximate Low Price: $959

John Deere GX85

Recommended

The GX85 is one of two Deere riders (the SX85 includes a foot-controlled variable drive and a more supportive seat for an additional $350) that are more stylish, more powerful, and less expensive than their predecessors. Convenient step-through design and hand-controlled cutting-height levels allow for easy operation. This conventional riding mower, with its tight 14-inch turning radius, is perfect for those tricky trimming jobs. Its in-line shift transmission and 13-horsepower long-life engine provides enough power to tackle the toughest jobs. You can even have the SX85's upgraded seat installed on the GX85.

Specifications: width, 30" deck; weight, 342 lbs.
Warranty: 2 years
Manufacturer's Suggested Retail Price: $1,799
Approximate Low Price: $1,599

Murray 30500X92

Budget Buy

What the economical 30500X92 lacks in features offered with more expensive machines, it makes up with quality, basic necessities. The leg room is spacious and the step-through design allows for easy access. Shifting and deck-height adjustments are conveniently located, allowing for smooth operation. Its 30-inch deck is equipped to mulch, side discharge, or bag. The mower's ten-horsepower engine provides ample power.

Specifications: width, 30″ deck; weight, N/A
Warranty: 2 years
Manufacturer's Suggested Retail Price: $759
Approximate Low Price: $629–$729

LAWN TRACTORS

14 HORSEPOWER OR LESS

Sabre 1438GS

✓BEST BUY

Becoming better known in the market because of its connection to John Deere, Sabre has plenty to offer in lawn tractors. Its 1438GS, for example, includes many attractive features, such as comfortable seating, at a reasonable price. Beneath the handsome styling, the 1438GS is powered by a premium quality Industrial/Commercial OHV engine. Plus it's fun to drive. It has a desirable 18-inch turning radius and an easy-to-use in-line shift transmission. Optional accessories include a mulching adapter, a rear bagger, and snow blades.

Specifications: width, 38″ deck; weight, 391 lbs.
Warranty: 2 years
Manufacturer's Suggested Retail Price: $1,399
Approximate Low Price: $1,279

Kubota T1560

Recommended

The T1560 is a sleek, streamlined mower made for comfort and easy maneuvering. An innovative Cushion-Ride suspension system provides desirable comfort. The Auto Throttle Advance System automatically adjusts speed from the mower's 14-horsepower engine, with or without engaging the power take-off lever, which operates the mower blades. Raising and lowering the deck is a snap, thanks to a lift-assist gas-charged cylinder. Cutting height can be adjusted with a single touch. Optional accessories include a mulching kit, a grass catcher, a front blade, a thatcher, and snowblower attachments.

Specifications: width, 40" deck; weight, 528 lbs.
Warranty: 2 years, including original mower deck
Manufacturer's Suggested Retail Price: $3,670
Approximate Low Price: $2,990–$3,380

MORE THAN 14 HORSEPOWER

Scotts 46572X8

✓BEST BUY

This well-designed tractor is loaded with appealing standard features, all residing on its wide-track platform. The rugged mower deck can be accurately leveled without tools and has a mulch kit installed. The tractor comes equipped with a 19-horsepower Briggs & Stratton V-twin OHV engine and a diagnostic dash that monitors its performance with service indicators. Driving is enhanced with a foot-operated automatic transmission and cruise control. Leg room is spacious and features Scotts' step-through design for easy accessibility. Because of the quality and the aforementioned convenience features, we've rated the 46572X8 a Best Buy.

Specifications: width, 46" deck; weight, N/A
Warranty: 2 years
Manufacturer's Suggested Retail Price: $1,899
Approximate Low Price: $1,899

Craftsman 27062

Budget Buy

The 27062 offers solid construction at an affordable price. It is powered by a long-life, 15.5-horsepower Briggs & Stratton turbo-cooled engine, and its seamless operation is due to its automatic drive. The EZ3 deck mulches, discharges, and rear bags (with an optional bagger) without changing blades. A handy gauge monitors battery charge. The 27062 is also available with a six-speed transmission (as model 2706, retail price $1,199).

Specifications: width, 42" deck; weight, N/A
Warranty: 2 years
Manufacturer's Suggested Retail Price: $1,379
Approximate Low Price: $1,049

STRING TRIMMERS

GASOLINE MODELS

Stihl FS36

✓BEST BUY

Frequently recommended as a top consumer choice, this twin-line, curved shaft trimmer is made to last, with a powerful, top quality 30.2cc engine. The engine controls are conveniently built right into the grip for easy starting. You can quickly advance the cutting line by simply tapping the head. Two important features for low maintenance and long life are the shaft liner and the permanently-lubed drive cable. This lightweight trimmer is perfect for the weekend gardener.

Specifications: width, 16" cutting swath; weight, 10 lbs. 13 oz.
Warranty: 2 years
Manufacturer's Suggested Retail Price: $140
Approximate Low Price: $129

Echo SRM-2601

Recommended

The brand new SRM-2601 is a durable trimmer designed for serious trimming. It features a 24.5cc commercial grade engine and a rigid steel straight drive shaft for smooth, quick acceleration. Heavy-duty engine vibration reduction mounts and padded handles substantially reduce vibration and increase comfort. The twin-line head is semiautomatic, and a shoulder harness is included for effortless mobility.

Specifications: width, 17" cutting swath; weight, 11 lbs. 8 oz.
Warranty: 1 year, commercial use; 2 years, parts and labor

Manufacturer's Suggested Retail Price: $350
Approximate Low Price: $329

ELECTRIC MODELS

McCulloch Trimmer/Edger 3600TE

✓BEST BUY

McCulloch's stylish new 3600TE trimmer/edger is pleasing to the eye and unbelievably fun to use. Equipped with a 5.5-amp motor, the 3600TE offers plenty of power. Its six-string head is more efficient with its use of multiple strings, and it snaps on and off for instant replacement. The trimmer has a telescoping shaft and quickly converts to an edger. The 3600TE also includes an adjustable assist handle, which adds comfort and convenience.

Specifications: width, 12″ cutting swath; weight, 5 lbs.
Warranty: 2 years
Manufacturer's Suggested Retail Price: $50
Approximate Low Price: $50

Ryobi 132r

Recommended

This unit is not only an effective trimmer but has the special ability to use nine attachments. These attachments work by removing the trimmer head and using the unit's two-speed, 5.2-amp motor to power them. A snow thrower, a mini-cultivator, and a blower are among the accessories that will attach to the 132r. When used as a trimmer, it has good balance, and its useful adjustable handles maximize comfort. It also has a dependable string advance mechanism, which advances premeasured line with a single tap.

Specifications: width, 15″ cutting swath; weight, 9 lbs.
Warranty: 2 years
Manufacturer's Suggested Retail Price: $59
Approximate Low Price: $59

CORDLESS MODELS

Craftsman 78354

✓BEST BUY

Craftsman's new 78354 cordless trimmer is an effective trimmer that also doubles as an edger. It runs up to 30 minutes on a 12-volt battery charge, which is more than enough to do the trimming tasks for a ½-acre lawn. A new feed system automatically feeds line so it is always ready to cut a full swath. After you finish, hang it in its wall-mount charger storage bracket until you're ready to use it again. The 78354 also includes an adjustable shaft and handle for comfort and convenience.

Specifications: width, 9" cutting swath; weight, 10 lbs. 5 oz.
Warranty: 1 year
Manufacturer's Suggested Retail Price: $90
Approximate Low Price: $90

Ryobi 150r

Recommended

Although selected as a Best Buy last year, the 150r continues to be the most effective and efficient cordless trimmer available. It will easily trim almost any average-sized lawn on a 12-volt battery charge and still have power for more. Then just hang it up in its wall-mount charger bracket until the next time you're ready to trim, and it will be ready to go. The bump feed mechanism is extremely effective and easy to use. The Ryobi 150r is perfectly balanced, making it one of the easiest available trimmers to operate.

Specifications: width, 10" cutting swath; weight, 10 lbs.
Warranty: 2 years
Manufacturer's Suggested Retail Price: $99
Approximate Low Price: $79

BLOWER/VACS

ELECTRIC MODELS

Toro Super BlowerVac 51582

✓BEST BUY

Rated as a Best Buy last year, the 51582 continues to be a best-selling favorite. Its 12-amp motor can generate a powerful 190-mph air speed. Many users will enjoy the easy, no-tools changeover from blower to vacuum. Its powerful vacuum with shredding action can reduce up to ten bags of leaves to one. It is hard to make these units perfectly comfortable because of the hanging bags, the shoulder straps, and the grips. We found the best comfort while operating in the vacuum mode, but this is a matter of personal preference.

Specifications: mulching ratio 10:1; weight, 7 lbs.
Warranty: 2 years
Manufacturer's Suggested Retail Price: $80
Approximate Low Price: $59

Black & Decker Super Vac 'N' Mulch BV1000

Recommended

The BV1000 operates and performs similarly to the Toro 51582. It has a two-speed switch to control air flow and a 12-amp motor that can generate air speeds up to 180 mph. It also quickly converts from blower to vacuum without the use of tools. One of its more interesting features is an optional kit consisting of a large, long vacuum hose and an elastic-rimmed fabric boot that fits neatly over a trash container so you can suck up debris, mulch it, and blow it directly into the container.

Specifications: mulching ratio 10:1; weight, 7 lbs.
Warranty: 2 years
Manufacturer's Suggested Retail Price: $79
Approximate Low Price: $59

GASOLINE MODELS

Weed Eater Barracuda SV30

✓BEST BUY

Appearing once again as a Best Buy, the SV30 still deserves this rating. Its gutsy 30cc engine can create up to 190 mph air speeds. It also powers the impeller blades, which have small flail devices mounted on the intake end of the impeller to aid in reducing debris in the vacuum mode. The SV30 has a good throttle design for controlling blower airflow plus it has anti-vibration handles. Switching between blower and vacuum modes is relatively easy. Options include a gutter cleaning kit.

Specifications: mulching ratio 16:1; weight, 13 lbs.
Warranty: 2 years (limited)
Manufacturer's Suggested Retail Price: $120
Approximate Low Price: $99

Echo Shred "N" Vacuum ES-2100

Recommended

The ES-2100 continues to be one of the best blower/vacs around, particularly because of its effective four-blade debris preshredder mounted in the impeller. While not the most powerful unit reviewed here, the small 21.2cc engine can generate air speeds up to a respectable 135 mph. The ES-2100 has an efficient mulching ratio and is quite comfortable when operating in the vacuum mode. An optional gutter cleaning kit is also available.

Specifications: mulching ratio 12:1; weight, 9 lbs.
Warranty: 2 years, parts and labor; lifetime, electronic ignition
Manufacturer's Suggested Retail Price: $199
Approximate Low Price: $169

FOOD PREPARATION

Today, the name of the game in cooking is speed. Few people can make a habit of spending hours in the kitchen turning out magnificent lunches and dinners. Still, no one wants to sacrifice quality and flavor in their daily meals. To respond to this need for efficient, quality food preparation, manufacturers have created a variety of appliances to handle every job, large and small.

BEST BUYS '99

Our Best Buy, Recommended, and Budget Buy food preparation products are listed below. Products within each category are listed according to quality. The best of the Best Buys is listed first, followed by our second choice, and so on. A Best Buy, Recommended, or Budget Buy designation only applies to the model listed—it does not necessarily apply to other models made by the same manufacturer or to an entire product line.

FOOD PROCESSORS

The food processor has earned its place in the kitchen, alongside the coffee maker, mixer, and toaster. What was once considered optional equipment for culinary artists, is now an everyday mainstay. The question is no longer "Do I need a food processor?" but rather "Which type of processor do I need?"

WHAT SIZE IS RIGHT?

Bigger, more powerful machines can knead dough for two loaves of bread, slice and shred produce for salads, slice and shred a party-size batch of coleslaw, or slice whole fruits or vegetables through an expanded feed tube. The biggest of these are the food preparation centers—machines that perform all the functions of the largest processors, but also come with added attachments that enable them to function as stand mixers (and, in some cases, blenders and choppers). Some models also come with fancy disc attachments for cutting julienne vegetables or French fry potatoes. Smaller models save work space and are perfect for smaller tasks such as processing a single onion, a handful of herbs, or a cup of mayonnaise. Mini choppers specialize in chopping small items such as garlic cloves, nuts, or bits of chocolate. These small units also are handy for making up single servings of baby food.

You may discover that one machine serves many purposes in the kitchen. The larger machines offer the most functions and versatility, while carrying a higher price tag. Smaller machines do an admirable job with smaller quantities. Compact models may be just right for singles or smaller families.

FEATURES AND TERMINOLOGY

The first-time processor owner may want a machine that is as uncomplicated as possible. Single-button or two-speed models offer the most ease of use. Masters of processor techniques may prefer the versatility of a variable-speed model. All models share the following features:

Motor Base: Generally speaking, the bigger the machine, the more powerful the motor, but some of the compact models pack a surprising punch.

On/Off/Pulse: These are the common speeds for a processor: "on" for continuous action; "off"; and "pulse," which provides short, consecutive rotations of the blade for more even chopping.

Stainless-steel Chopping Blade: Also called an "S" blade, this blade is used for chopping, mixing and blending, pureeing, or for kneading bread dough. Some machines have separate dough blades or hooks.

Work Bowl: This is usually transparent. Some machines include extra bowls as well as blender carafes for added features and convenience.

SAFETY TIPS

Once you've chosen a unit, read the instructions thoroughly to familiarize yourself with the functions. Be sure to follow all the safety precautions; keeping the unit stable and the cord out of the way is essential. Also remember that the blades are extremely sharp and should be handled with care. All manufacturers nowadays are taking precautions to make their units as safe and trouble-free as possible. Virtually every unit is now equipped with a safety interlock system that will not allow the unit to operate if the bowl and cover are not properly in place.

LARGE FOOD PROCESSORS

Cuisinart Food Preparation Center DLC-7SFP

✓ BEST BUY

For those who are serious about cooking but don't have hours to spend preparing everything by hand, the Cuisinart DLC-7SFP food preparation center offers a solution. Its powerful motor speeds through everyday tasks such as chopping vegetables and mixing pastry and bread dough. In addition, this unit comes with a whisk attachment that is perfect for whipping cream, egg whites, or mashed potatoes. The oversize 14-cup Lexan work bowl is large enough to accommodate more than two pounds of ground beef, batter for five 8-inch layer cakes, or dough for about 90 cookies in a single batch. You can even shred an entire head of cabbage without emptying the work bowl. Two fingertip switches—on and pulse/off—are easy to use. The DLC-7SFP comes with a stainless-steel chopping blade, heavy-duty plastic dough blade, medium slicing and medium shredding discs, a stainless-steel whisk attachment, a plastic spatula, and two covers—one compact cover for chopping and mixing and one standard cover with both large and small feed tubes for slicing and shredding both wide and thin produce. Because of its dual functions, the feed tube assembly may seem a bit challenging at first; however, anyone who has ever been frustrated by trying to feed larger produce items down smaller feed tubes will appreciate the added versatility. Optional attachments include a fine shredding disc; fine and medium julienne discs; a French fry disc; and ultra-thin, thin, medium, thick, and extra-thick slicing discs. All parts, except motor base, are dishwasher safe.

Warranty: 3 years (limited); 5 years, motor
Manufacturer's Suggested Retail Price: $440
Approximate Low Price: $300

KitchenAid 11-cup Ultra Power KFP600WH

✓BEST BUY

KitchenAid's reputation for quality is evident in its Ultra Power food processor. This unit features touchpad controls and a two-bowl system for versatility as well as performance. The KFP600WH comes with a clear 11-cup work bowl with chopping blade, a reversible thin slicing/shredding disc, medium slicing and medium shredding discs, a dough blade, a plastic spatula, and a mini chopping bowl and blade. The multipurpose chopping blade and mini chopping blade are made by Sabatier, the renowned knife manufacturer. Another innovative feature is an accessory storage box, which houses all the blades/discs when not in use. Three touchpad controls allow you to switch from on to off or pulse instantly. You can process up to six cups of chopped beef or produce, enough dough for one large pizza, or up to three cups of chopped nuts or peanut butter. A handy feature on this unit is the mini chopper attachment, which eliminates the need for a second appliance for chopping smaller amounts. The mini chopper bowl can handle up to one cup of semi-liquid ingredients or ½ cup of solids. The KFP600WH easily assembles and disassembles for effortless operation. Because there are no crevices for dirt to get trapped in, the unit is easy to clean. Bowls and blades are dishwasher safe.

Warranty: 1 year
Manufacturer's Suggested Retail Price: $250
Approximate Low Price: $200

DeLonghi Ultimate FP30

Recommended

The DeLonghi FP30 combines an old-fashioned chrome-and-black finish with state-of-the-art touchpad controls and superior performance. Billing itself as the "Ultimate Food Processor," the FP30 features innovative orbital mixing action, thanks to a slightly inclined work bowl and a contoured chopping blade that lifts and turns ingredients as it blends. Its powerful motor provides four electronic speed settings in on, off, and pulse modes that suit any processing task from slicing and shredding to pureeing and mashing. The three-quart work bowl has a watertight cover for processing small to large batches of dry or liquid ingredients. It will also knead dough for one loaf of bread, Fench-fry cut more than a pound of carrots and zucchini for a salad, or puree up to four cups of cooked vegetables. Included with this unit are a multipurpose serrated chopping blade; grating, slicing and French-fry discs; a citrus press; a spatula; and a full-color recipe book. An optional juice extractor is sold separately.

Warranty: 2 years
Manufacturer's Suggested Retail Price: $280
Approximate Low Price: $270

MID-SIZE FOOD PROCESSORS

KitchenAid Classic KFP500

✓BEST BUY

There is no substitute for reliable performance, a fact of which the KitchenAid Classic KFP500 attests. This unit combines a powerful motor and nine-cup capacity work bowl to tackle a shopping list of preparation chores. Its inclusion of a mini work bowl and blade provide the added functionality of a mini chopper for smaller chores such as chopping garlic cloves or a single onion. Features include a cover with feed tube and food pusher, a multipurpose chopping blade, a mini work bowl and blade, a plastic dough blade, a reversible thin slicing/shredding disc, a medium shredding disc, and a spatula/cleaning tool. Both the standard and mini chopping blades are made by Sabatier, a name that means quality among knife manufacturers. The smooth, rounded base sits firmly on your countertop. Touchpad controls for on, off, and pulse are easy to use. And since there are no crevices to trap food particles, the KFP500 is also easy to clean. All parts, except base, are dishwasher safe.

Warranty: 1 year
Manufacturer's Suggested Retail Price: $230
Approximate Low Price: $172

Cuisinart Pro Classic DLC-10S

✓BEST BUY

The Cuisinart Pro Classic DLC-10S combines high-performance features in a standard-capacity machine. This versatile unit allows you to chop, slice, or shred a variety of ingredients in a fraction of the time it would take to do by hand. The DLC-10S boasts power equivalent to its larger counterparts, yet its reduced size and price tag make it perfect for smaller families or those who cook or entertain less frequently. The Pro Classic comes with a seven-cup clear work bowl, a clear cover with both large and small feed tubes, a flat cover for use during chopping or mixing, a stainless-steel medium slicing disc, a medium shredding disc, a stainless-steel chopping/mixing blade, a plastic dough blade, and a spatula. The three-position lever switches from off to on or pulse in seconds. The multifunction feed tube assembly takes some getting used to but the versatility it offers (for processing whole cucumbers, for example) is well worth the extra effort. A how-to video is also included, which shows you step-by-step instructions on assembly and use. An assortment of thick and thin slicing and shredding discs are optional. All parts, except motor base, are dishwasher safe.

Warranty: 3 years (limited); 5 years, motor
Manufacturer's Suggested Retail Price: $260
Approximate Low Price: $190

Braun CombiMax K750

Recommended

The Braun CombiMax K750 calls itself a versatile food preparation center—and one look at the many attachments will explain why. Two work bowls sit side by side atop the motor base. The nine-cup capacity processor bowl can be used for basic tasks—chopping, slicing, shredding, blending, mixing, and pureeing—as well as some specialty functions, such as whipping cream or egg whites, cutting French fries, and juicing citrus fruits. The three-cup capacity processor bowl is designed to chop, mix, or blend smaller quantities. Attachments include standard chopping blades for both large and small work bowls, a plastic dough-kneading attachment, a blade carrier with fine and coarse grating and shredding inserts, a French-fry system, whisk and juicer attachments, covers for both work bowls, and protective covers to seal motor drives when not in use. You can select your speed along the variable-control dial, then turn the power dial to the on position or depress the pulse button. Because of its multiple speeds and innovative slicing system, the CombiMax K750 takes a bit more practice to master than other machines. But the meticulous cook will find its versatility appealing. Bowls and attachments are dishwasher safe. A juice extractor attachment is available separately.

Warranty: 1 year, limited
Manufacturer's Suggested Retail Price: $200
Approximate Low Price: $150

Hamilton Beach Food Pro 2 702R

Budget Buy

The Hamilton Beach Food Pro 2 is a no-frills affordable machine that performs basic tasks well. A seven-cup capacity work bowl allows you to process dough for one loaf of yeast bread, up to six cups of cracker or bread crumbs, or about two cups of mayonnaise or pesto sauce. The Food Pro 2 is also handy for chopping raw or cooked meat, pureeing cooked vegetables, grating cheese, or shredding coconut. Two speed settings and a pulse setting are designed to handle both hard and soft food items easily. Standard features include the clear work bowl and cover with feed tube, stainless-steel processing blade, and reversible slicing/shredding disc. Bowl and cover are dishwasher safe.

Warranty: 1 year (limited)
Manufacturer's Suggested Retail Price: $60
Approximate Low Price: $50

COMPACT FOOD PROCESSORS

Cuisinart Little Pro Plus LPP

✓BEST BUY

The Cuisinart Little Pro Plus is not restricted by its compact size. This unit features a space-saving design and a powerful, yet surprisingly quiet, motor. It comes with a clear three-cup Lexan work bowl for chopping and mixing, an opaque white bowl with a chute assembly for continuous slicing or shredding directly into a waiting bowl, a stainless-steel chopping/mixing blade, a thin slicing disc, a medium-fine shredding disc, and a spatula. The "Plus" is a citrus juice attachment with three stackable reamers for juicing lemons/limes, oranges, and grapefruit. The clear work bowl can accommodate up to three cups of sliced or shredded produce, a half pound of chopped meat, or enough dough for a 15-inch pizza. The continuous slicing/shredding chute attachment allows you to process unlimited quantities without emptying the work bowl. To operate, push the three-position lever up for on or depress and release for pulse action. All parts, except motor base, are dishwasher safe.

Warranty: 3 years (limited); 5 years, motor
Manufacturer's Suggested Retail Price: $140
Approximate Low Price: $90

Krups MasterPro Plus 704

Recommended

The Krups 704 is small enough to be considered compact yet large enough to handle the processing needs of an average-size family. It comes with a clear work bowl that can handle up to five cups of sliced or shredded ingredients, three cups of dry batter or light dough, or almost two cups of heavy dough. It also includes a stainless-steel chopping blade, a disc with stainless-steel inserts for slicing and shredding, an emulsifier disc with superblender crown for whipping egg whites or cream, and a plastic spatula. The feed tube-pusher assembly is divided into two parts to handle both large and small food items; the pusher also doubles as a measuring cup. Three large buttons let you select on, off, or pulse. An electronic variable-speed control slide lever has settings from 1 (low) to 4 (high) that can be set at the start of processing or adjusted as needed while the unit is operating. Also included with this unit is a creative cooking booklet that shows step-by-step how to use your processor, and also provides an assortment of recipes. All parts, except motor base, can be easily cleaned with warm soapy water.

Warranty: 1 year
Manufacturer's Suggested Retail Price: $95
Approximate Low Price: not available

MINI-MINCERS

Cuisinart Mini-Prep DLC-1

✓BEST BUY

For processing smaller quantities, the Cuisinart Mini-Prep processor is powerful, sturdy, and reliable. Composed simply of a motor base with a work bowl and a patented reversible stainless-steel chopping blade, the Mini-Prep does an excellent job with chores such as chopping onions or a handful of nuts. The clear 21-ounce-capacity work bowl is the larger in its class. This unit blends small batches of sauce or dressing, grinds coffee beans and spices, and grates chocolate and cheeses. Two push-button controls let you select low and high speeds with pulse control. Use the high speed with the blade's blunt edge for grinding and grating hard foods. Use the low speed and sharp edge for soft or watery foods. The Mini-Prep takes up minimal space and the hidden wraparound cord storage keeps counter clutter to a minimum. The work bowl and lid disassemble easily and are dishwasher safe.

Warranty: 18 months (limited)
Manufacturer's Suggested Retail Price: $48
Approximate Low Price: $30

Krups Speedy Pro Mini-Chopper 720

Recommended

The Krups Speedy Pro Mini-Chopper consists of a clear three-cup capacity work bowl, a stainless-steel multipurpose chopping blade, a clear cover with two openings for adding last-minute ingredients during processing, and a taller-than-average power base. Designed to speed through everyday chores such as chopping onions and mincing garlic, this unit's powerful motor also tackles hard cheeses, chocolate, and coffee beans. On/off thumb-control button features pulse action for achieving even results. For semi-liquid ingredients, such as sauces or baby food, the Speedy Pro's capacity is reduced to about 11 ounces.

Warranty: 1 year
Manufacturer's Suggested Retail Price: $45
Approximate Low Price: not available

Black & Decker 2-Speed Super Chopper SC400

Budget Buy

An oversize work bowl makes the Black & Decker 2-Speed Super Chopper useful for recipes that call for just a bit more than the standard one-cup yield of most mini-choppers. The two-cup work bowl can handle up to two medium onions, three hard-cooked eggs, or about 1½ cups of mushrooms. This model features an easy-to-grip contoured base, a work bowl with cover, and a chopping blade. To use, place food in bowl, lock cover in place, and depress one of two pulse buttons. Low speed is for coarse chopping, while high speed works best for fine mincing. Hold either button down for continuous processing. Bowl, lid, and blade are dishwasher safe for easy cleanup.

Warranty: 1 year
Manufacturer's Suggested Retail Price: $30
Approximate Low Price: $25

ELECTRIC MIXERS

For mixing batters, whipping cream, or mashing potatoes, there is still no substitute for the familiar and reliable mixer. With its unique beater design, the mixer is able to mix, whip, mash, or blend a variety of consistencies from thin cake batters to thick cookie dough. Plus many mixers now come with added attachments, such as dough hooks (for kneading bread or pizza dough), whisks (for whipping extra volume into cream or egg whites), and immersion blender rods (for blending frothy beverages). No other machine can surpass the mixer when it comes to aerating (increasing the volume by incorporating air into light batters, such as whipping cream or egg whites).

TYPES OF MIXERS

Traditional stand mixers, with their supplied work bowls, offer the most power. They also have the added advantage of hands-free mixing. These machines make short work of everyday jobs such as blending cookie dough or creaming butter with sugar. Portable mixers—or hand mixers—are less expensive and can be easily stored when not in use. A relatively new option is the stand/hand combination unit, which offers the convenience of both types of mixer—and usually costs considerably less than a traditional stand mixer. If versatility is what you're looking for, the combination unit is a sensible choice.

PORTABLE MIXERS

Cuisinart SmartPower CountUp HTM-9LT ✓BEST BUY

The Cuisinart SmartPower CountUp HTM-9LT is a nine-speed electronic hand mixer that automatically tracks mixing time. No more setting the timer when a recipe calls for a selected mixing time. To start the unit, just depress the power button to activate the machine on its lowest setting. The digital display shows mixer speed (1-9) and time elapsed in minutes and seconds. Electronic touchpad controls let you switch between speeds with a gentle touch on the + (increase speed) or - (decrease speed) buttons.

The mixer starts slowly to prevent splattering when working with dry ingredients. The lower speeds are well suited for folding or start-up mixing. Higher speeds are extremely fast for quick whipping and aerating. Sturdy wire beaters have no center posts for dough to climb and clog mixing action. Made of stainless steel, these beaters cut cleanly through even heavy cookie dough. The HTM-9LT also comes with an oversize stainless-steel whisk for use with whipping cream and egg whites. Other features include a rotating cord that is designed to stay out of the way during mixing and a plastic spatula for scraping bowl sides. Beaters and whisk are dishwasher safe for easy cleanup.

Warranty: 3 years (limited)
Manufacturer's Suggested Retail Price: $98
Approximate Low Price: $70

KitchenAid Ultra Power Plus KHM7T

✓BEST BUY

For households that prefer a smaller mixer without sacrificing power or performance, the KitchenAid Ultra Power Plus is a good alternative. This unit comes with stainless-steel Turbo-Beaters—wire beaters that cut through heavy batters and also act as efficient whisks with light batters. Because the beaters have no center posts, dough will not climb and clog mixing action. An on/off switch activates power and touchpad controls lets you move between speeds effortlessly. A digital display shows which speed you have selected. An electronic sensor automatically adjusts the power to maintain a consistent speed through any consistency. The mixer's handle is comfortable to grip even during extended mixing. Optional attachments include a liquid blender rod and stainless-steel dough hooks.

Warranty: 1 year
Manufacturer's Suggested Retail Price: $80
Approximate Low Price: $80

Hamilton Beach 62695

Budget Buy

The Hamilton Beach 62695 hand mixer is an economical machine that performs basic mixing chores efficiently. This unit comes with traditional beaters, which are suited for most mixing chores, such as blending pancake batter, mashing potatoes, or pureeing steamed vegetables. It also comes with wire beaters, which are designed with no center posts so that stiff or thick dough or frostings will not clog mixing action. It also includes a single whisk attachment that is designed to add extra volume during whipping. You can choose from six speeds along the thumb-operated speed-control lever. A QuickBurst button provides short bursts of power at any speed. Other features include a bowl rest for adding ingredients or draining beaters, a cord wrap for convenient storage, and a comfort-grip handle. Attachments are dishwasher safe for easy cleanup.

Warranty: 2 years
Manufacturer's Suggested Retail Price: $30
Approximate Low Price: $20

STAND MIXERS

KitchenAid Ultra Power KSM90

✓BEST BUY

For power and performance, the KSM90 Ultra Power is unmatched. This unit tackles the most strenuous chores effortlessly and is ready in a minute for all your light mixing needs. This unit features a powerful ten-speed motor, a 4½-quart stainless-steel mixing bowl with handle, a flat beater, a dough hook, a stainless-steel wire whisk, and a nonsealing bowl cover. Instead of rotating the bowl, this mixer has unique "planetary mixing action," which spins the beater and rotates it around the stationary bowl for maximum bowl coverage. For added stability, the bowl locks into the base of the mixer for hands-free mixing. Optional accessories include a food grinder, a pasta maker, a fruit/vegetable strainer, a rotor slicer/shredder disc, a grain mill, a citrus juicer, a can opener, an extra three-quart mixing bowl, extra bowl covers, a fabric cover, a food tray, and a two-piece pouring shield. The KSM90 is available in a variety of colors.

Warranty: 1 year
Manufacturer's Suggested Retail Price: $325
Approximate Low Price: $279

Krups Power Mix Pro 610

Recommended

In one compact unit, the Krups Power Mix Pro features both the hands-free convenience of a stand mixer and the versatility of a hand mixer. Detach the mixer from its stand to use as a hand mixer for quick blending in any container. The unit's powerful motor has three speeds plus a pulse option and turbo speed to satisfy all your mixing needs. Accessories include a three-quart plastic mixing bowl, a lightweight stand base, two self-cleaning stainless-steel turbo beaters, and two stainless-steel dough hooks. A thumb-control lever effortlessly clicks into each of the three speeds. Turbo speed can be activated at any speed by depressing a button located atop the mixer. To operate in manual pulse, depress and move the lever to the left. This movement may seem unfamiliar at first, but is easily mastered. The pulse option is great for slow stirring of dry ingredients or last-minute mix-ins, such as chips or nuts. The mixer also features automatic gear-driven bowl rotation and an oscillating power arm that can be set to move automatically from the side of the bowl to the center every 15 seconds for thorough bowl coverage. An automatic sensor adjusts power to maintain a consistent speed, even with heavy cookie dough.

Warranty: 1 year
Manufacturer's Suggested Retail Price: $100
Approximate Low Price: $100

BLENDERS

For crushing hard food items or for thoroughly combining liquids with solids (for example, when making soup), the traditional blender cannot be surpassed. The carafe and its added power not only crush the ice but also protect the user from flying ice particles and splashes. Carafe blenders vary by model, giving consumers a choice between glass, plastic, and stainless-steel carafes; push-button, dial, and touch-pad controls; and specialty features, such as separate ice-crushing and pulse switches.

IMMERSION BLENDERS

The newest addition to the blender market is the immersion blender. These long, thin blending rods excel at jobs involving soft food items, such as pureeing cooked vegetables or blending fruit or ice-cream drinks. The immersion blender also offers the added convenience of being able to go directly into a drink cup, saucepan, or other container for quick blending without having to transfer the contents to separate blender carafe. For added versatility, many immersion blenders also come with chopping or whipping attachments to help them function as mini choppers or hand mixers.

TRADITIONAL BLENDERS

Cuisinart SmartPower SPB-7

✓BEST BUY

The Cuisinart SmartPower SPB-7 blender is a state-of-the-art appliance that features touchpad controls that operate in either continuous or pulse mode. A separate ice-crush speed is strong enough to crush ice in seconds even without liquid. The SmartPower SPB-7 is ideal for mixing a batch of frozen daiquiris or making homemade salad dressing or salsa. Stir, mix, chop, puree, or liquefy—all with an effortless touch of your finger. The 40-ounce glass jar and stainless-steel blade assembly create a whirling "tornadolike" motion for fast, efficient blending with hot or cold liquids. Internal ribs keep the action focused down at the blade so solids do not go unprocessed. The two-piece plastic cover has a removable two-ounce cap so extra ingredients can be measured and easily added. Slip-proof feet add stability and a cord storage compartment prevents counter clutter. All parts, except motor base, are dishwasher safe.

Warranty: 3 years (limited)
Manufacturer's Suggested Retail Price: $120
Approximate Low Price: $80

Krups Power Xpert 250

✓BEST BUY

With its powerful five-speed motor, the Krups Power Xpert speeds through everyday blending chores from mixing a batch of fruit drinks to crushing ice for frozen beverages. This unit comes equipped with a large 40-ounce plastic carafe with a lid that has a removable two-ounce measuring cup. The motor base features a speed selector dial, as well as buttons for pulse, power burst, and ice crushing. A separate on/off button starts and stops the motor. The ice crusher and power burst buttons are touch-and-release, providing pulselike control. In addition, the Power Xpert includes a stable base (with rubber feet) and hidden cord storage.

Warranty: 1 year
Manufacturer's Suggested Retail Price: $85
Approximate Low Price: $50

Oster Osterizer 6635

Recommended

An innovative feature of the Osterizer 12-speed 6635 blender is its double-wall thermal jar. This is designed to keep frozen drinks cold for up to six hours, which is more than five times as long as average plastic or glass blender carafes. The double-wall design also prevents condensation from forming on the outside of the jar. Great for frozen cocktails or milkshakes, the Osterizer 6635 consists of the five-cup break-resistant thermal jar, a stainless-steel blade, a contoured cover with a removable two-ounce measuring cup, and a power base with 12 push-button speeds that can operate in continuous or pulse mode for controlled blending action. To operate, just select a high or low speed then press one of the six control buttons; or push and release the pulse button for stop-and-go blending action. Optional accessories include a milkshake blade and 8- and 30-ounce mini-blend jars, which are handy for blending and storing ingredients.

Warranty: 1 year
Manufacturer's Suggested Retail Price: $50
Approximate Low Price: $50

Hamilton Beach 56200

Budget Buy

The Hamilton Beach 56200 boasts commercial quality in a consumer appliance. This unit tackles routine chores, such as fruit smoothies, gravies, or pancake batters. It also goes to work on denser mixtures, such as cream cheese gelatins or guacamole dip. The 40-ounce glass carafe is well suited for varying temperatures. Eight push-button controls, along with a low/high switch, let you operate the unit in any of its 16 speeds from grating and grinding to liquefying and mixing. The off button also serves as an ice-breaker and pulse button. The 56200 will operate in short bursts when this button is pressed and released. A Quick Clean button lets you rinse the blender of any loose food particles when processing multiple batches of the same food.

Warranty: 2 years
Manufacturer's Suggested Retail Price: $50
Approximate Low Price: $38

IMMERSION BLENDERS

Braun Multiquick MR430HC

✓BEST BUY

The Braun Multiquick MR430HC is a compact, convenient appliance that performs multiple functions. The slim design lets you blend a milkshake in your own glass or puree soup right in the pan. The motor is extremely quiet in comparison to traditional carafe blenders. This unit consists of a slim blending rod with detachable shaft, a stainless-steel blade, a whisk attachment, a resealable one-pint mixing/measuring beaker, and a mini-chopper. To operate, simply press and release the control grip. To avoid splashes, first insert the hand blender into the mixing beaker then activate the motor. The up-and-down motion produces a smooth consistency. Use the whisk attachment for whipping cream or egg whites to stiff peaks. The seven-ounce chopper is perfect for mincing or chopping small quantities of onions, garlic, fruits, nuts, or cheeses. The MR430HC, however, is not designed for extremely hard food items, such as ice cubes, coffee beans, or chocolate. The double-function antislip chopper bowl base/lid seals the bowl to let you store unused quantities quickly and easily. To clean, rinse all parts, except motor base, in hot, soapy water. Shaft, chopper bowl, and mixing/measuring beaker are also dishwasher safe.

Warranty: 1 year (limited)
Manufacturer's Suggested Retail Price: $35
Approximate Low Price: $30

Cuisinart Cordless Rechargeable CSB-44

✓ BEST BUY

The Cuisinart Cordless Rechargeable hand blender is both powerful and versatile. Because there is no cord to restrict your movement either within or outside of your kitchen (a compact, detachable battery-pack handle plugs directly into a wall outlet for charging), the Cuisinart hand blender offers maximum versatility and convenience. You can blend a drink out on the patio or directly on the stovetop without worrying that the cord will get tangled or twisted. This unit is perfect for chores that involve stirring, mixing, or blending soft food items, or combining solids with liquids, such as when making soups. To use, simply assemble the unit by twist-locking the blade stem and power pack onto shaft. Then press the control switch on the handgrip to activate motor. An up-and-down pulsing motion provides the best results. This unit comes with a stainless-steel chopping/mincing blade, a plastic whipping attachment, a counter or wall storage unit, and a clear mixing beaker. The whipping attachment can be used for making milkshakes, whipped cream, or mashed potatoes. To clean the blender, simply rinse stem and blades under running water. All parts, except motor base, are dishwasher safe.

Warranty: 3 years (limited)
Manufacturer's Suggested Retail Price: $80
Approximate Low Price: $70

TOASTERS AND TOASTER OVENS

Toasters have occupied a prominent place in the kitchen for more than 70 years. During that time, other appliances have come on the market, including the toaster oven, but none has been able to replace the toaster in terms of performing its one basic function—toasting. Many manufacturers produce toasters, and it is not difficult to find inexpensive models at any department store—if toasting bread is all you want to do. The models listed here are top-of-the line toasters that offer a number of convenient options, such as defrosting and light pastry settings, as well as the ability to handle thicker food items, such as bagels.

TOASTER OVENS

Toaster ovens, on the other hand, perform the additional functions of baking and broiling. They come in handy for making open-faced sandwiches or other items that cannot be accommodated by the vertical slots of toasters. Toaster ovens come in a variety of styles from smaller models that can handle up to four slices of bread to larger models that can roast an entire chicken. Of course, the larger the capacity, the more room the unit will occupy on your counter, so be sure you choose the right capacity to suit your needs.

KitchenAid Ultra Power Plus KTT261

✓BEST BUY

The KitchenAid Ultra Power Plus KTT261 is a digital-control toaster with a single, extra-long slot for toasting bread slices up to one-inch thick, frozen waffles, and bagels. An electronic heat sensor combines with an Even-Heat System for even browning and to help retain moisture so breads don't dry out. To use, position bread in the slot, select toast setting (from 1:light to 9:dark) by pressing either the up or down arrow touchpad, and press the carriage lever down. The centering rack automatically adjusts to keep food upright. An indicator light signals that the unit is operating and a digital display shows the darkness setting. When toasting is complete, the carriage lever raises toast and unit shuts off. Other settings include "frozen," which first defrosts, then toasts the bread; "reheat," which warms previously toasted foods; and "bagel," which is specially designed for even toasting of bagels. To interrupt toasting at any time, simply press the stop/reset button and the carriage lever will raise immediately. Other features include a slide-out crumb tray, sturdy, easy-to-clean cool-touch housing, and wraparound storage.

Warranty: 1 year
Manufacturer's Suggested Retail Price: $100
Approximate Low Price: $100

Cuisinart Custom Control Total Touch CPT-60

✓BEST BUY

The Cuisinart Custom Control Total Touch CPT-60 is a state-of-the-art appliance that boasts "perfect" toast every time. A single, extra-wide (1¾-inch) slot accommodates a wide variety of breads, bagels, and pastries. Touchpad controls offer defrost, reheat, and shade control (lighter to darker) settings, as well as special settings for a bagel or a single slice of bread. There's also a cancel/reset button, which halts toasting at any time during the cycle. A lighted display shows which of the seven browning levels has been selected. Specialty items, such as muffins, pastries, croissants, and frozen convenience items are no problem for this unit—although additional toasting time may be required. Other features include a high-rise carriage for easy removal of cooked items, a cool-touch housing, self-centering bread guides, a cord storage, and a slide-out crumb tray.

Warranty: 3 years (limited)
Manufacturer's Suggested Retail Price: $98
Approximate Low Price: $70

Krups Compact Toaster 155

Recommended

The Krups Compact Toaster is a space-saving appliance that features two wide slots with self-centering guide wires for toasting thick or thin slices of bread or English muffins. It also toasts specialty items, such as bagels or pastries. The shade selector dial easily adjusts from reheat (low) to 6 (high) for minimum to maximum browning. Other features include a smooth cool-touch surface that easily wipes clean, a hidden cord storage, and a hinged crumb tray for simple cleanup.

Warranty: 1 year (limited)
Manufacturer's Suggested Retail Price: $40
Approximate Low Price: $40

TOASTER OVENS

DeLonghi Convection AS670

✓BEST BUY

The DeLonghi AS670 is more than a toaster oven—it's a scaled-down countertop convection oven. The exclusive turbo fan distributes heat within the oven for fast, even cooking. The heat distribution means quicker cooking time—up to 30 percent faster than standard ovens. The unit features multilevel cooking, with two racks for accommodating extra batches or two different items simultaneously. Three control dials let you select a function (broil, toast, bake, fan bake), oven on/toast color (from light to dark), and temperature (from keep warm/200°F degrees to broil/450°F). An indicator light signals when the oven has reached a desired temperature. Other features include an extra-large capacity that can handle oversize roasts, pies, and casseroles; a full-view glass door; a continuous-cleaning interior with an interior light that lets you monitor cooking progress; a removable crumb tray; and a cord storage. A pizza stone is available separately.

Warranty: 1 year
Manufacturer's Suggested Retail Price: $170
Approximate Low Price: $170

Krups Pro Chef Plus 553

✓BEST BUY

The Krups Pro Chef Plus does the work of both a toaster and a broiler. It offers four-slice capacity with settings from light to dark (as well as top brown, which is great for open-faced sandwiches). When toasting is complete, a bell timer signals and the unit automatically shuts itself off. Two dial controls let you select toast color and oven temperatures, which range from 150°F to 500°F—plus the broiling feature. The interior can accommodate a nine-inch pie plate, a mini loaf pan, or its own bake/broil pan. A full-panel glass door lets you monitor cooking progress but also hides fingerprints, thanks to a geometric grid dot pattern covering its surface. A handy feature of this unit is the slide-out rack, which moves forward as the door is opened, providing easier access to (and removal of) cooked food items. Other features include on/off indicator light, easy-care white exterior, coated continuous-cleaning interior, and hinged crumb tray for quick cleanup.

Warranty: 1 year
Manufacturer's Suggested Retail Price: $150
Approximate Low Price: $150

Toastmaster Breadmaker's Hearth 1193

Recommended

A truly unique machine, the Toastmaster Breadmaker's Hearth looks more like a microwave oven but is actually a toaster, countertop oven, and bread maker all in one. Functions include bake, broil, defrost, keep warm, top brown, and of course bread making. A bit more complicated than your average toaster oven, this unit is exceptionally versatile. To use the bake or broil functions, first slide the oven rack into place, then press the "oven" button to select a program. Set bake time by pressing up or down arrow key until desired time is displayed in clock window. Press the "temp" button to select your temperature (from 100°F up to 500°F). Toaster functions include programs for toasting (two or four slices) or top browning. The programming may seem unfamiliar at first so reading through the detailed instruction book is essential. Touchpad controls are a welcome addition. This unit also bakes a traditional horizontal two-pound loaf of bread, and it is great for dinner rolls, pretzels, or pizza dough. Accessories include a nonstick bread pan with kneading blade and handle, a mixer assembly cover, a bake/broil pan, and a wire rack. Bread making features include a 13-hour delay timer, 12 fully automatic cycles for breads, cakes or dough, a keep warm feature, and an automatic signal when it is time to add ingredients. A handy instruction video is included.

Warranty: 3 years
Manufacturer's Suggested Retail Price: $200
Approximate Low Price: $150

Oster Designer Toast Logic 6204

Budget Buy

The Oster 6204 is an attractive toaster oven that can easily accommodate up to six slices of bread, a whole roasting chicken, a frozen dinner, or two mini loaf pans. "Toast Logic" is an electronic sensor that monitors power usage and adjusts toasting time accordingly to maintain temperature for consistent results. Three rack positions let you bake, toast, or broil/grill at the appropriate level with proper airflow for even cooking. Features include a 60-minute timer with auto shut-off, which can be set to turn oven or broil/grill mode off at the end of cooking cycle; thermostat dial, which controls bake temperature (from 100°F to 500°F) and broil/grill function; an indicator light that signals when unit is in use; and a toast control dial to select darkness. The 6204 also features a toasting lever with auto shut-off, nonstick interior walls, a removable wire rack, a pull-out crumb tray, a heavy duty bake/broil pan, and a cord storage.

Warranty: 1 year (limited)
Manufacturer's Suggested Retail Price: $100
Approximate Low Price: $70

JUICERS/JUICE EXTRACTORS

Salton Juiceman Jr. JM1

✓BEST BUY

The Salton Juiceman Jr. JM1 is an efficient way to enjoy delicious vitamin-rich juice in minutes. It comes with a compact motor base, large pulp collector, stainless-steel extractor basket with micromesh screen to separate and strain pulp, clear dome cover, and food pusher. To operate, prepare fruits and/or vegetables by washing and trimming away any undesirable parts (brown spots, thick skins, stems, pits). Cut into pieces to fit feed tube. With juice cup in position, turn motor on and feed fruits/vegetables into the machine using the food pusher with gentle pressure. Pulp will automatically collect in the pulp container, which removes easily for cleaning. This unit also comes with its own fresh juice recipe book and a detailed instruction book. The unit disassembles and all parts, except motor base, rinse clean in warm soapy water.

Warranty: 1 year (limited)
Manufacturer's Suggested Retail Price: $100
Approximate Low Price: $90

Farberware Deluxe FCJ 300P

Recommended

The Farberware FCJ 300P features two cones that are suitable for juicing both small (limes, lemons) and large (oranges, grapefruit) citrus fruits. It comes with a 24-ounce capacity clear juice container with both liter and ounce measurements, stainless-steel strainer and base, juicing cones, and clear cover. To use, assemble juicer with the desired cone in place, place fruit over cone, and press. Apply even pressure as you gently squeeze fruit around the cone. The juicer will automatically stop when fruit is removed. To adjust pulp contents, turn container on base—left for lower pulp content, right for higher pulp content. Rubber feet help hold the unit in place and the cord storage eliminates unnecessary counter clutter. All parts on the FCJ 300P, except base, are top-rack dishwasher safe.

Warranty: 1 year (limited)
Manufacturer's Suggested Retail Price: $32
Approximate Low Price: $30

STEAMERS

Black & Decker Flavor Scenter HS2000

✓BEST BUY

The Black & Decker Flavor Scenter combination food steamer/rice cooker has its own container for direct steaming of vegetables, seafood, or other items. Steaming basket is oblong to accommodate longer produce, such as corn-on-the-cob or asparagus. A special screen insert allows you to add fresh or dried herbs for flavor enhancement. This unit also comes with a seven-cup rice bowl. To use, fill water reservoir with cold water. Lemon juice, broth, or white wine may also be added to enhance flavor. Attach drip tray with flavor scenter screen and place herbs or spices onto screen. Place food in steaming bowl, insert bowl in steamer, and cover in position on base. Set timer for desired cooking time (up to 75 minutes). The 3.5-quart steaming basket can hold up to five ears of corn, two pounds of red potatoes, or six cups of beans or broccoli florets. When steaming time has elapsed, the bell will signal and the unit will automatically shut off. Bowls, cover, and drip tray are all dishwasher safe for easy cleanup.

Warranty: 1 year
Manufacturer's Suggested Retail Price: $35
Approximate Low Price: $28

Krups OptiSteam 649

✓BEST BUY

The Krups OptiSteam 649 features a clear steaming basket that lets you prepare healthy steamed vegetables and rice, without the added calories of butter of cooking oil. The 14-cup steaming tray divides into two compartments, so cooking several different foods is effortless. Simply fill water reservoir, assemble unit, and place prepared foods into tray. Then set the automatic timer. Steam begins flowing almost instantly. The oblong tray is designed to accommodate longer foods, such as asparagus, corn-on-the-cob, or crab legs. A separate six-cup rice bowl converts the unit to a rice cooker. A thermal safety feature protects the unit from overheating if water tray becomes empty. Other features include a water-level indicator, external fill spout, 60-minute timer with automatic shut-off, and hidden cord storage. Tray and bowls are dishwasher safe for easy cleanup.

Warranty: 1 year
Manufacturer's Suggested Retail Price: $55
Approximate Low Price: $50

ICE-CREAM MAKERS

Krups La Glacièr 358

✓BEST BUY

The Krups La Glacièr ice-cream maker lets you enjoy a fresh batch of creamy ice cream without the hassle of ice-and-salt-powered machines. A double-insulated mixing chamber retains a frozen state longer for better results. A see-through lid with a feeder hole lets you watch the progress of the ice cream and allows you to add fruit, nuts, or chips without opening the container. To use, first freeze the cylinder for a minimum of eight hours. Note: Continual storage of the cylinder bowl in the freezer is recommended so that the unit is ready at a moment's notice. It will make up to 1½ quarts of your favorite ice cream. The unit includes an automatic mixing feature that stirs and scrapes the walls of the cylinder, blending air into the mixture for a creamy texture. It takes 20-30 minutes for ice cream to reach desired consistency. As mixture thickens and the paddle senses resistance, it will automatically change direction. Paddle and lid are dishwasher safe.

Warranty: 1 year (limited)
Manufacturer's Suggested Retail Price: $95
Approximate Low Price: $60

Toastmaster Automatic 6701

Recommended

The Toastmaster Automatic 6701 is a two-speed, salt-free ice-cream maker that uses a freezer bowl to provide chilling power during the ice-cream-making process. Features include compact motor base, freezer bowl, mixing paddle, and clear domed cover. Before using, freeze bowl until solid (approximately 15 hours). Prepare and prechill ingredients. Then assemble the unit and select desired consistency (hard or soft) using the control switch. As the freezer bowl begins to turn, pour ice-cream mixture into bowl. Additional ingredients, such as candies, nuts, or chocolate chips can be added near the end of the mixing cycle through a hole in cover. When ice cream reaches the desired consistency, turn unit to off. The Toastmaster is equipped with an automatic shutoff feature that turns machine off if too much resistance is encountered. This unit makes up to four cups of your favorite frozen dessert in about 25-30 minutes.

Warranty: 3 years (limited)
Manufacturer's Suggested Retail Price: $64
Approximate Low Price: not available

BREAD MAKERS

Salton Breadman Plus TR800

✓BEST BUY

The Salton Breadman Plus offers 54 bread settings, including a choice of three horizontal loaf sizes, three crust colors, and "normal" or "rapid" bake cycles. A digital display window shows your selection, with touchpad controls for crust color, loaf size, bread cycle, time, and start-stop. A separate row of indicator lights shows which function is being performed: knead, rise, bake, complete. A time function allows you to delay breadmaking start time for up to 15 hours. In the event of a power failure, the Breadman Plus stores the active program in memory and lets you return to breadmaking within an hour of the elapsed time. Start-to-finish bread baking takes as little as 3½ hours in the basic cycle or just over 2½ hours in rapid bake cycle. Bread pan and kneading paddle remove for easy cleaning in warm, soapy water.

Warranty: 1 year
Manufacturer's Suggested Retail Price: $180
Approximate Low Price: $150

West Bend Automatic 41089

Recommended

The West Bend 41089 bakes a traditional bakery-style loaf of fresh bread. This unit's innovative feature is its horizontal design with swing-open door and horizontal loaf pan, which produces either 1½- or 2-pound loaves of bread. Other features include a viewing window on the door and a digital display panel that lets you select bread and crust settings with a touch of your finger. This model also comes with a sample bread mix to help get you started. The unit is preprogrammed at the basic/specialty bread setting, medium crust, and 1½-pound loaf size. To operate, simply add ingredients to the pan (liquids first, followed by dry, and yeast last), and press start. Two kneading bars ensure thorough mixing of ingredients. Finished bread is ready in 3½ hours. Other features include a 13-hour programmable timer, a keep-warm function that operates for three hours after bread is finished baking, and an alert signal that tells you when to add additional ingredients, such as nuts or raisins. The horizontal design lets this unit keep a low profile so it can fit into tighter kitchen spaces where less height is available, such as under cabinets.

Warranty: 1 year
Manufacturer's Suggested Retail Price: $210
Approximate Low Price: $170

Oster Deluxe 5839

Budget Buy

An affordable simple-to-use machine, the Oster Deluxe 5839 programs everything there is to know about mixing, kneading, rising, and baking into one of eleven cycles. To make bread, attach the kneading blade, measure ingredients into the pan, and insert the pan into machine. A digital control panel lets you select a program, start the unit, or cancel operation in progress. The unit automatically mixes ingredients, lets dough rise, kneads it, and bakes it—all in 2¾ to 4½ hours. You can even set the 13-hour delay timer to delay completion. The 5839 has an automatic warming cycle that begins when baking is completed and runs for about one hour. Another plus is the clear and informative instruction booklet, which will even have first-time bread bakers turning out perfect loaves every time.

Warranty: 1 year
Manufacturer's Suggested Retail Price: $100
Approximate Low Price: not available

COFFEE MAKERS AND TEA MAKERS

With the multitude of coffee makers on the market, selecting the right model to suit your particular needs may seem an overwhelming task. You can narrow the choices considerably, however, if you first select the type and size of coffee maker you need.

Automatic-drip Coffee Makers: These units consist of a power base (with water reservoir), a filter holder, a carafe, and a built-in warming plate or a carafe stand. Optional features include permanent gold-tone or screen filters, which replace the standard disposable paper filters; digital clocks with timers to preset the start of coffee making; an automatic shut-off; and a pause-to-serve function, which lets you halt brewing long enough to pour a cup of coffee. The newest and most attractive offerings in this category include water filtration systems that remove chlorine, bacteria, and other contaminants from drinking water before brewing; flavor systems that can adjust the strength of the coffee—from mild to robust—to suit your taste; and even a combination machine that can grind coffee beans just prior to brewing for the freshest possible taste. Larger machines can make up to 12 cups but can usually be set for smaller servings. Personal-size machines make up to 4 cups at a time and save counter space. Single-cup machines are available, which, in many cases, brew directly into a travel mug for convenient on-the-road coffee consumption. All automatic-drip coffee makers require periodic cleaning or decalcifying to remove mineral deposits. This is accomplished by brewing a cycle with a special cleaning solution or a mixture of vinegar and water.

Electric Percolators: These are self-contained carafes with built-in brewing mechanisms, permanent filter baskets, and lids. Many have detachable cordsets. These units brew coffee by pumping hot water over and through coarse grounds at an incredibly fast (cup-a-minute) speed. Sizes range from 4 to 12 cups for standard percolators and anywhere from 12 to 30 cups and up to 100-cup capacities for the largest percolator urns.

Expresso/Cappuccino Makers: These machines operate by heating water and using steam or pump pressure to force the water through fine grounds quickly for maximum flavor extraction. Steam can then be diverted through a nozzle to foam milk for cappuccino. Of the two types, pump machines are the more powerful, heating water to the optimal temperature (190-197°F, as recommended by the Specialty Coffee Association of America) then propelling it through fine-ground beans in about 20-30 seconds. The fast rate of expulsion produces a rich layer of foam, known as crema, which is the mark of great espresso. Though steam machines do not possess the power of pump machines, they do produce a good, strong cup of espresso and are generally smaller and less expensive than pump models. Combination units are also available, which make regular brewed coffee as well as espresso and cappuccino.

Coffee Mills: Since a good cup of coffee starts with quality ingredients, always be sure to use fresh coffee. Grinding your own from freshly roasted beans is simple with a coffee mill. The mills, also called burr grinders, use wheels to produce a variety of grinds from very fine espresso grinds to coarser grinds for use in percolators. These units are larger and more expensive than standard blade grinders; however the increased capacity and ability to select from a number of different grinds make them ideal choices for the most discerning coffee drinker. Be sure to store your beans in an airtight container in your freezer and grind only the amount needed immediately before brewing.

AUTOMATIC DRIP COFFEE MAKERS

Krups Premium 253

✓BEST BUY

The Krups Premium 253 features a specially-designed carafe with an airtight lid that excels at keeping coffee fresh up to 20 percent longer than conventional carafes. An electronically-controlled flavor selector sets the brewing cycle for smaller quantities (1-3 cups) or larger quantities (4-10 cups) to ensure maximum flavor extraction. Specialty features include auto shut-off, which keeps coffee hot for two hours after brewing then turns appliance off; Stop 'n Serve, which lets you remove carafe during brewing to pour a cup of coffee; and a stainless-steel heating element for long-lasting and consistently superior performance. Other features include a permanent gold-tone filter, swing-away removable two-part filter holder, stainless-steel antidrip spout, easy-to-read water-level indicator, hinged water-chamber lid, and hidden cord storage.

Warranty: 1 year (limited)
Manufacturer's Suggested Retail Price: $160
Approximate Low Price: $120

Braun FlavorSelect KF187

✓BEST BUY

The Braun FlavorSelect KF187 offers a number of attractive features to satisfy a variety of tastes. Available in three vibrant colors, this unit has an hourglass design with a tapered filter holder and a carafe. Specialty features include a flavor selector dial that can be set at any point along a graduated scale for varying coffee tastes (mild to robust) and a multipath brewing system that distributes water evenly through grounds for optimum flavor extraction. The patented water filter reduces chlorine and other contaminants in water prior to brewing. A digital clock/timer lets you preset brewing time so coffee is ready when you are. Other features include automatic pause-to-serve, adjustable temperature control that can be set to maintain the user's preferred drinking temperature, adjustable auto shut-off, gold-tone filter, swing-out filter basket, water-level indicator, flip-back water-reservoir lid, and cord storage.

Warranty: 1 year
Manufacturer's Suggested Retail Price: $100
Approximate Low Price: $95

Rival Brew-Thru CM5500

Recommended

The Rival Brew-Thru CM5500 lets you brew up to eight cups of coffee directly into its own insulated carafe. A patented lid system is engaged when the unit rests on its base. Once removed for serving, the lid can be closed to keep steam and flavor locked inside. The carafe goes right to the table for serving and coffee stays hot for up to four hours. This model features a swing-out removable basket that uses a cone-shaped paper filters, an easy-to-read water-level indicator, and a single, easy-to-use on/off switch. A pause-to-serve feature lets you interrupt brewing long enough to pour a cup of coffee. Available in white or black, the carafe is attractively designed with a comfortable handle and smooth base that won't mar surfaces. Other features include a flip-back water-tank lid and hidden cord storage.

Warranty: 1 year (limited)
Manufacturer's Suggested Retail Price: $52
Approximate Low Price: $50

Sunbeam CustomBlend 3281

Budget Buy

The Sunbeam CustomBlend 12-cup coffee maker packs some attractive features into an affordably priced unit. The CustomBlend dial lets you adjust coffee taste to suit your preferences—from mild to robust. A programmable clock/timer lets you preset brewing time. Auto-shut-off keeps coffee warm for two hours after brewing, then switches itself off. Pause-to-serve interrupts brewing cycle, enabling you to pour a cup of coffee. Available in white or black, with a removable, dishwasher-safe filter basket, this unit doesn't sacrifice performance for price.

Warranty: 2 years
Manufacturer's Suggested Retail Price: $57
Approximate Low Price: not available

PERCOLATORS

Farberware FCP240

✓BEST BUY

The Farberware FCP240 Percolator is a small-capacity percolator that is well suited for singles or households with modest daily coffee consumption. This unit is made of heavy-gauge stainless steel, with a permanent stainless-steel filter basket assembly and detachable cordset. The base, handle, and lid knob are made of heavy black plastic to protect surfaces and provide safe handling. To operate, simply fill percolator with cold water to desired level (markings are given inside tank), measure grounds into filter basket, insert basket on pump assembly, replace lid, and plug in. Within minutes you'll have 2-4 cups of piping hot coffee. The unit switches to a keep-warm setting once brewing is completed. This unit's compact size saves counter space and stores away easily.

Warranty: 1 year
Manufacturer's Suggested Retail Price: $50
Approximate Low Price: $45

Cuisinart Classic Cordless PER-12

✓BEST BUY

The Cuisinart Classic Cordless sits atop a power base for brewing, then detaches for serving—at your desk or out on the patio. This unit prepares 4-12 cups of piping hot coffee in about ten minutes. The stainless-steel base and cover are built for consistent and long-lasting use. A clear knob on the lid allows you to monitor percolating. The lid must be allowed to cool down before it can be removed. A permanent coffee basket filter has convenient measurements etched on the side. Inside the percolator, water-level markings take the guesswork out of coffee making. Other features include a tapered no-drip spout, a cool-touch percolator handle, a "ready" light, and convenient cord storage.

Warranty: 3 years (limited)
Manufacturer's Suggested Retail Price: $98
Approximate Low Price: $70

COFFEE URNS

Farberware FSU236

Recommended

The Farberware FSU236 is both attractive and functional. Made of heavy-gauge stainless steel, this unit is designed to provide many years of use. It brews from 12 to 36 cups of fresh, hot coffee at a rate of less than one cup per minute. Once brewing is complete, the urn switches to keep-warm in order to maintain ideal drinking temperature. The base is made of superhard plastic to stay cool and protect surfaces. The unit's elegant design makes it suitable for display in the dining room, patio, or wherever coffee is to be served. The stay-cool handles and lid knob also provide safe and easy handling. Other features include a no-drip spigot for clean, easy dispensing of coffee; a break-resistant dishwasher-safe plastic brewing basket; and an indicator light that signals when coffee is ready.

Warranty: 1 year (limited)
Manufacturer's Suggested Retail Price: $175
Approximate Low Price: $150

West Bend Party Perk 57640

Budget Buy

The Party Perk offers an economical alternative for those who need a larger capacity coffee maker for entertaining but who don't want to spend a lot to get it. This unit's antique white plastic has double-walled insulation for a cooler exterior surface and also keeps coffee hot for up to two hours after brewing is completed. You can brew from 12 to 30 cups of coffee at a cup-a-minute speed. Other features include an automatic temperature control to maintain a consistent serving temperature, a two-way dripless faucet (lever locks in an up position for filling carafes), twist-lock lid, heat-resistant handles, a detachable cordset, and a "ready" light.

Warranty: 1 year
Manufacturer's Suggested Retail Price: $59
Approximate Low Price: $35

EXPRESSO/CAPPUCCINO MACHINES

Salton Spresso PE 1,2,3

✓BEST BUY

Perhaps the easiest way to enjoy rich espresso at home is with the Salton Spresso PE 1,2,3. Just fill the removable water reservoir with fresh water and switch the machine on. Then select "coffee" on the temperature switch and, when the green light indicates, drop in a ready-to-use "pod" or pouch prefilled with European roasted coffee. Enough pods are included with this machine to brew 50 cups. Then turn the function selector to dispense coffee. Coffee brews in approximately 10-15 seconds. For additional cups, repeat this process. When brewing is complete, the used coffee pod falls into its own container for quick, easy removal. The prefilled pods eliminate the need to fuss with exact measuring of fine coffee grounds. This unit features a universal water-filter holder, which uses any cylinder-type filter (not included). An additional steam function can be used to heat and froth milk for cappuccino or café latte. A step-by-step instructional video is also included.

Warranty: 1 year
Manufacturer's Suggested Retail Price: $250
Approximate Low Price: $250

Cuisinart ICAPP-4

Recommended

The Cuisinart ICAPP-4 iced cappuccino maker uses centrifugal force to extract the maximum flavor from fine coffee grounds. This unit prepares up to eight servings of hot espresso or four servings of iced cappuccino in approximately three minutes. To make iced cappuccino, fill water reservoir to desired level, add finely ground espresso coffee to the spinner cup, fill the milk container, and fill carafe with ice. Gently press down on the cover and turn milk dispensing knob to "heat" position; then press on/off button. A red indicator light signals that the unit is heating water to proper brewing temperature. A green light will signal when espresso is ready to flow into carafe. Turn milk-dispensing knob to dispense milk into carafe. The unit automatically shuts off when cycle is completed. You can make hot espresso by following the same steps, but omitting the milk and ice. This unit's unique design eliminates the need for packing down the grounds. Other features include a removable drip tray, a measuring scoop, and a recipe booklet. Milk container, spinner cup, and cover are dishwasher safe for easy cleanup.

Warranty: 3 years (limited)
Manufacturer's Suggested Retail Price: $100
Approximate Low Price: $100

Black & Decker Mio EE200

Budget Buy

The Black & Decker Mio provides an economical and simple alternative to other high-power, sophisticated machines. This unit consists of a water cup, funnel, coffee basket, filter, and brewer cup with handle and lid. You can brew traditional espresso, cappuccino, or latte in less than two minutes in a standard microwave oven. Rather than forcing water down through grounds, this unit uses steam pressure to brew espresso from the bottom up, just as traditional stove-top models do. Simply fill water cup, fill coffee basket with fine-ground coffee, reassemble unit, and heat in microwave on high for 1½ minutes. Espresso brews through the funnel and coffee basket into a brewer cup for easy pouring. The

EE200 kit also includes a recipe book, a measuring spoon, and an instant pump for frothing hot or cold milk to make cappuccino or latte. All parts are dishwasher safe for easy cleanup.

Warranty: 1 year
Manufacturer's Suggested Retail Price: $30 ($20 without frother)
Approximate Low Price: not available

COFFEE MILLS

Salton CM4

✓BEST BUY

The Salton CM4 is a compact, efficient unit that produces uniformly ground coffee for all types of coffee makers. Choose from varying degrees of fineness—from extra fine for espresso to coarse ground for percolators or urns. The bean chamber holds up to four ounces, which is enough for about 18 cups of coffee. A simple-to-use "on" button activates motor. Grounds are dispensed into a separate storage container. A safety interlock feature stops the grinder when the grounds container is not is position. Other features include detachable grounds container for easy dispensing and cleaning. A convenient cord storage is also included.

Warranty: 1 year
Manufacturer's Suggested Retail Price: $30
Approximate Low Price: $30

Braun KMM30

✓BEST BUY

This burr grinder uses grinding wheels instead of blades to produce a precision grind for all types of coffee. The KMM30 features an adjustable fineness control dial with 24 grind settings from coarse to extra fine. There's also an automatic quantity selector with timer, which determines the grinding time based on the number of cups of coffee desired. To shorten or stop the grinding process, return the timer to the off position. A conical bean container with lid holds up to eight ounces of coffee beans (enough for up to 60 cups of coffee). The coffee grounds are dispensed into a separate container with rounded bottom to allow easier removal with measuring spoon. The coffee-bean container, lid, and ground coffee container all remove for easy cleaning in warm, soapy water, or in upper rack of dishwasher. The KMM30 is available in white or black.

Warranty: 1 year (limited)
Manufacturer's Suggested Retail Price: $60
Approximate Low Price: $52

COFFEE AND TEA MAKER

Hamilton Beach 47291

Recommended

The Hamilton Beach 47291 is an automatic-drip coffee maker with a tea-making attachment that fits inside the carafe and holds either loose tea or teabag for steeping. This model includes a number of specialty features such as a programmable clock timer, an automatic shutoff, and an auto pause-and-serve for sneaking a cup of coffee during brewing. For regular coffee, fill water reservoir, add grounds to filter basket, and brew. To make tea, place tea in attachment and insert attachment in carafe. Fill the water reservoir with desired amount of water (up to ten cups). Water brews through the empty filter basket into carafe for steeping. Strength depends on length of steeping time. Tea attachment easily removes for serving. Other features include a nonstick warming plate, a removable filter holder, an accelerated brewing process, and an "on" light that signals when the unit is in operation.

Warranty: 2 years
Manufacturer's Suggested Retail Price: $60
Approximate Low Price: not available

MICROWAVE OVENS

Microwave oven manufacturers are constantly using technology to upgrade units in order to meet the needs of today's families better. For example, automatic sensors take away some of the guesswork in determining when food has finished cooking. These high-tech sensors measure moisture in the oven to determine reheating times and cooking levels. More recently there has been a movement to higher wattage and more spacious interiors. The wattage of an oven determines the cooking speed. Therefore, these higher wattage units cook faster than ever before.

Units are also gaining usable interior space, while outside dimensions remain consistent. Consequently, there is a new size category, referred to as a family-size unit. This unit is larger than the medium-size oven, yet smaller than the full-size models. Other innovative features include interactive displays, which now offer detailed, written instructions in the control panel window in as many as three languages. The key to getting the best buy is to select the right unit with the right features for your microwaving needs.

CHOOSING A MICROWAVE

Microwave ovens are available in various styles. Units may sit on a countertop or cart. They may be built-in or placed on a special microwave shelf. Another popular option is the over-the-range unit. This unit typically replaces the ventilation hood and light and is mounted over the cooking surface. It eliminates the need for a range hood and is more space-efficient. Since these units have a smaller usable interior than comparable tabletop units, you will want to select the most spacious one you can find.

Still another option is the microwave/convection oven. Although it is more expensive than other styles, it can offer many benefits to the user. This unit is both an oven and a microwave. It can microwave, bake, and roast foods and can be identified by its stainless-steel interior. Foods will brown and cook in one-third less time than if prepared in a conventional oven. A microwave/convection oven can serve as the sole oven in a small kitchen or as a second oven in a traditional kitchen. Although they may heat up to 500°F, their ability to broil is limited.

SIZE

Units are classified according to size. For all practical reasons, it makes sense to purchase the largest unit your kitchen can accommodate. A full-size microwave, for example, makes the best choice for built-in use or placement on a microwave shelf or cart. In this instance, it usually takes up no more space than a smaller unit.

A full-size unit measures from 1.5 to 1.9 cubic feet overall. If you intend to have the unit installed, make sure a built-in kit is available; not all manufacturers offer this option. For countertop use in the home, full-size, family-size, or medium-size units are usually best depending on the space available. A family-size unit measures from 1.2 to 1.4 cubic feet, while a medium-size unit measures from 0.9 to 1.1 cubic feet. For offices, where space is limited and where microwaves are used primarily for heating up lunch, a medium-size unit is usually sufficient. Compact units sell less frequently these days and are used primarily for dorm rooms, boats, and campers. Compact units are those measuring 0.7 cubic feet or less.

WATTAGE

Most microwave recipes and prepackaged foods cook best with an oven of 700 watts or more, but cooking power on today's ovens may go as high as 1,100 watts. As a rule, the larger the unit, the higher the wattage is likely to be. Compact units are usually rated at 700 watts or less. Medium-size, family-size, and full-size units are typically rated from 825 to 1,100 watts. It is probably wise to give more weight to features than wattage, providing wattage falls within this range. The features that fit your needs will pay off far beyond the minimal decrease in cooking time a few watts will offer.

BUYING TIPS

Microwave ovens are offered by many retail stores. Appliance stores, electronic stores, discount stores, national chain stores, and home centers are the most common places to find microwave ovens. For built-in products, convection microwaves, and over-the-range microwave ovens, appliance stores tend to have the best displays and best products available. Some home centers offer design centers that can be helpful with these items as well. National chains, discount stores, and electronics stores usually offer a nice selection of compact, medium-size, family-size, and full- size ovens. Typically the prices at these stores are attractive. Select carefully, as the advertised products do not always include the best selection of features.

Many manufacturers also have web sites that can provide a wealth of information about available products. Using your computer can save you lots of time on comparative shopping. It is also important to note that manufacturers often offer the same basic body of a microwave oven with slightly differing model numbers. Changes in model numbers may often indicate varying features or colors. Check model numbers carefully to insure you get the exact features and color you desire.

FEATURES AND TERMINOLOGY

Automatic Defrost: This feature allows the food's weight and type to be keyed into the microwave's panel. A built-in mechanism then determines the amount of defrost time required to thaw the food.

Automatic Sensors: The newest of microwave technologies, this feature determines when food is cooked by measuring vapors in the oven. The majority of manufacturers are not installing sensors in their microwaves. Once a sensor has sounded, the oven automatically shuts off. Food should still be checked to make sure it has been thoroughly cooked. Sensors are also used by some manufacturers to determine defrost time.

Browning Dishes and Trays: These are sometimes included with the microwave to create a more oven-cooked look for the food. Browning dishes have a metal content on the bottom that helps foods, such as French fries, get crispier. Browning trays work in the same way, though neither provides the amount of crispness provided by a conventional oven.

Instant-Action Keys/Easy-Touch Buttons: These features are on keypads that have preset times installed by the manufacturer to determine how long a dish should take to cook. Common instant-action keys are for potatoes, popcorn, pizza, and hot beverages. Some full-size and countertop microwaves have as many as 15 keys.

Interactive Displays: These are word prompts that high-end microwaves use to guide you through the cooking process. Some interactive displays will make the cooking process more complicated, especially if you have a lot of keys available at your fingertips.

Language/Weight: These options allow some models to show you cooking directions in other languages, generally Spanish, English, and French. Weights of foods can also be translated by these models between pounds and kilograms.

Microwave/Convection Ovens: These ovens provide a more complete cooking environment than a microwave oven. Convection technology uses an electric element to provide heat, which is circulated through the oven. The combination microwave/convection oven allows for baking and other cooking of recipes that cannot be done in a microwave alone. These ovens work best when the two technologies are combined to cook meats and other foods that are browned nearly as well as when prepared in a conventional oven. Some convection ovens have metal interiors that are hotter to touch when cooking is finished.

Turntables: These revolving plates, usually glass, inside a microwave automatically turn food as it cooks. Turntables eliminate the need to open the microwave and turn the food by hand. Nearly all full-size and countertop microwaves have turntables, and many compact and over-the-range models are now adding them. Some microwaves have turntables that automatically place the dish at the front of the oven when cooking is finished.

BEST BUYS '99

Our Best Buy, Recommended, and Budget Buy microwave ovens are listed below. Products within each category are listed according to quality. The best of the Best Buys is listed first, followed by our second choice, and so on. A Best Buy, Recommended, or Budget Buy designation only applies to the model listed—it does not necessarily apply to other models made by the same manufacturer or to an entire product line.

FULL-SIZE MICROWAVE OVENS

Sharp R-530

✓BEST BUY

Also our top choice in 1998, the R-530 excels in technology and value. It features a 16-inch turntable, which is large enough to rotate a 9×13-inch dish. Its 1,100 watts of cooking power will satisfy all your microwaving needs. You'll appreciate the interactive and easy-to-read trilingual display (English, French, Spanish), which provides easy-to-follow programming steps and cooking hints. It includes 14 sensor settings for cooking and defrosting all types of foods. Simply touch and go. A help-pad offers user assistance and a special key automatically reheats beverages to the ideal temperature. Its roomy 1.8 cubic feet of cooking capacity makes it ideal for built-in use. A built-in kit is available separately. The R-530 is available in black and white. Stainless steel is available at additional cost.

Specifications: Overall dimensions—height, $13\frac{7}{16}$"; width, $23\frac{15}{16}$"; depth, $19\frac{1}{4}$"; capacity, 1.8 cubic feet; cooking power, 1,100 watts. Interior dimensions—height, $10\frac{1}{16}$"; width, $16\frac{13}{16}$"; depth, $18\frac{5}{8}$"
Warranty: 1 year, parts and labor; 5 years, magnetron tube
Manufacturer's Suggested Retail Price: $179
Approximate Low Price: $169

Sanyo EM-P891W

✓BEST BUY

The EM-P891W is yet another large full-size microwave, offering a spacious 1.8 cubic feet of cooking space and

1,000 watts of power. The recessed 13-inch turntable enables you to cook with large rectangular dishes, then it returns the food to its original starting position for safe and easy removal. New double sensor keys are provided for efficient cooking and reheating. This model also features an automatic defrost, a trilingual display (English, Spanish, French), and a more/less time adjustment. The EM-P891W is offered only in white.

Specifications: Overall dimensions—height, 14¼"; width, 23⁷⁄₁₆"; depth, 17⅝"; capacity, 1.8 cubic feet; cooking power, 1,000 watts. Interior dimensions—height, 11¹¹⁄₁₆"; width, 16⁵⁄₁₆"; depth, 15⅞"
Warranty: 1 year, parts and labor
Manufacturer's Suggested Retail Price: $190
Approximate Low Price: $180

Panasonic NN-S768

Recommended

This full-size microwave has a 1.7-cubic-foot capacity with easy, single-touch sensor cooking for 15 foods. There's also a convenient reheat sensor for previously cooked food. A handy preprogrammed defrost and popcorn key make late-night cooking a breeze. Two interesting features are the one-minute key and turbo defroster, which incorporate Panasonic's advanced sequencing systems to defrost foods quickly. The NN-S768 is equipped with a turntable to help you achieve even cooking, and a trilingual display provides information in French, Spanish, and English. This model is available in black or white.

Specifications: Overall dimensions—height, 14"; width, 23⁷⁄₁₆"; depth, 16¾"; capacity, 1.7 cubic feet; cooking power, 1,100 watts. Interior dimensions—height, 10¹¹⁄₁₆"; width, 17³⁄₁₆"; depth, 15⁶⁄₁₉"
Warranty: 1 year, parts and labor
Manufacturer's Suggested Retail Price: $179
Approximate Low Price: $165

FAMILY-SIZE MICROWAVE OVENS

Sharp R-420

BEST BUY

This streamlined family-size microwave eliminates all the guesswork of microwaving. Its 1.3 cubic feet of cooking space makes it convenient for your countertop. Equipped with a 14-inch turntable and 1,100 watts of cooking power, the R-420 is ideal for family-size meals. It features action keys for cooking and reheating up to six servings of six different categories of foods. Easy-to-use sensor settings provide one-touch convenience for six varieties of microwaved foods. An automatic defrost program and an interactive display with helpful word prompts are also provided. A kit to convert it to a built-in oven is available at additional cost. Sharp offers this unit in black or white.

Specifications: Overall dimensions—height, 12⅜"; width, 21 11/16"; depth, 17⅜"; capacity, 1.3 cubic feet; cooking power, 1,100 watts. Interior dimensions—height, 8 11/16"; width, 15"; depth, 16¾"
Warranty: 1 year, parts and labor; 5 years, magnetron tube
Manufacturer's Suggested Retail Price: $149
Approximate Low Price: $140

Quasar MQS1385

Budget Buy

This economical family-size microwave offers an ample 1.3 feet of cooking space and a respectable 1,000 watts of cooking power. But the low cost does have its limitations. Although the MQS1385 lacks the preferred sensor feature, it comes equipped with preprogrammed reheating, defrosting, and cooking. It also includes a popcorn key and a one-minute pad for easy cooking. Quasar offers this model in white or black.

Specifications: Overall dimensions—height, 12"; width, 21⅞"; depth, 16¾"; capacity 1.3 cubic feet; cooking power, 1,000 watts. Interior dimensions—height, 9⅛"; width, 14 15/16"; depth, 15 13/16"

Warranty: 1 year, parts and labor
Manufacturer's Suggested Retail Price: $159
Approximate Low Price: $150

MEDIUM-SIZE MICROWAVE OVENS

Panasonic NN-S568

✓BEST BUY

The Panasonic NN-S568 features an oven capacity of 1.0 cubic foot and 1,100 watts of cooking power. At the touch of a button, the microwave's built-in sensor accurately cooks or reheats several foods. It offers a preprogrammed defrost feature, which will defrost most meats, fish, and poultry just by entering the food's weight. And for a late-night snack, a popcorn key is included. Other features include a one-minute selection and a more/less adjustment for individual tastes. The NN-S568 comes in black, white, or almond.

Specifications: Overall dimensions—height, 12″; width, 20″; depth, 14 3/16″; capacity, 1.0 cubic foot; cooking power, 1,100 watts. Interior dimensions—height, 9″; width, 13 7/8″; depth, 13 5/16″
Warranty: 1 year, parts and labor
Manufacturer's Suggested Retail Price: $159
Approximate Low Price: $150

Sharp R-320

Recommended

Although this is a medium-size microwave, the R-320 conveniently fits on your countertop. It offers 1.0 cubic foot of cooking space, 1,100 watts of cooking power, and a generous 13-inch turntable to satisfy most of your microwaving needs. It also boasts some of the most impressive timesaving features on the market. Included with R-320, for example, are a sensor for cooking and reheating, an efficient automatic defrost, and six preprogrammed cooking times. The user-friendly display tells the time and provides helpful instructions and cooking hints. A one-minute key and a separate popcorn setting are also included. The R-320 is offered in black or white.

Specifications: Overall dimensions—height, 11⅞"; width 20½"; depth, 15⅞"; capacity, 1.0 cubic foot; cooking power, 1,100 watts. Interior dimensions—height, 8⅜"; width 13¾"; depth 14⅞"
Warranty: 1 year, parts and labor; 5 years, magnetron tube
Manufacturer's Suggested Retail Price: $139
Approximate Low Price: $130

COMPACT MICROWAVE OVENS

Sharp R-230

✓BEST BUY

The Sharp R-230 is an affordable unit for those with limited space. It features 0.7 cubic foot of cooking space, a respectable 11⅝-inch turntable, and 700 watts of cooking power. Convenience cooking for one or two servings has been preprogrammed. Instant-start buttons are available for six different food categories. The one-touch defrost has a three-stage cycle for fast and efficient defrosting. The R-230 also includes a helpful one-minute timer and a digital display. Auto-touch controls allow for easy operation. Sharp offers this compact microwave in black or white.

Specifications: Overall dimensions—height, 11⅝"; width, 18⅛"; depth, 14⅝"; capacity, 0.7 cubic foot; cooking power, 700 watts. Interior dimensions—height, 7⅞"; width, 12⅜"; depth, 12⅝"
Warranty: 1 year, parts and labor; 5 years, magnetron tube
Manufacturer's Suggested Retail Price: $99
Approximate Low Price: $99

Sanyo EM-N105

Recommended

This compact microwave oven offers plenty of features for the price. The model boasts a 0.65-cubic-foot capacity and 600 watts of power. One nice feature is the 11-inch turntable that returns the food to its original starting position for safe and easy removal. Its four preprogrammed keys enable cooking for frequently microwaved foods, with a more/less adjustment to meet individual tastes. Quick cooking can be easily set using 30-second and one-minute touch pads. An optional bracket is available for mounting beneath a cabinet. Color selections come in black or white.

Specifications: Overall dimensions—height, 9$\frac{13}{16}$"; width, 18$\frac{3}{16}$"; depth, 13$\frac{5}{8}$"; capacity, 0.65 cubic foot; cooking power, 600 watts. Interior dimensions—height, 7$\frac{7}{8}$; width, 11$\frac{7}{16}$"; depth, 12$\frac{1}{4}$"
Warranty: 1 year, parts and labor; 5 years, magnetron tube
Manufacturer's Suggested Retail Price: $110
Approximate Low Price: $99

MICROWAVE/CONVECTION OVENS

Sharp R-930

✓ BEST BUY

This relatively large microwave boasts the ability to brown, bake, broil, crisp, and microwave. It supplies 1.5 cubic feet of cooking capacity and 900 watts of power. The user-friendly interactive display panel offers programming steps and cooking hints. A handy sensor provides effortless cooking for eight food categories, while no less than 12 preprogrammed times are included for convection use. Convection buttons that automatically compute broiling, roasting, and baking times are also included. A 15$\frac{3}{8}$-inch turntable is replaceable with two removable convection oven racks. The R-930's size and versatility make it an outstanding choice for built-in use. An optional kit to convert the oven into a built-in unit is also available. Sharp offers this model in charcoal or white.

Specifications: Overall dimensions—height, 14$\frac{7}{8}$"; width, 24$\frac{5}{8}$"; depth, 18$\frac{3}{4}$"; capacity, 1.5 cubic feet; cooking power, 900 watts. Interior dimensions—height, 9$\frac{5}{8}$"; width, 16$\frac{1}{8}$"; depth, 16$\frac{1}{8}$"
Warranty: 1 year, parts and labor; 5 years, magnetron tube

Manufacturer's Suggested Retail Price: $449
Approximate Low Price: $400

General Electric JE1390

Recommended

This multifeatured full-size unit offers the choice of microwave cooking, convection cooking, or the combination of the two. This model offers 1.3 cubic feet of cooking capacity and 850 watts of power. A helpful sensor is featured for easier cooking and reheating. The JE1390 includes two racks for baking and roasting, a turntable for thorough cooking, and an automatic defrost feature for efficient defrosting. It makes an excellent choice for built-in use, due to its ample size. An optional kit to convert the oven into a built-in unit is also available.

Specifications: Overall dimensions—height, 14⅞"; width, 22¼"; depth, 19⅞"; capacity, 1.3 cubic feet; cooking power, 850 watts. Interior dimensions—height, 10⅛"; width, 14½"; depth, 14½"
Warranty: 1 year, parts and labor; 9 years, magnetron tube
Manufacturer's Suggested Retail Price: $439
Approximate Low Price: $410

OVER-THE-RANGE MICROWAVE OVENS

General Electric JVM1460

✔ BEST BUY

The JVM1460 is a user-friendly, sophisticated microwave with advanced sensor cooking. It has a generous 1.4 cubic feet of cooking space and 950 watts of power for effortless preparation of eight categories of food. Custom pads allow programming of the most frequently used time settings and a help pad aids in problem solving. Helpful features include a turntable with an on/off switch and an interactive display, which coaches the user for the best results. Other features include automatic defrost and a temperature probe for cooking and roasting. Full cooktop lighting, a programmable night-light, and a ventilation fan are also provided. The JVM1460 also boasts a unusual message center, a convenience feature that allows the user to leave a 20 second audio message or reminder for family members. This model is available in stainless steel, white, black, or almond.

Specifications: Overall dimensions—height, 16 1/2"; width, 29 7/8"; depth, 14 5/16"; capacity, 1.4 cubic feet; cooking power, 950 watts. Interior dimensions—height, 9 5/16"; width, 19 5/16"; depth, 13 3/16"
Warranty: 1 year, parts and labor; 9 years, magnetron tube
Manufacturer's Suggested Retail Price: $499
Approximate Low Price: $460

Sharp R-1490

Recommended

This sleek microwave is a user-friendly, feature-enriched microwave with 950 watts of cooking power. The R-1490 offers a 13-inch turntable that can be turned on or off to accommodate a four-quart, 10×15-inch dish. A built-in sensor provides the easiest and most accurate cooking times for a variety of foods. This unit also includes a custom help key that provides users with hints and programming options. Other features include preprogrammed defrost and cooking. An interactive display makes programming and cooking easy, in your choice of French, English, or Spanish. The unit includes a two-speed ventilation system, which can be vented or nonvented (in which case a charcoal filter is included) for quick removal of smoke and steam. To round out the package, the R-1490 includes a work light and a night-light. This innovative model comes in white, black, or almond.

Specifications: Overall dimensions—height, 16 3/8"; width, 29 15/16"; depth, 15 1/4"; capacity, 1.1 cubic feet; cooking power, 950 watts. Interior dimensions—height, 8 3/16"; width, 20 1/4"; depth, 14 1/2"
Warranty: 1 year, parts and labor; 7 years, magnetron tube
Manufacturer's Suggested Retail Price: $399
Approximate Low Price: $360

Whirlpool MH7130XE

Budget Buy

This over-the-range microwave oven features preprogrammed time settings for a variety of prepared food categories. It has 1.3 cubic feet of cooking capacity, a turntable with an on/off switch, 900 watts of cooking power, and a bilevel rack. A friendly pop-up menu prompts the operator to make selections. You can even reprogram settings while in use. A fan for vented or nonvented use and lighting for the range top are also provided. Although this unit does not offer a sensor, Whirlpool will add a sensor at additional cost. The MH7130XE is available in black, white, or almond.

Specifications: Overall dimensions—height, 16 7/16"; width, 29 15/16"; depth, 15 3/8"; capacity, 1.3 cubic feet; cooking power, 900 watts. Interior dimensions—height, 8 9/16"; width, 19"; depth 14 5/8"
Warranty: 1 year, parts and labor; 5 years, magnetron tube
Manufacturer's Suggested Retail Price: $449
Approximate Low Price: $400

OVER-THE-RANGE MICROWAVE/CONVECTION OVENS

Sharp R-1850

✓BEST BUY

The Sharp R-1850 offers 850 watts of cooking power and 1.1 cubic feet of cooking space. This exceptionally versatile unit allows you to heat, brown, bake, and crisp with the microwave, convection, and combination options. The interactive display spells out programming steps for helpful cooking. A custom help key also offers cooking hints and instructions for operation. Two racks are included: a high one for preparation of more than one dish and a low one for baking and broiling. The sensor automatically determines microwave cooking or reheating times for eight prepared food categories. The 13-inch turntable enhances even cooking and can be switched off to accommodate oversized dishes. Included are a ventilation fan and a hood light.

Specifications: Overall dimensions—height, $16^{11}/_{32}$"; width, $29^{15}/_{16}$"; depth, $15^{9}/_{32}$"; capacity, 1.1 cubic feet; cooking power, 850 watts. Interior dimensions: height, $8^{1}/_{16}$"; width, $17^{1}/_{8}$"; depth, $13^{13}/_{16}$"
Warranty: 2 years, parts and labor; 7 years, magnetron tube
Manufacturer's Suggested Retail Price: $579
Approximate Low Price: $505

General Electric JVM1190

Recommended

The JVM1190 remains an excellent choice for an over-the-range convection microwave oven. It features sensor cooking controls for many commonly microwaved and reheated foods. A combination sensor allows the use of convection and microwave cooking to be used together, achieving the speed of microwaves and the crisp, browned surface of convection. A temperature probe is included for cooking with either microwave or combination settings. Defrosting can be done automatically or by time. The oven has 1.1 cubic feet of cooking space and 825 watts of power. The JVM1190 is available in white, black, almond, or stainless steel.

Specifications: Overall dimensions—height, $15^{1}/_{2}$"; width, $29^{15}/_{16}$"; depth, $14^{1}/_{4}$"; capacity, 1.1 cubic feet; cooking power, 825 watts. Interior dimensions—height, $8^{1}/_{16}$"; width, 18"; depth, $12^{1}/_{2}$
Warranty: 1 year, parts and labor; 9 years, magnetron tube
Manufacturer's Suggested Retail Price: $689
Approximate Low Price: $680

RANGES

There's really no more powerful or flexible cooking tool than a standard kitchen range. Today's ranges offer consumers more capabilities and greater flexibility than ever before and are designed to make the cooking process simpler, more consistent, and cleaner. Plus, ranges are available in a number of sizes, finishes, and designs, with special features and prices to suit everyone from the occasional cook to the serious chef.

MAKING THE RIGHT CHOICE

The basic choices that have to be made are determined by the kitchen the appliances are to be installed in. Usually appliances are purchased either to replace an existing unit or to be installed into a new or renovated kitchen. In a replacement situation, the size of the space and the available fuel will often dictate the choice. In a new or renovated kitchen, there is often a bit more room for flexibility.

Fuel choices today include electric, gas, or dual-fuel. Gas ranges tend to be more popular among home chefs because of their instant response time, easy control, and visible flame. Also, in many regions of the country, gas tends to offer a lower operating cost than electric appliances.

Historically, coil elements were the choice for electric ranges and cooktops. Today an increasing number of electric units are sold with smooth-top cooking surfaces. The ease of cleaning is the primary reason for this tremendous growth in popularity. Look for radiant ribbons encased in glass-ceramic surfaces, but be prepared to use only flat-bottom cooking vessels. Halogen elements are also available. They heat quickly, but cost a bit more and are not as common as the radiant ribbons.

In gas ranges and cooktops, ease of cleaning and smoothness of surface are the most popular features. For the most effortless cleaning, select sealed gas burners. Flush grates offering a smooth surface for moving pans are a nice feature, but one that still commands a fairly high price.

Dual-fuel kitchens usually have gas for the cooking surface and electricity for the oven operation. This can be accomplished in one unit or by using a cooktop and wall oven. Often dual-fuel is the choice of gourmet cooks and bakers. They enjoy the precision of gas surface units and prefer the evenness of electric baking, usually with a convection oven. Choosing dual-fuel, however, can significantly add to the cost of new appliances.

In addition to fuel, space and cabinets in the kitchen will determine selections. Not all manufacturers make built-ins to fit every space. The choices may be limited by the space occupied by the former appliance or by the design of the kitchen itself.

BUYING TIPS

Typically, ranges, cooktops, and wall ovens are purchased in a local appliance store or a national chain store. Local appliance stores often have the best selection of models on display and they tend to have a more knowledgeable sales staff. They often have products in stock and their own service departments. Because of this advantage, however, prices may be slightly higher.

Many national chains do not have an extensive display of products, especially built-in ones. Usually, they will order these products for you. On the other hand, items such as freestanding ranges are usually stocked and readily available. The selection usually includes the most common and less expensive choices. Ask about service, as it varies from store to store.

In addition to stores, knowledge regarding appliances is available to the public on the Internet. Most manufacturers have web sites, which describe their products and provide specifications as well as dealer services. A lot of time can be saved by doing comparative shopping with a computer and a modem, instead of going store to store.

It is also important to note that many manufacturers offer the same basic body of an appliance in different models. Each model number will vary slightly to indicate a change in features or colors. Check with your dealer to ensure you receive the exact features and color you desire.

RANGES

Ranges contain a cooktop and an oven in a one-piece unit. The most typical unit is 30 inches wide, although other sizes are available. For today's busy families, the range with a self-cleaning oven has become the standard.

The three styles of ranges are known as freestanding, drop-in, and slide-in. A freestanding unit is designed to sit on the floor by itself and has finished sides. The drop-in and slide-in units are made to fit between two cabinets and do not have finished sides. A drop-in typically hangs from the countertop and may require cabinetry at the bottom. A disadvantage of this may be the loss of the storage drawer. A slide-in literally slides between the cabinets and sits on the floor. Generally, slide-in and drop-in ranges are less expensive than freestanding units and offer a continuous countertop-to-range surface.

COOKTOPS

An alternative to the range is the cooktop. Cooktops fit into the top surface of a cabinet. They may be placed against a wall in an island. Units may range in size from 18 to 48 inches, containing two, four, six, or more burners. The average cooktop is 30-36 inches wide and fits in a cabinet 24 inches deep.

Modular style cooktops have bays, which accept various interchangeable elements and accessories. Accessories include griddles, grills, woks, rotisseries, roasters, and steamers. The griddle and grill are considered the most useful. Catalogs from the manufacturer will outline all the choices, as stores often do not have the space to display them all.

Ventilation is needed for every cooktop. Either downdraft or updraft ventilation must be selected. Updraft uses an overhead hood, while downdraft uses a powerful fan, which is located at the cooktop's surface and vented to the outside. Many modular cooktops require downdraft ventilation. Proper ventilation is imperative and should be described in detail by the dealer.

WALL OVENS

When a cooktop is selected, the next choice is the wall oven. Wall ovens today are usually built into a large cabinet. Convection, a feature where hot air circulates in the oven, is a useful feature for more even cooking and baking. It does, however add significantly to the cost of the oven. Ovens are available single, double, or in combination with a microwave. Gas ovens are sized for 24-, 27-, and 30-inch cabinets. Electric ovens are usually sized at 27- and 30-inch cabinets. In kitchens with limited space, 30-inch wall ovens are a nice choice and fit directly under many cooktops. Check with your dealer for compatibility.

COMMERCIAL-STYLE RANGES

We've included commercial-style ranges in this chapter for users who desire restaurant-quality kitchen equipment in their homes. Commercial-style ranges generally produce more heat than standard ranges. As a result, they require a high-powered ventilation system. The don't require special clearance or gas connections, though many manufacturers do recommend stainless-steel backsplashes between the cooktop and the hood because of the added power of the burners.

RANGE HOODS

A vital—and often overlooked—element to a successful kitchen is a proper ventilation system. Range hoods absorb, filter, and redistribute air in the kitchen. Usually positioned above the cooktop, they not only filter cooking odors and smoke, but also absorb residual fumes left behind by gas cooktops, making your kitchen safer, cleaner, and more comfortable.

Standard horizontal or vertical range hoods typically run a vented line through a hole in a wall or through a ceiling. Many modular cooktops have a downdraft ventilation system included with the unit. These systems come built into the range-hood system and must be used for the cooktop to operate properly.

When purchasing a ventilation system, it's important to make sure the hood is powerful enough to match the range and cooking applications. For example, a user who owns a powerful commercial-style range and plans on regularly deep-frying foods will require a much more powerful ventilation system than a user who owns a standard gas oven. Hoods are rated in cubic feet of air (cfm) moved per minute. A minimal recommendation is a hood that is rated at 180 cfm or more. Cooktops and commercial-style units will require additional cfm. Check with the range manufacturer for specific details and recommendations when choosing an appropriate range hood.

BEST BUYS '99

Our Best Buy, Recommended, and Budget Buy ranges, ovens, and range hoods are listed below. Products within each category are listed according to quality. The best of the Best Buys is listed first, followed by our second choice, and so on. A Best Buy, Recommended, or Budget Buy designation only applies to the model listed—it does not necessarily apply to other models made by the same manufacturer or to an entire product line.

GAS RANGES

FREESTANDING GAS RANGES

General Electric JGBP30WEA

✓ BEST BUY

The JGBP30WEA is a 30-inch gas range with easy-to-use electronic controls, including a handy clock and timer. The range is equipped with sealed burners, including a high-powered burner and a simmer burner. The grates are porcelain-on-steel and the cooktop is porcelain-enameled. Cooking is simple, thanks to a glass door with a large window and an in-oven broiler. Temperature in the oven is electronically controlled, and the door is removable for easy cleaning. For convenience, the oven contains a light and a roll-out storage drawer at the bottom. This product is available in almond or white.

Specifications: Overall dimensions—height, 46½"; width, 30"; depth, 26¼". Oven dimensions—height, 17"; width, 24"; depth, 19".
Warranty: 1 year, parts and labor
Manufacturer's Suggested Retail Price: $779
Approximate Low Price: $749

Maytag MGR5770

BEST BUY

With grates constructed of durable cast iron, this 30-inch full-capacity range offers dependable performance and easy cleanup. It offers four sealed gas burners, including two that offer a high-power feature. This self-cleaning range includes an automatic oven light and an exceptionally large viewing window in an attractive glass door. Included is a half-rack, which allows baking of smaller items while a large pan is in use. Convenience features include a convenient waist-high broiler and a storage drawer. The unit can also be converted to LP gas. Maytag offers this unit in white, almond, or black.

Specifications: Overall dimensions—height, 46¾"; width, 29⅞"; depth 26⅛". Oven dimensions—height, 16½"; width, 23"; depth, 18⅛".
Warranty: 1 year, parts and labor; 2 years, parts; 10 years, sealed gas burners (limited)
Manufacturer's Suggested Retail Price: $799
Approximate Low Price: $749

KitchenAid KGRT500F

Recommended

Although this 30-inch range is more expensive for similar features found on comparable models, its reputation for design performance and reliability is outstanding and worth the price. It includes an easy-clean tempered-glass cooktop with four sealed gas burners, two rated at 6,000 Btu and two rated at 10,000 Btu. The front-mounted controls are convenient and easy to reach, but may be a safety concern with small children. Electric ignition/reignition is also featured. The oven has full electronic controls for balanced baking and roasting, and the broiler offers variable time broiling. The oven also includes variable time self-cleaning. A convection oven option is available in this style at an additional cost. This full-featured range is offered in almond or white.

Specifications: Overall dimensions—height, $44\frac{3}{8}$"; width, 30"; depth, $25\frac{1}{2}$". Oven dimensions—height, $15\frac{3}{4}$"; width, $23\frac{1}{16}$"; depth, $15\frac{5}{8}$".
Warranty: 1 year, parts and labor; 5 years (limited); 10 years (limited)
Manufacturer's Suggested Retail Price: $1,199
Approximate Low Price: $1,169

DROP-IN/SLIDE-IN GAS RANGES

KitchenAid KGST300F

BEST BUY

KitchenAid's elegant KGST300F is a powerful and flexible slide-in range that is easily installed in any kitchen. It features an easy-to-clean tempered-glass cooktop with four sealed gas burners. Two of the burners are rated at 6,000 Btu and two are rated at 10,000 Btu. It includes electric pilotless ignition and infinite heat controls for precise cooking. The thermal oven is fully electronic, including a handy electronic graphic display. It offers variable-time self-cleaning, an automatic light with manual switch, and automatic baking. This unit is available with a convection oven at additional cost. KitchenAid offers this range in white or almond.

Specifications: Overall dimensions—height, 38"; width, $30\frac{7}{8}$", depth, $25\frac{3}{4}$". Oven dimensions—height, $15\frac{3}{4}$"; width, $23\frac{1}{16}$", depth, $17\frac{1}{8}$".
Warranty: 1 year, parts and labor; 5 years (limited)
Manufacturer's Suggested Retail Price: $1,199
Approximate Low Price: $1,170

General Electric JGSP44WEY

✓BEST BUY

GE's stylish, white-on-white, JGSP44WEY slide-in gas range is an ideal addition to any kitchen lineup. It features sealed burners, a standard simmer burner, and a maximum output burner. The grates are cast iron, the cooktop surface is glass, and the unit has electronic pilotless ignition. The self-cleaning oven has a delay clean option and boasts electronic controls. Convenience features include a storage drawer and effortless in-oven broiling. The oven door is removable for easy cleaning. This range is also available in black or almond glass.

Specifications: Overall dimensions—height, 36¼"; width, 30"; depth, 29½". Oven dimensions—height, 13"; width, 22 ¾"; depth, 17".
Warranty: 1 year, parts and labor
Manufacturer's Suggested Retail Price: $1,009
Approximate Low Price: $949

GAS COOKTOPS AND MODULAR GAS COOKTOPS

KitchenAid KGCT305E

✓BEST BUY

This black gas cooktop provides total cooking flexibility in just 30 inches of space. The surface is made of easy-to-clean tempered glass and the grates are made of durable cast iron and feature four sealed high-efficiency burners. Two of the burners have six towers instead of the usual four, providing additional coverage for the use of large cooking vessels. A kit is also available for conversion to LP gas. KitchenAid offers this cooktop in white or almond.

Specifications: height, 3"; width, 30¾"; depth, 21¾".
Warranty: 1 year, parts and labor; 5 years, burners and cooktop
Manufacturer's Suggested Retail Price: $680
Approximate Low Price: $500

Jenn-Air CVG4280

✓BEST BUY

This 30-inch downdraft, modular-style cooktop comes with two gas burners, one at 8,000 Btu and one at 10,000 Btu, and a grill element. The CVG4280 also accepts an optional two-burner module and various grill and cooktop accessories. Features include an electronic pilotless ignition, a two-speed fan, and porcelain-enameled cast-iron burner grates. Jenn-Air makes this model in black, white, or stainless steel.

Specifications: width, 29⅞"; depth, 21½"
Warranty: 1 year, labor, 2 years, parts; 5 years (limited)
Manufacturer's Suggested Retail Price: $849
Approximate Low Price: $799

BUILT-IN GAS OVENS

General Electric JGRP17WEW

✓BEST BUY

This GE oven is an excellent choice for replacing your existing 24-inch gas wall oven. The JGRP17WEW is self-cleaning with a delay clean option and control-lock capability. It also features a stylish, frameless glass door that opens and closes easily. Other features include electronic controls and pilotless ignition. The unit also boasts in-oven broiling and a storage drawer. The JGRP17WEW is available in white-on-white or black-on-black.

Specifications: Overall dimensions—height, 38⅜"; width 23¾"; depth 23". Oven dimensions—height, 15"; width 17"; depth, 18⅞".
Warranty: 1 year, parts and labor
Manufacturer's Suggested Retail Price: $889
Approximate Low Price: $799

Magic Chef 9112

✓BEST BUY

Magic Chef offers a more extensive selection of sizes of gas wall ovens than most manufacturers, including 24-inch and 30-inch units. And the 24-inch 9112 is one of its most impressive models, offering quality at a reasonable price. This standard-clean oven features electronic pilotless ignition and temperature control, including upper baking and lower broiling. An electronic clock, a window, a light, a removable door, and two racks are also included. Magic Chef offers this model in black or white glass, or white or almond porcelain.

Specifications: Overall dimensions—height, 39¼"; width, 23⅞"; depth, 22⅝". Oven dimensions—height, 14"; width, 18"; depth, 18½".
Warranty: 1 year, parts and labor
Manufacturer's Suggested Retail Price: $469
Approximate Low Price: $419

COMMERCIAL-STYLE GAS RANGES AND COOKTOPS

Dacor ERSD30

✓BEST BUY

The Dacor ERSD30's commercial-style gas range offers home chefs all the cooking power and quality of a professional range. Its 30-inch dual-fuel range features a gas cooktop and an electric oven. There are four sealed gas burners, rated at 15,000 Btu each. The top is sealed for easy cleaning and the grates provide a continuous surface for easy sliding of pans from burner to burner. Infinite controls allow for precise burner management and automatic reignition enables uninterrupted cooking. This self-cleaning, convection oven features an electronic touch pad, a digital clock, and a delay timed mode. For safety around children, the control panel may be deactivated. Dacor offers this range in white, stainless steel, black, or almond.

Specifications: Overall dimensions—height, 36"; width, 30"; depth, 25½". Oven dimensions—height, 59"; width, 24"; depth, 18½".
Warranty: 2 years, parts and labor

Manufacturer's Suggested Retail Price: $3,629
Approximate Low Price: $3,467

Viking VGSU161

✓BEST BUY

The Viking VGSU161 six-burner gas cooktop is designed to fit easily in virtually all 36-inch cutouts. It features sealed burners with porcelain/cast-iron caps and settings ranging from 950 Btu to 14,000 Btu. The flame ports are constructed of durable brass. This unit offers electric spark ignition/reignition and its burners light at any position on the knob and relight if extinguished. The heavy-duty, removable burner grates provide a continuous surface for easy movement of large pots. The knobs are large, easy-to-read, and childproof. Three spill collection areas are included and hold up to five cups of liquid. You can choose either natural gas or propane with a proper regulator. Available colors for the VGSU161 include black, white, or stainless steel. Various optional cooking accessories are available to fit this model.

Specifications: height, 4⅝"; width, 36¾"; depth, 21"
Warranty: 1 year, parts and labor; 5 years, surface burner (limited)
Manufacturer's Suggested Retail Price: $1,425
Approximate Low Price: $1,307

ELECTRIC RANGES

FREESTANDING ELECTRIC RANGES

General Electric JBP78WY

✓BEST BUY

This 30-inch self-cleaning range offers reliable performance at a reasonable price. Its easy-to-clean, flat glass-ceramic cooktop features four ribbon heating elements: one 8-inch, two 6-inch, and one dual 6-inch/9-inch. The dual feature adds cooking versatility. Each element has easy-view hot lights, which are an important safety feature. The oven is electronically controlled for accurate temperature management and offers delay bake, auto oven shut-off with override, and audible preheat signal. Dual elements in the oven provide even baking and roasting. Also included are an electronic clock, a storage drawer, and an exceptionally large viewing window. GE offers the JBP78WY in white-on-white, almond-on-almond, or black-on-black.

Specifications: Overall dimensions—height, $45\frac{3}{4}$"; width, $29\frac{7}{8}$"; depth, $25\frac{7}{16}$". Oven dimensions—height, 16"; width, 23"; depth, $17\frac{3}{4}$".
Warranty: 1 year, parts and labor; 4 years, cooktop (limited)
Manufacturer's Suggested Retail Price: $849
Approximate Low Price: $849

Maytag MER5730

✓BEST BUY

Maytag's MER5730 30-inch range comes with four radiant elements in an easy-to-clean, flat Ceran surface. The sleek cooktop features a durable porcelain back panel and removable knobs for easy cleaning. The oven is self-cleaning with electronic temperature control. It features a light, a window, an electronic clock, a delay start, and a storage drawer. An optional half-rack is available to increase usable space when roasting a large item. Hot surface lights are provided for safety. The unit comes in white or almond with a black door, or white or almond with a matching door.

Specifications: Overall dimensions—height, $46\frac{3}{4}$"; width, $29\frac{7}{8}$"; depth, $26\frac{1}{8}$". Oven dimensions—height, $16\frac{1}{2}$"; width, 23"; depth, $18\frac{1}{8}$".
Warranty: 1 year, labor; 2 years, parts; 5 years (limited)
Manufacturer's Suggested Retail Price: $699
Approximate Low Price: $669

KitchenAid KERC500E

Recommended

The KERC500E is a dependable oven with many advanced features. We list it as a Recommended product only because of its high price. Measuring 30 inches, this electric range features four powerful radiant elements, one of which is expandable to adapt to various pans. Infinite heat controls are included, as well as hot-surface indicators. The oven offers variable-time self-cleaning and a convenient storage drawer. Variable temperature broiling and an automatic light with manual switch are provided as well. This model comes in white or almond.

Specifications: Overall dimensions—height, $46^{13}/_{16}$"; width, $29^{15}/_{16}$"; depth, $24^{1}/_{2}$". Oven dimensions—height, $15^{3}/_{4}$"; width, $23^{1}/_{16}$"; depth, $18^{1}/_{4}$".
Warranty: 1 year, parts and labor; 5 years (limited)
Manufacturer's Suggested Retail Price: $1,049
Approximate Low Price: $930

DROP-IN/SLIDE-IN ELECTRIC RANGES

KitchenAid KESC300B

✓BEST BUY

KitchenAid KESC300B 30-inch slide-in range provides flush-to-cabinet installation for a stylish built-in look. The control panel is front-mounted, adding to the smoothness of design. It includes an easy-clean Ceran surface cooktop with four radiant elements, including one expandable element. Hot-surface indicator lights are added for safety as well. The oven features electronic controls and a variable-time self-cleaning system. Convenience features include automatic time baking, an automatic light with manual switch, and a removable storage drawer. The broiler also boasts a variable temperature selection. A optional convection oven is available. KitchenAid offers this unit in almond, white, or black.

Specifications: Overall dimensions—height, 38"; width, $30^{7}/_{8}$"; depth, $25^{3}/_{4}$". Oven dimensions—height, $15^{3}/_{4}$"; width, $23^{1}/_{16}$"; depth, $18^{1}/_{4}$".
Warranty: 1 year, parts and labor; 5 years (limited); 10 years (limited)

Manufacturer's Suggested Retail Price: $1,199
Approximate Low Price: $960

General Electric JSP40BW

✓BEST BUY

GE's JSP40BW is easy to install and has an attractive built-in look. This 30-inch black slide-in range has four powerful ribbon heating elements: two 8-inch, one 6-inch, and one dual 6-inch/9-inch. The surface features an easy-to-clean, flat glass-ceramic cooktop with four hot surface indicator lights for safety. Electronic controls offer precise cooking. The oven is self-cleaning with a delay-clean option, and has a frameless removable glass door with a viewing window. An electronic clock and timer are also included. This unit is available in white or almond.

Specifications: Overall dimensions—height, 35⅞"; width, 30"; depth, 28½". Oven dimensions—height, 15¾"; width, 22¾"; depth 17".
Warranty: 1 year, parts and labor; 5 years (limited)
Manufacturer's Suggested Retail Price: $1,269
Approximate Low Price: $1,109

ELECTRIC COOKTOPS

Jenn-Air CVE4270

✓BEST BUY

Jenn-Air's 30-inch downdraft modular cooktop remains a popular choice year after year. At the base price, it comes with a grill and an empty bay, which accepts various heating element cartridges at an additional cost. Typically, this unit is purchased with one or two surface element cartridges. Cartridge choices include solid element, conventional coil, halogen, and radiant elements. The plethora of available accessories serve to make this unit incredibly versatile. Accessories include a griddle, a grill cover, a wok, a rotiss-kebab, a cooker-steamer, and a big pot canning element. A two-speed fan and light bar are included as well. This cooktop comes in white, black, and stainless steel.

Specifications: width, $29\frac{1}{8}$"; depth, $21\frac{1}{2}$"
Warranty: 1 year, labor; 2 years, parts; 5 years (limited)
Manufacturer's Suggested Retail Price: $549
Approximate Low Price: $540

General Electric JP350

BEST BUY

This 30-inch frameless cooktop offers plenty of versatility in an electric cooktop. It features four ribbon heating elements: one dual 6-inch/9-inch, two 8-inch, and one 6-inch. For safety, there are four hot-surface indicator lights. The unit has flush-mount capability and an easy-clean patterned surface. Color selections include white, almond, or black.

Specifications: height, $3\frac{3}{8}$"; width, $29\frac{3}{8}$"; depth, $20\frac{1}{2}$".
Warranty: 1 year, parts and labor
Manufacturer's Suggested Retail Price: $599
Approximate Low Price: $530

BUILT-IN ELECTRIC OVENS

KitchenAid KEBI171D

BEST BUY

KitchenAid's 27-inch thermal oven provides stylish, flush-to-cabinet installation and may be installed under the counter as well as in the wall. The elements are hidden for more even heat distribution and easier cleaning. Included are fully electronic controls, variable-time self-cleaning, and variable temperature broiling. Convenience features include two halogen oven lights, a large viewing window, and a control lock function. These same features are also offered on the 24- and 30-inch unit. Convection and double-oven units are also available. KitchenAid offers this oven in white or black.

Specifications: height, $27\frac{3}{4}$"; width, $25\frac{1}{2}$"; depth, $23\frac{1}{4}$".
Warranty: 1 year, parts and labor; 5 years (limited); 10 years (limited)

Manufacturer's Suggested Retail Price: $1,049
Approximate Low Price: $899

Jenn-Air W27200

Recommended

Although slightly more expensive, this 27-inch built-in oven offers cooking perfection. Its most notable feature is dual-speed convection. Convection may also be selected for the broil mode. This large-capacity unit is self-cleaning with electronic controls and offers a large viewing window. It features a flush design and can be installed in the wall or under the counter. This unit is also offered in a double-oven version. Jenn-Air supplies this model in either black or white.

Specifications: Overall dimensions—height, 27¾"; width, 26¾"; depth, 24 7/16". Interior dimensions: height, 14¾"; width, 21"; depth, 18 9/16".
Warranty: 1 year, parts and labor; 5 years (limited)
Manufacturer's Suggested Retail Price: $999
Approximate Low Price: $729

RANGE HOODS

General Electric JV376V

✓BEST BUY

Also a Best Buy in 1998, this 30-inch vented hood features rotary knobs and a variable-speed fan control. Two cooktop lights and a night-light setting are also included. It can be used for vertical or rear exhaust rectangular duct installations. It is an ideal companion to any range or cooktop. The JV376V is available in black or white.

Specifications: height, 7"; width, 29⅞"; depth, 19¾".
Warranty: 1 year, parts and labor
Manufacturer's Suggested Retail Price: $279
Approximate Low Price: $219

Broan 463001

Budget Buy

A sturdy performer, this 30-inch economy range hood offers good ventilation. It is vented and can be converted to vent-free operation with the included filter, thus giving it versatility for different installations. This unit features an infinite rotary fan speed control and the capability to hold a 75-watt light bulb. A duct connector is included for vented installations. Broan offers this model in black or white.

Specifications: height, 7½"; width 30"; depth, 17½"
Warranty: 1 year, parts
Manufacturer's Suggested Retail Price: $135
Approximate Low Price: $99

REFRIGERATORS AND FREEZERS

Refrigerators and freezers are among the most expensive major appliances in the home—both in terms of purchase price and operating costs. A poor choice can be an expensive mistake; a wise choice, however, can provide real value in terms of cost and convenience.

There's a wide range of refrigerators on the market, from modest and inexpensive models with a basic design and few extra features to the deluxe models that offer a wide assortment of convenience and performance features. The refrigerators reviewed here are grouped as side-by-side, top-freezer, bottom-freezer, built-in, or compact models. Freezers are categorized as upright or chest models.

BEST BUYS '99

Our Best Buy, Recommended, and Budget Buy refrigerators and freezers are listed below. Products within each category are listed according to quality. The best of the Best Buys is listed first, followed by our second choice, and so on. A Best Buy, Recommended, or Budget Buy designation only applies to only the model listed—it does not necessarily apply to other models made by the same manufacturer or to an entire product line.

REFRIGERATORS

When choosing a refrigerator, selection comes down to two basic considerations—your budget and your family's needs. You can spend several thousands of dollars on a refrigerator with all the bells and whistles, or several hundreds of dollars on a basic version that may be smaller and have fewer features but still holds and chills food sufficiently. Manufacturers have concentrated their efforts on improving styling, performance, and convenience features. Today, the selection of refrigerators is broader and better than ever.

WHICH MODEL?

Side-by-side Refrigerators: These models are the most popular style of refrigerators sold today. They offer modern styling and large-freezer capacity. Unfortunately, these are also the least energy-efficient models. Through-the-door ice maker/water dispensers are now offered as an option on all side-by-sides. While this is a popular feature, it also increases repair needs and costs.

Top-freezer Refrigerators: These are the next popular choice. They are less costly to purchase and run than side-by-side models but have smaller freezer compartments. Top-freezers generally take up less space than side-by-side. They also put the freezer at eye-level, but the lower refrigerator section is less convenient to use.

Bottom-freezer Refrigerators: These models are relatively uncommon, with only a few manufacturers producing them. That's a shame, since bottom-freezers offer many advantages: Freezer sections are generally larger than those on top-freezer models, and the refrigerator section (which is typically used more frequently than the freezer) is at a more comfortable level, permitting access to fresh foods without stooping. Even better, a bottom-freezer is the most energy-efficient refrigerator configuration available.

Built-in Refrigerators: These models are essentially shallower versions of conventional models. They are available as either side-by-side or bottom-loading units. Their narrow depth help them fit flush (or almost flush) with kitchen cabinetry. Many models protrude less than two inches past normal counter depth. Special trim kits help customize their look, so they can blend in. Built-ins come with unfinished sides, but some manufacturers make shallow freestanding models with finished sides and tops.

Compact Refrigerators: These models are small enough to fit into college dorm rooms, offices, family rooms, and other limited spaces. They have small ice-tray compartments instead of actual freezer sections. Compact refrigerators aren't really replacements for larger models, but they do a creditable job of holding snacks, drinks, and even a moderate supply of groceries.

WHICH FEATURES?

Shelves: In-the-door storage for gallon containers is a handy feature on many new refrigerators, as are adjustable shelves and bins. Glass shelves with raised edges are easy to clean and help contain food spills. Height-adjustable shelves are a great convenience, particularly if they're split into half-width sections that can be arranged to suit your particular needs. Slide-out shelves are generally not adjustable, but they provide easy access to items stored at the back of shelves.

Storage Compartments: Well-featured refrigerators have an assortment of compartments designed to hold different types of products. Many basic models have one or two crisper drawers and a dairy locker on the door. Some units feature special bins that are designed to suit specific foods: butter enclosures that maintain a slightly higher temperature for easy spreading; meat bins that keep the meat at 32 degrees for longer and safer storage; and vegetable crispers that maintain a higher humidity level than is present in the main storage area.

Other Features: Today's refrigerators have an array of features designed to increase convenience and performance. Ice makers and water dispensers are handy features if you frequently drink ice water, but they also represent additional cost. Other features include wine racks and snack trays. It is wise to examine the full benefit of these features in each model. These are only conveniences if they fit your lifestyle. If they don't, they're simply space wasters that raise the price of your refrigerators.

SIDE-BY-SIDE REFRIGERATORS

General Electric TFX25JRY

✓BEST BUY

GE's TFX25JRY refrigerator offers great value and a plethora of features. With a cavernous 25.2 cubic feet of storage space, this model is well suited for a large or growing family. It features a through-the-door dispenser that delivers chilled water and crushed or cubed ice. The fresh-food compartment has 15.92 cubic feet of space, two adjustable humidity vegetable/fruit crispers, an adjustable temperature meat pan, three adjustable glass cabinet shelves, and a utility bin. In-the-door features include two handy adjustable gallon-size shelves, a condiment shelf, and a dairy compartment. The spacious freezer has 9.32 cubic feet of storage, with three adjustable wire shelves, door shelves, and a slide-out freezer storage bin. GE offers this model in white-on-white or almond-on-almond.

Specifications: height, 69¾"; width, 35¾"; depth, 32½"
Warranty: 1 year, parts and labor; 5 years, compressor (parts only)
Manufacturer's Suggested Retail Price: $1,099
Approximate Low Price: $999

Frigidaire FRS26ZRG

✓BEST BUY

The Frigidaire FRS26ZRG is a terrific choice for a large family. This model boasts a capacity of 25.6 cubic feet, divided into 16.1 cubic feet for fresh-food storage and 9.5 cubic feet for the freezer. This model has a through-the-door dispenser that provides both crushed and cubed ice. Convenience features include three adjustable shelves designed to contain spills, one clear adjustable crisper with a glass door, and an adjustable meat keeper. In-the-door features include a deli drawer, four gallon size adjustable bins, and a dairy locker. The lighted freezer has three wire shelves, four door shelves, a tall item rack, an automatic ice maker, and a wire basket. The FRS26ZRG is available in white, almond, or black.

Specifications: height, 67"; width, 35¼"; depth, 35½"
Warranty: 1 year, parts and labor; 2 years, ice and water dispenser; 5 years, sealed refrigeration system and liner
Manufacturer's Suggested Retail Price: $1,149
Approximate Low Price: $1,049

Whirlpool GD25DFXF

Recommended

Whirlpool's GD25DFXF is a nice choice for a medium to large family. Much of this refrigerator's 25.2 cubic feet of space is located on the doors. The four large adjustable gallon door bins will easily hold milk jugs and two- or three-liter bottles. The door includes a see-through dairy locker. In the main compartment, there are two see-through crispers, a temperature-controlled meat locker, a wine rack, a see-through snack bin, an egg bin, and three adjustable shelves with a spill saver feature. A through-the-door dispenser delivers crushed or cubed ice and chilled water through a filtration system that removes dirt, rust, chlorine, odor, and lead from the water. Its freezer includes four fixed-door bins, four shelves, and a wire basket. Whirlpool offers this model in white, black, or almond.

Specifications: height, 68⅞"; width, 35½"; depth, 33⅜"
Warranty: 1 year, parts and labor; 5 years, sealed refrigeration system
Manufacturer's Suggested Retail Price: $1,649
Approximate Low Price: $1,199

KitchenAid Superba KSRS25QG

Recommended

This exceptional model from KitchenAid boasts superb energy efficiency. It offers 25.1 cubic feet of capacity, with almost 10 cubic feet of space in the freezer compartment alone. The KSRS25QG also includes some convenience features, including a wine rack and a childproof lock on the built-in ice-and-water dispenser. In-the-door storage is spacious, including gallon storage space, can racks, and three other adjustable shelves. There is also a vegetable/meat locker, humidity-controlled crisper, and deli locker. The freezer has three slide out wire baskets and two shelves including one Quick Freeze shelf. KitchenAid offers the KSRS25QG in white, almond, or black.

Specifications: height, 68⅞"; width, 35½"; depth, 33"
Warranty: 1 year, parts and labor; 5 years, sealed refrigeration

system and door liners; 10 years, sealed refrigeration system (limited); lifetime, Slide N Lock can racks and door bins
Manufacturer's Suggested Retail Price: $1,549
Approximate Low Price: $1,549

Maytag RSW2400E

Recommended

Loaded with convenience features and a 23.6-cubic-feet capacity, Maytag's RSW2400E is a great unit for a larger, active family. The main refrigerator compartment boasts 15.3 cubic feet of fresh-food storage space. It includes two humidity-controlled crispers, a temperature-controlled meat drawer, three adjustable tempered-glass shelves, and a wine rack. The door has an adjustable gallon bin, a covered dairy compartment, a removable egg cradle, and four additional door bins. The freezer's 8.3 cubic feet storage space includes a through-the-door ice-and-water dispenser with an optional crushed-ice maker, an adjustable wire shelf, two tilt-out door baskets, three slide-out wire baskets, and three fixed deep-door baskets.

Specifications: height, 67½"; width, 35¾"; depth, 32⅛"
Warranty: 1 year, parts and labor; 2 years, parts; 5 years, sealed refrigeration system and cabinet liner
Manufacturer's Suggested Retail Price: $1,500
Approximate Low Price: $1,400

Magic Chef CSD2525AR

Budget Buy

With 16.43 cubic feet of space in the fresh food compartment and 8.35 cubic feet in the freezer, Magic Chef's CSD2525AR provides a lot of space at an affordable price. Within the refrigerator, there are three adjustable sealed cantilever glass shelves and three full-width bins. It also includes a see-through crisper drawer with humidity control, a temperature-controlled meat drawer, and a utility drawer. A wine storage rack and a lift-out egg tray are also featured. The door has a dairy locker and one fixed and four adjustable gallon-size storage shelves. One of the door shelves has a projection to prevent large bottles from toppling over when the refrigerator is opened. The freezer has three glass shelves and a wire basket, and the door has five deep storage bins. It also features a through-the-door ice-and-water dispenser with a crushed ice option. The CSD2525AR is offered in white or almond.

Specifications: height, 68⅛"; width, 32⅝"; depth, 35"
Warranty: 1 year, parts and labor; 5 years, sealed refrigeration system and cabinet liner
Manufacturer's Suggested Retail Price: $1,099
Approximate Low Price: $1,000

Hotpoint CSX22GAB

Budget Buy

With a capacity of 21.7 cubic feet and some performance-enhancing extras, the economical CSX22GAB is an excellent option. Fresh-food storage features include adjustable glass shelves, an adjustable humidity fruit and vegetable crisper, and a temperature-adjustable meat pan. On the door, you'll find four fixed shelves (two large enough for gallon jugs or two-liter bottles) and a full-width clear dairy locker. The freezer offers a clear pull-out bin, four adjustable wire shelves, six fixed door shelves, and an optional ice maker. A quiet package has also been added. This model is offered in white-on-white or almond-on-almond.

Specifications: height, 66⅝"; width, 33½"; depth, 32½"
Warranty: 1 year, parts and labor; 5 years, sealed refrigeration system and compressor; lifetime, sealed fruit and vegetable crispers
Manufacturer's Suggested Retail Price: $899
Approximate Low Price: $859

TOP-FREEZER REFRIGERATORS

Frigidaire FRT22QRG

✓BEST BUY

Hefty handles and 21.6 cubic feet all contribute to the FRT22QRG's Best Buy rating. This refrigerator has the look of more expensive units, with a surprisingly full array of features. With a fresh food compartment of 15.8 cubic feet, this refrigerator includes four adjustable half-width shelves, two glass-covered crispers with humidity control, and a deli drawer. In-the-door features include four gallon-size bins, an additional condiment shelf, and two dairy lockers. The lighted freezer compartment features an adjustable full-width shelf, two door shelves, and an optional ice maker. Frigidaire offers this model in white or almond.

Specifications: height, 67"; width, 32"; depth, 33"
Warranty: 1 year, parts and labor; 5 years, sealed refrigeration system and liner
Manufacturer's Suggested Retail Price: $739
Approximate Low Price: $700

Whirlpool ET18PKXG

BEST BUY

An economical 18.2 cubic foot refrigerator with a few surprising features, Whirlpool's ET18PKXG has a slim profile and is suited for smaller refrigerator openings. After opening the refrigerator using its bulky, easy-to-grip handles, there are two see-through crispers, a meat pan, two adjustable half shelves, and a full-width shelf. All shelves are made of glass and have been designed to contain spills. The door has a clear egg bin, a dairy compartment, three adjustable gallon door bins, and an additional condiment shelf. The freezer has one full-width adjustable shelf and two door shelves; it will also house an optional automatic ice maker. Whirlpool offers this model in white or almond.

Specifications: height, 65½"; width, 29½"; depth, 31⅛"
Warranty: 1 year, parts and labor; 5 years, sealed refrigeration system
Manufacturer's Suggested Retail Price: $699
Approximate Low Price: $600

Maytag MTB2456A

Recommended

This full-featured top-freezer boasts plenty of storage capacity and handy features that make it an excellent value. This model provides 23.7 cubic feet of storage, including 16.1 cubic feet for fresh food and 7.7 cubic feet for frozen foods. The fresh food compartment has four split tempered-glass shelves, two crispers with humidity control, and a sealed glass crisper shelf. The door features three gallon-plus storage bins, two additional shelves, a tilt-out bin, and a dairy compartment. Slidable package keepers, a 12-pack can rack, and a locking compartment round out the refrigerator options. In the freezer, the MTB2456A has expandable wire shelves, a slide-out wire drawer, a tilt-out door basket, and a freezer light. This model comes in white, almond, or black.

Specifications: height, 68 1/8"; width, 32 21/32"; depth, 33 1/2"
Warranty: 1 year, parts and labor; 2 years, free parts; 5 years, sealed refrigeration system and cabinet liner
Manufacturer's Suggested Retail Price: $1,300
Approximate Low Price: $1,000

Hotpoint CTX18DAB

Budget Buy

This economical 18.2-cubic-foot refrigerator includes features that are a pleasant surprise to find in this price range. Hotpoint's CTX18DAB will suit a small- to medium-sized family. In the fresh-food compartment, there are two split and one full-width spill-proof glass shelves, two see-through fruit/vegetable crispers, and a snack pan. Fixed-door storage includes one full-width and one half-width gallon-size shelves (both are tall enough for liter bottles), a half-width condiment shelf, and a clear dairy locker. Freezer storage includes a two-position, full-width epoxy wire rack, and ice trays and a bin; the door has two fixed shelves. This model is available in white-on-white or almond-on-almond.

Specifications: height, 64"; width, 29 3/8"; depth, 31 1/2"
Warranty: 1 year, parts and labor; 5 years, sealed refrigeration system and compressor; lifetime, sealed fruit and vegetable crispers

Manufacturer's Suggested Retail Price: $579
Approximate Low Price: $559

White-Westinghouse MRT18GRG

Budget Buy

This basic, 18-cubic-foot refrigerator is a nice choice for those who need a reliable unit without all of the bells and whistles. The MRT18GRG provides a good value for a medium-sized family on a budget. The fresh-food area has 14 cubic feet of storage space, while the freezer contains about 4.1 cubic feet. The main compartment includes two full-width adjustable sliding epoxy wire shelves, two clear crisper drawers, and a clear deli drawer. The door has two shelves, including one gallon-size shelf, and a clear dairy compartment. In the freezer, you'll find one full-width adjustable wire freezer shelf and an optional automatic ice maker. The MRT18GRG comes in white or almond.

Specifications: height, 64¼"; width, 29¾"; depth, 31½" (with handles)
Warranty: 1 year, parts and labor; 5 years, sealed refrigerant system (limited)
Manufacturer's Suggested Retail Price: $469
Approximate Low Price: $450

BOTTOM-FREEZER REFRIGERATORS

General Electric TCX22ZA

Recommended

GE offers smart styling, 21.7 cubic feet of storage capacity, and a nicely-featured interior in its TCX22ZA. While the refrigerator compartment provides easy accessibility, the freezer is designed to make it even easier to reach frozen food items. The TCX22ZA offers 15.23 cubic feet of storage in the fresh-food compartment. Out of the five door bins, four are adjustable and two have space for gallon containers. One crisper is sealed and the other has adjustable humidity. There's also a sealed snack pan and beverage rack, two dairy compartments, and four split shelves. The freezer features a tempered full-width glass shelf, a sliding storage basket, four door bins, and two ice-cube trays. GE offers this model in white or almond.

Specifications: height, 67⅝"; width, 32¾"; depth, 33¾" (with handle)
Warranty: 1 year, parts and labor; 5 years, sealed refrigeration system
Manufacturer's Suggested Retail Price: $1,200
Approximate Low Price: $1,000

Amana BX21T

Recommended

This refrigerator is rugged enough to withstand an active family's everyday usage. The Amana BX21T boasts a total of 20.5 cubic feet of storage capacity with a versatile design. This bottom-freezer refrigerator includes four adjustable glass shelves, a temperature-controlled deli drawer, and two humidity-controlled crispers. The freezer features an ice service rack, one stationary full-width shelf, and a pullout epoxy-coated wire basket. The BX21T comes in white, almond, or black.

Specifications: height, 67⅝"; width, 32⅝"; depth, 33½" (with handle)
Warranty: 1 year, parts and labor; 5 years, sealed system components and interior liners
Manufacturer's Suggested Retail Price: $949
Approximate Low Price: $900

BUILT-IN REFRIGERATORS

Amana BBI20TP

✓BEST BUY

Amana's BBI20TP refrigerator has an efficient bottom-mount design with 19.7 cubic feet of space that is sufficient for an active family. With 14.1 cubic feet of fresh-food capacity and 5.6 cubic feet of frozen-food space, the BBI20TP is stocked with an array of convenience- and performing-enhancing features. The refrigerator's interior has four adjustable split glass shelves, a temperature-controlled deli drawer, a humidity-controlled crisper, and a slide-out Deli Port storage compartment. The door has one fixed full-width and four adjustable half-width gallon-size bins plus two clear dairy lockers. One of the shelves has a tall bottle retainer that prevents toppling. The lighted freezer includes one full-width shelf, a pull-out freezer basket, and a nifty door rack that pivots to allow easy access. An ice maker is standard. Four panel kits are available to give this built-in a custom look. Amana offers this model in white, black, almond, or stainless steel.

Specifications: height, 68⅝"; width, 35⅝"; depth, 28⅛" (with handle)
Warranty: 1 year, parts and labor; 5 years, sealed refrigeration system and cabinet liner; 10 years, sealed system components (limited)
Manufacturer's Suggested Retail Price: $1,799
Approximate Low Price: $1,650

KitchenAid Superba KSBS20QE

Recommended

With hidden hinges and 19.7 cubic feet of storage capacity, this refrigerator disappears into its surrounding cabinetry for a built-in appearance in the cutout space of a freestanding unit. The model's factory-installed trim kit allows easy installation of custom front panels. This model has an ice and water dispenser with a crushed ice option and a night-light. The refrigerator door contains gallon door bins, a can rack, and three additional shelves. The main refrigerator compartment has two produce bins and a meat locker. It also includes three additional adjustable shelves. The freezer has two enormous slide out baskets, three shelves, and five door shelves. This model comes in white, almond, or black.

Specifications: height, 67½"; width, 35¾"; depth, 27⅞" (with handle)

Warranty: 1 year, parts and labor; 5 years, sealed refrigeration system and door liners
Manufacturer's Suggested Retail Price: $1,949
Approximate Low Price: $1,949

COMPACT REFRIGERATORS

Whirlpool EL05CCXFW

✓BEST BUY

Although compact, this 4.3-cubic-foot refrigerator offers some features found in standard-size models. This model is an excellent choice for college dorm rooms or other limited spaces. Special features include removable slide-out wire shelves, a full-size storage door with space for both small and large items, adjustable temperature control, and a removable meat/defrost tray. The freezer compartment includes an ice-cube tray. Whirlpool offers this model only in white.

Specifications: height, 34"; width, 18¾"; depth, 20⅞"
Warranty: 1 year, parts and labor; 5 years, compressor
Manufacturer's Suggested Retail Price: $229
Approximate Low Price: $229

General Electric TAX6SNXWH

Recommended

This compact refrigerator is a great choice for an under-bar application—an excellent choice for storing beverages and snacks. With 6.0 cubic feet, most of the unit's space (5.51 cubic feet) is in the fresh food storage area. The TAX6SNXWH includes two adjustable cabinet shelves, three full-width door shelves, a dairy compartment, and optional black, white, or woodgrain looks. The freezer holds two mini ice-cube trays.

Specifications: height, 34¼"; width, 23⅝"; depth, 25⅞"
Warranty: 1 year, parts and labor; 5 years, compressor (limited)
Manufacturer's Suggested Retail Price: $329
Approximate Low Price: $300

FREEZERS

While most refrigerators have a freezer section, it's often not large enough to handle the needs of people who shop infrequently enough, cook in large quantities, or grow their own produce and wish to store it. A home freezer provides this extra storage space. Like refrigerators, freezers can be expensive appliances to run. But a freezer pays for itself over the years with the money you save by purchasing bulk meat and produce.

UPRIGHT AND CHEST FREEZERS

When evaluating freezers for purchase, you need to consider two major factors: space and purpose. If you are planning to use the freezer to store items for several months at a time, and don't need quick access to all of your frozen foods, then a large chest freezer would be appropriate for you. An upright freezer takes up as much square footage as a refrigerator would. Upright freezers generally cost more than chest freezers and are less energy efficient. Some upright freezers offer an automatic defrost feature; all chest freezers are manual defrost.

FEATURES

Freezers that offer automatic defrost are clearly the most convenient type. Some manual-defrost models have a power defrost cycle that speeds up defrosting. Helpful freezer options include an alarm that sounds whenever the freezer's internal temperature drops below a safe freezing level. An often-overlooked features is a warranty against food spoilage—a breakdown that's relatively inexpensive to repair can cost a considerable amount in terms of spoiled food.

UPRIGHT FREEZERS

Whirlpool EV200FXGW

Recommended

The Whirlpool EV200FXGW is a 19.7-cubic-foot capacity upright freezer with ample storage for the large bulk-buying family. While this freezer is stylish enough for the kitchen, its probably better-suited for a garage or basement because of its large size. It includes four full-width wire shelves, a bulk storage gate, and an adjustable temperature control. The door's storage holds plenty of frozen goods on its five shelves. This manual-defrost model includes a drain with a cover for easy maintenance. The EV200FXGW also includes an interior light for easy product location. This model comes with a white textured steel cabinet and door.

Specifications: height, 66½"; width, 33"; depth, 29¼"
Warranty: 1 year, parts and labor; 10 years, sealed refrigeration system
Manufacturer's Suggested Retail Price: $599
Approximate Low Price: $599

Frigidaire FFU17M8G

Recommended

This solid, upright chest freezer has a spacious 17 cubic feet of storage space and can hold up to 599 pounds of frozen food. This manual-defrost model comes with plenty of design features to ensure efficient operation, including adjustable temperature control, an interior light, a lock with pop-out key, and both a power-on light and a temperature alarm system. Four door shelves and three compartment shelves hold frozen goods. This is a handsome and durable freezer, attractive enough to live in the kitchen. The FFU17M8G is offered only in white.

Specifications: height, 64½"; width, 32"; depth, 26½"
Warranty: 1 year, parts and labor; 3 years, food spoilage (limited); 5 years, sealed system (limited); 10 years, compressor (limited)
Manufacturer's Suggested Retail Price: $589
Approximate Low Price: $589

White-Westinghouse MFU12M2G

Budget Buy

Even though this moderately large, 11.6-cubic-foot upright freezer has a slim profile, it holds up to 406 pounds of frozen food. Inside you'll find three shelves and four door shelves. Adjustable temperature control ensures adequate freezing, while a magnetic door seals and a door closer ensures the freezer doors stay shut to keep cold air in. The unit also comes with a drain for easy defrosting and adjustable leveling legs. This model is only available in white.

Specifications: height, 54½"; width, 28"; depth, 26½"
Warranty: 1 year, full freezer (limited); 3 years, food spoilage plan (limited); 5 years, sealed refrigerant system (limited); 10 years, freezer compressor
Manufacturer's Suggested Retail Price: $349
Approximate Low Price: $329

CHEST FREEZERS

Frigidaire FFC07M5C

✓BEST BUY

This durable, compact manual chest freezer holds 7.2 cubic feet of frozen food in an economical and efficient package. The FFC07M5C includes a temperature alarm system that sounds if the interior temperature rises to an unsafe level. Other features include a power-on light, a lock with a pop-out key, and a defrost drain. A lift-out basket keeps often-used foods accessible. The FFC07M5C is only offered in white.

Specifications: height, 34¼"; width, 35"; depth, 23¼"
Warranty: 1 year, parts and labor; 3 years, food spoilage (limited); 5 years, sealed system (limited); 10 years, compressor (limited)
Manufacturer's Suggested Retail Price: $289
Approximate Low Price: $250

White-Westinghouse MFCI5M4F

✓BEST BUY

This affordable, manual-defrost freezer is suitable for the family that buys in bulk. With more than 14.8 cubic feet of storage, this freezer can hold more than 500 pounds of frozen goods. Features that provide ease of use and assure reliable operation include an adjustable temperature control, a removable basket, a defrost drain, and a lock with a pop-out key. The MFC15M4F is only available in white.

Specifications: height, 60¾"; width, 48"; depth, 29½" (including hinges)
Warranty: 1 year, parts and labor (limited); 3 years, food spoilage (limited); 5 years, sealed refrigerant system (limited), 10 years, freezer compressor
Manufacturer's Suggested Retail Price: $369
Approximate Low Price: $349

General Electric FCM55A

Recommended

This is a nifty, compact, 5.0-cubic-foot chest freezer that holds a deceptively large amount of frozen food. This manual-defrost freezer includes an adjustable temperature control and a recessed handle. With the addition of foam insulation in the cabinet and lid, the steel epoxy coated cabinet liner provides quiet and economical operation. For those with modest deep freezing needs, this is an excellent freezer choice.

Specifications: height, 35"; width, 23½"; depth, 25⅞"
Warranty: 1 year, parts and labor; 5 years, sealed refrigeration system and spoilage
Manufacturer's Suggested Retail Price: $329
Approximate Low Price: not available

DISHWASHERS

Although dishwashers have been around for a long time, they are still not universally accepted as major appliances (like ranges and refrigerators). One reason is that some people view dishwashers as more of a luxury than a necessity. In addition, you can't just carry one home and plug it in. Much like a washing machine, a dishwasher needs to be connected to hot water, electricity, and a drain. A dishwasher has the added limitation of only being able to be installed in a kitchen, where space is often at a premium.

For an increasing number of people, however, dishwashers have become a virtual necessity. They can significantly reduce mealtime cleanups. (They also offer a place to store unsightly dirty dishes until you have time to wash them.) Today's dishwashers do a sufficient job of cleaning most dishes, even without prerinsing. And hot water usage is typically nine gallons or less per load, which compares favorably to the amount of water many people use to wash dishes by hand.

BUILT-IN MODELS

Most dishwashers are 24 inches wide and are installed beneath a kitchen counter. They are wired into the electrical system of your home and connected to a hot water supply and a drain, often shared with the kitchen sink. General Electric offers a model that will fit under the sink; most other dishwashers are installed adjacent to it. Replacing an old dishwasher involves minimal installation costs. More complex installations can cost up to several hundred dollars, depending upon location.

PORTABLE MODELS

If space is a premium, if you're renting, or if you just want to avoid installation expense, a portable dishwasher is a worthwhile alternative. Many manufacturers offer models with casters for easy mobility. When operating, simply plug the unit into an electrical outlet, connect it to the faucet, and put the drain hose in the sink. A portable model is generally similar to the same manufacturer's mid- to low-end built-in dishwasher. Most portables can later be built in.

BUYING TIPS

Dishwasher prices range from less than $300 to more than $1,000, excluding installation. Models selling for more than $600 often include electronic controls, stainless steel interiors, extra dispensers and indicator lights, and extra noise insulation and sound dampening. However, there are many models in the $400 to $600 range that will satisfy almost any requirement. You may get more features on a more exclusive brand name by buying a more costly dishwasher, but most people will be satisfied with the more economical models.

FEATURES AND TERMINOLOGY

Controls: Push-button or dial controls are simple, reliable, and economical. Electronic touchpad controls add a contemporary "high tech" look, but can add up to $150 to the cost of the dishwasher. Electronic controls may also include indicators that tell you when a drain is clogged, whether the spray arms are obstructed, or how much time is remaining in the cycle. A child lockout feature, which prevents children from activating the dishwasher, may also prove convenient.

Cycles: Three cycles—normal wash, light wash (or water saver), and pots and pans—handle almost any load. Quick rinse (or rinse-and-hold) permits you to rinse a partial load and wait until you load more dirty dishes before adding detergent and washing a full load.

Rinse-aid Dispenser: This feature dispenses a special conditioner during the final rinse cycle, which aids in eliminating water spots and speeds up drying.

Sound Insulation: Today's dishwashers are much quieter than older models. Manufacturers use various approaches, from wrapping interiors with fiberglass blankets to using quieter-running motors.

Time Delay: Time delay is a worthwhile feature that delays the start of operation by as much as 12 hours. This allows you to take advantage of off-peak electric rates and to use hot water at a time when it is not being used by other household members.

Tub and Inner Door Materials: Stainless steel is a durable and expensive tub and inner door material. Polypropylene is just as durable and less expensive.

Washing Action: Multiple spray arms and/or additional spray heads help prevent a dish or pot from blocking the spray. Make sure that the rack arrangement will permit water to reach all parts of a load. Generally a three-level wash system will give the best results, but two-level systems can also be satisfactory.

Water Heating: Many models have an automatic water-temperature booster system that ensures consistently hot water (140°F) during wash and rinse cycles. This feature reduces the cost of operating your household hot water heater by permitting you to lower the thermostat as low as 120°F. Some dishwashers have a hot-rinse option that heats the water to about 160°F. Water at this temperature may be effective at killing germs.

BEST BUYS '99

Our Best Buy, Recommended, and Budget Buy dishwashers follow. They are divided into built-in, undersink, and portable models. Within each category, the units we consider to be Best Buys are listed first, followed by our second choice, and so on. A Best Buy, Recommended, or Budget Buy designation only applies to the model listed—it does not necessarily apply to other models made by the same manufacturer or to an entire product line.

BUILT-IN DISHWASHERS

KitchenAid KUDI24SE

✓BEST BUY

Although the KUDI24SE is the least expensive of KitchenAid's premium line of dishwashers, it still shares the same stainless steel interior, effective wash system, and sculptured exterior look of its more costly cousins. Touchpad controls include three wash cycles: pots and pans, normal, and rinse-hold. Helpful indicator lights display the water temperature and the cycle that's being used. Other controls are provided for high-temperature wash and energy-saving drying. Also included is a child lockout feature and a fixed four-hour delay-start. The well-designed interior racks feature flexible layouts that are not blocked by spray components. Soundproofing is adequate, but not as effective as other models in the same line. The KUDI24SE was also a Best Buy pick for 1998. It's available in white, black, or almond.

Specifications: height, 33⅞"; width, 24"; depth, 26"; water use, normal cycle, 9.5 gallons
Warranty: 1 year, parts and labor; 5 years, motor, electronic controls, and heating element; lifetime, tub and door
Manufacturer's Suggested Retail Price: $579
Approximate Low Price: $529

Frigidaire Gallery FDB636GF

BEST BUY

When you first glance at this midline model, you can sense that something is fundamentally different. The difference is a one-piece door (instead of a door-and-toeplate normally seen on most U.S. dishwashers), which gives the unit a more seamless, sculptured look. The innovative, redesigned washing system, which uses less water (and energy) and detergents than previous models, results in cleaner dishes. The system uses 100-percent filtered water to keep unclean particles off the dishes. A glass trap captures any small utensils or glass fragments resulting from accidental breakage. The dishwasher uses two compact motors rather than one larger one. The interior design features more room for flexible dish loading. It includes special holders for cups and stemware that fold down to accommodate pots and pans. The washer controls feature push buttons and a rotary dial, as well as helpful indicator lights for high-temperature wash, high-temperature rinse, and drying selections. Five wash cycles and a one- to six-hour delay are also included. The FDB636GF comes in white-on-white or black with a reversible color panel in either white, almond, or black.

Specifications: height, 33¾"; width, 23⅞"; depth, 22½"; water use, normal cycle, 6 gallons
Warranty: 2 years, parts and labor; 5 years, controls; 20 years, tub and door liner
Manufacturer's Suggested Retail Price: $369
Approximate Low Price: $352

Maytag Intellisense Plus DWU9962

Recommended

Maytag has pioneered the use of electronic sensors and controls in this top-of-the-line "thinking" model. When you push the "Smart Start" keypad, this appliance automatically adjusts water temperature and cycle times for optimum cleaning. It also adjusts for effective drying. Depending upon the load, the DWU9962 can save energy and water and cut down on wash time. If you prefer to make your own selections, the wipe-clean electronic keypad provides a full range of manual controls, including 12-hour delay-start, quick-wash cycle, rinse and hold, high-temperature scrub, delicate wash, and a water heating option. An electronic display shows time remaining in the cycle. An internal food disposer eliminates both soft and hard food wastes, and a filter traps and removes tiny food particles. The dishwasher uses Maytag's most effective sound insulation system for quiet operation. Loading is assisted by a terraced upper rack and adjustable fold-down tines on the lower rack. This model is available in white, almond, or black.

Specifications: height, 35¼"; width, 23⅞"; depth, 23½"; water use, normal cycle, 6.3 gallons
Warranty: 3 years, parts and labor; 5 years, wash system, sensor package, computer controls, and racks; lifetime, tub and door liner
Manufacturer's Suggested Retail Price: $799
Approximate Low Price: $699

General Electric Profile GSD4630Z

Recommended

GE extols the quietness of this model, which is loaded with features. It includes triple filtration and an antijamming hard-food disposer, which prevents dirty water from resoiling dishes and eliminates the need for prerinsing. A sensor automatically adjusts water usage to the most efficient settings for water temperature, water volume, and cycle time. An electronic touchpad controls normal-wash and rinse-only cycles, power presoak, and special cycles for glass, china and crystal, and pots and pans. There's a rinse-aid dispenser and a helpful indicator to tell you when it needs refilling. Inside, its durable nylon racks help prevent chipping. The dishwasher includes a lower rack with two rows of fold-down tines for flexible loading and two baskets for cutlery and other small items. The GSD4630Z is available in white, black, or almond.

Specifications: height, 34"; width, 24"; depth, 25⅛"; water use, normal cycle, 8.4 gallons
Warranty: 1 year, parts and labor; 2 years, parts; 5 years, racks and electronic controls; 20 years, tub and door liner
Manufacturer's Suggested Retail Price: $549
Approximate Low Price: $470

White-Westinghouse MDB531RF

Budget Buy

This dishwasher includes a reasonable number of features at an affordable price. It does an acceptable job washing with three wash levels, 100-percent filtered water, a self-cleaning polypropylene filter (with a trap for broken glass) and a macerator. In addition to five cycles, there is a one- to six-hour delay-start feature. In the pots-and-pans cycle, the dishwasher includes an automatic high-temperature wash. The controls are dial and push-button. This model is available in black only, with reversible color panels in black, white, or almond.

Specifications: height, 33¾"; width, 23⅞"; depth, 22½"; water use, normal cycle, 6 gallons
Warranty: 1 year, parts and labor; 2 years, water distribution system; 10 years, tub and door liner
Manufacturer's Suggested Retail Price: $429
Approximate Low Price: $329

UNDERSINK DISHWASHER

General Electric GSM2100Z

✓BEST BUY

This space-saving model can solve the problem of installing a dishwasher in a kitchen with limited counter space. Unlike the built-in models reviewed here, this model is designed to be installed directly under a sink, rather than next to one. The size of the door is comparable to other models, but the top of the washer is contoured to leave enough room for a sink and drain pipes. The combination of a single rotary dial and four push buttons allows you to select from five cycles—pot scrubber, normal, short wash, rinse-and-hold, and plate warmer—two wash levels, and a heated dry option. The dishwasher also includes a rinse-aid dispenser. The GSM2100Z is available in white or almond, and both include a black control panel.

Specifications: height, 34″; width, 24″; depth, 26¼″; water use, normal cycle, 8.2 gallons
Warranty: 1 year, parts and labor; 2 years, water distribution system; 10 years, tub and door liner
Manufacturer's Suggested Retail Price: $409
Approximate Low Price: $375

PORTABLE DISHWASHERS

Frigidaire FDP635RFR

✓BEST BUY

This portable model shares the same innovative three-level wash system as the manufacturer's built-in dishwashers. The system powers just one spray arm at a time to provide quiet operation and effective cleaning with low energy, water, and detergent use. Five cycles—pots and pans, heavy wash, normal wash, light wash, and rinse-and-hold—are available on a control panel dial; a start-delay is also featured. Buttons allow selection of high-temperature wash, high-temperature rinse, and heated dry. The unit moves easily on four casters and can be converted for built-in operation. The cabinet is white with a gray laminate top. The front is black with a reversible color panel in black or white.

Specifications: height, 33¾"; width, 23⅞"; depth, 22½"; water use, normal cycle, 6 gallons
Warranty: 1 year, parts and labor; 2 years, water distribution system; 10 years, tub and door liner
Manufacturer's Suggested Retail Price: $449
Approximate Low Price: $440

Whirlpool DP920QWDB

Recommended

This portable dishwasher features four automatic cycles, plus enough options to bring the total of cycle and option combinations up to 11, including a pots-and-pans cycle. It utilizes a three-level wash system with a heavy-duty macerator/disposer. The durable nylon racks have high sides for load stability. The upper rack has three position adjustments for loading versatility. There's an in-the-door silverware basket, adding to load flexibility and room. This model also has a console lockout to protect children. While the unit moves easily on four casters, it's suitable for built-in operation. The cabinet is almond and the front comes in black.

Specifications: height, 38⅛"; width, 24"; depth, 26¾"; water use, normal cycle, 7.2 gallons
Warranty: 1 year, parts and labor; 2 years, water distribution system; 5 years, electronic controls; 20 years, tub and door liner
Manufacturer's Suggested Retail Price: $549
Approximate Low Price: $499

FLOOR CARE

The era of the one-vacuum-cleaner household is fast becoming a thing of the past. The reason? Over the years, the vacuum cleaner has been refined and improved, giving rise to a new generation of specialized vacuums.

However, purchasing multiple cleaners doesn't simplify the shopping process. If you have several machines that aren't tailored to your home and habits, you will not get housework done as efficiently as you would with one cleaner that really suits your needs. So before you make any purchases, answer a few questions that will help you choose the right model (or combination of models).

CHOOSING THE RIGHT UNIT

What size is your home? There's no need for a huge model if your closet won't accommodate it or if you have a lot of bare floors. On the other hand, even a small home with thick carpeting won't be easy to tackle with a mini-machine.

What types of flooring do you have? If you have a sea of wall-to-wall carpeting, a powerful upright will probably be most effective. Lots of tile and wood will be maintained well with a suction-type canister or even a mini-broom vac. An even mixture of surfaces might be best cleaned with a powerhead canister or possibly an upright and handheld combination.

What type of vacuum cleaner are you most comfortable using? Logic may lead you to a certain type of cleaner, but if you're most at ease operating an upright and your home is crying out for a canister, it may be best to go with what you know. For some, vacuuming is unpleasant enough—there is no need to choose a machine style that goes against your grain.

BUYING TIPS

The best shopping tip of all is to be educated about the advantages and disadvantages of the various categories of cleaners. Before you get started, here are some basic facts about vacs:

Look for features that suit your needs, such as a HEPA (high efficiency particular air) system if you have allergies; good tools if you have a lot of furniture, molding, and drapes to clean; longer cords and hoses if you have a large space; and lighter-weight machines if you need to transport the unit between floors. Try out a vac and make sure the attachments are easy to use, the dirtbag is easy to empty, and the unit is easy to maneuver.

More and more vacs include a HEPA system, which refers to a sealed filtration system that retains almost all (estimates range from 99.97 to 99.99 percent) of the dirt, dust, pollens, and mites in the air. It supposedly filters better than any other system and it is used in hospitals. Don't be fooled by such special features. Even though a vacuum may have a HEPA suction system, that doesn't mean it is a perfect performer. For example, a vacuum's ability to pick up all the dust, dirt, and pollen possible depends just as much on the design of the whole vacuum as on its filter system. The same applies for recently-introduced dirt sensors. They only let you know when the vacuum has stopped picking up dirt, not necessarily if there is still dirt left in the rug because it doesn't actually detect the dirt in the rug.

Don't be misled by the amount of amps. More amps do not necessarily mean more power. Amps refer to the amount of current the unit draws when its power is on; it doesn't have anything to do with cleaning power.

TYPES OF VACUUM CLEANERS

Upright Vacuum Cleaners: These are best for rug and carpet cleaning. They are equipped with an agitator—essentially a beater bar outfitted with bristles—that digs up embedded dirt and grit even from high-pile carpeting. The newer uprights are more lightweight than earlier models, so they're easier to handle on stairs but still not as maneuverable as canisters. The upright is also usually less efficient than the canister in above-the-floor cleaning (upholstery, windowsills, and draperies, for example) because the attachments needed to tackle these jobs are often less accessible, and the upright doesn't roll along as easily as the canister. A new generation of upright cleaners, however, stores cleaning tools on the unit, and some come with a permanently attached hose for greater convenience on those above-the-floor jobs.

Canister Vacuum Cleaners: These units eliminate some of the shortcomings of uprights. They are usually quieter than uprights and do a fine job of cleaning bare floors and low-pile carpets. The canister nozzle's low profile permits better access under furniture, in tight spaces, and on stair treads. Easy-to-change attachments remove dust from walls, curtains, and lamp shades. Because it lacks the upright's agitator, the canister is less effective than the upright at removing dirt that has sifted down into the carpet pile. Most new canister models are extremely lightweight and maneuverable, but their suction is generally less powerful than the uprights.

Powerhead Canister Vacuums: A strong canister vacuum cleaner with a powerhead offers the best features of the upright and the standard canister. It has a canister's rolling tank (usually equipped with a tool caddy), hose, and nozzle, combined with a powerhead outfitted with an agitator similar to an upright's. When you shop for a powerhead canister, carefully examine its brush roll. Some units have independent motors that allow them to dig deeper into thick-pile carpet. Others have turbo- or suction-driven brush tools, which have less strength but may still be adequate for your needs. Remember, try it out before you buy it.

Mini Vacuum Cleaners and Brooms: Compact vacuum cleaners and broom-vacs are available in many shapes and sizes. Designed for quick spot cleanups or dry spills, these scaled-down units can be a great convenience as long as you remember that they are intended for smaller jobs. The motors on minis have less power, and the dust bags or cups must be emptied often. Cordless minis are supremely portable and ideal for room-to-room touch-ups and for car care. Corded models are more powerful and won't run out of juice, but they have the same outlet limitations as regular vacuum cleaners.

ALL-PURPOSE CLEANING MACHINES

Sometimes an ordinary vacuum cleaner just won't do the job, and you need a specialized cleaning machine. There are plenty of options on the market, some of which incorporate features that were once found only on industrial-strength vacuums.

Steam Cleaners: Once available only through rental services, carpet steam cleaners are now a significant presence at retail outlets. Typically, these vacs are bigger-ticket items than their conventional counterparts, but they offer a lot of added cleaning capability. Also known as spray extraction machines, these units dispense a cleaning solution into the carpet; then a brush connected to the head of the nozzle agitates the carpet pile to loosen dirt before the dirt and water are sucked back into the machine.

Wet/Dry Vacuum Cleaners: These machines handle messy chores, indoors and out, that conventional vacuums can't. They can clean a muddy garage, suck up soapy washing-machine overflow, and gobble up whole chunks of dirt. These units, however, are noisy and lack many of the convenient features of standard vacuums. For ease of use, you'll want an easy-to-maneuver machine with widely spaced wheels (for stability) and one that changes from wet to dry pickup with the flip of a switch. Also check to see how difficult it is to remove the tank lid and look for a long power cord, detachable blowers, and an extra-wide hose.

BEST BUYS '99

Our Best Buy, Recommended, and Budget Buy floor-care appliances are listed below. These products have been selected on the basis of convenience, performance, and overall value. Products within each category are listed according to quality. The best of the Best Buys is listed first, followed by our second choice, and so on. A Best Buy, Recommended, or Budget Buy designation only applies to the model listed—it does not necessarily apply to other models made by the same manufacturer or to an entire product line.

UPRIGHT VACUUM CLEANERS

Hoover Ultra Self-Propelled WindTunnel U6445-900

✓BEST BUY

This brand new model from Hoover, which features its superb patented suction system, is the Rolls Royce of vacuum cleaners. Its improved features, sturdier construction, superior cleaning capacity, and performance rival all other luxury brands in its class. It does a remarkable job of picking up dust and dirt, thanks to its WindTunnel technology. The U6445-900 is equipped with Hoover's special "Embedded Dirt Finder" feature: When the red light is on, the machine is in the process of removing dirt; when it turns green, the carpet is clean. Despite its size, this model is exceptionally maneuverable, thanks to its self-propelled feature. The design is sensible, with uncomplicated slide-button controls on the unit's base; an on/off switch in the handgrip; a durable snap-open easy-change bag compartment; and a powerful "dirt-finding" headlight. A six-piece tool kit (including a super-stretch hose, a crevice tool, a dusting brush, extension wands, and an upholstery nozzle) is conveniently placed at the top of the unit in a clear-plastic-covered storage box. This unit also includes a high efficiency filter, a brush roll that can be raised for hard floors, and edge groomers on both sides to clean baseboards. It also has a built-in handle so it can be carried between floors, an extra-long power cord (35 feet) for added flexibility, onboard storage for an extra dust bag and motor belt, and a bag-check indicator. This unit is a sturdy, well-built performer.

Warranty: 1 year
Manufacturer's Suggested Retail Price: $340
Approximate Low Price: $340

Panasonic MC-V7395

✓BEST BUY

This sleek, elegantly-designed vacuum from Panasonic is loaded with features that contribute to its superior performance. Its innovative energy-saving "smart handle" allows you to turn the unit on or off by gripping the handle. This unit employs HEPA filter technology, a seven-stage system that traps more than 99 percent of all dust, dirt, and pollen particles in the air. Other critical features include a motor bypass that channels dirt directly into the bag, thus eliminating the chance of hard objects breaking fan blades or the belt; an electronic dirt sensor that remains red when an area is dirty and turns green when it is clean; and a "QuickDraw" system that automatically switches suction to the attached cleaning wand when it is removed and used. This exceptional unit also includes standard features found on other top-of-the-line vacuums such as an automatic carpet height adjustment (including a setting for bare floors), dual-edge cleaning, a built-in headlight, and an easy-change bag. Also included is a wraparound rubber bumper that protects furniture, a 14-inch cleaning width, a 35-foot power cord with an automatic release, and a handle on the back to transport the unit between floors easily. Lastly, a handy five-piece onboard tool set (featuring a stretch hose that swivels 210 degrees, a dusting brush, an upholstery tool, a crevice tool, and a wand) allows for effortless cleaning. The MC-V7395 is an exceptionally quiet, efficient performer.

Warranty: 1 year, parts and labor
Manufacturer's Suggested Retail Price: $250
Approximate Low Price: $200

Eureka WhirlWind 4480

Recommended

Anyone who has ever run out of paper replacement bags for their vacuum cleaner while in the middle of cleaning will appreciate this remarkable new model from Eureka. The affordable WhirlWind 4480 features new "cyclonic action" technology that empties the dirt into a transparent (so you'll know when its full), easy-to-empty cassette on the front of the vacuum. It also includes a sealed True HEPA filtration system, which traps more than 99 percent of all pollutants (pollens, household dust). The unit also features an ergonomic Back Saver handle, a 15-inch-wide cleaning path, a bright headlight, and a 30-foot cord. For effortless cleaning, it includes a seven-position carpet height adjustment, a wraparound furniture guard, and a carrying handle. Onboard cleaning attachments include a transparent stretch hose, nested wands, a crevice tool, and a combination upholstery nozzle and dust brush. You'll be able to spot this durable model easily; the transparent cassette gives it a distinctive appearance compared with other models.

Warranty: 1 year (limited)
Manufacturer's Suggested Retail Price: $200
Approximate Low Price: $190

Hoover Convertible U5066-930

Budget Buy

If you think it is hard to find a vacuum that is a solid performer, has all the amenities, but comes at a relatively low price, look no further than this Hoover U5066-930. This model has virtually all of Hoover's most dynamic features, including outstanding cleaning capabilities and a solid, sensible design. It also features Hoover's new Allergen Filtration System, which traps more than 99 percent of all particles in the air, and does an admirable job of sucking up dust, dirt, and pollens. The U5066-930 is loaded with special features that make cleaning easy, such as a multiple-height adjustment, dual-brushed edge cleaning, a bright headlight, a grip to maneuver the vac for cleaning stairs, a toe-pedal that releases the handle so you can lay the unit flat for easy cleanup underneath low-clearance pieces (such as coffee tables). Its onboard tool set includes an attached hose, a crevice tool, a dusting brush, an upholstery nozzle, and two extension wands. Other features include a hard-bag cover that easily opens for quick and easy bag changes, and a 24-foot cord with a quick release. It's also lightweight enough to transport between floors easily.

Warranty: 1 year
Manufacturer's Suggested Retail Price: $180
Approximate Low Price: $180

Royal Dirt Devil Ultra Swivel Glide 086400

Budget Buy

This member of the Dirt Devil line does the racy name justice, since it's good looking, comes in bright red, and is loaded with exclusive "ultra-features" that increase its flexibility and performance. Some of these innovative features include a "power edger" tool (for baseboards and edges) that attaches directly to the front of the vacuum, and an "edge wedge" tool for stairs and corners. The rear-wheel-caster design makes pushing and maneuvering these vacs—which weigh only 12 pounds—extremely easy. Additionally, it features a "MicroFresh" filtration system that Royal claims can trap more than 99 percent of dust and allergen particles in the air; a "Motorguard System" that protects the motor; a set of five onboard cleaning tools and a convenient carrying handle. There's also a Hide-A-Hose system with a 20-foot extended reach so you can clean an entire flight of stairs without moving the vacuum. Model 086400 also features a full-bag indicator, a headlight, and a 32-foot quick-release cord. The sensible price and stylish design, coupled with all the extras, make this vacuum a good all-around unit you may not want to put away.

Warranty: 30 days, money back; 3 years, parts and labor; 6 years, motor
Manufacturer's Suggested Retail Price: $140
Approximate Low Price: $130

POWERHEAD CANISTER VACUUMS

Hoover PowerMax Supreme S3530

✓BEST BUY

With an aerodynamic look, the PowerMax S3530 is a well- priced, efficient entry into the powerhead canister vacuum market. Although the S3530 is not cheap, the price is fair considering the array of features included with this vac. This model has a motorized nozzle, a two-brush agitator (with brushed-edge cleaning on both sides), and a powerful headlight. The powerful motor does a superior job picking up dust and dirt, thanks to Hoover's Allergen Filtration System, which is designed to trap more than 99 percent of all dust, dirt, and pollen. Other features include a six-foot swivel hose, a full-bag indicator, a 25-foot retractable cord (with a foot-pedal rewind), and a large carrying handle for effortless transportation between floors. The unit also features molded storage compartments for easy access to the onboard tool set, which includes two chrome extension wands, a crevice tool, a dusting brush, a furniture nozzle, and a hardwood-floor tool.

Warranty: 1 year
Manufacturer's Suggested Retail Price: $330
Approximate Low Price: not available

Royal Dirt Devil Power Pak 082123

Budget Buy

This bright-red compact powerhead canister, which is similar to its "sister" can vac (also rated a Budget Buy), has chunky good looks and a powerful 12-amp motor; plus it weighs in at only 16 pounds. While the Power Pak offers decent cleaning power on bare floors (and moderate suction on carpets), its low price and weight make it a good option for consumers with wood floors or low-pile carpets. Power Pak's best points include its small size and its onboard tool set (with a seven-foot flexible hose, a crevice tool, a dusting brush, two extension wands, and a shoulder strap). Easy-roll wheels and a good-sized handle—located on its back—makes this an extremely maneuverable vac.

Warranty: 1 year
Manufacturer's Suggested Retail Price: $100
Approximate Low Price: $100

COMPACT CANISTER VACUUMS

Hoover PowerMax S3510

✓BEST BUY

This full-sized, full-power canister vac is the perfect alternative for a household that has lots of bare floors but needs the capabilities of a larger unit. It features Hoover's new Allergen Filtration System, which is designed to trap more than 99 percent of all dust, dirt, and pollens. With these features, plus its efficient motor and deluxe nozzle, which has two-sided edge cleaning capabilities, the PowerMax S3510 is a superb unit at a sensible price. This unit features a seven-piece onboard tool set, which includes a six-foot swivel hose, two extension wands, a crevice tool, a dusting brush, and a furniture nozzle. An extra-long 20-foot cord with wrap storage and a topside on/off pedal make the PowerMax a versatile machine. It incorporates an extra-large carrying handle and oversized wheels, making this unit remarkably easy and efficient to use.

Warranty: 1 year
Manufacturer's Suggested Retail Price: $170
Approximate Low Price: not available

Sharp EC-7311

Recommended

This suave, futuristic gray-blue unit is a bit pricey, but it is such an effective performer that the cost is merited. It boasts an outstanding efficient motor for a compact canister vac. Sharp features its triple filter system that the company claims traps more than 99 percent of all fine dust and pollen. The EC-7311 is small (10×14 inches), lightweight (just over 10 pounds), and has built-in attachments (a crevice tool and an upholstery tool with a detachable brush). With extra-large wheels and a low center of gravity, this unit proves to be smooth-moving and extremely stable. Best of all, it's extremely easy to change the bag on this unit (it has a simple, one-touch release) and there's an automatic rewind for its 16-foot power cord.

Warranty: 1 year, parts and labor (limited)
Manufacturer's Suggested Retail Price: $99
Approximate Low Price: not available

Eureka Mighty Mite 3685A

Budget Buy

The name Mighty Mite truly fits this unit, which looks like a sturdy little creature ready to pounce on dirt. Thanks to its light weight (just over 10 pounds) and clever design (oversized wheels and a large handle on its back), this vac is remarkably user-friendly. The unit is compact and easy to lift, so it can be used right where it's needed. It has relatively good suction for its size, though it works best on bare floors. It also features a True HEPA sealed filtration system, which filters out more than 99 percent of pollen, dirt, and dust, making this unit a real bargain for its price and performance. Eureka ingeniously conceals several onboard attachments (including a carpet nozzle, a crevice tool, a dusting brush, an upholstery tool, a crush-resistant hose, and two wands) that are designed to work on a variety of household surfaces (such as sofas and drapes). Other nice touches include dual-edge cleaning on the carpet nozzle, oversized wheels, a 20-foot power cord, and an extra-long seven-foot hose. The Mighty Mite is a great multipurpose vacuum that can complement an upright vacuum for carpets or suffice on its own in a residence that has mostly bare floors.

Warranty: 1 year (limited)
Manufacturer's Suggested Retail Price: $120
Approximate Low Price: $100

MINI VACUUM CLEANERS AND BROOMS

Hoover Twist & Vac S1147

✓BEST BUY

The Twist & Vac takes its name from the swivel nozzle that holds a powered brush roll, turns 90 degrees, and locks in place. This innovative nozzle gives the unit lots of cleaning versatility and the rotating brushes do an excellent job of picking up dirt. The ultra-slim design enables the vac to get under furniture, cabinets, and other hard-to-reach spaces. Other useful features include a see-through, quick-release "E-Z Empty" dirt cup (which eliminates the need for vac bags), a washable filter, a comfortable handgrip, and a 20-foot power cord. Hoover also makes a handy five-piece cleaning tool set (S1903) designed to improve the Twist & Vac's performance. The tool set includes a four-foot hose/converter that snaps onto the nozzle and enables a crevice tool or dusting brush to be used in place of the agitator brush. Thanks to the powered brush roll, the Twist & Vac is a perfect pick for carpeted stairs or cushy upholstered pieces.

Warranty: 1 year
Manufacturer's Suggested Retail Price: $55 ($13 for tool kit)
Approximate Low Price: $43

Bissell Spot Lifter 715-1

✓BEST BUY

Not much bigger than the traditional dust-busting hand vac, the lightweight Spot Lifter is a cordless rechargeable model designed for attacking messes, lifting out spills instead of blotting them in. Considering that this is a handheld vac, the Spot Lifter has a powerful deep-cleaning spray nozzle that can be adjusted for big or small spots. It includes an extra-wide scrub brush for stubborn stains, a squeegee for hard surfaces, and a detachable scoop for chunky surface messes that can't be sucked up. Thanks to its sensible design, the vac is virtually effortless. It features two transparent plastic tanks for cleaning solution (8 ounces) and dirt collection (12 ounces).

Warranty: 1 year
Manufacturer's Suggested Retail Price: $60
Approximate Low Price: $60

Royal Dirt Devil Scrub Devil SD100

Recommended

Royal believes anything that takes undue pressure off hands can be a welcome addition to a household. Which is why the cleverly-designed Scrub Devil is so ingenious. Just over one-foot long, it looks like a toy drill in bright red high-impact plastic with an enclosed grip. But the "Twist 'n Scrub" handle bends at about a

120-degree angle, so the unit can be used in hard-to-reach places. It also features three easy-to-switch attachments: a short, chunky swivel action scrub brush for large areas; a longer narrow detail brush for tight spots; and a scouring pad for tough stains.

Warranty: 1 year
Manufacturer's Suggested Retail Price: $50
Approximate Low Price: $40

ALL-PURPOSE CLEANING MACHINES

Bissell Powersteamer 1695

✓BEST BUY

Bissell's Powersteamer 1695 can be used to deep-clean carpets and upholstery, and it features onboard tools that include an attached ten-foot hose and upholstery and crevice tools for cleaning furniture and stairs. The Powersteamer features a "SmartClean" system that includes a powerful, three-motor system; a "DirtLifter Powerbrush" that attacks dirt on carpets and has a floating suspension for various height adjustments; a "SmartMix" regulating system that adjusts the amount of cleaning formula used for specific tasks (gentle, normal, or high traffic); and a pump that automatically pretreats difficult stains. It also has an easy-to-fill tank that uses tap water, an extra-wide cleaning nozzle, and it can clean in forward and reverse motion. For cleanups, the tank removes easily. Thanks to large wheels and a comfortable grip, the unit is extremely maneuverable. The 1695 is another economical addition to a home with lots of carpeting and upholstery.

Warranty: 1 year
Manufacturer's Suggested Retail Price: $189
Approximate Low Price: $160

Eureka Enviro Steamer 300

Budget Buy

Anyone who has scrubbed a ceramic tile or linoleum floor, or used a relatively messy mop, will truly appreciate this ingenious new steam cleaner from Eureka. The Steamer 300 makes it possible to clean and sanitize hard surface floors (including treated hardwoods) both quickly and effortlessly. Configured like an upright, this unit features a one-foot-wide, floor-hugging steamer. Simply fill it with tap water (it uses no chemicals) and watch it go to work. The steam it creates is 220 degrees, and it lodges in a washable, reusable waffle weave "Magic Pad" attached to the bottom of the steamer. The Steamer 300 comes equipped with a 25-foot cord, an adjustable handle, and an accessory pack that includes two pads and a tray to rest the unit on when warming or cooling it.

Warranty: 1 year (limited)
Manufacturer's Suggested Retail Price: $130
Approximate Low Price: $130

Royal Dirt Devil Wet-Dry Plus 081600B

Budget Buy

All-purpose cleaning machines are designed to handle chores above and beyond the typical vacuum, such as picking up chunks of dirt from a floor or sucking up spills from minor floods. Royal's Wet-Dry Plus 081600B is a superb performer that incorporates all the key features essential in an all-purpose cleaning machine. Royal designed this unit to be exceptionally stable, featuring an extra-wide wheel base. No matter what, home cleaning units are noisy, much harder to maneuver than regular vacs, and tend to be much heavier—and this unit is no exception. But it does an excellent job performing special tasks. The 081600B comes with a 20-foot cord and a 16-gallon capacity. Other features include two extension wands, an extra-wide seven-foot hose, and onboard attachments for floors, crevices, and upholstery. In addition, there's a removable tool caddy, a detachable blower, and an easy-to-use tank-drainage system.

Warranty: 2 years
Manufacturer's Suggested Retail Price: $100
Approximate Low Price: $100

LAUNDRY CARE

While there's been a great deal of speculation about future Department of Energy standards for energy use of laundry-care products, there has been little industry response. While some new machines designed to improve efficiency have already been introduced, the majority of washers and dryers available are essentially the same as what's been available for the past 40 years or so; improvements have been in details and convenience features.

BUYING TIPS

Picking the machine that's right for you is an exercise in deciding just what features fit your lifestyle. Convenience features can add to the price of a machine, and extra features you don't use simply waste money. On the other hand, a machine that lacks features that are important to you is no bargain at any price.

BEST BUYS '99

Our Best Buy, Recommended, and Budget Buy washers and dryers are listed below. Products within each category are listed according to quality. The best of the Best Buys is listed first, followed by our second choice, and so on. A Best Buy, Recommended, or Budget Buy recommendation only applies to the model listed—it does not necessarily apply to other models made by the same manufacturer or to an entire product line.

WASHERS

The front-loading washers that were popular in the 1940s were replaced by less-efficient top-loaders when energy was cheap and plentiful; the top-loaders offered greater load capacities, no-stoop operation, faster cycles, and lower cost. But in the interest of conserving energy, the industry is now considering taking a giant step back to the future: The horizontal, front-loading washer is making a comeback in a considerably updated form. The front-loading washer offers significant energy savings, but its disadvantages—notably its considerably higher price—have prevented it from gaining wide acceptance. Although they use less water (hot and cold) than do their top-loading counterparts and have a more effective spin-dry cycle (reducing dryer operating costs), they have smaller load capacities, longer cycles, and are not as easy to load. Most washers available on the market today are top-loaders.

FEATURES AND TERMINOLOGY

Bleach and Fabric-softener Dispensers: If you use liquid bleach and/or fabric softener, these dispensers can be a convenience. They automatically add the liquids at the optimum time in the wash cycle.

Capacity: A washer's tub size is rated in terms of volume—ranging from "large" (roughly 2 to 2½ cubic feet) and "extra large" (about 2½ to 3 cubic feet) to "super large" (3 to 3½ cubic feet). Unless you're washing bulky items such as comforters and ski parkas, figure on about a 10- to 12-pound maximum load for large-capacity machines and 14 pounds or less for extra-large and super-large models. Front loaders typically can handle 7 to 8 pounds.

Controls: Push-button electronic controls look high-tech, but they do not offer any advantage over the older rotary controls. They break down more often, as well.

Cycles: To a great extent, the number of cycles a washer has depends on how many points the manufacturer paints on the dials. Basic cycles are regular, delicate, and permanent press. On many machines, the water temperature and machine speed are automatically preset when you choose a cycle; we prefer machines where water temperature and machine speed can be independently adjusted. A water-level control is a money-saver if you often wash small loads. Many washers, in the interest of energy-saving, limit you to a cold-water rinse on all the cycles; we prefer the ones that permit a warm rinse.

Efficiency: A washer's energy efficiency depends almost entirely upon how much hot water it uses, although reducing cold-water usage can reduce water and sewer bills in many communities. For maximum efficiency, match the load to the water level.

Speeds: Most washers have two speeds—one for regular and one for gentle wash.

Water Levels: Some lower-priced machines have only one water level; as you go up in price, more levels are available.

TOP-LOADING WASHERS

General Electric WKSR2100T

✓BEST BUY

This super-large-capacity washer is ideal for a large family. It has enough versatility to handle almost any type or size load. It uses a combination of four rotary dial controls that allow you to select from three different water levels, two wash/spin speed combinations, three wash/rinse temperatures (no warm rinse is available), and ten wash cycles. The WKSR2100T also includes a self-cleaning lint filter. This model is available in white or almond.

Specifications: height, 42"; width, 27"; depth, 25½"; volts/amps 115/15
Warranty: 1 year, parts and labor; 5 years, suspension and transmission (parts only); 10 years, outer tub; 20 years, basket
Manufacturer's Suggested Retail Price: $470
Approximate Low Price: $470

Frigidaire FWX645RF

✓BEST BUY

This Frigidaire super-large-capacity washer features a heftier-than-usual ¾-horsepower motor and a rugged polypropylene tub. It has a five-rotary-dial control panel that provides a wide choice of washing conditions, including four wash/rinse temperature combinations (including one with a warm rinse), four wash/spin speed combinations, an adjustable water-level control, and 11 wash cycles. A self-cleaning lint filter and a fabric softener dispenser are also included. This model is only available in white.

Specifications: height, 43⅝"; width, 27"; depth, 27"; volts/amps 120/15
Warranty: 1 year, parts; 5 years, transmission (limited); 25 years, washer tub
Manufacturer's Suggested Retail Price: $399
Approximate Low Price: $360

Maytag LAT9806

Recommended

The Maytag LAT9806 is a super-capacity washer loaded with washing options. It features a combination of one rotary dial control, three sets of push buttons, and a slide control that provides a continuous variation of water levels. It also offers 14 cycles, four speed combinations, and four wash/rinse temperature combinations (including a warm/warm selection). Extra rinse and spin options can also be selected. Other features include a double-wash cycle, a quick cycle, and a "LoadSensor" agitator that changes its wash action to match the size of the load. There's a self-cleaning lint filter as well as bleach and fabric softener dispensers. This high-performance washer is available in white or almond.

Specifications: height, 41¾; width, 25½"; depth 26¾"; volts/amps 120/15
Warranty: 1 year, parts and labor; 2 years, parts; 5 years, washer motor (parts only); 10 years, outer cabinet rust-through
Manufacturer's Suggested Retail Price: $649
Approximate Low Price: $649

Amana LWA10AW

Budget Buy

This economical Amana is an extra-large-capacity washer, with plenty of capacity for a large family. It features a stainless-steel wash tub and a three-rotary-dial control panel. One rotary dial selects one of three water levels, another selects the wash/rinse water temperature from three options (excluding warm rinse), and a third selects one of six available cycles—essentially timing variations of regular, delicate, and permanent press. This model also includes a helpful self-cleaning lint filter. The LWA10AW is only available in white.

Specifications: height, 43"; width, 25⅝"; depth 26"; volts/amps 120/10
Warranty: 1 year, parts and labor; 5 years, transmission (parts and labor), cabinet rust-through; 10 years, transmission (parts only); 20 years, stainless steel tub (parts only)
Manufacturer's Suggested Retail Price: $419
Approximate Low Price: $350

Hotpoint VVSR1040

Budget Buy

Although this is rated a Budget Buy, this super-capacity washer packs a fair amount of versatility for the price. It provides two available water levels and three wash/rinse water-temperature combinations. There's a single speed for both wash and spin. The control panel, with a pair of rotary knobs, is uncluttered and simple and allows you to choose among four cycles, with a shorter version for delicate fabrics. The VVSR1040 comes equipped with a convenient self-cleaning lint filter.

Specifications: height, 42"; width, 27"; depth 25½"; volts/amps 115/15
Warranty: 1 year, parts and labor; 5 years, transmission (parts only); 20 years, basket (parts only)
Manufacturer's Suggested Retail Price: $329
Approximate Low Price: $310

FRONT-LOADING WASHERS

Frigidaire FWT449GFS

✔ BEST BUY

Frigidaire's FWT449GFS is a full-featured front-loading washer that has all the advantages of a horizontal-rotation machine. It has a 2.7-cubic-foot drum, and the control panel features four rotary knobs that allow you to select from four wash/rinse temperature combinations (including a warm rinse) and two wash/spin speed combinations. Water level automatically adjusts to match the load. Basic cycles are regular, permanent press, and knits/delicates; prewash and extra rinse cycles can also be selected, as can the length of each cycle. A handy drawer on the face of the washer contains dispensers for detergents (liquid or powdered), liquid bleach, and fabric softener. The wash drum is stainless steel, whereas the outer tub is made of polypropylene plastic. The FWT449GFS is only available in white.

Specifications: height, 36"; width, 26¾"; depth 27⅛"; volts/amps 120/15
Warranty: 2 years, parts and labor; 5 years, drive system (parts only); 25 years, stainless-steel drum (parts only)
Manufacturer's Suggested Retail Price: $849
Approximate Low Price: $800

ASKO 11505

Recommended

The ASKO 11505 is a high-quality—and extremely expensive—Swedish-built front-loading washer. While this design has several advantages, including compactness, quietness, and extremely effective spin drying, the unit's major claim to fame is its economy: The ASKO uses about 11 gallons of water per load as compared with the 40-plus gallons required by a typical top-loader. It also reduces the need for using hot water: The ASKO 11505 is connected only to your home's cold water line and heats the water as it's required, meaning that your laundry will never interfere with your other hot water needs. The washer's1.7-cubic-foot stainless-steel drum may be misleading because you can fill the drum up only to the level of the door opening. This limits load size to roughly nine pounds, instead of a similarly-sized top-loader's 12 to 14 pounds. Controls consist of a combination of three push buttons and two rotary knobs, which permit you to select water temperature (hot, extra hot, warm, or cold), a basic cycle (regular, permanent press, or delicate), and the duration of the cycle, as well as prewash and soak options. Water level automatically is set to match your load. There are two spin speeds and an extra rinse program. Both inner and outer tubs are stainless steel, and there's a fabric softener dispenser provided. This model is only available in white, although the washer face can accept designer panels.

Specifications: height, 32¼; width, 23½"; depth 24¾"; volts/amps 220/30
Warranty: 1 year, parts and labor; 5 years, pump and motor (parts only); 25 years, tank (parts only)
Manufacturer's Suggested Retail Price: $1,149
Approximate Low Price: $1,100

DRYERS

Dryers are relatively simple appliances. They consist of a rotating perforated basket that holds damp clothes, a fan to blow air through the load, and a heater to keep the airstream at the desired temperature. The heater can be either gas or electric.

ELECTRIC OR GAS UNITS

For most people, there's really little choice between a gas and an electric dryer. If your home doesn't have natural gas, you'll buy an electric one. If you have an option, gas dryers are considerably less expensive to operate than electric ones in virtually all locations; they're also faster. A gas dryer, however, will cost $50 more than an electric one, and it will cost more to install, as it requires an outside vent and a piped-in gas connection.

FEATURES AND TERMINOLOGY

Alarm: Most machines with a wrinkle-protection cycle are equipped with an alarm that signals when the drying cycle is complete, and then periodically sounds during the cool-down cycle. A control that enables you to adjust the volume, or turn it off completely, is a handy convenience.

Cycles: Dryers typically offer a choice between a timed cycle, which lets you select how long you want the dryer to run, and automatic cycles, which can be set for how dry you want the clothes to be. The two basic automatic cycles are regular and permanent press. The permanent-press cycle introduces a cool-down period of about five minutes, during which the clothes are tumbled with no heat to minimize wrinkling. To these cycles a delicate cycle is often added; this cycle runs on reduced heat.

Drying Sensors: There are two ways of controlling an automatic-dry cycle: Either the machine measures the temperature of the air leaving the clothes, or a humidistat (a device that directly measures the moisture in the clothes) can be used. Both methods work, but humidistats provide more precise control.

Efficiency: The efficiency of a dryer depends on how good the washer's spin-dry cycle is and how fully the dryer is loaded. If you normally dry small loads, you're better off with a smaller-capacity dryer. Using automatic instead of timed-dry cycles also helps.

Temperature: In some dryers the temperature setting is preset for each cycle; in others it can be independently adjusted. We prefer dryers that allow you to adjust temperature independently.

Wrinkle Protection: Clothes left in a dryer after the dry cycle is finished can wrinkle, especially if they're warm. Many machines have an automatic cycle that will tumble the clothes intermittently, circulating unheated air through them, for up to 2½ hours.

KitchenAid KEYS750G/E

✓ **BEST BUY**

KitchenAid calls this 7.0-cubic-foot dryer a "Super Capacity Plus" model. It uses a combination of switches and a rotary knob to control its various functions. One switch selects the drying temperature, another activates the extended no-heat Extra Care cycle on and off, while a third turns the end-of-cycle audible signal on or off. A rotary knob allows you to choose sensor, timed, or air tumble cycles, with a degree-of-dryness setting within each cycle. Automatic cycles are humidistat controlled. The automatic-dry cycle has settings for normal and permanent-press loads. There's an interior light, and a drying rack is an optional accessory. This model is available in white or almond.

Specifications: height, 42"; width, 29"; depth, $27\frac{13}{16}$";
volts/amps, 240/30 (electric), 115/15 (gas); heater, 5,400 watts (electric), 22,000 Btu (gas)
Warranty: 2 years, parts and labor; 5 years, motor and controls; 10 years, drum and top cabinet assembly
Manufacturer's Suggested Retail Price: $529 (gas model)
Approximate Low Price: $499

General Electric DWSR473

✓BEST BUY

This is a super-capacity dryer with a 7.0-cubic-foot capacity. It uses three rotary knobs to provide three drying temperatures plus an air-fluff or no-heat setting, an extra-care anti-wrinkling cycle, and an off/medium/loud signal setting. Another rotary knob is reserved for a manual start switch, while a fifth knob selects timed dry, automatic permanent press, or automatic regular dry. Automatic drying is controlled by a temperature sensor. An interior light is another useful feature of this model, which is available in white or almond.

Specifications: height, 42"; width, 27"; depth, $25\frac{1}{2}$";
volts/amps, 240/24 (electric), 120/6 (gas); heater, 5,600 watts (electric), 22,000 Btu (gas)
Warranty: 1 year, parts and labor; 5 years, dryer drum (limited)
Manufacturer's Suggested Retail Price: $429 (gas model)
Approximate Low Price: $400

Frigidaire FDE/G848GF

✓BEST BUY

The Frigidaire FDE/G848GF is a 5.7-cubic-foot dryer that features Frigidaire's two-way tumble dry system: The drum rotates clockwise for a period of time ($4\frac{1}{2}$ minutes for electric dryers and $7\frac{1}{2}$ minutes for gas models) and then reverses its rotation for 25 seconds to help untangle the load. A push-button panel provides four temperature settings (including no heat), and a rotary knob adjusts the sound level of the end-of-cycle signal. Another rotary knob selects timed dry, automatic regular, automatic permanent press, or automatic delicate. The automatic cycles allow you to select the degree of dryness you prefer; the timed cycle has a cool-down section at its end. This model comes in white or almond.

Specifications: height, 43⅝"; width, 26⅞"; depth, 25¾"; volts/amps, 240/30 (electric), 120/15 (gas); heater, 4,500 watts (electric), 20,000 Btu (gas)
Warranty: 2 years, parts and labor
Manufacturer's Suggested Retail Price: $439 (gas model)
Approximate Low Price: $409

Hotpoint NWXR473GT/ET

✔BEST BUY

This 6.0-cubic-foot-capacity dryer features an array of rotary knobs on a striking black backsplash. Features include a manual start, three drying temperatures plus no-heat air fluff, an extended cool-air anti-wrinkle cycle, and an adjustable end-of-cycle signal. There are three cycles to choose from: timed, automatic permanent press, or automatic regular. Automatic cycles are controlled by a temperature sensor. An interior light is also provided. This model is available in white or almond.

Specifications: height, 42"; width, 27"; depth, 25¾"; volts/amps, 240/30 (electric), 120/15 (gas); heater, 5,600 watts (electric), 22,000 Btu (gas)
Warranty: 1 year, parts and labor; 5 years, drum (parts only)
Manufacturer's Suggested Retail Price: $379 (gas model)
Approximate Low Price: $359

Amana LEA90A/LGA90 AW/L

Recommended

This top-of-the-line 7.2-cubic-foot-capacity dryer has just about any feature you can imagine. The easy-to-clean electronic touchpad controls nine automatic dry cycles (all humidistat controlled) and an adjustable-duration timed cycle, with settings for more dry, less dry, and no heat. There are five temperatures available. There's also an extended anti-wrinkle cycle. This model features a stainless-steel wash drum, a stationary drying rack, a fluorescent panel light, and a drum light. The chime used as an end-of-cycle signal has an adjustable volume. Amana offers this model in white or almond.

Specifications: height, 43"; width, $26\frac{7}{8}$"; depth, $27\frac{3}{4}$"; volts/amps, 240/30 (electric), 120/15 (gas); heater, 5,350 watts (electric), 22,500 Btu (gas)
Warranty: 5 years, parts and labor, 20 years, drum (parts only)
Manufacturer's Suggested Retail Price: $599 (gas model)
Approximate Low Price: $550

General Electric DBXR453

Budget Buy

This dryer, while it lacks some of the bells and whistles found on more expensive models, has a full six-cubic-foot capacity and enough versatility to satisfy a large family's needs. Its three rotary-knob controls provide four temperature settings (including a no-heat air-fluff setting), a manual start control, and a selector for timed dry, automatic cotton, and automatic permanent-press cycles, with variable time settings within each cycle. Its major limitation is its lack of an anti-wrinkle cycle. Dryness sensing is done by temperature. The DBXR453 is available in white or almond.

Specifications: height, 42"; width, 27"; depth, $25\frac{1}{2}$"; volts/amps, 220/30 (electric), 115/15 (gas); heater, 5,400 watts (electric), 22,000 Btu (gas)
Warranty: 1 year (limited); 5 years, DuraDrum interior
Manufacturer's Suggested Retail Price: $379 (gas model)
Approximate Low Price: $350

Hotpoint NVLR333

Budget Buy

This large-capacity dryer—5.4 cubic feet—is a plain-vanilla model that's ideal for a small family or one on a tight budget. It features automatic permanent press and automatic regular cycles as well as a timed-dry cycle. There are three temperature settings, which are built into the various cycles. The only other control is a start switch. This model, which was also picked as a Budget Buy in 1998, is available in white or almond, with a black backsplash.

Specifications: height, 42"; width, 27"; depth, 25¾"; volts/amps, 240/30 (electric model), 115/15 (gas); heater, 5,600 watts
Warranty: 1 year, parts and labor
Manufacturer's Suggested Retail Price: $309
Approximate Low Price: $299

COMPACT WASHER

General Electric WSKS2060T

✓BEST BUY

This little unit is ideal for situations where space is at a premium and washing requirements aren't heavy. It's a top-loader with a 2.0-cubic-foot capacity and a control panel with a trio of rotary controls that enable you to select from two wash and spin speeds, three temperatures, and four water levels. The six cycles include a spin-only cycle. The WSKS2060T has dispensers for bleach and fabric softeners and an easy-to-clean lint filter. It's available either as a portable or as a stationary unit, and you can purchase an optional rack that allows you to mount a compact dryer over the washer. This model is available in white or almond—both with a black control panel.

Specifications: height, 34¼"; width, 22¼"; depth 24"; volts/amps 120/15
Warranty: 1 year, parts and labor; 5 years, transmission

Manufacturer's Suggested Retail Price: $529
Approximate Low Price: $500

COMBINATION WASHER/DRYER

White-Westinghouse MLCE52RC

✓BEST BUY

A viable alternative to stacking a compact washer over a compact dryer is to purchase a ready-assembled high-rise combination—or, more formally, an integrated laundry center. The White-Westinghouse MLCE52RC is a single unit, combining a large capacity top-loading washer with a matching dryer into one unit with a single integrated control panel. The washer has three wash/rinse water temperature selections and a three-position water-level control. Control cycles are regular, permanent press, and delicates; soak and prewash cycles are also available. The washer's two speeds are determined by the cycle selected. The washer's operation is controlled by three rotary knobs; the dryer uses a single rotary control and a push-to-start button. There are two automatic-dry cycles for regular and permanent press loads. There is also a timed dry cycle and a no-heat air-fluff setting. The dryer has an end-of-cycle alarm and an easy-to-clean lint filter. The MLCE52RC is available in white or almond.

Specifications: height, 71¾"; width, 23⅞"; depth 27¼"; volts/amps 240/30 (electric dryer), 120/20 (gas dryer)
Warranty: 1 year, parts and labor; 5 years, parts and washer transmission; 25 years, tub (parts only)
Manufacturer's Suggested Retail Price: $849
Approximate Low Price: $849

SEWING MACHINES

Basic machine-stitch formation hasn't changed in the 150 years since Elias Howe patented the sewing machine. What has changed are the machine's capabilities beyond the straight stitch and the ease with which it can accomplish an ever-increasing variety of sewing techniques on a wide range of fabrics. Some new models also feature an endless variety of embroidery stitches. These machines are on the pricey side but well worth the cost for consumers interested in both craft and utility sewing.

FEATURES

Even if you'll never use half the stitches available on today's sewing machines, you will appreciate their time- and effort-saving features: electronic control, stronger motors, improved feeding systems, jam-free hooks, and more consistent thread tension. Easier operation often expands the fabric choices and techniques you're able to try. At the upper price range, hobbyists are discovering new pleasure in elaborate hooped embroidery, previously possible only on professional equipment but now standard on several top-of-the-line home models.

COMPUTERIZED SEWING MACHINES

Computerized machines feature electronic operation plus a "memory." Select a stitch at the push of a button and the machine automatically adjusts for the ideal settings (though you can change those settings if you wish). Most models include memory buttonholes, so you can repeat as many identical buttonholes as desired.

Increased computer memory is responsible for the tremendous expansion of the sewing machine's creative capabilities. The excitement began when it became possible to combine, or "program," stitches into elaborate borders or patterns and to "write" with a machine's built-in alphabet and numerals. The latest technology enables machines to interface with a personal computer for customizing designs and converting them into stitchery.

NONCOMPUTERIZED SEWING MACHINES

Since noncomputerized machines have no memory, their stitches are usually less complex than computerized machines. You also have to adjust the stitch length and width manually. But some of these models do have electronic circuitry. The most common electronic element is speed control, which allows full needle penetration power of any fabric weight even at the slowest speed. Electronic control also allows more precise reaction during the start and stop of motion, enabling the machine to make one stitch at a time for precise accuracy.

A mechanical foot control, by contrast, loses power as it loses speed, so it can be difficult to pierce heavy fabrics without "flooring" the foot pedal. Electronic regulation allows constant speed changes without the foot control heating up, thus prolonging sewing machine life. In general, electronic machines are more reliable and quicker to repair than mechanical models.

BUYING TIPS

Before you buy, spend time alone at various machines sewing with your preferred fabrics. How does each machine feel and sound? Does it sew balanced stitches without skipping or jamming, even on hard-to-sew fabrics? How easily and efficiently does it stitch a buttonhole? Examine the owner's manual for readability. Compare any problems and suggested solutions of the various machines you test. Perform the same tests on all machines for comparison.

As you shop, assess dealers' knowledge, services, and reputation as well. After all, few appliances involve as many variables for proper operation—thread, fabric, needle, technique—as sewing machines. Do they have on-site parts and repair services? Will they keep you up to date on new accessories and techniques? Will they stand behind the product if you're not satisfied? Ask about their trade-in policy should you decide to upgrade.

Prices may be enticing at discount and mail-order outlets, but information and service can vary greatly or be nonexistent. That's why it's worth the additional expense to buy the machine from a dealer that guarantees continued satisfaction.

BEST BUYS '99

Our Best Buy, Recommended, and Budget Buy sewing machines are listed below. Products within each category are listed according to quality. The best of the Best Buys is listed first, followed by our second choice, and so on. A Best Buy, Recommended, or Budget Buy designation only applies to the model listed—it does not necessarily apply to other models made by the same manufacturer or to an entire product line.

COMPUTERIZED MACHINES

Pfaff Tiptronic 6270

BEST BUY

Pfaff combines strength and durability with an extremely straightforward control system and a creative selection of stitches. Its 6270 offers more than 500 built-in stitch programs, including 128 built-in utility, stretch, and decorative stitches, all at the touch of a button. It can also be used with software to create endless customized designs. The 6270 is an all-purpose machine, ideal for the sewer who wants the versatility of special stitching and the ability to combine them easily. The LCD screen allows you to preview all the stitches, including the modifications (such as stitch width, length, and density) you make to them in the planning stages. The 6270 is loaded with innovative features that reflect Pfaff's state-of-the-art engineering, such as their respected dual-feed system that feeds the fabric from above and below at the same time and exerts more control so it will not slip. There's also twin needle sewing, full needle-piercing power at half-speed, automatic needle threading, a jam-proof rotary hook, and a high presser foot lift for sewing thick fabrics or multiple layers. The 6270 is also equipped with a large swing-out accessory tray for storage that is built into the base of the machine, instant flat-bed to free-arm conversion for sewing cuffs, a "needle up/down" button that allows you to stop with the needle in or out of fabric, and a "basting stitch" button for quick fitting tests. Overall, this is the best choice for sewers who aren't interested in full-blown embroidery functions.

Warranty: 2 years, electrical components; 25 years, defects in material and workmanship
Manufacturer's Suggested Retail Price: $1,799
Approximate Low Price: $1,499

Viking Husqvarna Rose

Recommended

This sewing machine is designed to do it all, from everyday jobs to intricate needlework. And because of its sturdy construction and smart engineering (which Viking is renowned for), the Husqvarna Rose fits the bill. This machine is cleverly designed to set stitch length and width automatically and make recommendations about both presser foot and thread tension. It offers a full array of 40 built-in decorative and utility stitches, which can be combined to make patterns and motifs or be used for sewing, darning, blind hemming, and making buttonholes. These options are all touch-activated on a large, easy-to-read keypad, and displayed on an LCD screen. Other handy features include a range of options for sewing ease such as adjustable speed control, a front load drop-in bobbin, instant and permanent reverse stitching, and three built-in thread cutters. When the slide-on embroidery unit is attached, the Rose converts into a professional quality embroidery machine in seconds. You can even use optional software to create your own designs. In addition, designs can be purchased for the unit over the Internet and are available for viewing on the Husqvarna Embroidery Shop, a CD-ROM On-Line catalogue and file editor in one (it also organizes the embroidery files you already own and allows you to cut and paste designs). The Husqvarna Rose comes with a 4×4-inch embroidery field (an optional 4×8-inch is available from the manufacturer).

Warranty: 1 year, labor; 5 years, electrical components; 20 years, defective parts
Manufacturer's Suggested Retail Price: $2,249
Approximate Low Price: $1,900

NONCOMPUTERIZED MACHINES

Bernina 1008

BEST BUY

The reputable Bernina is so straightforward and easy-to-use, directions are practically unnecessary. It is a sturdy machine, which is often used in school home economics programs to teach sewing. Tension is self-gauged by the machine (via the CB-hook system), making it adjustment free. Simple operating controls are logically arranged and clearly marked for quick and easy adjustments, making it simple to alter stitch width and length. There are 16 practical and decorative stitches, including straight, zigzag, blind, and buttonhole, as well as special stitches for stretch fabrics.

Warranty: 2 years, electric; 3 years, circuit board; 20 years, defects in material and workmanship
Manufacturer's Suggested Retail Price: $900
Approximate Low Price: $749

Viking Husqvarna Sew Easy 330

Recommended

The Sew Easy 330 (part of Viking's 300 series) fits its name perfectly. It offers astonishing utility, extremely user-friendly controls, and loads of features that make it a superb selection for any home sewer. Its 44 built-in stitches cover a wide variety of stitch types (including buttonholes). Other important features include an easy and efficient control system; a feed system that feeds all weights of fabrics evenly; a free-arm design for sewing cuffs, sleeves, and hems; an accessory tray and flatbed extension for sewing large items; drop-in jam-proof bobbins; adjustable stitch widths and lengths; an up-front horizontal spool system; twin needle sewing; a built-in bobbin winder; and electronic speed control.

Warranty: 1 year, labor; 5 years, electrical components; 20 years, defective parts
Manufacturer's Suggested Retail Price: $799
Approximate Low Price: $699

ENVIRONMENTAL APPLIANCES

Making our home environments comfortable and healthy has become a priority in this modern era of air pollutants, heat indexes, and high pollen counts. These environmental control appliances can help ensure that your house is a clean, comfortable place for you and your family.

BEST BUYS '99

Our Best Buy, Recommended, and Budget Buy environmental appliances are listed below. Products within each category are listed according to quality. The best of the Best Buys is listed first, followed by our second choice, and so on. A Best Buy, Recommended, or Budget Buy designation only applies to the model listed—it does not necessarily apply to other models made by the same manufacturer or to an entire product line.

CEILING FANS

Ceiling fans move large amounts of air in the home and can reduce cooling costs by providing air circulation throughout the house. Ceiling fans range in price from $30 to $1,000. Generally speaking, the more expensive the unit, the better it will perform and the more attractive the design. Unless you are looking for a ceiling fan that is a focal point in a room, a good low- to medium-priced fan will offer excellent air circulation and last for years.

QUALITY

Lower-priced fans are usually noisy. This is commonly caused by a poorly balanced motor and blades, poor bearing tolerance, or loose motor windings. For medium- to high-priced units, expect a sealed, well-balanced motor and blades; heavy-duty castings; attractive design features, such as brass fittings and center mounted blades; and sealed bearings.

An important concern with ceiling fans is how low they hang in a room. Most ceiling fans are designed to be installed in a room with standard eight-foot-high ceilings. If you have low ceilings but would like a ceiling fan, look for a unit that mounts flush to the ceiling or has blades that extend from the sides of the motor rather than below it. Also keep in mind that a light fixture below the fan will further reduce headroom. On the other hand, if you have high ceilings, consider an extension tube for the fan to lower its height to the ideal eight-foot level.

FEATURES

The majority of ceiling fans have five blades, although four-blade models are also available in the smaller sizes. Blade-size ranges from 29 to 62 inches across, with 52 inches being the most popular. Most fans have a pull chain for turning the unit on/off and changing speeds. There's also a switch for reversing the direction of the spin. In theory, a ceiling fan pushes air down to cool the room during the warm months, and pulls cool air up (which forces warm air down) during the heating season. Most fans have a light fixture or offer an optional lighting package.

Beverly Hills Rio Outdoor 1250

✓BEST BUY

The Beverly Hills Rio Outdoor, as the name implies, is designed and UL-rated for use outdoors, which makes it an excellent choice for an outdoor porch or covered deck. The motor is sealed and the blades are made of acrylic for long life in wet conditions. This unit contains a low-wattage light fixture that provides a soft, gentle light; a three-speed, reversible motor; and four 52-inch white blades. Installation is simple and can be flush-mounted, standard-hung, or sloped (up to 35 degrees). Accessory items include wall-mounted controls, acrylic light kit, and extension rods for high ceilings.

Warranty: lifetime (limited)
Manufacturer's Suggested Retail Price: $216
Approximate Low Price: $216

Beverly Hills Stratos

✓BEST BUY

The Beverly Hills Stratos is a 52-inch designer fan with a three-speed, reversible, sealed motor. The four blades extend from the side of the motor rather than from below. The basic Stratos extends 17½ inches down and is better suited for ten-foot-high ceilings. An optional flush-mount kit should be purchased for standard eight-foot high ceilings. A wall-mounted control switch is included with this unit. Standard colors are white, black, or brushed aluminum. Optional accessories include matching extension rods (12 to 72 inches), 12-volt halogen light kit, slope ceiling kit, dual-slide three-speed wall control, and a computerized fan and light control. A 42-inch unit is also available.

Warranty: lifetime (limited)
Manufacturer's Suggested Retail Price: $375
Approximate Low Price: $300

Hunter Master Suite 21904

Recommended

The Hunter Master Suite is a dependable, remote-control ceiling fan. This unit features a quiet, three-speed, reversible motor in an attractive brass housing. It has five reversible rosewood/dark walnut blades that measure 52 inches long. One other model is available with white blades and white motor cover (#21906). The innovative remote controls three fan speeds, six light intensities, and features one-touch reverse. The Master Suite comes with a four-arm, 240-watt light kit; optional light kits are also available. Installation is simple with three mounting options: flush to the ceiling, standard height, and extra long or angled.

Warranty: 50 years, motor (parts only)
Manufacturer's Suggested Retail Price: $300
Approximate Low Price: $300

Hunter Whisper Wind 2000

Recommended

The Hunter Whisper Wind ceiling fan is available in white with five white/oak reversible, 52-inch blades. (For an additional cost, the 2000 comes in five other colors.) The patented AirMax three-speed motor is quiet and reversible. A white, four-light (60 watts each) fixture is also included. Installation is simple and includes three position options: flush to the ceiling, standard height, and extra long or angled (optional extension tubes are required for ceilings higher than eight feet). Accessories include wall-mounted switch, remote control, optional light kits, and extension tubes. This is a dependable, medium-priced ceiling fan that should provide years of service.

Warranty: lifetime, motor and parts
Manufacturer's Suggested Retail Price: $225
Approximate Low Price: $140

AIR CONDITIONERS

When shopping for a room air conditioner it is important to choose a unit with enough cooling capacity for your space without getting one that is too large for your needs. A unit that is too small won't cool the room enough. A unit that is too large will waste energy and won't dehumidify the room properly. As a rule, it is better to buy several small units than to use one large air conditioner to cool several rooms.

Area to be cooled *(in square feet)*	**Cooling capacity needed** *(in Btu)*
up to 150	4,000-5,000
150-250	5,000-6,000
250-450	6,000-8,500
450-600	8,500-11,000
600-900	11,000-14,000
900-1,200	15,000-19,000

INSTALLATION

The majority of air conditioners are designed to be installed in conventional single- and double-hung windows (which open up from the bottom). Some models can also be installed in sliding windows. Air conditioners cannot be installed in casement or louvered windows. Measure your window before you go shopping for an air conditioner. All units have accordionlike wings that pull out sideways to seal the space between the air conditioner and the window frame.

In addition to installing an air conditioner in a window, most units can also be installed through the wall. In a room with only one window, this may be the only way you can have cooling and still use the window. Through-the-wall installation means cutting a suitable-size hole in the wall and exterior siding, then adding a frame to support the unit. Through-the-wall installation is a lot of work—and may not be suitable for all types of homes (brick or masonry, for example)—but it provides a much quieter, much more secure installation. You'll have less air leakage in a through-the-wall installation, making your unit more effective in the summer and keeping the warm air in during the winter. If you are handy, consider doing the work yourself. If not, get a few estimates from licensed contractors. In most cases, the work can be completed in about a half day.

MAINTENANCE

Air conditioners are not maintenance free. Clean the foam filter in the front of the unit at the beginning of the season and at least once a month. Simply remove the filter, rinse it under running water, let it dry, and reinstall. The exterior fins perform the actual heat exchange and should be kept as clean as possible. These fins are made of thin metal and bend easily, so work carefully when dusting. If any of the fins become bent, carefully straighten them out with a piece of rigid plastic, such as a credit card. Rinse the fins on the exterior of the unit as well.

BUYING TIPS

When shopping for air conditioners, pay close attention to the large yellow Energy Efficiency Ratio (EER) stickers on the front of the units. Since January 1, 1990, the federal government has required all room (window) air conditioners to have an EER of at least 8.0. The EER is computed by dividing cooling capacity, measured in British Thermal Units (Btu) per hour, by the watts of electricity used. The higher the EER, the more efficient the unit, and the less it will cost to operate.

5,000-12,000 BTU

Sears Kenmore 78071

✓BEST BUY

The Sears Kenmore 78071 is a medium-capacity air conditioner with a Btu/hour rating of 7,000 and an EER rating of 9.5. This unit features the exclusive View-Saver design from Sears and is only 9 inches high inside the window (12 inches high outside the window), and therefore does not obstruct as much of the window view as other air conditioners. It includes a three-speed fan and exhaust air and fan-only settings. It has an automatic thermostat, a comfort sensor, and a four-way side-air discharge. It features a rigid mesh, E-Z Out filter, and a Quick Mount system for easy installation.

Specifications: length, 20⅜"; height, 9" inside window, 12" outside window; depth, 19½"; weight, 55 lbs; 115 volts; 740 watts
Warranty: 1 year, full; 5 years, sealed cooling system
Manufacturer's Suggested Retail Price: $400
Approximate Low Price: $350

Panasonic CW-806TU

✓BEST BUY

The Panasonic CW-806TU is a high-efficiency (EER rating of 10.0), window-mount air conditioner. It has a Btu/hour rating of 7,800. This unit can be installed in a double-hung window, a sliding window, or through the wall. It features a slide-out chassis for easy installation. A double-layered top panel adds strength and reduces vibration. Extra sound-absorbing insulation in the cabinet and the location of the compressors contribute to the unit's quiet operation. Other features include a one-touch air filter, two cooling speeds, a separate thermostat, ventilation control, two fan speeds, and an economy operation mode.

Specifications: length, 17 23/32"; height, 13 5/8"; depth, 20 7/8"; weight, 66 lbs; 115 volts; 780 watts
Warranty: 1 year, parts and labor; 5 years, compressor (limited)
Manufacturer's Suggested Retail Price: $480
Approximate Low Price: $440

Carrier TCB051B

Recommended

The TCB051B is part of the Siesta series of lightweight air conditioners from Carrier. This model is a good choice for a bedroom or other small living area. It has a Btu/hour rating of 5,100. The unit weighs only 46 pounds and has a built-in carrying handle for easy moving. The filter, which is located in the front, is easy to remove and clean. It has two fan speeds and an automatic thermostat. Built-in sound reducers that isolate moving parts, a rust-proof fan and blower wheels, and a high-efficiency fan motor contribute to this model's quiet operation. This unit has factory-installed expandable wing panels and special locking screws to prevent removal of the unit and entry by intruders. It has an EER rating of 9.0.

Specifications: length, 19"; height, 14"; depth, 11"; weight, 46 lbs; 115 volts; 570 watts
Warranty: 1 year, parts and labor (in-home service); 5 years, sealed system (limited)
Manufacturer's Suggested Retail Price: $289
Approximate Low Price: $275

12,000-18,000 BTU

Panasonic CW-1805SU

✔BEST BUY

The Panasonic CW-1805SU is a large-capacity room air conditioner with a Btu/hour rating of 18,000. This unit can be installed in a double-hung window, a sliding window, or through the wall. It has an innovative air swing feature—which spreads cool air side to side during operation—or you can direct the flow of air in a single direction. It has two cooling speeds and two fan-only speeds. Other worthwhile features include a four-way air deflection system, a ventilation control, a one-touch air filter, an economy operation mode, and a slide-out chassis. The CW-1805SU has an EER rating of 8.8 and requires a 220-volt electrical outlet.

Specifications: length, 26"; height, $16\frac{7}{8}$"; depth, $28\frac{25}{32}$"; weight, 139 lbs.; 230 volts; 2,050 watts
Warranty: 1 year, parts and labor (in-house service); 5 years, compressor (limited)
Manufacturer's Suggested Retail Price: $750
Approximate Low Price: $666

Sears Kenmore 78186

BEST BUY

The Sears Kenmore 78186 is a large-capacity air conditioner with a Btu/hour rating of 18,000 and an EER rating of 9.5. It has three fan speeds, an automatic thermostat, a comfort sensor, and separate settings for exhaust, fan only, and fresh air. There's also a rigid mesh, E-Z Out filter, and a condensate drain. It has a four-direction top-air discharge, a slide-out chassis, and a Quick Mount mounting system.

Specifications: length, $26\frac{1}{2}$"; height, $16\frac{5}{8}$"; depth, $25\frac{5}{8}$"; weight, 146 lbs; 230 volts; 1,850 watts
Warranty: 1 year, full; 5 years, sealed cooling system
Manufacturer's Suggested Retail Price: $760
Approximate Low Price: $580

AIR CARE APPLIANCES

The air in our homes is important for good health. A number of factors can determine overall quality of the air. During the heating season, for example, household air tends to be dry, the end result being a dry throat. Conversely, during the warmer months, air in the home tends to be laden with moisture, thus feeling warmer. Internal air can also contain a variety of airborne particles—from pets, carpeting, furnishings, and smoking—and breathing this type of air can cause respiratory problems. There are a variety of appliances designed to improve the quality of household air.

Humidifiers: If, during the heating season, you walk across a carpeted room and get a static electricity shock when you touch a door knob or light switch, or you wake up with a dry, sore throat, you should consider increasing the humidity of your home. Tabletop units are the most portable and simple to use. These units can be used in one room during the day and in a bedroom at night. They also have replaceable filters to trap airborne particles and odors.

Dehumidifiers: These units are not just for keeping a basement dry year-round. In the summer, they can help keep your house cool by reducing the amount of moisture in the air. Stand-alone units typically run quiet and can be centrally located in the home.

Air Filters: These units come in a variety of sizes, capacities, and styles. Look for models with HEPA (High Efficiency Particulate Air) filters, which remove the smallest of pollutants and pollen from the air. (HEPA filters remove more than 99 percent of all particulates in the air.) If you have asthma, allergies, or respiratory problems, a unit equipped with a HEPA filter may help you to breath easier. Portable models, which can be mounted on a table or small stand, add convenience.

HUMIDIFIERS

Hunter 33350

✓ BEST BUY

The Hunter 33350 is a quiet, dependable unit for home use. It features a "PermaWick" filter that never needs replacement. A patented anti-bacterial system provides 100 percent protection against bacteria, mold, and spores. Special polymers are molded into the plastic parts of the unit to prevent the growth of bacteria and other microorganisms. A regulated release system eliminates stagnant water around the filter to further prevent bacteria and germs. A refill light indicates when the unit is low on water. There's also an auto shut-off feature in case the unit runs out of water. It has an adjustable humidistat, a two-speed motor, and an automatic moisture regulation system. The specially designed and balanced water tank makes for easy refilling of up to $3\frac{1}{2}$ gallons of water. This unit will cover 1,600 square feet of floor space.

Specifications: length, $20\frac{5}{8}$"; height, $14\frac{1}{8}$"; depth, $15\frac{5}{8}$"; weight, 12 lbs.
Warranty: 1 year, parts and labor; 5 years, motor
Manufacturer's Suggested Retail Price: $105
Approximate Low Price: $75

Bemis 338000

✓BEST BUY

The Bemis 338000 is a quiet, tabletop unit that can put up to 4.5 gallons of moisture into your home per day. It can cover up to 1,000 square feet of floor space in a 24-hour period. This unit features a replaceable two-wick system and two replaceable air cleaning filters. It has three fan speeds, a special night setting, and an automatic humidistat for maintaining a desired humidity level. This unit has two water containers (1.6 gallons each) that are easy to remove and fill.

Specifications: length, $19\frac{1}{2}$"; height, 12"; depth, $13\frac{1}{4}$"; weight, 10 lbs. 8 oz.
Warranty: 1 year (limited)
Manufacturer's Suggested Retail Price: $80
Approximate Low Price: $80

DEHUMIDFIERS

Emerson Quiet Kool DG50G

✓BEST BUY

The Emerson Quiet Kool is a high-capacity dehumidifier. It features an easy-to-remove front tank. This unit can also be connected to a hose, instead of the tank, for automatic drain ing. The air filter, located on the front, can be rinsed and reused. The controls, which are mounted on top of the unit, are easy to read and adjust. Additional features include automatic shut-off, a special de-icing control, easy-glide caster-type wheels, and an automatic humidistat.

Specifications: length, 17¼"; height, 21⅜"; depth, 13½"; weight, 58 lbs.
Warranty: 1 year, parts and labor; 5 years, sealed refrigeration system (limited).
Manufacturer's Suggested Retail Price: $200
Approximate Low Price: $200

Sears Kenmore 5751

Recommended

The Sears Kenmore 5751 is a large-capacity unit that features a two-speed fan, a generous 24-pint collection bucket, a water-level control, and a connection for a drain hose. The unit automatically shuts off when the collection pan is full. It can remove up to 50 pints of moisture per 24 hours. Other features include an automatic de-icer control, a humidistat, and four swivel caster-type wheels for easy movement.

Specifications: length, 13"; height, 24½"; depth, 15"; weight, 61 lbs.
Warranty: 1 year, full; 2 years, sealed refrigeration system
Manufacturer's Suggested Retail Price: $250
Approximate Low Price: $250

AIR FILTERS

Honeywell Enviracaire 12520

✓BEST BUY

The Honeywell Enviracaire 12520 is a large-capacity model that features true HEPA air filtration. It is cylindrical in shape and therefore takes in, filters, and discharges clean air in a 360-degree circle. On high speed, it can recirculate the air in a

16×20-foot room six times an hour. The HEPA filter will remove 99.97 percent of all the particles in the air, including the most common allergens and pollutants. A wraparound pre-filter extends the life of the HEPA filter and should be replaced every three months. This unit is lightweight and has a convenient top-mounted carrying handle for moving it from room to room.

Specifications: height, 12¾"; diameter, 17¾"; weight, 17 lbs.
Warranty: 5 years, (limited)
Manufacturer's Suggested Retail Price: $200
Approximate Low Price: $200

Bemis 200-001

✓BEST BUY

The Bemis 200-001 is a highly efficient air purification system in a triangular design package. It features true HEPA air filtration and has a pre-filter to extend the life of the HEPA filter. A sensor monitors the air flow in this unit and signals when the filter needs replacement. This unit will clean the air in a 17×20-foot room five times an hour. The easy-to-use electronic controls are located on the top of the unit.

Specifications: length, 20¼"; height, 19"; depth, 14³⁄₁₆"; weight, 24 lbs.
Warranty: 5 year (limited)
Manufacturer's Suggested Retail Price: $225
Approximate Low Price: $170

PORTABLE HEATERS

Portable heaters come in many different sizes and fuel types. Only operate a portable heater on a sound, flat surface. Keep any heater away from flammable materials, especially curtains, blankets, and other fabrics. Extension cords should not be used with portable electric heaters. Plug the unit directly into a wall outlet with a 20-amp breaker rating.

Lakewood 7096

✔ BEST BUY

The Lakewood 7096 is an efficient, clean source of heat suitable for any room in the home. It resembles a miniature old-fashioned hot-water radiator in style with seven steel fins to disperse the heat. The unit comes filled with diathermic oil, which is heated by internal elements and disperses heat quickly and evenly. (The unit is sealed at the factory and never needs refilling.) There are three heat settings—600, 900, and 1,500 watts—the seven-foot power cord can be plugged into any 20-amp grounded household outlet. A thermal fuse shuts off the unit to prevent internal overheating. Other features include a separate thermostat (to maintain a constant temperature) and automatic on/off cycling.

Specifications: length, 16"; height, 25½"; depth, 6½"; weight, 28 lbs.
Warranty: 1 year (limited)
Manufacturer's Suggested Retail Price: $55
Approximate Low Price: $49

Duracraft Surround Heat CZ-2200

✔ BEST BUY

The Duracraft Surround Heat CZ-2200 is a compact, efficient electric heater for home use. It features two heat settings (750 and 1,500 watts), and has an adjustable thermostat to help maintain a desired temperature. The CZ-2200 can disperse heat in a 360-degree circle or in one direction only. There is also a fan-only setting. This unit has twin internal circuit breakers to prevent overheating. Other features include a patented child-resistant switch and a tip-over switch that turns the unit off if it is knocked over.

Specifications: length, 9⅞"; height, 12½"; depth, 8⅞"; weight, 5.7 lbs.
Warranty: 5 years (limited)
Manufacturer's Suggested Retail Price: $40
Approximate Low Price: $40

BABY EQUIPMENT

Choosing the best baby products can be overwhelming for new parents. These days, the baby equipment industry is more innovative than ever, with companies racing to develop the most advanced products at the most competitive prices. That's great news, but it means the market can be confusing for the inexperienced shopper.

BUYING TIPS

When buying baby equipment, keep in mind that your first considerations are safety, comfort, ease-of-use, and convenience; looks are a fringe benefit. But given the demands of the market today, most of the following products have come a long way and are quite stylish. Most products today sport tailored or classic motifs and sleeker lines.

Baby products are also available in many different types of stores. Although mass retailers almost always beat department stores when it comes to price, they don't offer the same services. For instance, the latter will often deliver and set up large pieces of equipment (such as cribs) or have repair departments. Ask about the services a store provides when making purchases.

SAFETY TIPS

Several organizations monitor juvenile products. The Juvenile Products Manufacturers Association (JPMA) rigorously tests and certifies products in categories not covered by government regulations. Products that pass the JPMA test may state this on their labels, so look for the JPMA seal of approval.

Make sure all hinges and rough parts are covered so that they cannot pinch or scratch your baby's fingers or toes. Look for baby-safe materials such as plastic and rubber; avoid metals because they can heat up from the sun. Also look for soft, comfortable fabrics, such as cotton.

Make sure that small parts are firmly secured. Small objects that could come loose represent a choking hazard for your baby.

Any product meant to hold your baby should have a sturdy

frame that won't tip over. Look for a high chair with a wide base and for a stroller with large wheels and a substantial body that won't tip when you hang your bag on the handlebars. Look for straps on car seats and high chairs, and check to see that these will hold your baby securely.

Once you've made your purchase, it's important to stay on top of recall information in case the product turns out to be faulty. The U.S. Consumer Product Safety Commission keeps track of most children's products that have been recalled. The National Highway Traffic Safety Administration tracks recalled car seats. Also local newspapers routinely publish information about baby equipment recalls if a large manufacturer is involved.

BEST BUYS '99

Our Best Buy, Recommended, and Budget Buy baby equipment products are listed below. Products within each category are listed according to quality. The best of the Best Buys is listed first, followed by our second choice, and so on. A Best Buy, Recommended, or Budget Buy designation only applies to the model listed—it does not necessarily apply to other models made by the same manufacturer or to an entire product line.

PORTABLE CRIBS AND PLAY YARDS

Play yards (or playpens) are the portable cribs that sport bassinet attachments. Even though classic playpens and portable cribs can be used interchangeably, it's better to use each of these products exactly as specified by the manufacturer. A piece of equipment intended only for use as a portable crib should not be used as a play yard, and vice versa. It's also important to stop using these units when your baby outgrows them; for the most part, they are intended for children less than 34 inches tall or weighing less than 30 pounds.

FEATURES

A portable crib is a handy piece of equipment for travel or for overnight visits to friends and relatives, but it should not be used on a permanent basis in place of a full-size crib. Most portable cribs are rectangular and have sturdy metal or plastic frames, hard bottoms covered with padding, and fabric sides with mesh panels. Generally, these cribs fold down into a compact package that fits inside the carrying case.

Some play yards closely resemble portable cribs, while others are a bit roomier and have mesh sides that allow parents a full view of the child inside. Some also have drop-down sides that make it easier to fold the unit away. These sides, however, should always be raised when the play yard is in use.

QUALITY

When purchasing either a portable crib or a play yard, first make sure that it's sturdy. Give it a shake to see whether the unit will tip over or accidentally collapse. Look for tightly woven mesh, so small fingers or buttons on baby clothing cannot get caught. Also be sure that the mesh is securely attached to the top rail and floor of the unit and that any vinyl on the unit is sufficiently thick. Otherwise, when a baby sucks on it—or chews it when he or she is teething—small pieces can get stuck in the child's throat. For this same reason, make sure no foam is exposed for tiny fingers to pick at. Watch for sharp points or edges and exposed seams or hardware.

PORTABLE BASSINETS/PLAY YARDS

Kolcraft Corner Suite Travel Play Yard with Bassinet 18184

✓BEST BUY

The Kolcraft 18184 is the most innovative combination bassinet/play yard on the market, thanks to a unique triangular shape and plethora of both standard and extra features. This model can be assembled and collapsed quickly (even with the bassinet attached) into its own travel bag. The surprisingly elementary configuration offers substantial advantages over the usual rectangular models; it can easily fit in a corner to save floor space and can provide a baby with more interior play space (42 inches wide, 42 inches deep, and 31 inches high). The removable bassinet attachment (which suspends about nine inches down from the top rail of the unit) also features a built-in support pad that provides extra firmness for infants and a zippered compartment that can be used to store baby needs safely. The construction on this play yard is sturdy but lightweight. The 18184 incorporates padded railings so all corners are smooth, and strong nylon mesh on all sides allows parents to better see babies that are in the unit. Kolcraft covers this model in an exceptionally attractive tailored navy-and-white plaid fabric.

Warranty: 1 year
Manufacturer's Suggested Retail Price: $130
Approximate Low Price: $120

Fisher-Price Travel Tender with Soothing Bassinet 79525

Recommended

The contemporary, colorful looks of this multifunctional travel crib—bassinet, portable crib, and small play yard all in one—make it very appealing. Its clever design, reasonable price, and extra features (such as a battery-powered motor that makes soothing vibrations to calm babies) make it a sensible choice. This sturdy, lightweight unit is well constructed with smooth corners and padded guard rails. It sports durable wheels for easy maneuvering from room to room and is easy to assemble and collapse. The bassinet attachment is suspended about 10 to 11 inches down from the top rail of the play yard and spans the full area of the unit (which measures 40 inches long and 26 inches wide). The Travel Tender has mesh on three of four sides for viewing the baby and has its own carrying case.

Warranty: 1 year (limited)
Manufacturer's Suggested Retail Price: $116
Approximate Low Price: $99

PLAY YARDS

Kolcraft Octagon Playard 18503

✓BEST BUY

Measuring about 40 inches square, the Kolcraft Octagon is one of the roomiest play yards on the market. Despite its large size, it is still relatively easy to set up and take down. The unit conveniently folds in half (the double-drop sides have sturdy Stay-Loc hinges), which makes it manageable for storage or travel. It includes a built-in carrying handle and only weighs 24½ pounds for easy maneuverability. But one of the nicest features about this unit is the visibility it allows parents. While the strong steel frame and floorboard are covered with padded nylon casings and mats (available in vinyl or Cozy-Soft cloth pad), the sides of the unit are fabricated in a strong mesh that is easy to see through. The unusual design of the frame, which features center support legs that extend diagonally to the unit's outside edges (instead of posts at each corner), allows parents to view a child from every angle. It also allows the child much more play room than the average play yard.

Warranty: 1 year
Manufacturer's Suggested Retail Price: $70
Approximate Low Price: $65

Graco Canopy Pack 'N Play 9047FB

Recommended

Designed like the combination bassinet/play yard units, the Graco Pack 'N Play has a large, snap-on sun canopy, complete with a zip-open mesh panel that lets plenty of light in but keeps insects out. It is made of a special aluminized fabric that screens out some of the UV rays, making this one of the few play yards on the market that is suitable for use outside. The only difference is that it lacks a bassinet attachment. The play yard (measuring 40 inches long, 28 inches deep, and 32 inches high without the canopy) is sturdy and well constructed with smooth corners and padded rails. It is easy to use and can be assembled or collapsed in a few minutes. It's lightweight and extremely portable and features an innovative attached carrying case with a support board that folds up to encase the unit. It sports strong nylon mesh on all four sides and a roll-down flap on one side that can act as a sun and draft guard. Large swivel wheels with locks (instead of casters) on one end of the unit give it outstanding mobility. A colorful fabrication in primary colors makes it exceptionally attractive. A large accessory bag included with the Pack 'N Play is ideal for traveling.

Warranty: not available
Manufacturer's Suggested Retail Price: $127
Approximate Low Price: $119

Cosco Padded Playard 05-396

Budget Buy

The Cosco Padded Playard includes all the essential features in a sensible, economical package. The unit measures a roomy 36-inches square (the double-drop sides have sturdy lockable hinges), which brings it down to a manageable size for storage, travel, or merely moving the unit from room to room. Its sturdy construction includes a durable powder-coated steel frame and padded top rails and rail caps. The floorboards feature padded vinyl mats (in a variety of patterns and colors) that can be removed for cleaning. Visibility is superb because the sides of the unit are made of strong nylon mesh that is easy to see through. The frame features support legs that extend diagonally to the unit's outside edges (instead of posts at each corner), allowing parents to view a baby from every angle. Unfortunately, this unit does not have carrying handles, which makes it a bit awkward to transport.

Warranty: 1 year (limited)
Manufacturer's Suggested Retail Price: $40
Approximate Low Price: $40

SWINGS

When you shop for a swing for your baby, stability should be the most important concern. After that, you want to consider the ease of setting up and taking down, the padding and comfort of the seat, the winding mechanism or motor, and possibly the portability or adaptability of the swing. Some swings double as car seats and/or car beds. This may be the deciding factor for you, or you may decide not to pay for features you don't need.

Cosco Dream Ride Plus 08-980

✓BEST BUY

It's refreshing to find an old-fashioned idea with innovative new twists, and this classic windup swing from Cosco is the perfect example. To begin with, the removable swing seat can be used as either a rear-facing car seat or a side-facing car bed. As a swing, the seat can be switched from a sideways (cradle-style) position to a conventional forward-facing position with a simple rotating motion (instead of removing the whole seat). And unlike most of the deluxe models, it operates on a winding mechanism instead of batteries. The crank is unusually quiet to operate, the swing runs for a full 30 minutes, and the unit features a Minute-Minder to time the mechanism as it winds down. When used as a car bed, this is the only infant restraint that can be used in an air bag seating position. Overall, the Dream Ride Plus offers outstanding flexibility for a fair price.

Warranty: 1 year (limited)
Manufacturer's Suggested Retail Price: $100
Approximate Low Price: $100

Graco Open-Top Swing 1434

Recommended

The configuration of this open-top swing eliminates the need for a bar across its top, which makes it easier to get the baby in and out of the seat and gives the unit a streamlined appearance. The clever design, plus an advanced electronic drive, makes the Graco Open-Top an excellent all-around swing. An innovative, A-shaped frame makes the unit easy to set up and allows the seat to be suspended from the sides of the swing. The seat, covered in thickly-padded removable and washable cloth (available in a variety of patterns), includes a head support and a tray with a toy bar. It also can be set in four positions that range from sitting to reclining. The motor features three speed variations and a low-battery indicator. The motor should run for up to 200 hours on four D batteries. The Graco 1434, however, cannot be used for other functions, such as a car seat or carrier.

Warranty: 1 year, parts
Manufacturer's Suggested Retail Price: $94
Approximate Low Price: $90

Cosco Quiet Time Elite 08-989

Budget Buy

There's nothing more frustrating than running out of batteries when a baby is cranky and wants to swing, which may account for the popularity of the good old-fashioned windup model. The Cosco Quiet Time is a great choice if you opt for a traditional swing because it is well designed, quiet (with whisper-quiet winding and running operations), and—most importantly—swings for a full 30 minutes after being fully wound. It even has a convenient Minute-Minder gauge to show how much running time is remaining. This unit easily folds for storage or travel and features removable soft padded covers. Other features include a wide-stance sturdy steel frame and overwind protection. It also has an ergonomically designed seat, a t-bar with a push-button release for security, and a three-position reclining seat. This is a solid workhorse that will always be ready to perform.

Warranty: 1 year (limited)
Manufacturer's Suggested Retail Price: $55
Approximate Low Price: $55

NURSERY MONITORS

Nursery monitors can help put your mind at ease when you're not in the same room as your baby. Keep in mind, however, that monitor systems are sensitive to interference from other environmental sources (such as physical obstructions or cordless phones), and they are no substitute for periodic in-person checks on your baby.

FEATURES

The monitor's transmitter stays in the baby's room and relays noise—from soft cooing to loud crying—to your receiver. Most transmitters pick up sounds within a 6- to 10-foot radius and can relay them as far as 150-200 feet, depending on the environment. Modern monitors come with extra features: Some come with night-lights, others are cordless for greater mobility, and some very expensive models feature video display units. One highly desirable feature is a range finder that beeps when the transmitter is too far from the monitor (so there's no more guessing about whether you'll be able to hear your baby if you're in the backyard).

Fisher-Price Cordless Nursery Monitor 71562

✓BEST BUY

The concept of a cordless phone is also applied to nursery monitors. The compact design and excellent reception of this unit make it one of the best cordless models available. The receiver is designed to be portable during the day and rechargeable at night in a charging base (which is included with the unit). The unit also remains operational while charging. This concept eliminates the need for frequent and expensive battery changes (the receiver includes a charging indicator to ensure optimal battery performance). The 71562 operates on two separate channels to guarantee good reception. The receiver and transmitter both have AC adapters and durable, rubberized antennas.

Warranty: 1 year (limited)
Manufacturer's Suggested Retail Price: $50
Approximate Low Price: $50

Graco UltraClear Monitor 2750GM

Budget Buy

This old-fashioned audio monitor is still an effective—and far less expensive—way of getting a handle on what's going on in the room. The Graco UltraClear comes with a monitor and two receivers—one for each parent to take to their various locations in the home. This unit has superb reception, thanks to an advanced telephone technology that compresses the signal and narrows it for better transmission. The UltraClear features a variable light display (so parents can distinguish between a yawn or a cry), rotary volume control, and flexible antennas on both the transmitter and receiver. Its receiver and transmitter can work on a nine-volt battery or AC power (adapters are included). The channel selector and volume control are easy to use.

Warranty: 1 year, parts
Manufacturer's Suggested Retail Price: $45
Approximate Low Price: $35

CAR SEATS

Car seats for infants and young children are mandatory in all states, and newborns may not be released from hospitals unless a parent has an appropriate restraint system to use on the trip home. All car seats are required to conform to Federal Motor Vehicle Safety Standards, but this does not mean that all seats are suitable for all children. It is important to be aware of the many varieties on the market so you can choose the appropriate car seat for your child. Options include infant-only, convertible, and booster car seats.

INFANT CAR SEATS

Infant car seats, which can also be put to good use outside the car, are intended for newborn babies up to about 20 pounds (a weight usually reached between 9 months and 1 year of age). These car seats are used only in a rear-facing position in the car and must not be used in the front seat if the car is equipped with an air bag. If an air bag is deployed, it would strike the back of the infant's car seat at over 200 miles an hour (the base speed for such devices), and the impact of this violent blow to the baby's head could cause brain damage or death.

Outside the car, however, these seats can double as carriers, feeding seats, or even rockers. This type of seat is also the best choice for low-birth-weight babies, because the convertible car seats that also accommodate older infants or toddlers are likely to be too large—even in the infant position—for smaller newborns. Remember, if the child does not fit correctly in the seat, the seat cannot provide optimum protection.

CONVERTIBLE INFANT CAR SEAT/STROLLERS

These products can come in handy as car seats, strollers, and infant carriers. Many parents enjoy the convenience of being able to take the baby from the car to the stroller without undoing and refastening complicated harnesses. If you're shopping for a convertible infant car seat/stroller, first read the introductions for car seats and for strollers to make sure the model you're considering has all the safety and comfort features recommended for a car seat or a stroller. In addition, check the fasteners that hold the car seat to the stroller—they should be sturdy and secure—and try it out to see whether conversion from car seat to stroller and back is quick and easy enough to suit your needs.

INFANT CAR SEATS

Fisher-Price Safe Embrace Infant Car Seat 79725

✓BEST BUY

The 79725 is a refreshing addition to the car seat market because it is just one piece (many infant car seats come with bases that they snap in and out of). This seat offers a combination of safety features that make it an exceptional performer. It features a specially contoured base with a position indicator that makes it easy to see if the seat is installed properly. The restraint is exceptionally easy and fast to adjust, thanks to a sliding track system and a five-point harness system. Locking clips are included for installation in certain types of vehicles. This unit also includes a special Secure-Lock Attachment that locks the car seat in place when it is in a shopping cart. It also features a thick, retractable canopy to shield a baby from the sun.

Warranty: 2 years
Manufacturer's Suggested Retail Price: $70
Approximate Low Price: $70

Century SmartFit Plus 4529

Recommended

One of the major considerations when purchasing a car seat is whether it's compatible with your type of vehicle (or multiple vehicles). Also, can it work with older and newer car models? Century has designed the SmartFit infant car seat with these issues in mind. The unit's sculpted base is contoured to fit more of today's vehicle seats, and its higher slots on the base accommodate the raised seat-belts found in most newer cars as well as older configurations. The four-position handle quickly adjusts for carrying, rocking, feeding, playing. An "All-Ways grip" on the handle adapts to a variety of comfortable carrying positions. Other features include a single-hand car seat release, a patented built-in level indicator to ensure proper installation, and a two-piece harness tie that makes it easier to secure and remove infants.

Warranty: 1 year (limited)
Manufacturer's Suggested Retail Price: $79
Approximate Low Price: $79

CONVERTIBLE CAR SEATS

Fisher-Price Safe Embrace Convertible Car Seat 79700

BEST BUY

The Safe Embrace 79700 is the first car seat on the market that features a built-in tether strap. The strap attaches to the top of the car seat (when used in its forward-facing position), anchoring it directly to the vehicle's frame. In a crash, the tether strap reduces the forward motion of the car seat and the child, significantly reducing the risk of injury. The Safe Embrace 79700 features color-coded belts that make it easier to position and buckle children in correctly (blue for rear-facing infants, burgundy for forward-facing toddlers). The car seat also features a five-point harness system, built-in locking clips (for easy installation with the seat-belt), and virtually universal vehicle compatibility, thanks to the careful design of the unit. The unit was just introduced in July 1997 and is currently under evaluation by the National Highway Traffic Safety Administration, which may someday require this type of tethering system on all vehicles.

Warranty: 2 years
Manufacturer's Suggested Retail Price: $135
Approximate Low Price: $135

Century Ovation with SelectFit T-Shield Car Seat 4635

Recommended

The superb Ovation is an update of Century's award-winning STE line, but has been redesigned with a contoured base that easily adapts to the sculpted seats found on many newer vehicles. This unit features one infant and two toddler positions, which can be easily adjusted with a recline lever. A raised buckle area and beveled buckle guides help locate slots for effortless buckling. A level indicator helps properly place the seat in a rear-facing position. It also has a front access vehicle belt routing flap that makes installation faster and more convenient. Other features on this unit include a three-position harness for growing children and a soft easy-chair pad design that removes for easy washing. This car seat accommodates children from birth to 20 pounds in the rear-facing position and up to 40 pounds in the forward facing position.

Warranty: 1 year (limited)
Manufacturer's Suggested Retail Price: $95
Approximate Low Price: $90

BOOSTER CAR SEATS

Century NextStep Stage II Car Seat 4920

✓BEST BUY

This innovative car seat redefines the booster category. It uses its own shielded five-point harness system for children from 20 to 40 pounds, and it uses the car's own harness and seatbelt for children from 30 to 65 pounds. For smaller children, it has a removable, height-adjustable head-support pad and uses a convenient two-piece harness system. For the older child, a belt-routing system makes it easy to use the car's own seat-belt and chest harness. A Comfort Clip with three adjustable positions keeps the chest harness in the proper position (and off little necks) and adjustable side supports pivot down so it is easy for the child to get into the seat. Included on the 4920 are two seating positions (slightly reclining or full upright) for comfort at any age. This ingenious seat eliminates the need for three products (infant, convertible, and booster seats) because a child can use this until ready for the typical car seat.

Warranty: 1 year (limited)
Manufacturer's Suggested Retail Price: $110
Approximate Low Price: $100

Fisher-Price Safe Embrace Booster Car Seat 79750

Recommended

This brand-new booster seat consists of a thick, seat-shaped pad (with a high back) that surrounds the child's body and lifts him or her several inches off the seat of the car. In this raised position, the child is the perfect height for the car's own three-point harness system (which is required in newer-model vehicles). It features a lap belt positioner that keeps the belt across the child's hips (instead of abdomen) to better withstand the force of a crash. And the high back helps keep the child upright—even while sleeping—so the vehicle's belts remain safely positioned even if an accident should occur. Minimum and maximum shoulder-height indicators are imprinted right on the seat to check if a growing child is the right size for the seat.

Warranty: 2 years
Manufacturer's Suggested Retail Price: $60
Approximate Low Price: $60

CONVERTIBLE CAR SEAT/STROLLERS

Kolcraft Secura Travel System 36851

✓BEST BUY

This combination unit lets you move a sleeping baby from a car to a stroller with ease. It offers five functions in one by teaming an infant car seat with a lightweight stroller. The infant car seat/carrier has an ergonomic handle with a built-in, one-handed release for the car seat. Kolcraft's Glide 'n' Lock allows the car seat to be locked into place with a loud, reassuring snap. The stroller is also loaded with features, such as an adjustable sunshade canopy and large "hugger wheels" with locking mechanisms. Other features include a three-position seat back with a full recline and adjustable footrest, weather boot, and a large storage bin. This unit is easy to use and can be assembled or adjusted without a screwdriver. This particular system uses the Kolcraft Secura Infant Car Seat, which is the only infant car seat that passes testing at speeds 15 percent greater than U.S. government safety standards.

Warranty: 1 year
Manufacturer's Suggested Retail Price: $150
Approximate Low Price: $150

Century 4-in-1 System Adventure 11-770

✓BEST BUY

Century was the first to develop a 4-in-1 System, and has continued to make innovations on the product over the last three years. Today, it offers the same kind of versatility and convenience as Kolcraft's infant car seat/stroller combination. The 11-770 features Century's new SmartFit Plus car seat, which has an adjustable base with a level indicator to ensure proper positioning, raised belt slots that adapt to more of today's vehicle seat-belt systems, an All-Ways handle with a soft grip, a sculptured base designed to fit more cars, an easy one-hand release for removing the carrier from the base, and a two-piece easy-to-use harness design. The stroller, which accepts the car seat in a forward- or rear-facing position, is also easy to fold and includes a reclining seat back, an extended canopy for extra sunshade protection, oversized all-terrain wheels with brakes, a removable and washable canopy and pad, and an extra-large storage bin. Like Kolcraft's, it is also easy to assemble and can be adjusted without a screwdriver.

Warranty: 1 year
Manufacturer's Suggested Retail Price: $180
Approximate Low Price: $180

STROLLERS

Many parents tend to buy infant carriages or standard strollers in addition to the umbrella strollers that can be carried around easily in the car. Today, however, the best strollers grow with your baby, combining the luxury of a carriage and the practicality of an umbrella stroller. Look for a lightweight, easy-to-fold stroller with removable padded seats, reversible handles, and large, durable wheels.

Kolcraft Imperial Carriage Stroller 46540

✓BEST BUY

The Kolcraft Imperial Carriage Stroller is a good option for parents who can afford only one stroller. It's loaded with all sorts of practical features at a sensible price. Some of the features include a well-engineered folding mechanism that collapses the stroller; a height-adjustable reversible handle to convert the stroller into a "carriage" position; an extra-wide frame; a three-position reclining seat; "parking brakes"; a removable, adjustable three-tier canopy (with peekaboo window); a padded guard rail; and a footrest. This model comes with an extra-large storage basket on the bottom of the stroller and a storage bag built into the canopy. The steering is relatively effortless, the suspension system is good, and the extra-large wheels ensure a smooth ride. Overall, it is substantial enough to be a principal piece of equipment for daily use, but light enough to stash in a car trunk and use on the go.

Warranty: 1 year
Manufacturer's Suggested Retail Price: $130
Approximate Low Price: $120

Evenflo EX-3 All-Terrain Stroller 370101

Budget Buy

This three-wheeled stroller is similar to the high-performance models engineered for athletes who run with their babies. Evenflo combines the traditional offerings of a stroller with the design of a sports model into its 370101. This stroller is exceptionally rugged and includes lots of special features. It boasts an ergonomic two-position handle that adjusts to height, a multiposition reclining seat, a retractable canopy, a large storage bin behind the seat, a padded three-point harness, and extra-large sturdy wheels. Additionally, it is easy to collapse and it remains in the upright positioned after it is folded. This unit is slightly narrower than traditional full-featured units.

Warranty: 1 year parts and labor.
Manufacturer's Suggested Retail Price: $130
Approximate Low Price: $130

HIGH CHAIRS

A voluntary safety standard created by JPMA exists for high chairs, which basically calls for restraining belts, dependable chair and tray locks, stability, a design with no protruding or sharp edges, and good instructional literature (which covers assembly, maintenance, cleaning, and use). It also addresses issues such as slipping out of the chair under the tray (many models have restraints between the legs that reduce this hazard) and other performance issues. Chairs that meet this safety criteria have a JPMA seal of approval.

FEATURES

When purchasing a chair, seat-belt latches and tray operation are critical considerations since you will be using this product several times a day. Look for models that allow you to operate the tray with one hand, are sturdy, have no parts (such as legs or trays) that wobble, and have easy-to-use locks on the safety belt. Chairs should also be comfortable for the baby (most wooden models have no padding) and easy to keep clean (plastic and metal chairs are easiest to wash down).

Special features on high chairs run the gamut. Some fold up, some offer reclining positions for bottle-feeding, and others offer different height positions and convert into booster chairs. Fold-up models are great if space is at a premium, but make sure the legs have sturdy locking mechanisms. Make sure high chairs with different settings are easy to manipulate, or the settings will be too inconvenient to use.

When a child is in a high chair, it is critical to always fasten the seat-belt and never let the child stand in the chair. According to statistics, children under the age of one are most vulnerable to high-chair accidents.

Graco Height-Adjustable Reclining High Chair 3845

BEST BUY

Thanks to its sturdy construction and flexibility, this high chair is perfect for any household. It reclines in three different positions (so it can be used with young infants) and has six different height adjustments. It also features a deluxe, fully-padded leatherette seat pad that's easy to clean; a t-bar to keep the baby from sliding out of the seat; an extra-large, adjustable wraparound tray; and a removable snack tray. The A-frame legs collapse easily, so the highchair can be conveniently stored away when not in use. The 3845 is offered in a variety of patterns.

Warranty: 1 year
Manufacturer's Suggested Retail Price: $80
Approximate Low Price: $80

Century Grow With Me 16-710

Recommended

This sturdy, white wood high chair is a stylish addition to contemporary kitchens. The flexible 16-710 easily converts to a reclining position for infant feedings. Its most innovative feature, however, is a tray that can be attached to the side of the unit to hold food and utensils for such feedings. The unit has a four-position wraparound tray that can even be used as a booster with a regular dining table. The two-piece seat pad detaches and is machine washable, and the tray has a t-bar design to keep a baby from sliding off the seat. This model neither collapses nor includes a height adjustment.

Warranty: 1 year (limited)
Manufacturer's Suggested Retail Price: $110
Approximate Low Price: $110

Cosco Options All-Plastic High Chair 03-286

Budget Buy

From the inventors of the first plastic high chair 50 years ago comes this new version from Cosco. The economical 03-286 has plenty of flexibility and style for the price. It features seven height adjustments, reclines for infants, and can be used without the tray as a booster seat at the table. The tray can be set in four different positions, includes a t-bar design that keeps baby from sliding off the seat, and can be removed or adjusted. The high chair also folds up easily for quick and convenient storage.

Warranty: 1 year (limited)
Manufacturer's Suggested Retail Price: $50
Approximate Low Price: $50